BRITISH CARS OF THE SIXTIES

BRITISH CARS
OF THE SIXTIES

DOUG NYE

PARKER
HOUSE

Parker House Publishing Inc., PO Box 756, 1826 Tower Drive,
Stillwater, MN 55082, USA
www.parkerhousepublishing.com

ISBN-13: 978-0-9796891-6-1
ISBN-10: 0-9796891-6-3

Manufactured in Indonesia

10 9 8 7 6 5 4 3 2 1

Contents

Acknowledgements

I would like to offer sincere thanks to those who have helped in the preparation of *British Cars of the Sixties*, in particular to David Hodges, who suggested it, and James Shepherd, who steered it through its final phases. Thanks also to photographer Geoffrey Goddard, whose loan of his magazine library is a gesture I find difficult to return adequately. Without the enthusiasm and skill of staff members of *Autocar* and *Motor* magazines, any chronicle of road-car development in this country would be exceedingly difficult to compile. In common with most other enthusiastic motorists, I think I should record my gratitude to that indefatigable champion of free speech and free motoring, William Boddy, editor of *Motor Sport,* for his uncompromisingly honest road-car assessments.

Warm thanks, too, to the manufacturers, and in particular to M. G. Wright and K. Judd of A C Cars; H. B. Light, Alvis historian; F. C. Nursall, of Aston Martin Lagonda; Denis Miller-Williams, of Rolls-Royce; S. Frampton, of Bond Cars; D. W. Sevier, of Bristol Cars; Harry Calton, of Ford Motor Company; Air Vice-Marshal Bennett, of Fairthorpe Cars; Bob Walklett, of Ginetta Cars; Bob Berry and Jim Graham, of Jaguar Cars; G. J. W. Powell, of Jensen Motors; Peter Morgan, of the company which bears his name; Malcolm Ginsberg, of the Lotus Group; W. N. R. Harrison, of Marcos Cars; A. G. Cooper, of the Reliant Company; Keith Kent, of Rover; Bob Gerard, for giving valuable information on Turner Cars; Roy Wood, of T V R; D. C. Goatman and Tom Dobbyn, of Vauxhall Motors; Simon Pearson, of Standard-Triumph; and the Rootes Group Press Office; and Tony Dawson and Stephen G. Harrison, of the British Leyland Motor Corporation.

The following very kindly made available the illustration photographs, for which I am extremely grateful: AC Cars Ltd; Aston Martin Lagonda Ltd; 'Autocar'; Bond Ltd; British Leyland Motor Corporation; Ford of Britain; Gilbern Cars Ltd; Geoffrey Goddard; Jensen Motors; Lotus Group; Marcos Cars; Nicholas Meyjes; Charles Pocklington; Reliant Motor Company; Rolls-Royce Ltd; Rootes Motors Ltd; The Rover Co Ltd; William B. Turner; T V R Engineering Ltd; Universal Power Drives Ltd; Vauxhall Motors Ltd; Stuart White.

Thanks also to Angela Cook and Jane Moore for retyping much of my original manuscript; something which I am sure was a most unenviable task.

Acknowledgments 2008 edition

Sarah Hutton, Brands Hatch Morgans; Clive and Anna Rooke, Nostalgia; Gordon I Gandy, www.mywarrington.me.uk; Andrew Actman, Peter Rix and Julian Booty, Lenham Sports Cars; Motorbase; Simon Percival, Percival Motors; Edward Gibson, Heritage Classics; Mike Abbas Classic Cars; Adrian Oliver; Malcolm McKay; Stephanie @ Compomotive Wheels; D. Malins, Tempest

British Cars of the Sixties
New Edition

By Doug Nye

In 1970 I had been working as a motoring journalist for seven years, which seemed like a very long time as it does when we are only in our twenties and haven't yet begun to appreciate just how little we yet know or understand about anything.

I had learned the ropes with John Blunsden and Cyril Posthumus at *Motor Racing* magazine, and then spent a short period as Bill Boddy's assistant on *Motor Sport* where I struck up a close friendship with another of the great mentors I was fortunate enough to find, Denis Jenkinson. In August 1968 I had gone freelance, and two years later I was still finding it a struggle but increasingly people seemed to be coming to me with commissions, instead of me having to lay in ambush to buttonhole them… Week by week, month by month, I was producing feature stories and race reports, in return for a tenner here, twenty pounds there…

Then one day the telephone rang and it was a friend of Cyril's, a former colleague on *Motor* magazine, named David Hodges. He had left the magazine world to become a book editor, working for the 'Sixties dynamic new *enfant terrible* of the industry Paul Hamlyn, and at that time for Thomas Nelson. He was, he explained, setting-up a new series of titles for Nelson, and one he was keen to produce could involve me as a debutant author.

We met, and he showed me a copy of a useful little book produced in the 1950s by David J. Culshaw, entitled *The Motor Guide to Makes and Models*. In effect it told us in brief everything we might need to know – and a lot I personally would never wish to know – about the products of the British motor industry. "I think there's a real niche for something similar right now, covering British cars of the 'Sixties," he said. And then he added that Nelson would pay a lump sum advance against royalties – a whole £250 if I recall rightly - there would be refreshers upon delivery of an acceptable manuscript, and then a small royalty paid on every copy sold.

Now you have to understand, that while life as a freelance motoring journalist was incredibly fulfilling and addictively good fun, the pay wasn't worth a damn. By the age of 22 I'd already appreciated the fact I was never going to be a millionaire – I think I was averaging about £14 a week - but the prospect did not matter to me one iota. I was utterly absorbed in my interest, and in effect if my hobby could pay sufficient to keep roof over head, gorgeous girlfriend happy, grub on the table and a fire in the grate…then what more could one need? And so it has been ever since, and today that girlfriend of 1970 has been my lovely wife of 37 years so something must have gone right. I guess some blokes are just too dull to change their ways…

So, against this background of the arrival of a pay cheque being such a rare event it called for flags, banners, a parade in the street and an extra log on the fire, the offer of an advance grabbed my full attention. What's more, the notion of producing something to be published between hard covers also appealed to me, a small enduring footprint to leave behind. And as things worked out, this became the first footprint in quite a long trail which we have laid down over the past 38 years.

I was no expert in the motor industry then, nor did I ever become one. From the age of six I had been entranced by the racing car, and the racing car alone – absolutely not the production car. But I was still eager to do a good job for David Hodges, and for Nelson – the original publisher – and for myself.

So against this background I was both delighted and staggered when Colin Gower – the committed bookman and publisher, in cahoots with Tim Parker, former raison d'etre for my *Cooper Cars* and *Dino: The Little Ferrari* books – suggested this modern-style reprint of *British Cars of the Sixties* – and very happy to help. Today every one of the cars described in the following pages is to varying degrees a collectible classic. And I hope very much that young enthusiasts today will learn as much about them from reading this, as I did from researching and writing it all those summers ago.

Let's kick off with my original introduction; penned in eager anticipation of seeing my book on a bookshop shelf, back in 1970…

Introduction

The nineteen-sixties have proved to be a turbulent time for the British motor industry, and a fateful period for several of the less well-founded manufacturers. In 1959, at the beginning of the period covered by this volume, the motor industry was a *mélange* of three large combines, two autonomous giants and myriad smaller manufacturers. In the main, these were selling rather staid and uninspiring, though generally dependable, cars for the masses. Enlightenment had begun to dawn with the British Motor Corporation's release of the Mini ranges designed by Alec Issigonis. But the other major manufacturers – Ford, Vauxhall and the Standard-Triumph and Rootes Groups – were still concentrating on cars of widely differing appearance and appeal, but nearly all sharing those basic features of dependability and total conventionality.

Standard-Triumph were continuing their go-ahead, new image with the all-independently suspended Herald saloon, and the range of Triumph sports cars were naturally continuing their large-scale export and home market sales. The Standard marque itself was there to appeal to the Standard owners of old who were still attracted by the appeal of the well-proven family saloon. But it was not to last long, production being discontinued in May 1963 as the ever-growing Triumph range extended to larger saloons. Standard-Triumph itself continued to grow throughout the decade, to become the major partner in the pre-eminent British Leyland Motor Corporation.

The British Motor Corporation, the other major component to form BLMC, presents a split personality in retrospect. Their transverse-engined front-wheel drive saloons were unconventional in the extreme in 1959, and as the theme was developed through the 1100 Hydrolastic models of 1963 to the larger 1800 of 1964 it was obvious that a trend had been initiated which was being followed by some other manufacturers more seriously than ever before. Yet while such technical advances were being made in one production stream the solid old dependables – the Farina 1500s, A40 and in particular the Morris Minor – were still being produced in considerable numbers to supply a somehow very British market. Very few modifications or changes were made during the production runs of these models, change for change's sake in American style being completely alien to BMC's policy. Even the advanced front-wheel drive machines had comparatively few modifications made to them until the post-BLMC 1300s and Mk II variants appeared in the last years of the period.

Jaguar and Daimler had been taken into the BMC/British Motor Holdings fold early on as financial and marketing considerations (as discussed in the pertinent chapters) prompted grouping of the major indigenous elements of the British industry. Rover had taken over control of Alvis, and this combination then, too, became part of the BLMC consortium. Obviously the birth of such a large interconnected family of companies has led to a number of rationalization moves, moves which must continue well into the 'seventies before their full extent can be realized, but one of the first of these was the demise of the Riley marque in 1969. As the end of the decade approached, the country's financial health declined, and the industry was very hard hit indeed by a depressed home market. Few real innovations were made therefore towards the end of the period, although the all-new Austin Maxi did appear; this was disappointing despite having been delayed to reach its full development.

While British Leyland was evolving from two of the original major British combines, the Rootes Group was suffering a series of problems, not fully resolved by the infusion of American money from Chrysler. The rear-engined Imp saloon range, first introduced in 1963 and representing a huge investment on the Group's part, evolved into a well-planned and extensive range of variants, but does not quite appear to have completely fulfilled the faith put into its development. Rootes at the end of the period were a combine suffering from the effects of a depressed market, but with the introduction of the Hunter-based range of lightweight shells and smooth 1725-cc engines their products began to look more attractive than some of the uninspired offerings of the mid-sixties. At the beginning of the period the sporting range of Sunbeam models had, of course, been very much in the public's eye with race and rally successes (later to prove so valuable to BMC and Ford) making good advertising copy. The Rapier and Alpine sports both had a strong following at the time, and later the Ford V8-powered Sunbeam Tiger proved the value of lazy American power in a well-developed British chassis – it was a pity that the Ford tie could not survive Chrysler's interest in the Group.

But the outstanding success story of the decade must be that of the Ford Motor Company, for they have evolved from manufacturer of indifferent family saloons to producer of some really outstanding models – more a product of extensively developing nineteen-fifties' design thought than of any original design genius. The initial 105E Anglia saloon range of 1959 introduced the short-stroke engine which was to become the basis of early-sixties sales success, and when the Cortina series appeared to replace the ill-starred Classic/Capri range, demand for the light, roomy and quick saloon was enormous. The 105E engine had been found particularly suitable for competition tuning, and Ford rapidly found themselves with a competition image built for them by a number of independent tuning companies.

From this there developed the tie with Colin Chapman's Lotus concern, and the production of the Lotus-Cortina using a twin-cam headed variant of the basic 1500 Ford block. The larger Corsair followed the Cortina theme, major restyling changes producing a boxy but still attractive Cortina Mk II in mid-period. In the upper strata of the Ford range the Zephyr Zodiac series culminated in the Vee-engined Mk IVs which have not been so successful as might have been expected. Also the change from in-line to Vee engines in the Corsair range was initially received with a certain amount of dismay. Gone was the silky smoothness of the high-revving, five-bearing in-line engine; lumpy roughness from the inherently inbalanced V4 was a poor substitute. Subsequent development improved matters considerably, although with the introduction of crossflow heads and bowl-in-piston combustion chambers the in-lines, too, lost some of their almost legendary willingness. Right at the end of the period the vast Capri (*née* Colt) range was introduced; a range in more states of trim and tune than any previously attempted by any manufacturer. Here a customer could order himself a virtually unique, personalized motor-car, and although the early Capri was not without its vices, the car's attractive styling and considerable development background form one of the most attractive British products of the 'sixties.

The Anglia's replacement, the Escort, is cast in very much the same mould, although lacking the vast range breadth of the Capri, and although Ford Germany were deeply involved in both models they must be regarded as two of the outstanding British cars of the decade.

General Motors' British subsidiary, Vauxhall, have spent a decade true to form, alternating major mechanical modifications with restyling each year, and although their saloon car products have been aimed very much at the 'average motorist' they have produced some nice engine/transmission packages in generally large and comfortable (if often garishly decorated) shells at competitive prices. Their re-entry into the small car market after many years' absence with the Viva HA made considerable inroads into other manufacturers' preserves, and the restyled HB range quickly grew to become a large and many-faceted one. Finally the belt-driven single overhead cam-shaft inclined engines of the late 'sixties provided the type of advance rather lacking until that time.

For the smaller members of the British industry the 'sixties could have been a very hard time indeed, but some, such as Lotus, Marcos and Morgan, have prospered. Many of their contemporaries at the beginning of the period have fallen by the wayside, or suffered such chequered careers as TVR before finally reaching apparent security and producing some quite attractive road machinery. In 1959 the production of shells for Ford mechanical parts was quite big business, and through the decade this developed into a variety of companies producing shells to accept Mini components. Many of these companies rose and fell, but Unipower, with the most attractive of all the Mini variants, have achieved considerable success. Most of these specialists are dealt with in a final chapter in this volume, two of the companies which ceased production in the period (Tornado and Turner) being chosen as separate chapter subjects to illustrate typical situations. Of the larger manu-facturers, Alvis, Armstrong-Siddeley and Standard all ceased production during the period and these, too, have chapters to themselves.

One theme which will be found to recur again and again in the text is that of the US Federal Safety Regulations, for these have shaped the design of many of our cars in the latter part of the period – they have made the Jaguar E-Type ugly, and also (temporarily) precluded Morgan from one of their largest markets.

After the design and development doldrums of the 'fifties, the acceler-ating pace of competition in the 'sixties has produced some very fine and advanced machinery. The safety engineering of the Rover 2000 series is particularly notable, as are the advances built into the Austin 3-Litre, Rolls-Royce Silver Shadow and Jaguar XJ6 saloons. In the sporting market the period opened with the Jaguar E-Type nosing its way into the enthusiast's heart, and closed with the Aston Martin DBS V8 about to be announced. With such vehicles as the quantity-production Lotus Plus 2 adding to the image, these are the British cars of the sixties which will be remembered.

This is by no means intended to be the definitive work upon road cars of the period, but it is designed to give a quick and concise reference to the design and development background of any model. Particularly trend-setting vehicles are dealt with in greater detail than less interesting ones, but as a dating guide the majority of changes and modifications made during any model's run are also described. I must add that any opinions expressed in the text about individual models or makes are purely personal ones and are based either on my own experience of them as a motoring journalist, or on the road test reports of the time.

Where identical vehicles have been produced under different badges, as in the case of the Mini range and the Rolls-Bentleys, a full description of the type is generally given under the marque that appears first in alphabetical order.

Finally, full specification tables of the decade's major manufacturers' models are included in an appendix, and will, I hope, complete a picture of ten years' automotive development.

Please note that for convenience the following abbreviations have been used in addition to others in more general use:

bhp	brake horse power
cr	compression ratio
fwd	front-wheel drive
ifs	independent front suspension
irs	independent rear suspension
mpg	miles per gallon
mph	miles per hour
ohc	overhead camshaft
ohv	overhead valve
rpm	revolutions per minute
sdp	single dry plate

1 AC

When John Weller, an engineer, designed a 2-litre six-cylinder engine for use in the cars built by his company, Autocarriers Ltd, in 1919, he could scarcely have foreseen that this would be a unit of outstanding longevity. Not until 1963 was production of the engine (albeit in much modified form) finally discontinued. The 1991-cc engine, with aluminium alloy block, renewable wet cast-iron cylinder liners and inclined valves operated from a chain-driven overhead camshaft, was offered in the period covered by this book as an alternative power unit for A C's Ace, Aceca and Greyhound production models.

The Ace, its well-balanced chunky lines based on the 166MM Ferrari of the early 'fifties, was a most attractive machine – if costly at around £1,500 – which performed extremely well. With the optional Bristol 1971-cc six-cylinder engine fitted (producing some 125 bhp at 6,000 rpm), the Ace was found by *Autocar* to have a top speed of 118 mph and to accelerate from 0–60 mph in just 9·1 sec. The chassis was formed from two 3-inch diameter tubular members, and was based closely on a John Tojeiro competition design with transverse leaf-spring independent suspension to all four wheels. The ride was firm and well controlled – only really rough pavé surfaces could make it feel uncomfortably harsh. The Ace's handling qualities were a major selling point. With negligible pitch and roll, carefully controlled suspension movement and a very high adhesion limit with the standard Michelin X tyres, the car was very fast and safe on smooth and twisty roads. On a circuit it took a lot of pushing to make the Michelins reach their rather sudden limit of adhesion and then the chassis was so well balanced that after an initial oversteering tail-slide the front wheels could be broken away too, and the whole car would slide through bends in a precisely balanced drift. The high-geared steering (with two turns lock-to-lock) made it possible to place the car exactly, and finger-tip movements were sufficient to maintain control – above all else the Ace *was* controllable! Girling 11-inch drum brakes with Wellworthy Al-Fin drums provided powerful retardation, and other highly praised features were a slick and quick gearbox (with synchromesh on the upper three ratios), the long-range fuel tank capacity of 13 gallons, and the smooth torquiness of the Bristol engine, pulling cleanly from 2,500 rpm to the 6,000 rpm limit. Bad points commented on were slightly inadequate lights for the car's performance and, until one got the knack, difficulty of entry and egress with the sound- and flap-free hood in position.

Similarly well thought of was the Aceca two-seat coupé, based on the same chassis, announced in 1954 in prototype form, and featuring a basically similar body style to the Ace. But in fact this shell had been totally redesigned to blend in with the fixed roof, and the result was extremely attractive. The rear window was let into a large tailgate, opening into a roomy luggage boot, and the whole body was coach-built in aluminium panelling. Quality of workmanship throughout was extremely high – an A C hallmark – and the aerodynamics of this closed body, fitted to a firmly sprung and sporting chassis similar to the Ace, gave an impressive top speed of over 128 mph. *Autosport* was moved to remark that 'for sheer driving pleasure it is almost impossible to equal'. Its predictable and controllable handling combined with straight-line speed and acceleration in the order of 9·4 sec from 0–60 mph made the Aceca-Bristol a most desirable motor-car. The Bristol unit's three Solex downdraught carburettors limited fuel consumption figures somewhat, but driven hard the Ace-Bristol could be expected to return around 21 mpg and the more aerodynamic Aceca 22–3 mpg. With such performance potential this was very reasonable.

The four-seat Greyhound GT model was added in October 1959, production commencing in November the following year. Once more the 1971-cc Bristol 'six' was used, in this case the B-type 105 bhp unit, coupled with the usual four-speed gearbox. Alternatively the D-type Bristol engine with its 120 bhp could be specified, providing extra performance at the expense of a little refinement. At the other end of the scale a few 2216-cc Bristol 406 engines were offered at extra cost, again producing 105 bhp but at lower rpm than the B-type. Laycock de Normanville overdrive on top was standard with this engine and an attractive option with either of the 2-litre engines. Later on in its run, the Greyhound was also offered with AC's own 1991-cc engine. Recent development had given this a nitrided crankshaft, Vandervell main and big-end shell bearings and a compression ratio of 9:1 to produce 102·5 bhp at 5,000 rpm.

It was in its chassis and suspension layout that the Greyhound differed most from its predecessors. To accommodate four passengers the engine had to be moved further forward in the frame, and to allow this move the Aceca's transverse leaf spring was dispensed with. In its place there appeared coil spring and double wishbone ifs, while at the rear a system was adopted which owed something to an experimental Ace which had finished eighth in the 1958 Le Mans 24 Hours race. Each rear wheel was located by a two-piece trailing wishbone radius arm with a single transverse arm to absorb cornering loads. These units were mounted on a chassis frame formed around two longitudinal 3-inch steel tubes in normal AC style, but this time with extra rigidity offered by a body-supporting space frame of small square-section tubes. Panelling was in aluminium, and the body shape – though not quite so well balanced as that of the smaller Aceca – was still attractive. With lengthened tail fins, a separate boot lid, wrap-round screen and long bonnet with a square-cut nose and bonnet top air-scoop, the Greyhound looked purposeful from ahead and comfortable from the rear. The braking system was unique in having twin hydraulic systems, and featured 11⅝-inch front discs as standard with 11-inch Al-Fin drums at the rear.

When announced, the Greyhound was priced at £2,891 and about 150 were built, upholding all the best AC traditions of individuality. With its sound-deadening qualities, comprehensive equipment, walnut and leather trim and laminated glass throughout, the striking Greyhound was not over-priced.

Then in 1961 there began the great partnership between AC cars and Ford engines, with Ruddspeed-modified 2553-cc six-cylinder Ford engines being offered in the rebodied 2·6 Ace and otherwise unchanged 2·6 Aceca models. The oversquare Ford engine produced only 85 bhp at 4,400 rpm in standard form, but five stages of tune were offered, including a modified-head with triple 1¾-inch SU H6 carburettors and a triple DCOE2 Weber set-up with six-port light alloy head and lightweight pistons. Power output ranged from 90 bhp (touring) to 170 bhp (racing).

The body of the Ace was modified with a lowered bonnet line, which gave it a much improved sleek appearance and smaller grille, and from their introduction in March 1961 (Ace) and July 1961 (Aceca), these 2·6 models appeared concurrently with the well-established Bristol- and AC-engined vehicles. The initial price was £1,780 for the 2·6 Ace (compared with £1,889 for the AC-engined car and £2,261 for the Bristol), while the 2·6 Aceca was priced at £2,196, compared with £2,266 (AC engine) and £2,636 (Bristol) – the Ford-engined models' attraction was obvious.

In the autumn of 1961 American ex-GP driver Carroll Shelby had approached the company with an idea for fitting 4260-cc American Ford V8 engines into Ace shells and chassis. In October 1962 he visited the Thames Ditton works, and the first prototype of what was to become the Cobra was commenced then. This machine, with inboard rear brakes, was tested briefly in England by W. D. Hurlock, head of the company, and was then freighted to the States for subsequent development. This was also in October 1962, and after modifications to the engine and cockpit cooling systems, the rear suspension, wheel hubs and diff mountings, the 4·2-litre Shelby American AC Cobra, using AC-made chassis and shells, went into production in December. This was quick work indeed, and after the first seventy-five production Cobras had been fitted with 250-bhp 4·2 litre (260 cubic inch) Ford V8 engines, the larger 4·7-litre (289 cubic inch) 271-bhp V8 was dropped into subsequent vehicles. The cars were built virtually in their entirety at Thames Ditton, were painted, trimmed and wired there, and were then shipped out to Shelby American in Santa Fé, and later in Venice, California, to be fitted with their engines and gearboxes.

The Cobra 289 appeared in November that first, crowded year, and so great were demands on the modest Thames Ditton plant that production of the all-British ACs was brought to an abrupt end. First the Bristol B-type and D-type engine options for the Greyhound were curtailed, and then in November production of the 2·6 Aceca was discontinued. In January 1963 the Bristol-engined Aceca also passed into limbo, and in February the AC-engined Aceca was also discontinued. Demand for Ace/Cobra shells continued to grow, and with production working up to twelve cars per week the small but quality-conscious company ended work on the standard AC and Bristol-engined Greyhound and Ace models – production of Weller's six-cylinder engine ceasing in its forty-third full year! But in that same month the first Cobras were produced for the European market, and Cobra business generally was booming.

In early 1963 rack and pinion steering had replaced the original worm and peg system, and in July louvres were standardized aft of the front wheel arches to extract hot air from the surprisingly still-spacious engine compartment. Larger brake discs and calipers and wider rims (6 inch) were also fitted.

In October 1964 came a major change with the deletion of the transverse leaf spring suspension system, and more sophisticated coil springs and unequal length upper and lower wishbones were introduced. The first coil-sprung machine went to America on 23 October 1964. But slowly the Cobra's AC parentage began to be submerged, the model being known as the 'Ford Cobra' even though the traditional AC script still appeared in the centre of the bonnet badge and on the wheel spinners.

The next major step forward came in October 1965 with the 7-litre Ford V8 engine being squeezed in to form the Cobra 427 (using a 6997-cc, 425-bhp – 427 cubic inch – unit).

However, the Cobra family provided a genuine sports car, endowed with a lot of power and torque, firm and predictable – indeed, a little vintage – handling abilities, combined with a high degree of comfort. Top speeds of 145–50 mph and touring fuel consumption figures of 18–20 mpg put the Cobra 289, priced at just over £3,000 in March 1968, in a class of its own, and for a time gave AC the distinction of producing both the fastest and the slowest (the AC invalid carriage) production cars in the world.

With the introduction of the Cobra 427, however, AC moved again into the refined quality car field. The standard 289 twin-tube coil suspension chassis was lengthened to accept a strikingly beautiful Frua-styled two-seat convertible body, originally powered by the 427-cubic inch engine and accordingly being dubbed the AC 427. The long and broad body with its bold sweeping lines and 'nostril' nose was once again a study of balance and taste in automotive styling, recalling the grace of the Aceca and Greyhound. With its 6997-cc engine, the 427 was built in small numbers until October 1966 when the 428-cubic inch 7016-cc V8 engine replaced the earlier unit to form the AC 428 model, and in 1967 convertible production started. The two-seat, two-door machine was very much a car for the wealthy enthusiast at £5,177 standard or £5,324 with automatic, and in March 1967 the 428 coupé version with a most attractive fastback body by Frua was announced. Production began in October that year and with the last Cobra shell being produced at Thames Ditton in late 1968, total production capacity was centred upon these two big and beautiful 428 models. In all, about 1,500 Cobras were built, two-thirds of them 289s and the last, a 289, was finally delivered on 24 February 1969.

The 428s had 345 bhp available at 4,600 rpm, and with the three-speed automatic gearbox gave a maximum speed of 145–50 mph, and a 0–60 mph time of a mere 5·4 sec. Initial production entailed shipping the chassis to Frua in Italy for the lightweight all-steel body to be welded on. The complete shell was then shipped back to England for trimming and painting.

With extremely high standards of fitting and finish, performance, handling, workmanship and sheer aesthetic appeal, AC have ended the decade with these 428 fastback and convertible models in just the way they entered it with the Ace, Aceca and Greyhound.

2 Alvis

The first Alvis car, the 10/30 produced by T. G. John Ltd in Coventry in 1919, was the first of a line of advanced and attractive sports and touring cars to appear under the Alvis name. In 1921 John's firm had taken the name of the Alvis Car and Engineering Company Limited, and in 1936 this was simply abbreviated to Alvis Limited as aero engine and armoured car production became vital to its economy.

In post-war years car production became centred around an entirely new six-cylinder 2993-cc push-rod engine with seven-bearing crankshaft released in October 1950. Special bodies were built around this engine by Carrosserie Herman Graber in Berne, Switzerland, and in 1958 – after only a handful of the expensive Graber-bodied 3-litres had been sold at around £3,500 each the previous year – a new agreement was made with Park Ward to build modified versions of the Swiss shell, producing the quietly stylish and handsome Alvis TD21 saloon and drop-head coupé. A low waistline was coupled with a high roof to give plenty of glass area and a light appearance, while the bonnet top and nose were given a greater curve than their Graber-made predecessors. Both saloon and convertible had two wide doors with full four-seater accommodation, although the saloon, without the requirement for hood stowage of the convertible, was more roomy in the back. A small one-piece rear screen was featured in the saloon, and on this original 1958 model automatic transmission and front disc brakes were attractive options. In 1959 a new cylinder head with de-siamesed ports, different SU carburettors and a modified exhaust system raised the engine's output from 104 bhp at 4,000 rpm to 120 bhp at 5,000 rpm. These individually made and attractive vehicles cost new £2,827 (saloon) and £3,111 (convertible) in 1960. In October slight changes were made fitting larger sidelights, chrome-surround quarter lights, blocked-in rear overriders and offering Laycock de Normanville overdrive as an optional extra.

But while production of the TD21 was running at a modest rate, the Coventry works was busy making Saladin armoured cars, Salamander fire crash tenders and the Leonides fourteen-cylinder radial aero engine. By the end of 1960 the Alvis Stalwart cross-country vehicle had also appeared to compete for production capacity with the private cars, but TD21 production was still continued. The 3-litre engine's net output of 115 bhp was enough to give the large and conventional car a top speed of 103 mph, while 0–50 mph acceleration was brisk for a ton-and-a-half motor-car at 9·3 sec. But the engine did tend to be top-endy and inflexible, and while 80 mph cruising was smooth and quiet, engine and wind noise both increased sharply at higher speeds. The gear-change tended to be notchy too, but otherwise it seemed that Alvis had thought of the driver first; the driving position was excellent, vision was superb and the Burman recirculating ball steering light and precise. Ride was pronounced excellent by *Autocar*, the coil and wishbone ifs and semi-elliptic rear suspension with Armstrong telescopic shock-absorbers cushioning road shocks most effectively. Quality was evident in the obvious care with which the body had been built (for example, the doors were hung first and

5

panelled later to ensure their fit), but with an average of about 17 mpg and very high regular maintenance requirements the Alvis owner obviously had larger-than-average running costs to bear.

In April 1962 the 3-litre TD21 Series II was announced, featuring Dunlop disc brakes all round, fog lamps recessed into fresh-air ducts either side of the grille (these ducts feeding both the heater and the carburettors), and a redesigned rear number plate mount flanked by vertical reversing lights. In October German five-speed ZF gearboxes were fitted as standard and the overdrive option removed, the combination of the 152·3 lb ft torque from the seven-bearing engine, this beautifully-engineered gearbox and Park Ward's fine bodies making the Series II Alvis very much a prestige product.

January 1963 saw the introduction of the still further improved Series III models, with the appearance of the nose made rather heavier by the addition of twin sealed-beam headlights set vertically on either side of the upright grille, and rectangular sidelamp/flashing indicator fittings placed beside the grille. Modifications were also made to the steering and front suspension, and engine power was increased to 130 bhp net at 5,000 rpm with 165 lb ft torque at 3,250 rpm. With a reduction in purchase tax, sales were aided by a drop in price to £2,532 (saloon) and £2,774 (convertible). With these changes the series number was changed to TE21, and this model was supplemented in March 1966 by the release of the TF21 Series IV. Engine output had been raised, compression ratio rising from 8·5 to 9·0:1 power going up by some 15 per cent to 150 bhp at 4,750 rpm, and torque being 185 lb ft at 3,570 rpm.

The fascia in the TF21 was redesigned with repositioned controls and instruments, a bigger heater was fitted and an electrically heated rear screen, self-adjusting handbrake, variable rate springing and new-setting Woodhead-Monroe telescopic dampers were also added. Automatic transmission became an optional extra and, with this option removed from the Series III TE21 at the same time, the two types were both available in limited numbers. With the revised front suspension, steering, springs and dampers, ride was even further improved and better silenced, and the already light manual steering was supplemented by ZF power assistance (this having been offered as an optional extra since October 1964).

During this period of the mid-'sixties Britain's industries had been grouping together and consolidating their reserves in order to absorb the new trading atmosphere which would prevail should our application to join the European Common Market be successful. In particular the motor industry became increasingly streamlined – some would say monolithic – and during this period Alvis were in an especially difficult situation.

Demand for the company's piston aero engines was still surprisingly high, but with Government sponsorship now going to the jet-engine combines the writing was obviously on the wall both for the piston engine and for its specialist manufacturers. The cross-country and military vehicle programmes could not be considered secure since they depended so much on the policies of many different Governments, and of course the small-scale production of quality cars was a difficult programme to justify. On 22 July 1965, the Rover Company bought the whole of Alvis Ltd's share capital and then, in December 1966, the Leyland Motor Corporation made a takeover bid for both companies. In March 1967 this takeover was finalized and the Rover

Company – incorporating Alvis – became a wholly-owned subsidiary of the
Leyland Group.

In May the decision to curtail Alvis car production went into action with the ending of the TE21 Series III machines at chassis number 27367, and then, on 20 August 1967, TF21 Series IV number 27472 was completed at the Holyhead Road works in Coventry. Unless a decision is made some time in the future to revive the Alvis motor-car, this was the last of the proud line, begun in 1919, to bear the name.

3 Armstrong-Siddeley

This company's story as a car manufacturer began in 1919 and was brought to an abrupt end in 1960 by economic factors. The first 30-hp Armstrong-Siddeley produced immediately after World War I was ponderous and unwieldy, and it would not be unreasonable to apply this phrase to most subsequent cars of the marque. But the final model, the Star Sapphire, introduced in saloon form in October 1958 and as a limousine in October 1959, was different. Its staid, upright appearance gave little clue to the mechanical refinement, performance, and handling potential, which lay beneath its stylized skin.

Both the saloon and the limousine were built around a 4-litre six-cylinder engine of oversquare dimensions. In the saloon this had twin Zenith 42W1A carburettors and, with inclined push-rod operated overhead valves, produced 165 bhp gross at 4,250 rpm. This was transmitted via a three-speed Borg-Warner automatic transmission through a Hardy Spicer divided prop-shaft to the hypoid rear axle. Coil-and-wishbone ifs was used, with semi-elliptic rear springs and Armstrong telescopic shock absorbers, while the 16-inch front wheels were directed by Burman power steering. Interior accommodation – for four to six – was opulent, extending to separate heating systems for the front and rear seats. A wide range of tools were supplied as standard in a rubber-lined drawer, and with such detailed equipment this vehicle was well worth its price of £2,498.

Braking was powerful to drag the Star Sapphire's $34\frac{1}{2}$ cwt back from its 100 mph top speed, the 11·8-inch Girling discs at the front and 12-inch rear drums being servo assisted. The automatic transmission system was unusual in including a variable speed setting for the intermediate gear hold, the middle ratio engaging automatically when the throttle was opened below the pre-set speed; 35 mph in bottom and 65 mph in intermediate were normal top speeds. The car would cruise all day at 80 mph and just top 100 mph, but its 16-gallon fuel tank gave a range of only about 200 miles, 17 mpg being a normal cruising consumption (but this plunged to 10 mpg in traffic). The handling of this big car was solid and predictable, a fairly smooth ride being achieved without the expense of added roll and pitch.

The limousine was beautifully appointed. Special attention was paid to sound-proofing the interior, with the aid of a glass-fibre-coated front bulk-head, and the rear springs mounted on Metacentric rubber bushes at the front and Contrasonic inclined rubber cushion shackles at the rear. A positive air-cooling plant was also provided. But the engine was less powerful than in the saloon, for the design team considered a maximum of 90-plus mph quite sufficient for a vehicle by definition so sedate as a seven-seat limousine. A single Zenith 42W1A carburettor was therefore fitted, limiting output to 140 bhp gross at 4,000 rpm. The price for the limousine was £3,149.

In June 1960 the directors of Bristol-Siddeley Engines Ltd – the parent company – let it be known that car production was to cease with the end of the then current financial year, on 31 July. The decision had been made with great regret, but production was said to be no longer an economic proposition. Traffic conditions, taxation and competition from the larger manufacturers had caused the market for large luxury cars priced at over £2,000 to decline very considerably, the Star Sapphire falling victim to its own production limitations. An undertaking was made to make spares and service available for some ten years to come and production workers, some 165 in all, were absorbed into other branches of the parent group. Another marque had met its end.

4 Aston Martin

This name, synonymous with high-performance, expensive and luxurious sports coupés, entered the 'sixties with just one basic model – the 3·7-litre six-cylinder DB4. This was available in standard close-coupled four-seater form or as the two-seater DB4 GT sports coupé, production at the Feltham works having commenced in January 1959.

The six-cylinder light alloy engine boasted chain-driven twin overhead camshafts and a seven-main bearing crank. Its dimensions were perfectly 'square' with a bore and stroke of 92 mm × 92 mm, and its capacity was 3670 cc. With twin SU carburettors on a trifurcated manifold in standard form, output was 240 bhp net at 5,500 rpm, and this was transmitted through a 10-inch single dry-plate clutch and four-speed all-synchromesh manual gearbox to a hypoid bevel final drive. The body shell itself was styled by Carrozeria Touring in Italy, and built to their Superleggera lightweight system, with aluminium panelling supported by a strong tubular superstructure, mounted in turn on the box-section chassis platform. Coil-and-wishbone ifs was standard, with a well-located rigid rear axle also suspended on coils and located by paired trailing links and a Watt arrangement. This basic four-seater was opulently and comfortably equipped, its seats being rather confined at the rear, but offering excellent support and location at the front. Price for the DB4 stood at £3,755 on introduction, and this race-bred vehicle was fast and easy to handle, topping 140 mph, sprinting from rest to 50 mph in just over 7 sec and returning around 17 mpg. The rack-and-pinion steering was direct and precise, while the combination of $11\frac{1}{2}$-inch front and $11\frac{1}{8}$-inch rear Dunlop disc brakes with servo-assistance was powerful and reassuring. Noise level was fairly high, and this big-feeling vehicle was very much a 'man's car'.

The GT variant had been announced in September 1959, featuring large Girling disc brakes all round, a limited-slip differential, triple twin-choke 45DCOE4 Weber carburettors, 30-gallon twin-filler fuel tank, front-hinged bonnet and faired-in headlamps as standard. Wheelbase was reduced by 3 inches and overall length by 5 inches, and, with the standard 3670-cc engine the GT had 302 bhp at 6,000 rpm to propel its 26 cwt. Non-servo $12\frac{1}{16}$-inch front discs and rear 11-inch units provided 'stop' for such considerable 'go', and price was £4,534. Later a stroked-out 3749-cc block was to become available, making this already potent machine even more torquey.

During 1960 Series 2 modifications included fitting a front-hinged bonnet to the four-seater, with chrome window frames brightening the appearance. The front brakes were increased to $12\frac{1}{2}$-inch diameter, with $11\frac{1}{8}$-inch rears, while another increase was in sump capacity – from 14 to 17 pints. A new-style front bumper was also added at this point, but the Aston engineers still did not consider lubrication to be sufficient, and in April 1961 the further-modified Series 3 DB4 appeared with 21-pint sump capacity from chassis number DB4/491, improved silencers, an electric tachometer, separate rear lamps, twin bonnet props and an improved heating and demisting system. The chassis frame was also modified slightly to allow the fitting of overdrive as an optional extra – at £43. The overall new price was £4,084 at this time and the model continued until, in September 1961, the Series 4 model appeared. This featured a twin-plate clutch, ballasted coil, lower and smaller bonnet air scoop, modified grille, hooded tail lamps, larger rear squab roll and an insulated rear shelf. An oil cooler duct was added beneath the front bumper, and while the trusty six-cylinder engine was still kept at 240 bhp, the car was becoming more and more refined.

In October 1961 the Convertible version was released, a handsome vehicle retaining the chunky Superleggera lines beneath the waistline, with two doors and four deep close-coupled seats. Necessary chassis/body stiffening held the weight to 27 cwt, and the standard-tune 3·7-litre engine was fitted. This latest model was priced at £4,445, and at this time the GT was the most expensive of the DB4 range at £4,667.

In March 1962 a high-performance Vantage model appeared with the special series high-compression (9·0 instead of 8·25:1) engine, delivering 260 bhp at 5,750 rpm as standard. Appearance was improved by using sleek fairings over the headlamps in GT style, while a GT-type fascia was also used. The price of this refined model was set at £3,746 and Series 4 DB4 Vantage production was to total forty-four cars. Then, in October 1962, the full GT engine was fitted to the well-equipped Vantage to form the Vantage GT. The four-seater had a carburettor air box, vacuum advance distributor, dipping mirror, electric radiator fan, $2\frac{1}{2}$-inch prop-shaft and a modified steering box fitted. Smaller front brakes, longer rear wings, Keiper seat mechanisms and standard safety belts completed this new Series 5 model. Its weight was up to 27½ cwt, and a three-speed automatic transmission also became optional equipment.

So the Series 5 DB4, DB4 GT, DB4 Vantage GT and DB4 Convertible ran on into 1963, but not for long. In March the GT sports coupé was discontinued, only seventy-five having been completed in its 2½-year run. In July the Convertible followed suit with a total of seventy vehicles on the road, and finally in August the remaining models were discontinued – total production figures standing at 898 (all series) for the four-seater and 134 for the two Vantage variants. A total of twenty-five special Zagato-bodied competition-type GTs had also been built in the period, a bulbously aggressive vehicle underlining the Aston Martin's masculine image.

Replacing these handsome DB4s in September 1963 were the DB5 range of 4-litre six-cylinder engined machines, sports saloon and Convertible models being announced simultaneously. Four- or five-speed manual gearboxes were available, while the 3995-cc engine, aspirating through triple SU carburettors, produced a smooth 282 bhp at 5,500 rpm in standard form. Automatic transmission was optional, windows were electrically wound, headlamps were faired-in. There were red rear lights on the door trailing edges and an alternator and twin-plate diaphragm spring clutch were also standard. Overdrive was optional with the four-speed transmission, but only for three months, the five-speed ZF system and a single-plate clutch being standardized in December 1963. Weight was up to 29 cwt and, apart from being slightly longer than the DB4, the new model shared its attractive lines.

While the DB4 had been a really impressive sporting machine, the DB5 was more refined, handling and performing just as well yet adding a quietness and a smoothness which made it much more relaxing to drive. The new gearbox was crisp and quick, and its synchromesh on all ratios powerful, but it was rather intrusively noisy. The 4-litre engine, however, was delightful, producing a lot of power throughout its rev range and peaking at 282 bhp at 5,500 rpm. The standard DB5 price was £4,248 for the saloon and £4,635 for the Convertible, while a particularly handsome variant was the hardtop Convertible, with a steeply raked wrap-round rear screen and really rakish lines.

The new DB5 Vantage appeared in October 1964, following the removal of the automatic transmission option for the range in September. The Vantage's triple-Weber carburated engine produced 314 bhp, and with its high-performance potential this attractive machine was priced at £4,603.

Modifications followed in January 1965, with Armstrong Selectaride shock absorbers being fitted as standard, and then in August 1965 it seems that demand caused the resurrection of the automatic transmission option. Mechanical changes included the fitting of higher radial-pressure piston rings to ease oil consumption, changes to the distributor advance curve and the adoption of a 10-inch diaphragm clutch. Avon GT tyres were specified as standard, and finally winding handles were fitted in a 'belt-and-braces' development to augment the electrical window winders. But in August that year, DB5 production was ended after just two years, 1,150 units of all types having been produced in that time. The company had moved to spacious premises at Newport Pagnell, and there preparations were being made to introduce the DB6.

The new model was released in October, still sharing the basic shape of the earlier models, but with a 4-inch wheelbase increase and restyled cut-off tail carrying a spoiler lip bringing many advantages. These included much-increased rear seat room, a reduced drag coefficient, and aerodynamic down-thrust on the rear wheels at high speed. Mechanically the new model was identical to the DB5 apart from altered spring rates, and with this much-improved interior accommodation the standard four-seater was joined by the new Volante Convertible. The Volante was more like the DB5 in design, with minor alterations such as divided wrap-round bumpers and altered tail lights.

Optional automatic transmission, the Borg-Warner Model 8, now offered engine braking in all gears, and both standard DB6 and Volante were priced at £4,998 – this price to include specified options such as basic Vantage engine, limited-slip or normal differential and a heated or normal rear screen. Weight had leapt up once again, this time to 29½ cwt, and Aston Martin were getting further and further away from the image of big and tough GT cars – leaning now towards much more refined and generally more pleasant high-speed transport in Bristol and Jensen vein. The DB6 was, in fact, a very fast car indeed, and with the optional 325 bhp Vantage engine it could top 150 mph, and streaked from 0–50 mph in a mere 4·9 seconds. It gulped fuel in the process, however, managing around 13 mpg.

In September 1966 power-assisted steering became a further option to refine the DB range, and then in October 1967 the long-lived Superleggera DB4 foundation styling was replaced by the DBS.

This new styling was based on a design exercise produced in 1966, and since Touring of Milan had wound up their coach-works, Aston Martin did their own design for the new production four-seater. The result was a sleek and graceful knife-edge styled shell which was beautifully balanced, long, low and wide. Bill Towns, the designer, had done an excellent job, for the new shell combined obviously Aston Martin appearance with a totally new look, a spacious interior and boot and good all-round visibility. The new body was again panelled in aluminium over a tubular frame, but with a widened version of the DB6 sheet steel chassis platform this was to be no lightweight, turning the scales at over 2 tons all-up.

Major suspension changes had been made with the adoption of a De Dion system at the rear. This was as had previously appeared on the Lagonda Rapide produced by the company in the early 'sixties, and similar to the earlier DB3S and DBR1/300 sports-racing cars. Roller-spline BRD-made drive shafts were used for the first time, however, preventing the suspension from locking up under load (a defect of the simply splined shafts), and tube location was by parallel trailing arms and a Watt linkage. Armstrong Selecta-ride adjustable shock absorbers were fitted, and rear unsprung weight had been cut from the DB6 figure of 287 lb to just 177 lb by mounting the 10·8-inch Girling rear brake discs inboard. Front discs were 11½ inches in diameter, and operation was again by a dual hydraulic system with tandem master cylinder and twin vacuum servo-assistance. Much thought had gone into interior layout and design, the cabin combining comfort and convenience with strict adherence to the new United States Federal Safety Regulations.

The standard DB6 or Vantage engines were specified and the DBS ran concurrently with the normal DB6 and Volante models, priced at £5,500. The

11

new model was received with almost unprecedented acclaim, for despite its great weight, its 4-litre engine (in Vantage form with now undisclosed power output) rocketed it from 0–50 mph in 5·6 sec and to 100 mph in only 18 sec. Maximum speed was around 145 mph, but the most striking feature of the car was its sure handling and with the £133 extra ZF power-steering it could really be thrown around with almost complete safety. The ZF five-speed manual gearbox was as smooth as ever, and better sound-insulated, while the only drawbacks were inaccessibility of some controls when strapped in and a weak demisting and ventilation system.

And so into 1968 for the development of the final Aston Martin models of the decade. In homage to the new United States exhaust emission laws a triple Zenith-Stromberg CD Duplex carburation system was developed for export models, and while the DBS, DB6 and Volante Convertible range were generally little altered, prices now ranged from £4,497 for the DB6, through £5,062 for the Volante to the DBS at £5,718.

With this range of three models, still with the well-proven all-alloy 4-litre standard and Vantage engines, the company reached the end of a decade which had seen their products mature into some of the finest high-perform-ance Grand Tourers on the road. In 1967 their Chief Engineer, Mr Tadek Marek, had produced a 5-litre V8 prototype unit for competition use, and with the prospect of this being fitted beneath the DBS's capacious bonnet, the affluent enthusiast has good cause to look forward to the 'seventies with interest.

5 Austin

As a main element of the British Leyland Motor Corporation, the Austin company of Longbridge is one of the largest of British motor manufacturers. At the start of the last decade many models of all sizes were available. These ranged from the Austin 7, counterpart of the revolutionary Morris Mini, released in August 1959, through the A35, A40 and A55, to the A105 standard saloon and luxury Vanden Plas model.

To detail them in this order, the transverse front-engined, front-wheel drive ADO15 Seven was one of the major attractions at the 1959 Earl's Court Motor Show. Designed under the direction of Alec Issigonis, the new model presented reasonable accommodation for four people in a minimal overall package, endowed with fair performance by its 848-cc A-Series engine and phenomenal cornering capabilities by its rubber suspension units developed by Alex Moulton. Apart from the upper half of the engine, which incorporated well-proven parts from the existing A40 and Morris Minor ohv models, the new Austin Seven was completely new. The undersquare engine was mounted transversely in the nose of a unitary construction two-door shell, driving through a Newton & Bird single dry-plate clutch to a four-speed gearbox, with weak synchromesh on the upper three ratios. Gear-change was by an inordinately long central lever, with the sump-located gearbox being driven from the conventionally placed clutch by helical spur gearing. Further helical spur gears took the drive to two constant-velocity jointed drive shafts driving the front wheels. The 848-cc engine breathed through an SU HS2 carburettor, and with a cr of 8·3:1 produced 34 bhp net at 5,500 rpm.

The rubber suspension used had two main advantages; one, that it did not occupy much space, the other, that its progressive rate absorbed load changes in the car without altering the already rather limited standard of ride and the excellent, extremely stable and 'swerveable' handling characteristics. Wheel location was by front transverse links and rear trailing tubular arms, suspended by rubber cones with Armstrong dampers all round. Very direct rack-and-pinion steering was employed and the joys of hurling one of the new Austin Sevens through a corner in controlled understeer were soon amply demonstrated to spectators at motor race meetings (or in quiet country lanes when 'nobody was about'!). Tiny 7-inch Lockheed drum brakes were used, in 10-inch wheels for which special tyres had had to be produced. The major attraction of the car was economy, for at £496 for the standard model and £537 for the better-trimmed De Luxe, running costs were extremely low, and spares were ridiculously cheap. BMC had produced one of the greatest small cars of all time.

The previous small-capacity saloon, the A35, was discontinued in July 1959, only the Series AP5 Countryman version continuing into the 'sixties. But the angular Farina-bodied A40, with its estate styling and let-down tail-board beneath a fixed rear screen, was continuing, and in January 1960 both saloon and Countryman models were available. The engine was a 948-cc version of the A-Series unit, with a Zenith 26VME carburettor and, with a cr of 8·3:1, producing 34 bhp net at 4,750 rpm. This drove through a Borg & Beck 6½-inch sdp clutch to a four-speed manual gearbox with synchromesh on the upper three ratios, and from there a Hardy Spicer open prop-shaft transmitted to a hypoid bevel back axle. Coil-and-wishbone ifs was used with the conventional semi-elliptically sprung live back axle. Using Lockheed drum brakes all round, 8-inch front and 7-inch rear, this uninspiring but very solid, reliable and well-selling car was offered in standard trim at £638, De Luxe at £650 and Countryman at £659.

The A55 Mark II was one of BMC's typically solid and dependable Farina-bodied saloons, called, in this instance, the Austin Cambridge. Using an undersquare 1489-cc engine, producing 53 bhp at 4,350 rpm, the Cambridge, with its oblong radiator grille, rather obtrusive tail fins and generally austere and handsome looks, was a well-trimmed four-door family saloon, costing £801 basic or £829 in De Luxe saloon forms. Again a reliable but large gearbox was used, with synchromesh on the upper three ratios only, and with 9-inch drum brakes all round, coil-and-wishbone ifs and a semi-elliptic live rear end, the machine was conventional and generally unexciting but excellent transport for the average motorist.

Also cast in this mould but with rather more power was the A99 Westminster, with its C-Series 2912-cc engine, producing 108 bhp at 4,750 rpm, and with a three-speed all-synchromesh gearbox with overdrive on second and top as standard. Borg-Warner fully automatic transmission was an optional extra, and suspension was as usual, but Lockheed servo-assisted disc brakes were used at the front ($10\frac{3}{4}$ inches in diameter) with 10-inch rear drums. Steering was by Cam Gears or Bishop cam-and-peg, and this most opulent of the standard Austin range was priced at £1,148 standard manual with overdrive, or £1,219 with automatic.

Perhaps it would be simplest to deal with the Mini series development next. In March 1960 the Countryman model was first produced, having a 4-inch longer wheelbase than the saloon, with an attractively lengthy wood-trimmed estate body, four seats and extensive luggage accommodation. The new model was released in September, and in October the saloon had padding added to each side of the instrument cluster and in the doors and side panels, while modified telescopic dampers were used in place of the original orifice type.

On to June 1961, when the first Austin Seven Super was produced, to be announced in September that year. The radiator grille had twelve straight vertical chrome bars with nine horizontal wavy ones; duotone paintwork was introduced and with better trim and sound-proofing, lever-type door handles, and triple circular instruments in an oval panel it was much refined.

Big news had come in August, however, when an association between B M C and the Cooper competition car company was announced, in the form of the high-performance Mini-Cooper Mark I. Externally this little bullet resembled the new Super models apart from a Cooper badge and eleven horizontal grille bars. The engine had a slightly smaller bore and longer stroke, capacity rising to 997-cc, and with two SU HS2 inclined carburettors power was raised to 55 bhp at 6,000 rpm. An up-rated close-ratio gearbox was fitted and Lockheed 7-inch diameter front disc brakes overcame an inherent weakness of the standard vehicles. Engine oil capacity was 9 pints instead of $8\frac{1}{2}$, and turning circle was slightly down on the saloon's rather unimpressive 29 feet 6 inches.

In January 1962 the Austin Seven title, an unattractive attempt to revive the name of the company's famous small car of the between-wars period, was discarded, the Mini tag being adopted for both Morris and Austin products. In March Vynide replaced cloth upholstery on the basic saloon, and in October the De Luxe and Super models were discontinued, being replaced by the single Super de Luxe with more refined interior trim and the oval instrument panel. Some models were fitted with baulk-ring synchromesh on the upper three ratios from this time onwards, and an all-metal Countryman model, minus the attractive wooden trim, was introduced for the home market. Prices at this time ran from £509 for the Cooper, £605 for the all-metal Countryman and £627 for the half-timbered model.

March 1963 was the next landmark in Mini development, with the introduction of the Cooper 'S' variant, using a $70\cdot61\text{mm} \times 68\cdot26$ mm oversquare engine for the first time, with a capacity of 1071 cc. With 9·5:1 cr and twin SU HS2 carburettors, this tuned unit produced 68 bhp at 5,700 rpm, with 62 lb ft torque at 4,500 rpm. A BMC $7\frac{1}{8}$-inch sdp clutch was used with the same semi-synchromesh gearbox, although a close-ratio unit could be specified with an alternative 3·444:1 final drive ratio. The price of this marvellous little car, with its $7\frac{1}{2}$-inch large diameter front disc brakes, 94 mph top speed, 9 sec 0–50 mph time and 30 mpg economy, was £695.

In the same month a much-improved heater system was adopted on the

997-cc Cooper and standard models, and in May improved window catches were introduced throughout the range. In September 1963 improved telescopic dampers were fitted to the 997 Cooper, and in January 1964 this engine was discontinued, being replaced by a 998-cc unit with reduced stroke and increased bore. In March the 1071-cc Cooper 'S' was discontinued, and in April a new Cooper 'S 1275' was introduced, its 1275-cc capacity being derived from dimensions of 70·64 mm × 81·33 mm. Basically it was similar to the 1071 model, but with a high cr of 9·75:1 and enormous oil consumption the engine produced a healthy 75 bhp net at 5,800 rpm, with 79 lb ft torque at 3,000 rpm. A Lockheed vacuum-servo assisted the 7½-inch front disc and 7-inch diameter rear drum brakes, and with a close-ratio gearbox as standard this little car could touch 98 mph, rush from 0–50 mph in under 8 sec and still return some 30 mpg. The standard 850 Mini, at the same time, was reaching 74 mph flat-out, taking a respectable 17 sec from 0–50 mph and returning a genuine 40 mpg.

Major modifications came in 1964, when the Hydrolastic interconnected fluid suspension system of the 1100s was adopted in the Mini ranges. This system, with its unique self-levelling characteristics providing a smooth and constant ride, was in some respects a great improvement over the old rubber system, its ride being much less choppy on bumpy and poor surfaces. The Hydrolastic characteristic of increased tail-dip under acceleration and increased dive under braking was still present in the Minis, however, and they seemed to have lost a fraction of their inherent road-hugging precision so evident in the earlier vehicles. On the new models a combined ignition/starter switch was introduced, deleting the floor starter button used previously, and courtesy lights, oil filter warning lights, and crushable sun visors became standard. The 998 Cooper, 970 'S' and 1275 'S' all had gear levers mounted in rubber block inserts to cure an annoying buzz, while crushable sun visors and plastic-framed rear-view mirrors were added. All, of course, were converted to Hydrolastic suspension.

In October 1965 an excellent Automotive Products automatic transmission system was introduced as optional equipment, giving four-speed control with a complete manual over-ride in a central floor-mounted fore-and-aft notched gate. Girling telescopic dampers were fitted all round on the Hydrolastic suspension displacer units, and with diaphragm spring clutches the new basic and Super de Luxe models were respectively priced at £470 and £515 (manual) or £561 and £606 (automatic).

In January 1966 twin fuel tanks and an oil cooler became standard on the 1275 'S' models, and these were continued into 1967 without major change until October, when the original Mark I series cars were all discontinued, to be replaced by modified Mark II variants. The A2S7 basic saloon, A2S7S De Luxe and A/AW7 Countryman (in November) were replaced by the new Mark II A/A2SB standard and A/A2SBS Super de Luxe models with altered grilles containing eleven horizontal bars – instead of nine – and a thicker, more angular chrome surround. A wider rear window appeared with ugly protuberant tail lights and massive tail badge reading 'Mk II 850'. The Super de Luxe had chrome window surrounds, hinged rear quarter lights, oval instrument nacelle, heater, carpets, revised switches and restyled seats as standard. The 998-cc engine was made standard in the Mini 1000, with

15

remote gear-change as used previously on the Coopers, and also appearing in metal and wooden Countryman styling. The 850 engine was also to be made available to order in Super de Luxe trimmed shells, but with the bigger engine came an increase of 4 bhp and more torque, allowing a higher final drive ratio to be used (3·44:1 from 3·76) for easier high-speed cruising. Modifications to the brake drums gave lower pedal pressures, and steering changes resulted in a turning circle reduction to just 28 feet.

The Mini-Cooper Mark II appeared in C/A2SB form developed from the original Series C/A2S7 model, with similar external and internal changes to those already mentioned, although the disc/drum braking system was unaltered. The C/A2SB Mark II 1275 'S' was also released, and with this wide and refined Mini range, Austin went into 1968, and thence, in scarcely changed form, into 1969 and the end of the decade.

Meanwhile the little A35 Countryman had continued into the 'sixties, the original AP5 model being modified in March 1962 to the AP6-type, with flashing trafficators replacing the outdated and dangerous semaphore type, white-painted grille and road wheels, and a brightly painted moulding along the waistline. This produced an attractive dumpy-looking little machine, and it continued to sell reasonably well until finally discontinued in September 1962.

The longer Farina A40 reflected, in its continued production well into the 'sixties, BMC's staunch stand against making change just for change's sake. The 948-cc engined A40, with its enclosed rear luggage space accessible either through the tail-gate or from within the car, was offered in basic saloon form and, with folding rear seats and a fully-opening rear, as a Countryman true estate. The Countryman was introduced in September 1959, and in March 1960 a major modification – for the A40 – was the adoption of a longer dipstick! Prices at that time were £638 for the basic saloon, £650 De Luxe, £659 Countryman, and £671 Countryman De Luxe, and these extremely economical prices made the A40 range very attractive indeed for the family man who wanted reliable, steady transport for the family and a fair amount of baggage.

In September 1961 the A40 Mark II (Series A/A2S8) saloon and A/AW8 Countryman models were released, having a horizontal grille of seven bars, winding windows, redesigned fascia incorporating a glove box and a folding rear seat squab as standard. Wheelbase had been increased by about 4 inches, increasing passenger space very noticeably, and with an SU HS2 carburettor replacing the Zenith one used previously power was up to 37 bhp at 5,000 rpm from 34 at 'four-eight'. An anti-roll bar was added to the coil-and-wishbone ifs system, and the new prices for the mark IIs ranged from £657 to £715. The new saloon could top 75 mph, had a 17-sec 0–50 mph time and returned about 35 mpg. The ride was fairly comfortable, with well-controlled roll and a basic slight understeer characteristic.

In September 1962 the standard 948-cc engine was discontinued, being replaced by a bigger bore and longer-stroke 1098-cc unit. With a standard cr of 8·5:1 (an optional 7·5 export head also being available) the new engine produced 48 bhp net at 5,100 rpm and appeared in saloon and Countryman bodies in standard and Super de Luxe trim. Baulk-ring synchromesh was adopted on the upper three manual gearbox ratios, and reductions in purchase tax allowed prices to be reduced slightly for this much improved model. The A40 series continued happily into 1963, improved telescopic dampers being introduced in March and more noticeable changes following in September 1964. The fascia design was then extensively revised, with heater controls being placed vertically on either side of the switch panel, redesigned front seats and crushable sun visors with a plastic-framed mirror also being added.

In this basic trim the A40 was not further modified before its production finally ceased in November 1967. The 1098-cc Mark II was no ball of fire, managing a maximum speed of about 76 mph, and a 0–50 mph time of 16 sec, but with such a capacity it was very economical at about 40 mpg. If conventionality, simplicity and economy were what the people wanted they certainly found it in the A40 series. Prices on discontinuation stood at only £586–£629, a figure commendably stable throughout the model's production run.

The A55 Cambridge Farina saloon, in the meantime, had become a symbol of middle-class affluence slightly lower than the P4 Rover series, and offered comfortable accommodation, a solid, stable air, and reasonably effortless transport. Using the 1489-cc engine, a Countryman version joined the basic saloon Mark II model in May 1960, being announced in September with the same overall dimensions as the saloon. The Mark II models lasted until October 1961, when the A60 Cambridge replaced them, using a big-bore 1622-cc engine. With an 8·3:1 cr, and single SU HS2 carburettor, output was 61 bhp at 4,500 rpm, with torque figures of 90 lb ft at 2,100 rpm. Drive was via a Borg & Beck sdp clutch to the usual heavily synchromeshed four-speed gearbox. Automatic Borg-Warner three-speed transmission was optional, and with 9-inch drum brakes all round, suspension featured the normal coil-and-wishbone ifs with a semi-elliptic back end. Cam-and-peg steering was standard, and prices stood at £854 saloon, £883 saloon De Luxe and £978 for the Countryman. With the change from A55 to A60 the standard shell had been modified slightly, with lowered rear wings, cut-back fin tips and restyled rear lights. There were now slight variations in size between the saloon and Countryman, increasing space particularly in the latter model.

New rear springs were fitted to the saloon in June 1962, and October saw duotone paint schemes introduced, together with 'rimbellishers' and screen washers – which had been standardized on the Countryman in September 1960. New rear springs and the rimbellishers were added to the A60 Countryman the following month, and not until September 1964 were further major changes made, the steering mounting being modified, a greaseless prop-shaft adopted and the crushable visors and plastic-framed mirror (modifications of the complete BMC range) being added. In late 1967 the A60s were selling for around £770; far from expensive for a biggish, very solid, dependable and comfortable family saloon. A diaphragm spring clutch was standardized and, though still lacking synchromesh on first and generally beginning to look rather dated, the A60 line soldiered on into 1969. At this time prices ranged from £837 to £951, and the A60's survival is a remarkable example of automotive conservatism. How, in the face of their stern and so much more sophisticated opposition, the range still sold is an interesting reflection on the buying public.

Between July 1959 and September 1961, the A99 Westminster had been at the top end of the pure Austin saloon scale, with its 2912-cc engine producing sufficient power and torque for a three-speed gearbox to be deemed sufficient (albeit with overdrive on the upper ratios). The car had been selling in 1960 for just over £1,000, as related earlier, and in March that year new cam-and-lever steering and modified and more comfortable seats were adopted. Both overdrive and automatic models struggled on until they were deleted in September 1961 being replaced by the similar six-cylinder 3-litre engined A110 Westminster model. This had a 2-inch longer wheelbase than the A99, improved rear seating and generally more refined and luxurious interior trim, while a twin exhaust system raised the 3-litre engine's power output to 120 bhp at 4,750 rpm, torque peaking at 163 lb ft at 2,750 rpm. Three-speed all-synchromesh manual transmission with overdrive as standard was retained, while the Borg-Warner three-speed auto variant was also still available. The Lockheed disc/drum braking system was servo assisted, and both cam-and-peg steering and the ifs/semi-elliptic live axle suspension had been modified. At the rear a telescopic damper was employed in Panhard rod style to locate the live axle further, damping road shocks and axle deviations quite effectively. The manual overdrive saloon was priced at £1,269 with the automatic model at £1,342.

In July 1962 power-assisted steering and air conditioning became optional extras for the new Westminster, and from August 1963 an interior boot-light came on automatically when the lid was opened. In March 1964 a Mark II version replaced the Mark I, a four-speed gearbox being fitted with overdrive as an option rather than standard equipment. Small 13-inch wheels replaced the original 14-inch ones, while self-adjusting brakes were also standardized. Aluminium mesh grille and bonnet scoop were anodized bright trim, while Vinyl upholstery and a simpler fascia looked rather like economy measures. But this was a good, rugged five-seater, with a 100 mph maximum speed, 0–50 mph time of 10·5 sec and consumption of around 18 mpg. Practicable and fast, this big saloon cost £997 in basic form. In October a sealed prop-shaft and safety visors were fitted, and in January 1965 a De Luxe variant was introduced, similar to the Super de Luxe but minus the handsome veneer fascia and door cappings and without the handy picnic tables – a genuine luxury feature. This model survived for just over a year, being deleted in February 1966, and then in January 1968 the standard saloon and Super de Luxe machines were discontinued in favour of the new 1800-based 3-litre model, which had been announced the previous October, and of which more later.

In September 1963 a new ADO16 transverse front-engined 1098-cc variant had been announced, the Austin 1100. This was the Longbridge version of the Morris model announced the previous year, and with its larger, roomier shell, a direct development of the Mini theme, used the A40-sized A-Series engine with spur gear drive to the front wheels. With an 8·5:1 cr, and single SU HS2 carburettor, the 1100's engine produced 48 bhp net at 5,100 rpm. Lockheed 8-inch disc brakes were standard at the front, with similar size rear drums, and the Hydrolastic independent suspension system introduced in the Morris model of 1962 was used, later to be developed for use in the Mini range too. The Austin 1100 was priced at £593, the same as the Morris at that time, but had a grille comprising eight wavy horizontal bars with a central

Austin badge fore and aft. Two- and four-door models were available, and the De Luxe featured over-riders, twin horns, stainless steel window frames and several other minor refinements in advance of standard trim.

The two-door model was originally for export only, and typically BMC minor modifications on an already advanced and sophisticated original concept took place thereafter. A diaphragm spring clutch and redesigned gear-change was fitted in September 1964 with crushable sun visors and mirror common to the rest of the range, a heater was standardized on the De Luxe model in March 1965 – very late to be standardizing such a vital item – and, in October 1965, the excellent AP four-speed automatic transmission with manual over-ride control was offered as an optional extra.

In March 1966 a new Countryman two-door model was announced, with an opening tail-gate and good interior accommodation for such a small overall package. Prices of the Austin 1100 range at this time ran from £625 for the standard model, through £717 for the automatic, to only £712 for the new all-steel Countryman. The standard 1100 was endowed with a top speed of just under 80 mph, could get from 0–50 mph in under 15 sec, and averaged some 35 mpg, and with the Mini these two transverse front-engined models were selling in great quantities to all parts of the world. In addition the Minis were piling up competition successes, both in saloon car racing and international rallying, and more than one twin-engined device had appeared with a transverse engine at either end!

In May 1966 reclining front seats became an attractive optional extra, and the Mark Is continued basically unchanged until October 1967, when the new Mark II models were introduced in saloon De Luxe, Super de Luxe two-door and four-door, and Countryman versions. These had a similarly restyled grille surround to the Mark II Minis, with repeater indicators standard on the front wings, cut-back tail fins with larger rear lights (apart from on the Countryman) and with the new 'Mk II' insignia on the tail. The central instrument panel was finished in wood with a circular speedometer replacing the previous ribbon type and tumbler switches being standardized. The seats were restyled and improved while the Super de Luxe and Countryman models also had additional chrome on the window surrounds and a full-width fascia in silver finish still using a strip speedometer. The Countryman had also developed a simulated-wood side stripe, and the new Mark IIs occupied a price range from £647 to £745.

In that same month a new model was released using the basic Mark II 1100 body shell, but powered by a low-compression (8·8:1) version of the 1275-cc Cooper engine, producing – with a single SU HS4 carburettor – a smooth 58 bhp net at 5,250 rpm. Torque was 69 lb ft at 3,500 rpm, and for the first time an all-synchromesh gearbox was introduced on a BMC front-wheel drive car. A Borg & Beck 7½-inch single dry-plate diaphragm clutch was used, with the AP automatic transmission an optional extra. Standard manual ratios gave the new Austin 1300 a top gear speed of 16·8 mph per 1,000 rpm, the same as the automatic system, and the well-trimmed and nicely appointed machine was available in two- and four-door versions, standard and Super trim, prices beginning at £672 and running to £770 for the Countryman. In comparison with the 1100's performance figures, the 1300's maximum speed was raised to about 88 mph, 0–50 mph acceleration time was cut to well under 12 sec and fuel consumption was down only slightly to about 33 mpg average.

The 1968 announcement of the 1969 1100 and 1300 models revealed few changes, BMC adhering to their well-developed policy of no change purely for change's sake, and still the smaller capacity models were without all-synchromesh gearboxes, although an overdrive option was introduced for the 1100 and 1300s. Prices were considerably higher at between £698 to £750 for the 1100 saloons, the Countryman having been discontinued in this form, and £750 to £826 for the 1300s, including the only Countryman model still to survive.

The 1100 had long been the only medium-size model between the fwd small-capacity Minis and the big conventional saloons, but a further model had been added in October 1964. This was the ADO17 1800 Mark I, using an extremely spacious and rather handsome four-door body in typically BMC transverse-engine style. Headlamps were in bright metal trimmed recesses on either side of a deep grille, tapering towards its bottom and carrying the Austin badge on a bold horizontal rail across its centre. The car was a full five-seater with enormous bench seats front and rear and, although comfortably trimmed, was rather simple and 'empty' within. An undersquare 1798-cc five-bearing engine was fitted, developed from the MGB unit, with a standard cr of 8·2:1 (only 6·8:1 being optional), and with a single SU HS6 carburettor this unit produced 84 bhp at 5,300 rpm, and 99 lb ft torque at 2,500 rpm. An all-synchromesh four-speed gearbox was introduced with a standard top gear speed of 16·4 mph per 1,000 rpm. Optional ratios increased this to 17·7 mph per 1,000. Front transverse links and rear trailing arms located the wheels while suspension was by the now well-proven Hydrolastic fluid system, interconnected front to rear. The usual Cam Gears rack-and-pinion steering system was employed, but with lower gearing, making it rather unresponsive, and this big car, turning the scales at 22½ cwt, was found deceptively fast. Although appearing rather sluggish and unexciting, its top speed was in fact about 92 mph and 0–50 mph time 11 sec. It was roomy and comfortable: good transport for the conventional BMC big-car customer. With a consumption of about 25 mpg, and a selling price of £833 (in 1965), however, its performance was sufficient to make it attractive.

The De Luxe model also featured a full-width parcels shelf with air vents at either end, overriders, a passenger's side sun visor, leather upholstery, twin horns, grab handles, full carpeting, hinged quarter-lights and wheel trim discs. In November reclining front seats and a rear-seat centre arm-rest became optional extras, and from then on the A/HS10 1800 model continued virtually unchanged until May 1967, when a walnut-veneer fascia and door cappings were introduced, with a centre console, altered heater controls and pile carpets. Seat upholstery in the De Luxe was changed from hide to Ambla, and then in September power-assisted steering was also offered as optional equipment.

During this period the 1800 had been developed for rally and racing circuit use, and as modified it was – although still a rather large car – extremely stable and almost utterly reliable, while also actually feeling a fast and accelerative machine much belying its standard trim and tune.

In May 1968 the 1800 Mark II model was released, shell changes being the reverse of the 1100s with the rear wings being extended to form fins carrying vertical tail-light units. A restyled grille was adopted with four horizontal bars and centre badge and the sidelight/indicator clusters were enlarged. 'Mk II 1800' insignia appeared on the tail, and rocker-type control switches and flush-fitting door handles were also standardized. Extra power was obtained by increasing the cr to 9·0:1, output rising from 81 bhp net in 1967 to 86 bhp at 5,400 rpm in 1968. In addition 14-inch wheels had replaced 13-inch ones, so acceleration times were unchanged in favour of slightly less fussy high-speed cruising characteristics. Maximum speed was 93 mph, 0–50 mph time 11 sec, and fuel consumption was still not bad for 1800 cc at about 25 mpg. The price for the De Luxe was over £1,020 in 1969.

Back in October 1967 news of a very odd-sounding hybrid had been released, this being a conventional longitudinal engined rear-wheel drive saloon, based on the spacious 1800 centre section and entitled the 'Austin 3 Litre'. This machine used the latest MGC-type 2912-cc six-cylinder C-Series engine, with seven main bearings, still undersquare for smooth and effortless power, and fitted with twin SU HS6 carburettors. The cr was 8·2:1, and maximum power was 118 bhp net at 4,500 rpm, with 152 lb ft torque at 2,500 rpm. Drive was taken via a Borg & Beck diaphragm clutch to a four-speed all-synchromesh gearbox with optional overdrive, producing a direct top gear road speed of 18·33 mph per 1,000 rpm. Borg-Warner 35 automatic transmission was optional, and the big saloon, with its rather strange appearance, a long bonnet with 1800-type grille and rectangular headlamps grafted on to an 1800 centre section with an apologetic-looking boot glued on at the tail, used all-round independent suspension of a more sophisticated Hydrolastic type.

At the front the displacer/spring units and wheel locating links were all carried in a massive light-alloy casting bolted to the body shell, while at the rear separate displacers and rubber springs were used, the wheels being located on semi-trailing malleable cast-iron arms. An Armstrong Auto-Levelling system was built-in, sensing increases in vehicle load and pumping extra fluid into the system to compensate. In order to prevent this leveller from compensating for normal suspension movement, an 18-second delay in correction was allowed. This meant that nose-up attitudes under load were automatically corrected, handling characteristics would remain more constant, and also that the drive shaft universal joints would now have an easier time. New Girling '17/3' disc brake calipers were used, with triple pistons, on the stepped 10·4-inch diameter front discs, while 9-inch drums were again standard at the rear. Power-assisted steering was used, and prices stood at around £1,475 when models finally became available (with overdrive and fully-automatic Borg-Warner 35 transmission options). Cornering power of the new car was surprisingly high, regardless of a large degree of roll, and the low noise level and standard of ride were both most commendable. Maximum speed was about 98 mph, and the big car could accelerate from 0–50 mph well inside 12 sec. Fuel consumption was fair at 17 mpg, and the new 3 Litre was a very worthy vehicle for the head of such a generally advanced and sophisticated range, although still retaining such peculiar conservatism in some aspects.

Only about 1500 of these original 3 Litres were produced, however, in an

21

effort to judge initial market reaction, and for 1969 a new 3 Litre De Luxe was released for general consumption. Final drive ratio was 3·54:1 compared with the prototypes' 3·91 gearing, and with extensive sound-proofing, a redesigned fascia, revised steering wheel with a horn ring and modified secondary controls, and wider new seats the new model price was increased to £1,558.

But right at the end of the period, in April 1969, BLMC announced the long-awaited replacement for the 1½-litre Farina saloons, named the Austin Maxi. This model had been on the stocks for a long time, its release sensibly having been delayed until it had been produced in sufficient quantity for all major dealers to have examples available at once. Previously the British Motor Corporation had tended to release new cars before reasonable stocks were available.

The Maxi featured a new single ohc 1485-cc undersquare engine, producing 75 bhp net at 5,500 rpm. This was a major new design task, for it is intended to be developed well into the 'seventies as a basic power unit. Some £16 million were invested in its development, and its unusual undersquare dimensions were chosen to allow the production of a compact six-cylinder engine suitable for similar transverse mounting using the same tooling. The new engine had a single SU HS6 carburettor, and featured an unusual head design, with valves inclined away from each other, producing a long inlet and short exhaust tract. Much attention had been paid to ease of maintenance and service of the overhead camshaft installation.

An all-new five-speed transmission was used, located in a strong alloy sump casing and with cable selection from a rubber-mounted central gear-lever. Pot joints replaced the earlier Hooke types on the fwd drive shafts, dispensing with the original splines which could lock up under power. Engine, gearbox and Hydrolastic front suspension were all mounted in a common sub-frame. This in turn was mounted on an extremely strong unitary construction body shell, owing much to the 1800 in looks and construction. With four large side doors and a full-width upwards hinging tail-gate, the Maxi derived its strength from heavy gauge sills, exhaust pipe tunnel, double-skinned scuttle, and front and rear-seat platforms. Double-skinned pillars fed torsional loads into the roof panel, which was also doubled around its periphery. Austin 3 Litre-type Hydrolastic suspension was used, with separate pitch damping and individual wheel control. Forged arms replaced wishbones locating the front wheels, while trailing arms were used at the rear. Lockheed swinging caliper front disc brakes, 9·68 inches in diameter were standard with 8-inch rear drums and vacuum servo-assistance. A pressure limiting valve restricted locking tendencies in the rear brakes.

Internally, the Maxi offered reclining front seats forming a fairly comfortable bed, combined with a folding rear-seat squab to give useful freight space, accessible through the full-width tail-gate. Very few extras were offered in a diametrically opposed approach to that of Ford with their Capri model announced two months earlier, and price on introduction was £979.

The Maxi was roomy and comfortable, but very sluggish through the gears with little torque low down and a lot of noise high up. Like the gear-change on the 1800, the Maxi's was rather notchy, and fifth gear was very much an overdrive, offering about 10 per cent improved economy at cruising speeds.

Top speed was 87 mph in fourth, or only 85 mph in fifth, and 0–50 mph time 11·3 sec. Fuel consumption was not particularly good, averaging about 28 mpg.

But in typically British Leyland manner, the Maxi felt tough and solid, and cornered fast with almost neutral characteristics and rather more roll than its smaller brethren, being more softly suspended to improve the ride. It was big, spacious and practical, and although by no means a fast car, was very attractive to the man with a family who envisaged touring holidays.

6 Austin-Healey

In October 1952 the Healey Motor Company of Warwick had shown a glamorous 2·6-litre model at the Earl's Court Motor Show, and so great was the new model's attraction that the small works was completely swamped with orders. The Austin concern stepped in to help with production amenities, and the new model eventually appeared as the Austin-Healey 100. From that time on the combine never looked back in sports car mass production, becoming one of the country's leading car exporters.

The marque entered the 'sixties with the AN5 'bug-eyed' Sprite and the BN7/BT7 two- and two-/four-seat Healey 3000 machines. The attractive little Sprite had been modified in 1959 with a more easily erected and stowed hood, an effective hood/windscreen seal, a modified radiator and stronger wheels; among optional equipment available for the little two-seater was a useful hard-top. The undersquare 948-cc four-cylinder ohv A-Series engine had two SU H1 carburettors, a cr of only 8·3:1 and produced only 42·5 bhp net at 5,000 rpm. A Borg & Beck sdp clutch of 6¼-inch diameter transmitted drive to a four-speed gearbox. This had synchromesh on the upper three ratios, and there was rather a large gap between second and third, although third and top ratios were commendably close. A Hardy Spicer open propshaft was used with a hypoid final drive.

Independent coil-and-wishbone front suspension was used, with a live rear axle sprung on quarter elliptic springs with radius arm location. Girling lever-arm shock absorbers were fitted, and there were tiny but effective Lockheed 7-inch diameter drum brakes all round. All-up weight was only 12¾ cwt, and while the really diminutive Sprite was no road-burning 'man's car' it provided many enthusiasts with open-air motoring for the low initial price of £631, and very economical running costs thereafter.

The 3000, on the other hand, had all the attributes of a 'traditional' sports car. It was fast, easily handled in a muscular sort of way and was available as a pure two-seater or, with an enlarged cockpit area, as a two-/four-seater in the manner of the Sunbeam Alpine, with room for two small children or one transverse-seated adult. With the hood down, more could travel in fair comfort, but many found this to be illegal when they were spotted trying it.

23

The body shell was similar to the old 100-Six model, with long bonnet, a sloping nose and handsomely kicked-up rear wings with a sloping tail. The 2912-cc engine with normal push-rod ohv had a 9·03:1 cr with twin SU HD6 carburettors, and produced a healthy 124 bhp net at 4,600 rpm. A 10-inch Borg & Beck sdp clutch transmitted drive to a heavy four-speed gearbox with the usual quota of synchromesh on all but first, while Laycock de Normanville overdrive was optional. Again a Hardy Spicer open prop-shaft combined with a hypoid final drive, while coil-and-wishbone ifs with a semi-elliptic live rear axle was used, Girling 11¼-inch front disc brakes and 11-inch rear drums providing powerful retardation for this 21¼-cwt machine. Cam Gears cam-and-peg steering was used, as opposed to the same concern's rack-and-pinion system on the highly manœuvrable little Sprite, and prices for the 3000 models were £1,168 (two-seater) and £1,175 for the two-/four-seat version. Top speed was about 117 mph, and 0–50 mph acceleration took only 8·5 sec. Consumption was about 21 mpg, and with a mild oversteer characteristic the 3000 was fast, and cornered well.

In March 1960 sliding side-screens, previously standard only with the hard-top were standardized on the Sprite, and in April and May protective shrouds were applied to the two- and two-/four-seat 3000's discs.

A Mark II Sprite appeared in May 1961, replacing the Mark I with its attractively curved lines and protuberant headlights. The new model had a completely new body of flat, rectangular and singularly unimpressive appearance. The new AN6 model was available in De Luxe and standard forms, with a close-ratio gearbox standard, the De Luxe model featuring additional bumpers, overriders, screen washers and a rev-counter. The 948-cc engine was modified with compression raised to 9:1 and a twin SU HS2 induction system raising power output to 46·5 bhp at 5,500 rpm, with 52·5 lb ft torque at 2,750 rpm. Drum brakes were retained, together with rack-and-pinion steering and coil-and-wishbone ifs with the live rear axle. An opening boot-lid was new, however, access to the Mark I model's boot having been through the cockpit. The big improvement in the Mark II was at the top of the range, where acceleration continued well into the red at 6,000 rpm. Top speed was about 85 mph, 0–50 mph time was 13·2 sec and fuel consumption was a remarkable 38 mpg. But it was through corners that this car proved its sporting heritage, riding firmly but well, with minimal roll, slight understeer and great stability.

In June that year Mark II 3000 models had also been introduced, featuring convex vertical radiator grille slatting, triple SU semi-downdraught HS4 carburettors, a re-profiled camshaft and stronger valve springs. Compression ratio was unchanged, and this big six-cylinder now produced 130 bhp net at 4,750 rpm, with allied 167 lb ft torque at 3,000 rpm. The new models were kept at £660 for the standard Sprite, £674 Sprite De Luxe, £1,202, 3000 two-seater, and £1,210, 3000 two-/four-seater. The 3000 returned a maximum speed of about 123 mph for this price, covered 0–50 mph runs in fractionally over 6 sec and managed a reliable 18 mpg or so, and was everything that a sporting two-seater (or two-/'four'-seater) of the time should be, although handicapped by poor ground clearance.

The Sprite, however, was still rather underpowered, not comparing very well at all with several saloon cars of the day. In October 1962, therefore, the

AN6 948-cc version was discontinued, and in its place there appeared the Series AN7 Mark II using the enlarged 1098-cc four-cylinder A-Series unit, and with several other detail improvements. Power output was up to 55 bhp net at 'five-five', on a cr of 8·9:1, and net torque was 61 lb ft at 2,750 rpm. Lockheed front disc brakes were adopted, together with an electronic rev-counter, screen washers, padded mouldings on the cockpit surrounds and fascia, carpets in place of rubber matting, the baulk-ring synchromesh on the upper three gearbox ratios. Wire wheels were a pleasant optional extra, and the new 1098-cc Sprite was a rather more self-respecting sports car now, for although top speed was still only just under 90 mph, 0–50 mph time was down to 11 sec and fuel consumption was still over 30 mpg.

In June that year the pure two-seater 3000 had been discontinued, and production then concentrated on the two-/four-seat model as racing and rally successes continued to accumulate for all Austin-Healey variants. In January 1963 the 3000's rear cockpit moulding was redesigned to prevent damage to the folded hood, and in April a completely new hood assembly was standardized. At the same time felt slides and compression springs were adopted for the Sprite's antique sliding side-screen system, and then in February 1964 the Mark II Healey was discontinued, a new Mark III Series BJ8 model replacing it. Modifications to the engine, including a change to twin SU HD8 carburettors, had produced a vast power increase to 150 bhp at 5,250 rpm, with commensurate torque increase to 173 lb ft net at 3,000 rpm. Girling servo-assistance was introduced on the 11¼-inch front disc and 11-inch rear-drum brake system, while a wood-veneer fascia, with lockable glove box and a central console-mounted gear-lever were noticeable refinements. Overall weight was up slightly to 22¾ cwt.

In March the Mark II AN7 Sprite was deleted, to be replaced by the H/AN8 series Mark III model. This featured a curved windscreen, lockable doors with externally operated push-button door handles, fully winding side windows and hinged quarter-lights. Tachometer and speedometer were placed in a binnacle dead ahead of the driver with supplementary instruments in a central panel, and engine modifications raised output to 59 bhp net at 5,750 rpm.

Further modifications occurred in May 1965, with a greaseless prop shaft appearing on the Sprite, and in October 1965 separate rounded flasher indicators appeared on the 3000. Major change came to the Sprite in October 1966 with the replacement of the 1100 Mark III by the 1275 Mark IV model. This H/AN9 series machine was fitted with a version of the Cooper 1275-cc engine, with a 9:1 cr and twin SU HS2s, producing a healthy 65 bhp at 6,000 rpm, with 72 lb ft torque at 3,000 rpm. This was still notably less than the higher-compression Mini-Cooper 'S', however, and this seems a strange parallel between a sports saloon and a 'true' sports car. Synchromesh was still lacking on bottom gear, but a 6½-inch diaphragm clutch was standard, and Lockheed 8¼-inch front discs with 7-inch rear drums were fitted. Separate brake and clutch master cylinders appeared, and the folding hood was now an integral, non-removable fixture and operated very well – proving extremely weather-proof. The price of this much refined model was £672, and meanwhile the 3000 Mark III continued at £1,126. Both models continued to sell well throughout 1967, but January 1968 saw the introduction of far-reaching new United States Federal safety regulations, and it was decided that the cost of suitably modifying the 3000 for export to this country, one of the firm's largest customers, would be disproportionately high. Therefore, the 'big Healey' was discontinued, its passing causing many a silent tear.

But the Mark I V Sprite was better placed in both home and export markets, and as such continued in slightly modified form into 1968. Compression was reduced slightly to 8·8:1, and with twin SU HS2 carburettors and other modifications, a maximum of 64 bhp was produced at 5,800 rpm, while peak torque was greatly improved at 139 lb ft at 3,000 rpm. In 1968 the 1969 model Mark IV was announced as having similar power, with a respectable top speed of 96 mph, a 0–50 mph acceleration time of only 9·2 sec and still good consumption figures of about 33 mpg. The price for the car in this trim was £724.

During the decade the Healey range contracted noticeably, and with the passing of the 3000 model, production of the traditional, masculine and rugged Austin-Healey was at an end. However, the Mark IV Sprite at last introduced some genuine sports-car performance into the always under-powered smaller model.

7 Bentley

The Rolls-Bentleys of the 'sixties have lacked a little of the status of the true Rolls-Royce models, but that Gothic radiator style still retains something of a sporting air, even if the rest of the car has become progressively more and more opulent and luxurious.

In August 1959 the company's new 6230-cc V8 engine appeared in the S2 models, the unit being formed from light alloy castings, and weighing no more than the 4887-cc six-cylinder, which it replaced. With push-rod-operated inclined overhead valves, an 8:1 cr and twin horizontal SU carburettors, this new engine produced an undisclosed but 'sufficient' number of horses, and used an antiquated automatic transmission, with hydraulic coupling. This system had been originally designed in America some twenty years previously, and was now showing its age in its wide ratios and lack of a torque converter to multiply effort. Its jerky gear-change was to mar 'the world's best car' for most of the decade. It had been modified slightly to transmit increased torque, however, and a divided open prop-shaft drove to a hypoid bevel back axle. Final drive ratio was also higher than previously, giving a higher cruising speed, and some minor suspension alterations had been made to improve stability at these high speeds. Basically, the suspension system incorporated coil-and-wishbone ifs with a rigid rear axle on semi-elliptic springs located by a 'Z-bar', and the lever-arm hydraulic shock absorbers and power-assisted cam-and-roller steering were of Rolls-Royce manufacture. A dual hydraulic braking system was standard, with a gearbox-driven mechanical servo giving something like seven times multiplication, much more than usual with a vacuum servo. Massive $11\frac{1}{4}$-inch drum brakes were fitted all round, and the Bentley S2 was available in four basic forms complete.

These included the basic four-door all-steel saloon, an attractive convertible coupé by H. J. Mulliner, and special long-wheelbase versions built by James Young and Park Ward. All were to the usual almost legendary standards of finish and equipment, and prices ran from £5,660 and £7,457 to £8,316 or £8,942 respectively. Among the luxury equipment available, incidentally, was a full air-conditioning system (both heating and cooling), and the body shells were insulated from the massive chassis by rubber cushioning. Another interesting feature, and a modification from earlier models which expected the driver to operate a one-shot lubrication system pedal, was the addition of chassis lubricant reservoirs, extending greasing service intervals to around 10,000 miles, or one year.

Using the same lightweight V8 engine was the Bentley Continental, fitted with a lighter body shell and higher gearing. Speed per 1,000 rpm in top gear was up from 27·3 mph (for the S2) to 28·9 mph, and again a number of body styles were available, built and fitted by selected specialist coachworks. The cheapest of these was the Park Ward convertible coupé at £7,856, and the range progressed through a two-door sports saloon and 'Flying-Spur' four-door saloon at £8,118 each to James Young's two-door saloon at £8,196 and four-door model at £8,295. In view of the Continental's increased performance potential, four-shoe front brakes were fitted in place of the S2 models' two trailing shoe type. Disc brakes, as yet, could not compete for quiet performance with Rolls' sophisticated drum system.

So the Bentley range entered the 'sixties, minor additions such as map lights, revised rear lamp designs and trim alterations being made until October 1962, when the short-wheelbase S3 series models were introduced. Virtually identical to the Rolls-Royce Silver Cloud III, the new Bentley had a lowered bonnet line improving forward vision, and dual sealed-beam headlight units were mounted in the broad flared wings, flanking the traditional radiator design. Fog-lights beneath the outer sealed-beam units were retained, but these no longer did double duty as indicators, separate lights being added to the leading edges of the curved wing styling. The V8 engine had its cr raised to 9:1, and 2-inch SUs replaced the $1\frac{3}{4}$-inch original units. The engine's bottom-end was strengthened to accommodate a 7 per cent – otherwise unspecified – power increase, and other changes included more steering assistance, increased leg-room and a modified independent heating and ventilation system as slowly developed in the S2s and earlier Silver Clouds. The gearbox-driven brake servo was unaltered, and these huge saloons were remarkably sporting in performance if not in feel, comfort and appearance. The huge tyres generated a lot of grip and with a basically neutral handling characteristic the big Rolls-Bentleys could be cornered at remarkably high speeds. Cruising was quiet and effortless at 100 mph, and the new S3 was offered for a basic price increase of around £260. The Continental also had twin headlamps and modified power-steering, and from October 1963 Mulliner and Park Ward bodies became combined under the 'H. J. Mulliner, Park Ward' title, the combined concern becoming a Rolls-Royce subsidiary. In March 1964 the headlamp fairing surfaces were raised to incorporate the 'B' monogram on the S3s and four-door Continentals, while on the two-door lightweights the monogram was incorporated on a flat headlamp surround.

In October 1965 the all-new T-series appeared, being the Bentley equivalent of the Rolls-Royce Silver Shadow. Designed by a team under Chief Engineer Harry Grylls and styled by John Blatchford, the new model was something of a sensation. This was a slightly shorter, much lower, and more sleek model than the previous S-series cars, retaining the same amount of internal accommodation and more luggage space. Replacing the standard steel-bodied Rolls-Bentley saloons – the other chassis continuing unchanged as produced for specialist coach-builders – the two vehicles differed from one another only in radiator design. A monocoque shell was adopted, with independent suspension all round to provide the best combination of ride and handling from the lighter machine. The steel monocoque derived much of its strength from longitudinal members formed under the door sills, linked by a combination seat and wheel arch structure at the rear and scuttle and bulkhead at the front. Envisaging the possibility of providing a bare basic structure for coach-building specialists to practise their art, the roof was largely unstressed, but even so the complete structure proved torsionally stiffer than most other British production cars, and second only to the outstandingly strong BMC 1800 shells. In order to keep noise and road-shock level to a minimum, sub-frames were attached at front and rear to carry the suspension, and these were insulated from the body by Delaney-Gallay 'Vibrashock' steel-wire cushions. Hung on these at the front was a welded sheet steel sub-frame, carrying upper and lower wishbones with interposed coil-spring/damper units, Saginaw power-assisted steering, engine and automatic transmission. At the rear, a cross-member mounted on Vibra-shock insulators carried robust trailing wishbones, and compliance was allowed in the cross-member by attaching its lower edges to trailing arms on either side. This allowed the cross-member to rock slightly, its upper edge carrying the wishbones being allowed to move fore-and-aft, complying with road bumps and shocks, and so reducing their effect on the car's occupants. But at the same time the trailing arms prevented the cross-member from skewing and giving rise to rear-wheel steering. The differential was rigidly mounted to the sub-frame, and co-axial coil-spring damper units picked up on the wishbones forward of the drive shafts. One feature of the suspension system as a whole was its built-in resistance to dive under braking. Very soft springs were used, and a high-pressure hydraulic self-levelling system was adopted to give automatic height control and prevent the available wheel movement being used all the time. Disc brakes were also fitted all round, with dual circuits and a sophisticated 'fail-safe' system. Girling and Rolls-Royce engineers believed that they had at last got over the problem of squeal which had deterred them from using discs for so long, and with twin front disc calipers and single rears, powerful servo-assistance was standard.

Minor alterations had been made to the 6230-cc V8 engine, including relocation of the sparking plugs to make them more accessible, and an air filter was mounted under the off-side wing. The much-criticized jerky change from third to second gear in the automatic transmission had been improved, and electrical selection replaced a mechanical linkage. Although the rather outmoded four-speed transmission was retained on home-market models, export versions used a new three-speed transmission with torque converter based on an American GM400 design. This was very smooth, very slick and very desirable. Alternators were standard on air-conditioned models, and electrically operated front-seat adjustment, winding side windows, heated rear screen, extending radio aerial and fuel filler cover were also basic equipment. An extremely complex heating and ventilation system was fitted, and the interior was the usual quietly opulent mixture of deeply padded hide upholstery, best-quality carpet and beautifully finished wooden veneer.

Here was a Bentley which looked more like a motor-car and less like an armoured vehicle, and prices on release stood at £6,496 for an advanced and sophisticated machine which was looked upon very much as the British new car of the decade.

A two-door James Young saloon version was announced soon afterwards, and in March 1966 another two-door model appeared from the H. J. Mulliner, Park Ward works. At the end of 1965 the Bentley Continental series had been discontinued in favour of the sophisticated new T-series variants, and in January 1967 the standard four-door model and two-door Mulliner-Ward variant continued, the James Young model being discontinued. Standard saloon price stood at £6,608 at this time, and the Mulliner model was available for £9,958.

Then, in September 1967, Mulliners introduced a drop-head coupé model with a power-operated hood. Late in 1968 the GM400 transmission, with its ultra-smooth change and effort-multiplying torque converter, was adopted as standard on home as well as export markets. With this modification the only serious source of criticism of the Crewe company's products was at last eradicated.

8 Bond

Laurie Bond built his first minimal three-wheeler in 1948 and production was continued by Sharps Commercials Ltd during the 'sixties. This inexpensive transport, powered by Villiers two-stroke engines, attracted a small but fanatically enthusiastic band of owners – the self-styled 'Bondoliers' – although the attractions of the motorcycle-inspired three-wheelers are not obvious to everybody who has travelled in them. They are noisy, shaky and a little unstable; they do not go very quickly but they do give the occupants an impression of endeavour, of team effort made actually to travel somewhere. Thus they were very much a throw-back to the vintage days. Bond three-wheeler offerings of the early 'sixties included the 250G tourer, with a box-like body, folding three-position hood, winding windows, and a locking boot. Without a reverse gear, this little two-seater with a steerable nose wheel was taxed as a motorcycle, and with a 250-cc Villiers engine was priced at £388.

Reverse was available, pushing the price up to £394, and an Estate version was also produced, prices running from £406 for a non-reversible single-cylinder model to £440 for a twin-cylinder reversible. These machines offered economic transport to impecunious families and their low prices were difficult to better.

In 1966, however, the hard-core 'Bondoliers' were shocked to hear of their ideal's replacement by the Bond 875. This featured an all-enveloping glass-fibre body shell, with two doors, sliding side windows and a rear-mounted de-tuned Hillman Imp *car* engine. This four-cylinder light-alloy single ohc unit had a capacity of 875-cc, and with an 8:1 cr it produced 34 bhp at 4,700 rpm. It drove through a smooth four-speed gearbox. Suspension was independent front and rear, a coil-spring/damper suspended leading arm locating the single front wheel, and trailing arms with separate coils and dampers being used at the tail. Those 34 bhp were sufficient to propel the little Bond from 0–60 mph in 16 sec – a speed which felt almost frighteningly quick within the frail-looking cockpit structure! However, it was an extremely manœuvrable and utilitarian little vehicle, with a phenomenal fuel economy of over 50 mpg. Soon it was joined by a 40 cubic foot van version, and eventually was restyled as the Mark II, with a restyled nose and grille incorporating rectangular headlights, which lost the 'down-in-the-mouth' expression of the Mark Is.

But while the Bond works were continuing with their three-wheeled economy cars, they had embarked on a programme of economically priced GT car production, using basic Standard-Triumph parts. The original four-wheeled model, the Bond Equipe GT, had been introduced in May 1963. This was the parent company, Sharp's Commercials', first foray into the four-wheeled world, and used the Triumph Herald backbone chassis with a partially stressed glass-fibre body shell bolted to it. The 1147-cc twin SU HS2 carburated engine was fitted, producing 63 bhp net at 5,750 rpm. The basic Herald suspension was used all round, and with a Spitfire-like disc/drum braking system the new model was marketed through Standard-Triumph's dealer system under their normal warranty.

An attractively styled glass-fibre shell was used, incorporating two Vitesse doors and blending them into a contemporary GT shape with a gently drooping nose, full-width radiator grille and sloping fastback tail flanked by small fins. But the overall height was dictated by Triumph saloon parts, and the result was a rather dumpy shape which limited maximum speed rather to around 82 mph. Acceleration from 0–50 mph was reasonable, at just under 12 sec, and the Triumph engine was as usual economical, giving around 35 mpg. In handling, and braking, the GT naturally was as good as the Herald, with the same ultimate limitations of understeering tyre scrub causing the nose to dip, the tail rising until the rear swing axles up-edged the tyres and caused final oversteer. But, sadly, the body left much to be desired, in both execution and design. The rear seat leg and headroom were severely limited (even for a 2+2), while the boot space was accessible only through a rear seat squab, which folded down. On the road the whole structure rattled and shook. With extras to be added to a basic price of £786, the original Bond GT was rather expensive.

However, the company persevered, and in October 1964 announced a modified Equipe, the GT4S with a modified, and aesthetically less satisfactory, body shell. The tail was clipped off short into a Kamm-type transom to increase boot space (a conventional boot-lid was also added), while dual headlights appeared in heavily lipped wing mouldings. On introduction the price was £817.

The 2+2 was discontinued on the announcement of this new model, and in February 1965 the 4S was fitted with the latest Spitfire Mark II engine as standard. From June wire wheels became optional, along with a heated rear screen from February 1966. In January 1967 the last Spitfire Mark II-engined Equipe was produced, and in February the GT4S 1300 made its debut. This used a 1296-cc 75 bhp engine, again of Triumph origin.

Then in August, a Vitesse-based six-cylinder 2-litre model appeared. This had the chassis, engine and gearbox from the Triumph model, in a still deep-chested but rather cleaner four-light body with GT styling. A large flat rear window surmounted the knife-edged tail and twin headlights were placed in a recessed full-width grille. A number of sophisticated extras were offered, including an electrically heated rear screen, and interior accommodation on this model was much improved, a Vitesse rear bench seat combining with Bond-adapted GT6-type bucket seats at the front to give comfortable and positive location. The price of this attractively styled and now well-built GT was £1,095 on release.

Quantity production of the 1300 and 2-litre models continued into 1968, and then in October two new models were announced: the 2-litre Mark II and a 2-litre Convertible. The Mark II coupé used the modified Vitesse rear suspension (described in the Triumph chapter) which limited camber change at the wheels and thus gave more predictable handling qualities, while the more powerful engine also adopted gave a top speed of over 100 mph. In addition to cornering and straight-line power improvements, some trim changes were also made, the result being a quiet and comfortable motor-car. It was priced at £1,197.

The Convertible version looked less happy, for with the hood lowered its high waistline and tapered nose and tail gave it something of the appearance of a military amphibian. However, it offered full four-seat accommodation, which was unusual for a vehicle of this type. With an integral 'disappearing' hood, its price was £1,277.

Early in 1969 the Reliant company acquired Bond's production interests, but the two marques continued unchanged and outwardly independent towards the 'seventies. Nevertheless, it will be interesting to see if the marriage to a Ford-oriented parent company will dictate any changes of allegiance.

9 Bristol

After World War II the Bristol Aeroplane Co. Ltd was left with spare plant and space at its Filton, Bristol, factory and primarily at the instigation of one of the firm's directors, Mr (now Sir) George White, a car-producing division was formed to make use of it. The first Bristol car to appear was based on the sporting German BMW 328 'six' of the immediate pre-war years, and this original Bristol 400 model was produced to scrupulously high aviation standards of design, manufacture and inspection. Design was in the hands of Mr Dudley Hobbs and his assistant, Mr D. W. Sevier, and they have since been responsible for the design of every subsequent model. The select Bristol team were convinced that workmanship of the highest standard in a car of medium size, coupled with high performance and good handling characteristics, would sell readily to a particular type of wealthy enthusiast. The market was, and is, small, but the Bristol products have catered for it admirably in the past twenty-five years.

Introduced in 1958, the Bristol 406 was just such a car. A roomy two-door four-seater, the car was similar in appearance to the later A C Greyhound with a straight waistline from square nose to tail, and large glass area. Transverse leaf ifs was used, while at the rear a rigid axle was located by Watt linkage and sprung by longitudinal torsion bars. A single central arm controlled torque reaction. Power came from a 2216-cc six-cylinder Bristol engine fed by three downdraught Solex B32 PB1/7 carburettors and producing 105 bhp at 4,700 rpm. Transmission was via a four-speed gearbox with Laycock de Normanville overdrive on top to a Salisbury 4·27:1 back axle. The 406 body was aluminium-panelled over an all-steel frame and this was welded to a very stout box-section chassis. Extensive sound-deadening was provided by Mutacel lining; deep Reutter reclining front seats were used with a Bristol modification in the form of an adjustable head-rest, and at the rear the bench seat was formed into two individual squabs, with large arms and side cut-outs to give roomy elbow rests. Rheostat-controlled lighting illuminated the comprehensive instrument panel, while a telescopic steering column, cigar lighter and washer/wiper sweeps were standard. The whole interior was trimmed in top-quality leather, while there was also extensive crash padding, and a walnut-veneer fascia and door cappings. The size of the carpeted boot was effectively increased by placing the spare wheel in the nearside front wing, a hatch opening aft of the front wheel arch to give access (the battery was in the offside wing).

At just under 27 cwt dry the Bristol's 105 bhp gave vivid acceleration and a top speed of over 100 mph in overdrive top, while consumption was around 20 to 24 mpg.

In October 1959 a mesh grille replaced the original vertical slat styling, and fog lamps were added to the powerful Marchal headlamps, fitted to external mounts within the radiator air intake. The price was £4,244, and in this form the Filton factory produced the 406 in small numbers until October 1961.

Then the model was replaced by the Bristol 407, and in this car the quiet running and immense torque of a large American V8 engine was used, in place of the company's own BMW-based 'six'. The V8 chosen was of Chrysler manufacture and 5130-cc capacity. But, characteristically, this was no 'ordinary' V8. The oversquare engines were built in Canada to special order and had the usual hydraulic tappets removed to allow higher rpm. With a four-barrel Carter carburettor this compact and quiet engine (twin electric fans saving space and cutting noise) produced 250 bhp at 4,400 rpm and 340 lb ft torque at 2,800 rpm. It was mated to a torque converter and three-speed automatic gearbox; press-button control allowed lower ratios to be selected at will, while a kick-down engaged first when the throttle was floored below 29 mph, and second below 60 mph. Normal upchanges were at 37 and 70 mph flat out, but, driven gently, the car would go along in top at very low speeds.

The body was still in steel-framed aluminium coach-built panelling and welded to the box-section frame, but coil-springs and ball-jointed wishbone ifs were now standardized in place of the transverse leaf. Dunlop discs all round with Lockheed servo-assistance provided powerful braking, while interior trim was still to the same exceptionally high standards.

The 407 was a smooth and comfortable car, with firm and well-controlled suspension and steering which was heavy at low speeds, but lighter further up the speed range. A slight oversteer characteristic and first-rate tractional qualities provided fast, safe and predictable cornering. From 0–100 mph took 25·9 sec, 0–60 mph 9·2 sec, and with a maximum speed of over 126 mph, consumption of this 32-cwt car was fair at 12·5 mpg. Price at introduction was £4,848, falling shortly afterwards with purchase tax reductions to £4,260.

In October 1963 the 407 was made available to special order only, upon release of the 408. Lower and sleeker than its predecessors, the 408 had a wider and less square grille with a second set of headlamps sunk into it, but substantially it was similar to the 407. Electrically adjustable Armstrong telescopic dampers were added to the torsion bar live rear axle. Overall weight was 32 cwt, yet this purposeful high-performance luxury car would hold a 2+2 Ferrari over the standing half-mile and out-accelerate an E-type Jaguar in top gear! With enough understeer to be stable at high speeds and a slight degree of oversteer for 'fun' cornering the Bristol could be said to be Britain's true counterpart of the Italian performance car. Its £4,459 list price was reasonable indeed.

Two years later the 408 was replaced with the 409, which featured a 5211-cc V8 engine, widened front track and Girling hydraulic servo-assisted disc brakes on all four wheels. It was slightly lighter than the 408 and higher geared, maximum speed rising to 132 mph. Weight distribution had been altered, the front roll centre raised and softer front suspension adopted with new-setting dampers fore and aft. These gave a gentler low-speed ride. The radiator intake shape had been revised for better air flow over the new sealed system lightweight radiator core, and a hold was provided on each of the three gear ratios. New 'long-life' stainless silencers were fitted and an electrically heated rear screen was also standardized. Finally a silent 'pre-engaged' starter motor was fitted and customers could specify paint and leather colour in their orders. The price was £4,849 on release, but with the introduction of power-assisted steering in October 1966 it rose to £5,373. With further suspension softening and steering developments the type was slowly developed away from its sporting background, becoming more and more a luxury 'grand touring car' in the true sense of the term.

More sporty versions could still be ordered, the 407 and 408 still being available in October 1967, when the Bristol 410 appeared. Very similar to the 409, the 410 was externally distinguished by its two full-length chrome side strips instead of just one-and-a-half, repeater indicator units ahead of the front wheel arches, and rectangular slots in the disc wheels instead of the round ones in the ugly old wheels. Dual system hydraulic Girling disc brakes were used, while track was increased and height reduced. Gear hold selection was by a floor-mounted lever instead of push buttons, but otherwise the car was essentially similar to the 409 which, again, would still be produced to special order. The price of the new model was £5,898 on introduction, rising to £6,127 in spring 1969.

In the meantime, Bristol-Siddeley Engines had closed down Armstrong-Siddeley car production in mid-1960, and had then decided to back out of car production altogether. In 1961 Bristol Cars Ltd became a separate entity under the directorship of Sir George White and Anthony Crook, a well-known motor racing personality, whose interest and support for the marque had fostered its many competition successes until its pursuit of an exclusive market lured it away into the realms of the pure, sophisticated and beautifully appointed high-performance quality car.

10 Daimler

This company can trace its foundation back to the very dawn of the motoring age, and in its recent history has gained a reputation for smooth, quiet and refined motor transport for the gentry, with lavish equipment and standards of mechanical refinement second only to the Rolls-Bentley products. Surprise was understandable, therefore, when the V8-engine format appeared in 2½-litre form in the SP250 sports car in 1959, the model joining the imposing and sedately fast Majestic and 4·5-litre saloon and limousine range.

The SP250 Dart was shown in prototype form at the New York Motor Show that April, based on a short, strongly cross-braced chassis frame with a wheelbase of only 7 feet 8 inches, and which passed below the live rear axle. A well-designed and engineered V8 engine with oversquare dimensions of 76·2 mm × 69·85 mm, had the cylinders disposed in a 90-degree formation, the inclined overhead valves being operated by a single central camshaft. Light alloy cylinder heads were used with a compression ratio of only 8·2:1, and the 2500-cc unit produced a genuine 140 bhp at 5,800 rpm. Twin SU HD6 carburettors were used, mounted within the Vee, and drive was taken to a four-speed close-ratio gearbox, with synchromesh on all but first, via a 9-inch Borg & Beck sdp clutch. An open Hardy Spicer prop-shaft transmitted drive to the hypoid rear axle, and attractive options included overdrive and fully automatic transmission.

Braking was by Girling discs all round, 10·625-inch diameter front and 10-inch rear, while Cam Gears cam-and-lever steering was fitted. Front suspension was of coil-and-wishbone independent type, while at the rear semi-elliptics were used. The whole thing was clad in an ugly but purposeful-looking glass-fibre body, with a high domed bonnet blending in with short bulbous wings and thrusting forward ahead of them into a protruding air intake, carrying a low and wide representation of the classic fluted

Daimler grille. Two wide-opening doors were used and the rear wings swept up into prominent fins with a roomy boot accessible through a large squared-off hinged lid wrapping over the tail transom. Accommodation included comfortable and well-wrapped-round front bucket seats with fairly limited leg-room and a small occasional bench seat in the rear of the cockpit for children or the usual 'transverse adult'. Soft and hard-tops were available and this lightweight machine, with its glass-fibre shell contributing to a figure of 18¾ cwt dry, was a vivid performer. Top speed was 120 mph, and the smooth and quiet V8 accelerated the machine from 0–50 mph in only 7·3 sec. In addition economy of the order of 20–25 mpg could be expected, and for £1,395 on release the new Dart was a very attractive and genuinely sporty buy.

Unfortunately the chassis did have its limitations, flexing under hard cornering with adverse handling results, and distortion in the glass-fibre body made incidents of doors flying open in corners fairly commonplace!

Running concurrently with the Dart was the Majestic saloon, using a six-cylinder 3794-cc engine producing 147 bhp at 4,400 rpm. This unit was fitted with twin SU HD6 carburettors, and had a cr of 7·5:1, was smooth and quiet in true Daimler tradition and matched the stylish four-door saloon body very well in terms of refinement and finish. Borg-Warner three-speed automatic transmission was standard, and giant Dunlop disc brakes were used all round, 12-inch diameter front and rear. Coil-and-wishbone ifs was used, with semi-elliptics springing the live rear axle; and with Newton telescopic shock absorbers and Burman recirculating ball steering the Majestic offered very high standards of ride comfort. All-up weight was a massive 34½ cwt, and this Series DF316/7 Majestic was priced at £2,495.

Generally similar but newly released at the 1959 London Show was the Majestic Major saloon, incorporating various improvements and using a new 4½-litre version of the SP250 sports model's V8 engine. The unit's oversquare dimensions had risen to 95·25 mm × 80·1 mm, giving a capacity of 4561 cc, and output was up to 220 smooth and manageable bhp at 5,500 rpm. Twin SU HD8 carburettors were used and the water pump and fan were located between the cylinder blocks with the dynamo moved to a new mounting low down to the right. Tappet arrangement had been modified slightly, and two cylindrical air cleaners were mated to the carburettors, dominating either side of the engine bay. But a major advantage of the new V8 unit was that it saved 26 lb over the 3·8-litre 'six'. Otherwise the Major was similar to the basic Majestic model, apart from a higher final drive ratio (3·77:1 replacing 3·92:1), larger front brake calipers, Girling telescopic dampers and Dunlop Road Speed tubed tyres as standard. The boot was extended by some 6 inches, and internally a new fascia was adopted.

The Majestic Major had a velvet-smooth top speed of over 120 mph, and went from 0–50 mph in only 7·1 sec. Cornering was surprisingly good, but the soft suspension bottomed easily on undulations. Very light controls made it a large car that was easy to drive, and, with such performance, very distinctive. Finally, Daimler had their small-quantity production DK400/A standard and DK400/B De Luxe Limousines, using a six-cylinder 4617-cc engine in a long, roomy and very opulent sleekly styled body shell. Again with two SU HD8 carburettors and a 7:1 cr, this unit produced 167 bhp gross at 3,800 rpm, with the normal coil-and-wishbone ifs and semi-elliptic rear end, and huge

35

13-inch Girling servo-assisted drum brakes were used all round. Dry weight for these monster limousines was over 2 tons, the 'A' model having three occasional seats and a sliding partition between chauffeur and occupants, while the 'B' luxury version had two occasional seats and a drop division. Prices were £4,215 and £4,340 respectively, and for cars in this class they were reasonably inexpensive.

Following its export announcement as the Daimler Dart in April 1959, the V8 sports model entered production in September, and in October the home market SP250 right-hand drive vehicle began to leave the Coventry works. In March 1960 a new style fascia and different final drive ratio was adopted, and at the same time the 4½-litre Limousines were discontinued. October saw power-assisted steering introduced as an optional extra for the Majestic, and quantity production of the Majestic Major commenced in November, with minor trim and instrument changes and the new power-assisted steering option.

In April 1961 the body shortcomings of the SP250 were recognized and largely removed by the adoption of 'Spec. B' models, using a strengthened glass-fibre shell structure. Bumpers, adjustable steering column, petrol reserve unit and switch, screen washers and exhaust embellishers were all standardized where before they had been optional extras. In September a new eight-seater Limousine model was released, using the 4561-cc V8 engine from the Majestic Major in a similarly styled but very much enlarged version of the same shell. The wheelbase was 2 feet greater than that of the saloon, and dry weight was up from 35½ cwt to a massive 40¾ cwt. A sliding glass partition divided chauffeur from passengers, and luxury trim, twin heating systems and power steering were all standard. The new model sold for £3,995 complete, and bare chassis were made available to be bodied by approved coach-builders at £1,825 basic.

Since the Jaguar-Daimler merger of 1960 the appearance of a combination model had been prophesied and was, indeed, awaited with considerable interest. In October 1962 the resultant model appeared, Sir William Lyons having characteristically combined the best that both concerns had to offer in an aesthetically attractive and sophisticated model, the Daimler 2½-litre saloon. Using the Jaguar Mark II body shell, with its coil-and-trailing wishbone ifs system, and live rear end on cantilever leaf springs with radius arm and Panhard rod location, the new car was powered by the SP250 V8 engine, producing 140 bhp gross at 'five-eight'. Borg-Warner Model 35 three-speed automatic transmission was standard, with over-riding manual control, and a throttle kick-down switch, while drive was taken via an open divided Hardy Spicer prop-shaft to a Salisbury hypoid bevel final drive. A Powr-Lok limited slip differential was available. Dunlop 11-inch front and rear disc brakes were used and to keep the automatic transmission cool – this being the most powerful engine this particular system had yet been mated to – an oil heat exchanger was built into the engine radiator.

The V8 slotted in neatly to the existing engine bay, and was lighter than the six-cylinder XK engine, so suitably modified spring rates were adopted to make the most of the more even front/rear weight distribution thus afforded. Internally the new Daimler was similarly trimmed and comfortably appointed to the standard Mark II Jaguar range, which always offered phenomenal value for money, although a split front bench seat was new, offering individual adjustment for two occupants, or full-width comfort for three. Total price was £1,783 and the new model filled a yawning gap at the foot of the Daimler range. Very low-geared power steering was optional, and the deceptively quiet Daimler returned a 111 mph top speed, a 9·6-sec 0–50 mph time and about 18 mpg.

The six-cylinder Majestic was discontinued, giving place to the new 2½-litre model in December 1962. Then, in April 1963 the popular SP250 sports was further modified to 'Spec. C' trim with a heater, cigar lighter and even a trickle charger socket as standard, and in July the 4·5-litre Limousine appeared with electrically operated screen washers, a rear compartment heating system warning lamp and improved occasional seats.

April 1964 saw D1/D2 transmission control introduced on the 2½-litre saloon, and in October power-assisted steering became standard on the 4·5-litre Majestic Major. Prices ranged from £1,647 for the 2½, through £2,703 for the Majestic Major to £3,497 for the limousine, for the SP250 was discontinued at the end of the year, the company again concentrating on saloons after their brief single-model excursion into the sports-car market.

A new model appeared in August 1966, with initial production of the 4235-cc six-cylinder-engined Daimler Sovereign. The new car was announced in October, using the Jaguar 'S' type shell with a modified nose carrying the fluted Daimler radiator, four headlamps with separate sidelights and wrap-round indicators, and rectangular air intakes on either side of the grille base. The 4·2-litre XK Jaguar engine was used, mated to either the new all-synchro Jaguar gearbox with overdrive or a Borg-Warner Model 8 with dual drive range. Independent all-round suspension and four wheel discs were retained while Varamatic power steering, dual hydraulic braking systems, selective interior car temperature control and alternator were standardized. Also equipped with a pre-engaged starter, heated rear screen, transistorized clock, leather hide upholstery, reclining front seats with centre arm rests front and rear, the Sovereign had a fully carpeted boot and twin rear-wing-mounted fuel tanks.

With 245 bhp being produced at 5,500 rpm from the XK engine, the new model could reach 117 mph maximum, rush from 0–50 mph in only 6·7 sec and return some 17 mpg, and was initially priced at £2,120 (manual) or £2,198 (automatic).

The 2½-litre saloon was further modified in February 1967 when the Jaguar manual gearbox with optional overdrive was introduced in one variant, and in October the 1968 model was announced as the Daimler V8-250. In right- or left-hand drive forms, the new car inherited some of the Sovereign's trim features such as reclining front seats and a heated rear screen, and an alternator replaced the original dynamo. Mechanically the V8 was basically unchanged, and with the XK-engined Sovereign and the stately Majestic Major and 4½-litre Limousine models Daimler entered the last year of the decade.

Finally, for 1969, the 4½-litre Limousine was replaced by an all-new model with craftsman-built coachwork by Vanden Plas. Using the six-cylinder 4·2-litre twin ohc XK engine it disappointed many people, for they were expecting to see a smooth new Jaguar Vee engine under the car's shapely bonnet. The body style retained a Sovereign-like nose with a long waistline dipping down sharply to a lipped tail line beneath a slightly protruding boot. The roofline rose in a curve forward from the boot-lid running forward over the eight-seater passenger compartment to a large and quite steeply raked windscreen. The XK unit's 245 bhp was transmitted via a Borg-Warner Model 8 transmission, with four-wheel disc brakes, power steering, all-independent suspension and extreme luxury as standard. It was still an inexpensive chauffeur transport for £3,827, and, as the only new Daimler model for 1969, marked the end of a decade of Jaguar development in true Daimler traditions of luxury, comfort and refinement.

11 Elva

Frank Nichols's company made its name in racing during the late 'fifties and early 'sixties with a line of light and successful single-seaters and sports cars. In 1959 he branched out into road-car production with the two-seater MG-powered Elva Courier, and after considerable export success with the car it was introduced to the home market in kit form. This was in January 1961, when the car was exhibited in coupé form at the Racing Car Show.

Based on a large-section tubular ladder-frame chassis, the Courier used a rather unattractive glass-fibre body shell in open or 'notch-back' coupé form, and was powered by a 1588-cc MGA engine. Coil-and-wishbone ifs was used with a rigid axle on coil springs at the rear. It was rough, raucous and reasonably fast. Early in 1962, when some 700 had been sold, mainly to the American market, Nichols signed an agreement with Trojan Ltd of Purley for road-car production. These were sold in kit form for around £650, or £1,000 assembled, with the latest 1622-cc MGA power unit, which had been adopted on its release.

Despite the announcement of the 1798-cc MGB engine, Trojan persisted in using the MGA 1600 unit until demand dictated otherwise (its 78 bhp proving sufficient to give a maximum speed of about 103 mph). Disc front brakes were standard, although drums as on the original models could be specified, costing slightly less. The basic price for the sports two-seater was £701, rising to £848 with tax. The coupé model with its Ford Anglia-like reversed rear screen was priced at £723 (£875 complete), reasonable enough for the performance it offered. BMC and Triumph components were used extensively in these Mark III models to provide adequate spares supply; the rack-and-pinion steering, for example, originated from the Triumph Vitesse.

Then, for 1963, a new all-independent occasional four-seater was introduced, using Salisbury irs components, radius arms, wishbones and coil springs. This Elva 4GT Coupé looked generally unhappy – rather hunch-backed with a high rear roofline curving down steeply between the tall tail fins terminating the rear wings.

But at the end of the year the Mark IV appeared as the Mark IV T-Type, by contrast with its predecessor a sleek and well-finished looking sports two-seater. The 1798-cc MGB engine or the 1498-cc Ford Cortina GT unit was installed, the former producing 98 bhp net at 5,400 rpm from its twin SU HS4 carburettors and 8·8:1 cr, while the Ford unit smoothly turned out 78 bhp. Gearboxes matched the proprietary engines chosen, while the all-round independent suspension carried $10\frac{5}{8}$-inch front disc brakes and 9-inch rear drums. Prices were £1,000 complete with the BMC unit, or £995 with the Ford engine.

In 1964 a lightweight 'Sebring' Courier was introduced in small quantity, and was raced with either Cosworth-Ford or tuned MGB engines, magnesium alloy road wheels and a limited-slip differential. But it was not particularly successful, and the Mark IV continued as the basic production model, the major part of the output still being exported. It was continued basically unchanged into 1965.

By this time, however, Nichols's design concern had become embroiled in competitive sports–racing development in conjunction with Bruce McLaren, and Trojan eventually took on production of the McLaren sports–racing cars. Their production facilities eventually became fully committed to pure competition cars – most of them still being exported – and Ken Sheppard Customised Sports Cars of Radlett took over contract Courier production. The latest 1500-cc Ford or MGB engines were fitted, and production continued in earnest for another couple of years before tailing off, eventually to peter out when the company changed hands early in 1969. At this time three complete units remained at the works, and these had stood there for some eighteen months.

The rather spartan performance sports car so prevalent and so popular at the start of the decade had been superseded by the more advanced and better-finished products of the select brand of successful and progressive sports car manufacturers, and as development of the Courier lagged behind production it eventually became obsolete and unwanted.

12 Fairthorpe

This little company has spent many happy years producing myriad kits and, lately, completely assembled performance cars, noted for their unorthodox styling and design features, and in the latter part of the period for a very advanced and unique suspension system. Moreover, Air Vice-Marshal D. C. T. Bennett's Fairthorpe company has survived the decade in which so many of its competitors have failed.

The company had begun production in 1955, right from the start placing excellent handling qualities at the head of its priorities – ahead of refinement, comfort and sometimes finish, too. The exception was their tiny Atom, which was designed as the ultimate in economy transport – costing £254 and returning around 75 mpg from its motorcycle engine.

In 1959 Fairthorpe were producing four models, ranging from the Atomota, the Electron Minor and Electron, and the Zeta. All were based on very rigid chassis frames and clad in glass-fibre shells, a material which Bennett had used since the earliest days.

Smallest of the range was the Atomota, with a twin-cylinder 646-cc motorcycle engine producing 35 bhp gross at 5,700 rpm. This drove through a 6¼-inch Borg & Beck clutch to a four-speed gearbox with non-synchromesh bottom gear, thence through a Hardy Spicer prop-shaft to a hypoid bevel final drive. Girling 7-inch drum brakes were fitted all round, and coil-and-wishbone ifs was used with a rigid rear axle located by trailing wishbones and, again, coil-sprung. Burman worm-and-bevel steering gear was fitted, and this tiny economy car, with a weight of only 8 cwt dry, was priced at £408 in kit form or £447 complete, but less purchase tax. It was paired with the Atom Major which cost £446 as a kit.

The larger sports cars all shared similar square-section chassis frames, the Electron Minor being the cheapest and simplest with a 948-cc Triumph Herald coupé engine. Fitted with twin SU H1 or H2 carburettors, this unit produced 45 bhp gross at 4,800 rpm. Also borrowed from the Herald were the gearbox and Girling 7-inch drum brakes, while suspension was similar to that of the Atomota. Price of the Minor in kit form was £446, or £713 assembled, which was not expensive for a car in the Austin-Healey Sprite class, say, but endowed with better handling and performance.

Coventry Climax power appeared in the Electron, which used the 1098-cc single overhead camshaft FWA engine (10·5:1 cr; twin SU H4 carburettors; 93 bhp gross at 7,000 rpm). Alternative units were the 1220-cc FWE or 1960-cc FPE Climax engines, producing 85 bhp at 6,300 rpm or 170 bhp at 6,500 rpm respectively. Chassis changes compared with the Minor included 11-inch Girling front disc brakes, combined with 10-inch rear drums, and with plenty of power in only 10 cwt of motor-car, the good handling and very well-braked Electron was available at £1,145 (1098-cc complete) or £734 in kit form.

At the head of the range was the Zeta, still using substantially the same chassis frame and body shell but now with the six-cylinder 2553-cc Ford engine. In three stages of tune, this 'six' was offered in standard Zephyr form with a single carburettor, with an Alexander-tuned cylinder head and triple SUs, or finally using a Raymond Mays BRM-modified head with either six Amal carburettors or, again, triple SUs. With six Amals, power output was 137 bhp gross at 5,500 rpm, and prices for cars with engines in the three states of tune listed above were respectively, £1,198, £1,281 and £1,407. The kit price in basic form was around £740.

The Atomota and Atom were discontinued right at the start of the decade, and the three states of tune for the Zeta were announced in March 1960. In October a new model appeared to supplement the two Electrons and their larger brother. Named the Electrina, this was a two-/four-seater sports saloon, rather bizarre in appearance with a bulky superstructure on the standard basic shell. Very small side windows with thick pillars were notably ugly features, and power came from a modified Standard 10 948-cc engine producing around 50 bhp. Price on release was £799 factory-assembled, or £498 as a kit.

The Fairthorpes were very functional, but with rather spartan trim, finish and equipment. They undoubtedly handled well, the Zeta in particular being seen a lot in club races that season. Top speed was just under 120 mph, with 0–50 mph acceleration in 5·8 sec and 0–100 mph in only 23·5 sec. The Moss gearbox was as usual quick but crunchy, with the weak synchromesh which spoiled Jaguar products for so long. The Alford & Alder rack-and-pinion steering offered excellent control, and although the Zeta's ride was uncompromisingly hard, cornering benefited, for with a slight understeer characteristic it cornered flat and fast with negligible roll and plenty of traction even in the wet. But it was noisy, not particularly comfortable, had minimal luggage space and was not too well finished.

In 1961 the Electron was modified to reduce unsprung weight, and overall weight was, in fact, cut by some 1¾ cwt. Smaller 9-inch front disc brakes and smaller wheels aided these reductions (the back axle ratio was raised to compensate for the wheel-size change and to maintain the original overall gearing). The nose air intake was reduced to a single opening instead of two, and the whole of the bonnet panel hinged forward to reveal the Climax engine. Ford 105E and 109E engines were being offered in the Minor while Zeta and Electrina continued virtually unaltered.

A new model was added in September 1962, using the Triumph Vitesse 1596-cc six-cylinder engine in the Zeta frame, clad in a slightly modified glass-fibre body shell. The combination 9-inch front disc/7-inch rear-drum braking system was retained, and apart from its odd appearance (with the centre headlight of three being mounted in a pod on the nose) the new Rockette was smoother than its Zephyr-engined big brother. Price for the standard model was £997 on release, falling to an attractive £625 as a kit. Overdrive was an optional extra at £70.

Unfortunately, the Rockette did not set off to a very good start, since Fairthorpe's annual attendance at the Earl's Court Motor Show was jeopardized by labour troubles. However, business soon proceeded as usual, part of the production being exported, and in February 1963 the price of the Zeta Super Sports was reduced by about £100, for both complete and component cars.

September that year saw change in the Minor model, an untuned Triumph Spitfire 1147-cc 63-bhp engine replacing the Herald unit and the name being changed to the Fairthorpe EM Three. Offered in basic form with a GT hard-top, a folding hood could be specified and the usual policy of marketing complete or component forms was continued – prices being £755 and £599 respectively.

The range continued with three basic models now, the EM Three, Rockette (which had the peculiar central headlight removed) and Electron, while the Zeta could also be supplied to special order. But all the time competition from the more styling-, comfort- and finish-conscious oposition was increasing. Consequently development began in terms of cleaning up rather fussy body shapes and improving finish, the EM3A and Rockette models carrying on through 1965.

October that year saw the announcement of a new-look Fairthorpe – the

TX1. Designed by Torix Bennett, son of the Air Vice-Marshal and head of his own Technical Exponents Ltd concern, the new car featured a clean and uncluttered knife-edge body shell reminiscent of the later model Sprites and Midgets but with a low horizontal air intake beneath a rolled nose, with headlights recessed into deep cut-outs. The tail was sharply cut off with a flat, slightly recessed transom, and with the normal chassis and ifs combination a new departure was the adoption of a rear suspension system designed and patented by the younger Bennett. This employed a transverse rod system, linking the suspension units on either side and making the wheels bank slightly *into* corners, motorcycle style, to maintain a constant track, maximum traction and grip. The TX1 used a 78-bhp Ford Cortina GT 1499-cc engine and gearbox, and its specification included full instrumentation, reclining seats and adjustable hydraulic dampers. The unusual rear suspension reduced boot space, and so the spare wheel was carried under the bonnet. A price of £1,420 complete was quoted, but it was not to be produced, the prototype acting purely as a suspension test-bed.

This prototype was the beginning of the evolution of an entirely new range of cars, however, the EM and Rockette running together through 1966 and then being joined in 1967 by the TX-GT. This used the new 2-litre Triumph GT6 1998-cc engine, which had a 9·5:1 cr and twin side-draught 150 CD Stromberg carburettors, and produced 95 bhp gross at 5,000 rpm, with peak torque of 117·3 lb ft at 3,000 rpm. The standard gearbox was used, with the new Torix Bennett rear suspension system allied to a conventional coil-and-wishbone ifs system. Alford & Alder rack-and-pinion steering was retained, and 9·7-inch front disc brakes combined with 8-inch rear drums to give the traditional Fairthorpe standard of powerful braking.

The new GT was clad in an attractive glass-fibre fixed-head coupé shell, again with knife-edge styling and carrying rectangular headlights above a low and shallow horizontal air intake. The whole thing was based on a Triumph GT6 backbone chassis, and offered a lot of interior space although, in early form at least, it was still rather spartan. But with the new suspension system, its handling was far superior to that of the GT6. Ride was fairly good when travelling at speed and the car was eminently swerveable, taking sudden changes of direction with few qualms. Prices stood at £1,361 assembled, or £954 component form, which again were reasonable for an efficient and now quite advanced motor-car.

In October 1968 there came the announcement of the 1969 models, and the Bennetts produced a flock of new models. The basic EM appeared in Mark IV form, with a very much cleaner body than previously used, and with the 1296-cc 1300-type four-cylinder engine, twin SU HS2s, producing 75 bhp at 6,000 rpm with a peak of 75 lb ft torque at 3,750 rpm. Transverse leaf spring irs was used and with a top speed of around 108 mph and a 30 mpg economy this little sports car was offered at £636 in kit form. This kit consisted of chassis frame, front and rear suspension assemblies, steering, engine, braking system, body panels, fittings and instruments – typical of its *genre*. Complete car list price stood at £908.

But new to the more sophisticated closed coupé line were the TX-GT Mark II, TX-S and TX-SS, production models all using the Torix Bennett transverse rod irs system with co-axial coil spring dampers providing the springing medium. The GT Mark II was a more refined version of the original model, with quarter windows added to improve visibility, and offered complete with full instrumentation, alternator, heater, windscreen washers, map reading light, reversing light, seat belts, tool kit, jack and spare wheel. The 104 bhp standard GT6 engine gave a top speed of 112 mph, and 0–60 mph acceleration was quoted as 9·5 sec, believable since the car's power/weight ratio was 143 bhp/ton.

The other coupé models, the TX-S and SS were virtually identical, both using tuned versions of the 1998-cc six-cylinder engines. The S used twin Stromberg carburation, producing 112 bhp at 5,300 rpm, while with fuel-injection the SS achieved 140 bhp at 6,000 rpm. Maximum speeds for the cars, which were very similar externally, were 115 mph and 130 mph, with claimed 0–60 mph figures of 8·8 and 7·4 sec respectively.

Prices for all these models, again available in both complete and component forms, were £1,433 (GT Mk II), £1,545 (TX-S) and £1,658 (TX-SS) complete, and £1,110, £1,198 and £1,286 respectively in kits.

So Fairthorpe came to the end of a decade of accelerating development in which Air Vice-Marshal Bennett and his talented son Torix evolved a line of very advanced and attractive, yet inexpensive, high-performance cars.

13 Ford

During the 'sixties Ford emerged as a manufacturer of family cars with very well-developed sporting qualities, skilfully contriving to combine these characteristics with the possibly more saleable attributes of reliability and value for money.

In 1960 Britain's cheapest family car, the £494 100E Popular, was at the foot of the Ford range, with the 100E Escort Estate, the 107E Prefect and the much more advanced 105E Anglia grouped as compact four-seater transport above it. At the other end of the scale were the larger four-/five-seat Mark II Consul, Zephyr and Zephyr Zodiac saloon, estate and convertible series. Between these two clear-cut types, the small economy saloon and the larger, faster, more expensive and better-appointed – though still low-priced – 'prestige' cars, there was nothing.

In September 1959 the cigar-box-shaped 100E Anglia had been replaced by the all-new 105E, and at the same time the old upright Popular model, which had provided basic motoring for six years, was discontinued. In its place appeared the standard and De Luxe 100E Popular, using the same rectangular, plain but still handsome body, and the same antique 1172-cc side-valve engine and three-speed gearbox.

The 100E Escort had first appeared at the end of 1955, a two-door four-seat estate car with 100E Anglia frontal treatment, with the better-equipped wood-trimmed Squire as a more costly alternative. But the Squire was

FORD

discontinued in September 1959, the small 100E-engined Escort continuing alone until replaced by the 105E Anglia Estate in 1961.

September 1959 saw the appearance of the 105E Anglia saloon, and in this car advanced lines, with reverse slope to the rear window, two wide-opening doors and a large glass area combined well with mechanical advancement for a Ford product. Until this time the company had been markedly conservative with three-speed wide-ratio gearboxes, well-proven suspension systems and utter conventionality of design.

But the two-door 105E Anglia featured a very compact, lightweight, high-revving and well-oversquare engine with much scope for further tuning (as future Formula 3 racing was to prove) mated to a beautifully slick and precise four-speed gearbox with synchromesh on the top three ratios. These, and the classic Ford suspension system, with ifs by Macpherson coil-spring/damper struts and a well-controlled semi-elliptic live axle at the rear, produced a well-balanced and stable integral body/chassis of pleasing appearance and considerable straight line and cornering performance. At 76 mph flat-out, the new Anglia was considerably faster than the earlier 100E model, and acceleration was also improved. Yet it was about 30 per cent more economical at 40 mpg. Speeds in the gears of 19 mph in first, 33 mph in second and 61 mph in third were extremely good for a 1-litre saloon of the time, although they betrayed the annoying ratio gap between second and third.

This 996·6-cc engine was also available in the 107E Prefect De Luxe four-door saloon, which featured the same well-worn 100E body shape but had a vastly improved and more economical performance with the new ohv engine and its slick gearbox. Lower gear ratios were used, giving the car 14·6 mph per 1,000 rpm in top as opposed to the Anglia's 15·7 mph. The 100E Popular De Luxe was sold at £515 in 1960, the 105E-engined four-speed Prefect was £621, and astonishingly the new Anglia was cheaper at only £603 – Ford seem to have decided to educate the public with sheer economy.

In the larger model range, the Consul Mark II, introduced in 1956, was being offered in standard, de luxe, convertible and estate car versions, and in February 1959 all models were revised with a lower roofline, stainless steel surrounds to the windscreen and rear window, chromed headlamp bezels, restyled rear light clusters and a rectangular instrument fairing (the estate cars were conversions built by Abbott of Farnham). All the models in the Consul range were powered by oversquare 1703-cc four-cylinder engines at this time and with prices ranging from £773 to £1,006 they were extremely competitive and well received.

At the top of the ladder were the Zephyr and Zephyr Zodiac models, using the same common body shells but with much more lavish trim in Zodiac form. All were identical mechanically, using a six-cylinder 2553-cc engine, and all underwent the same modifications in February 1959 as the Consuls. Borg-Warner automatic transmission was an optional extra, and in standard form the Zephyr was priced at £865, ranging through to £1,044 (automatic); the standard Zodiac cost £957 and the automatic version, £1,120. The most expensive model in the whole range was the Zodiac Farnham Estate with automatic transmission, priced at £1,432. In October 1960 disc brakes became an optional extra on the front of all Consul and Zephyr versions.

Then, in May 1961, they became standard equipment with the release of

44

the Consul 375 model, which also featured sealed-beam headlamps among its detail changes. These were also made standard Zephyr and Zodiac fittings at the same time and price increases of about £30 were made throughout the range. In this guise the Mark IIs came to the end of their six-year production run in March and April 1962, the Zephyrs and Zodiacs being replaced by the new Mark IIIs while the Consul name tag appeared as a prefix to the Classic, Capri and Cortina names of the 'new generation' medium-sized cars.

As chief passenger car engineer, Mr Fred Hart had been responsible for the production of the 105E Anglia in 1959, and with the Escort being discontinued in April 1961, and the 107E Prefect disappearing in March, this became Ford's small passenger car market mainstay, with the 100E Popular, in unchanged form, soldiering on with its side-valve 1172-cc engine and (in 1961) a £529 selling price appealing to the less adventurous or more impecunious motorist.

In August that year the attractive estate car version of the Anglia first rolled off the production lines, to be announced in October. With its upward-opening rear door, the tail sloping to a convex V-shape at waist level, the more aerodynamic shape of this estate gave it a more streamlined, though less pert, appearance than the saloon. Standard and De Luxe versions were offered, the former with a painted, metal-framed wooden floor, and the latter with a laid lino floor, alloy rubbing strips, lockable glove box, opening rear quarter-lights and a full-width radiator grille. Prices of these versions were £671 and £691 respectively, and for the four-seats and bulky luggage accommodation combined with compact size and high performance potential these estates offered, this was very reasonable.

But while the small 997-cc engine was generally quite capable it could become a little breathless on long and steep hills, and in tight corners when driving hard the gap between second and third gears could be a great embarrassment. So in October 1962 the larger, stroked, 1197·8-cc 123E engine with the common 80·96-mm bore became available as an optional unit for the De Luxe saloons and estates. Top speed was up to 82 mph, acceleration from 0–50 mph took 14 sec and fuel consumption was still reasonable at 33 mpg.

The next Anglia series change was in October 1964, when all controls, switches and steering wheel were finished in black and the screen-washer and heater systems were offered as standard on the De Luxe models only. Then, in September 1965 the 1200 De Luxe saloon was removed from the range, this engine only being available from then on in the De Luxe Estate. On the 997-cc saloons and the lone estate external trim modifications resulted in separated sidelights and trafficators, and a new 'Shepherd's Crook' heater control, and in this guise the 105E and 123E Anglia range (which sold well over 1,250,000) ran on until discontinued in favour of the new Escort saloons in November 1967. Although the Escort was not announced until January 1968, production had been started the previous November, and immediately upon its announcement the new Escort became generally available in large numbers: sound policy so typical of Ford's close attention to promoting an image of quick and efficient customer service.

But in June 1961 the company had taken the first of two steps towards producing a car to fill the gap between the small saloon car family and their larger brethren. In that month they announced the 109E Classic two- and four-door four-seat saloon, powered by a four-cylinder ohv engine with the standard 80·96-mm bore, a stroke of 65·97 mm giving a capacity of 1340 cc.

The Classic has often been looked upon as a rather unfortunate styling example, its reverse angle rear screen inherited from the Anglia looking rather out of place on the larger car, and its large tail fins apparently never quite 'clicking' with the public. Twin headlamps were fitted side-by-side in broad wings with circular sidelights mounted outboard, while twin rear lights were provided on either side. Front disc brakes were standard with the usual Macpherson strut ifs and semi-elliptic/live axle rear end, and standard and De Luxe saloons were offered. The De Luxe was duotone-finished inside and out, with extra applications of chrome strip and moulding, concealed door handles and a steering column gear-change as an optional extra. Both the two-door and four-door models could be provided in De Luxe form, and prices ran from £766 to £825.

A special two-seat two-door version also appeared, christened the Capri coupé. This was styled very closely after the Classic below the waistline, but had a forward sloping rear screen in what would later be termed 'fast-back' styling, although a separate horizontal boot-lid was retained. Both column- and floor-change models were available and standard Capri price in 1961 was £915.

In July 1962 the 1340-cc engine was discontinued and replaced by the 116E 1498-cc engine, this having been stroked out to 72·7 mm, and featuring a very rigid five-bearing crankshaft now allied to a new all-synchromesh four-speed gearbox. The modified Classic also had greaseless steering and suspension joints to minimize maintenance, and it was followed by the Capri in having the original 'thirteen-forty' unit replaced by the new long-stroke 1498. Here was a two-seater which looked fast and sporty; but in fact it was neither to any great degree, and a logical development was the introduction in February 1963 of the higher-powered Capri GT. By that time the new Cortina had appeared, and this latest coupé version of the Capri used a 9:1 cr, Weber-carburetted version of the 116E engine as used in the Cortina GT, again mated to Ford's excellent all-synchromesh four-speed gearbox. The engine produced 78 bhp at 5,200 rpm, but the Capri was priced at £900, and this did not sell well when only £749 was asked for the similarly engined Cortina. It was faster, at 94 mph compared with 92 mph for the Cortina, but 0–50 time was about 10 sec as opposed to the Cortina's 8·6 sec and consumption was about the same at an unimpressive 27 mpg.

Production figures for both the Classic and Capri models were modest for Ford, totalling 130,000 units. But where the Classic and Capri had failed to attract the public with their 'American' styling and rather cheap and nasty appearance, the opposite was to be true of the company's second line of attack in this medium saloon car range – the Cortina.

In September 1962 Ford Germany had just announced their medium-sized Taunus 12M – a thoroughly unconventional machine with V4 engine and front-wheel drive – when the Dagenham company released news of their thoroughly conventional Cortina. The new car was handsome and practical, with a reversion to forward rake on the rear screen, two doors, and an 1198-cc engine mated to an all-synchromesh four-speed gearbox. Some £12 million and four years' work had gone into the car's development and in most dimensions it was almost identical to the Classic, yet was over 2 cwt lighter. This weight-saving allowed a comparable performance to be obtained from the 113E 1200-cc engine, based on the common Anglia/1340 Classic cylinder block. Standard cr was 8·7:1 and with a single Solex carburettor the unit produced 48·5 bhp at 4,800 rpm. Cable-operated column change with a front bench seat or central floor change with separate buckets were offered, and with the usual Macpherson ifs, live rear axle and drum brakes all round, the new model was priced at only £639 standard or £666 De Luxe. The car was an instant success, and in the first three months over 60,000 Cortinas were sold – Ford had found a winner.

In October four-door Cortina saloon production started, and then in January 1963 the 1498-cc engine from the Classic/Capri series was offered as an optional unit for the De Luxe models. At the same time the Cortina Super was announced with the larger engine as standard, bigger brakes, improved interior trim and with chrome strips outlining the prominent fluted styling line along the body's side. The Super could top 81 mph, get from 0–50 mph in 12·8 sec and was still good for over 30 mpg. Wheel trims and a heater were standard in this model – although it seemed rather late in the development of the motor-car to be introducing a heater as such!

Meanwhile Ford of Dagenham successes and interest in all classes of competition had grown enormously since 1960 with the introduction of Ford-engined single-seater cars in Formula Junior, and racing and rally successes with the Anglia and Cortina began to mount up. The Lotus concern in particular were receiving a lot of Ford works support, both from Dagenham and, later, from Detroit, and in 1962 had produced a Harry Mundy-designed twin-overhead camshaft version of the 997-cc Anglia engine. When applied to the larger capacity blocks, this combination proved really potent in competition form, and in January 1963 the 125E 'Cortina-developed-by-Lotus' road saloon made its bow. Based on the two-door saloon shell, the Lotus-Cortina's engine was bored and stroked to 1558 cc, and had inclined valves operated by two chain-driven overhead camshafts. Two Weber 40DCOE2 carburettors provided mixture, and this very racy unit produced 105 bhp at 5,500 rpm. Macpherson ifs was retained with zero wheel camber and a stiffer anti-roll bar, while the live rear axle was mounted on coil springs and located by radius arms and a hefty A-bracket. Larger disc/drum brakes were fitted, using servo-assistance, while 5½J wide-rim wheels, wood-rim steering wheel and special front seats with a central glove box, and full instrumentation, completed an extremely fast and uncompromisingly 'sporty' saloon. Top speed was 108 mph, 0–50 mph took only 7·5 sec and fuel consumption was not bad at 21 mpg.

The standard and Super Estate cars followed in March 1963, having four-door styling with an attractive tail configuration similar to that of the Anglia Estate variants. On the standard model the 1498 or '1500' engine was optional, while a chrome flash was the only concession to extra external trim. The Super Estate on the other hand had the 1500 engine as standard, was better appointed inside and had exterior 'wooden' trim outlined in the genuine article. Top speed was around 80 mph.

The next development came in April, with the release of the higher-powered Cortina GT model using front disc brakes as standard with the 78 bhp Weber-carburetted engine. This state of tune and much improved standards of trim and interior comfort was offered in both two- and four-door body styles, and a central gear-change was fitted to take full advantage of the quick and precise gearbox, although a gap between second and third gears still persisted. Circular instrument dials in a neat binnacle above the steering column and greaseless chassis appeared in September 1963 while Borg-Warner automatic transmission became an optional extra on both 1500s and the Cortina Super in December.

There followed a major innovation in the Cortina range when, in September 1964, Ford released their 'Aeroflow' ventilation system. With omni-directional air vents on the fascia, and extractor ducts on the rear quarter pillars this was a major step forward in mass-production car ventilation. Cool air playing on the driver's face cut down fatigue, and the constant flow of fresh air through the cabin minimized the dangerous effects of cigarette smoke or exhaust and petrol fumes. Allied with this modification came external trim and badge changes, a smaller mesh grille incorporating sidelights and amber flashers, while 'Cortina' lettering appeared on bonnet and boot replacing the earlier 'Consul' block. Front disc brakes became standard on all models while heater and screen washers were made standard on all but the basic 1200.

In September 1965 semi-elliptic rear springs replaced the coils used hitherto on the Lotus-Cortina, to soften the ride, and the A-bracket (which had been causing differential casing distortion) was dispensed with. The standard Cortina 1200 saloon was discontinued and the column gear-change option removed. On the Cortina Super Estate the rather cheap-looking simulated wood panelling was replaced by chrome body strips and a two-tone paint finish, and fixed quarter-lights appeared on all models, the efficiency of Aeroflow ventilation having rendered them largely obsolete – perhaps aided by the laws against dropping litter and sweet papers on the public highway! The following month the close-ratio Corsair V4 gearbox (of which model more later) appeared as standard in the Lotus-Cortina, but these were to be the final major changes in the life of the 'Mark I' Cortina range for a major restyling was imminent.

September 1966 saw the announcement of the chunky, neatly squared off 'Mark II' Cortina body shell, having the same wheelbase as the earlier cars, but being slightly shorter and wider overall. These were introduced as 3014E variants with 1297-cc engines, retaining the common bore of 80·96 mm but having a 62·99-mm stroke. With five main bearings the 1300 engine was offered in new two- and four-door shells, with a full-width front grille incorporating head and side-lamp clusters. Wrap-around rear light fittings replaced the triple-segment circular lights of the 'Mark I', while curved doors and windows gave increased room inside. The waistline featured a fashionable upsweep over the rear wheel arches, while steering column change, bench seats and automatic transmission were optional extras. The 3016E 1499·9-cc engine became standard on the rebodied Super saloon, while chrome body strips below the doors, over the wheel arches and round the windows were added externally. This 3016E engine was also optional on the standard models, while the newly-bodied GT variant bore suitable badges instead of the chrome strips and had its four supplementary instruments – ammeter, oil pressure, temperature and fuel gauges – removed from the centre of the well-padded fascia to a podded binnacle mounted above its centre. The Lotus-Cortina in new form was eventually put into production in February 1967, and announced in March. It had a matt black grille and wide wheels, and 'side-winder' body stripes were an optional extra. Although it still had a vivid performance, the beautifully taut-feeling Lotus-Cortina was now a much more refined and civilized road car. Top speed was down slightly to 105 mph, and 0–50 mph time was up to 7 sec, but consumption was slightly improved.

In November the previous year, the Mark I Estate had been deleted, and in December the 3014E Estate appeared, with fold-down rear seats, convex vertical rear light units and column gear-change and bench seat options. Then, in July and August 1967 came the next modifications with cross-flow headed engines using bowl-in-piston combustion chambers to replace the original units with the 3034E 1298-cc standard and 3036E 1599-cc Super series. The new engines both had a 9·0:1 cr and Ford down-draught carburettors, producing 58 bhp at 5,000 rpm and 71 bhp at 5,000 rpm net respectively. The new pistons were considerably heavier than hitherto, however, and this increased reciprocating mass led to vibrational problems not encountered with the smooth and high-revving earlier units.

The standard Cortina models had black Vinyl fascia-lining in place of the painted metal used previously, Aeroflow controls were simplified with twist regulators set into the vents themselves, carpeting replaced rubber floor mats and '1300' lettering appeared on the tail of the 3034E cars. The 3036E 1600 Crossflow engine replaced the 1500 unit, in similar body shells; reclining front seats were optional on both the 1300 and 1600 variants, and worth while in that they made possible much improved driving positions.

Internally the 3036E Cortina Supers were given similar modifications to the standard vehicles, while the Super saloon was modified to have a remote GT-type central gear-change and on the GT itself a clock was added to the centre console and radial ply tyres were fitted as standard. The new 1600 model had a maximum speed of 88 mph, managed 0–50 mph in 10·5 sec and retained 27 mpg, while the 1300 figures were about 81 mph, 13 sec and just 28 mpg respectively.

At the same time a new model, the Cortina 1600E, was announced. This vehicle, cast in the 'executive' mould with normally optional equipment fitted as standard, was based on the new four-door shell, with GT mechanical parts and lowered Lotus-type suspension. With a Weber twin-choke carburettor, the GT engine produced 88 bhp net at 5,400 rpm, and standard equipment on this attractive motor-car included a wooden fascia and door cappings, wide-rim sculptured road wheels, an aluminium leather-rimmed steering wheel, reversing lamps and radial ply tyres. Overall trim and finish was of a very high standard, and with a contrasting coachline along the side and '1600E' insignia, this was great value for £1,073. Then, in October that year, the Lotus-Cortina gained a centre console clock and a similar wheel to the 1600E, and lost the Lotus badge from the tail, 'Twin Cam' lettering appearing in its place.

Final alterations occurred in late 1968, when the 1969 models appeared with single rail gear-change selector mechanisms developed in Germany for the Escort range, new individual front seats for the GT, 1600E, Super and Super Estate models (fully reclining seats becoming available for the first time on two-door shells), interior bonnet releases and fully fused electrical systems.

Other alterations included the use of twin shaped bucket rear seats in the 1600E, redesigned fascia panels on the GT models with the supplementary instruments back on the panel proper rather than in a pod, and the provision of floor-mounted central handbrakes in place of the handy glove box-cum-arm rest. Prominent 'Ford' capital lettering appeared on bonnet and boot-lid, while the 1600E and GT also featured a black tail panel styling, and matt black detail paintwork appeared on the new grilles.

So much for the ultra-successful Cortina range, over 1,600,000 of all models having been built between September 1962 and Spring 1969, but back in October 1963 a slightly larger, rather less handsome five-seater had been produced to provide yet another medium stage between the small and large saloons – the Corsair.

With a tapering nose line and otherwise angular shape, the 120E Corsair was cast very much in the conventional Cortina mould. Macpherson strut ifs and an elliptical leaf-spring suspended live rear axle were retained, with disc brakes at the front, column gear-change and a deep bench-type front seat. The 1498-cc engine was used, and a 120GT series version was also introduced, being offered in two- and four-door form with bucket front seats and a central gear-change as standard. In January 1964 two- and four-door Corsairs were available in standard, de luxe, GT, floor- and column-change versions. The standard model reached 84 mph flat-out, had a 0–50 mph time of about 14 sec, and did 26 mpg, while the GT was quicker than the Cortina at 94 mph, 9·9 sec 0–50 mph and still managing about 27 mpg.

But in September 1965 Ford of Dagenham followed the lead of Ford Germany and introduced a V4 engine for use in the Corsair range. This 1663-cc 3004E unit suffered from the inherent imbalance of such a configuration and a separate balance shaft had to be built in to smooth this out. In the early cars it was not altogether successful, the engine being lumpy and noisy at high speed, in contrast to the smoothness of the beautiful high-revving in-line engines. However, teething troubles were ironed out, and the new model continued with external 'V4' badges to distinguish it, larger front discs, self-adjusting rear drums and Aeroflow ventilation as standard. Top speed was up to 88 mph, 0–50 mph time was down to 10·6 sec and down, too, was fuel consumption to 23 mpg.

In September 1965 the 1996-cc V4 3006E GT appeared with optional automatic transmission, 'GT' badges on the boot and quarter panels and with chrome strips beneath the doors. In March 1966 a four-door GT Estate with the new 2-litre engine appeared, in September the new Cortina gearbox and gear-change were fitted, using a smaller floor tunnel, and then, in November, the GT was discontinued in favour of the more refined middle-class 'prestige' car, the Corsair 2000. Also using the 1996-cc 3006E engine, the new model was announced in January 1967 in de luxe saloon and estate car versions, with servo-assisted brakes, wide-rimmed wheels and radial tyres as standard. The rear springs of the estate version were up-rated but it was otherwise mechanically identical. The 2000E Executive model was also introduced, with seven horizontal grille bars, twin reversing lamps, name strip across the boot, walnut-veneer fascia, reclining front seats, padded central arm-rest and a roof covered externally in black Vinyl. It could top 98 mph and 21 mpg, and was generally an acceptable car. In May 1967 a wooden fascia was added to the 2000 with chrome window surrounds and in September the Aeroflow modifications common to the rest of the range were incorporated, while bucket-formed rear seats and a console clock were added to the 2000E. The prices of the V4s in May 1968 varied from £902 for the standard saloon, to £1,196 for the automatic 2000E and £1,305 for an automatic 2000E Estate.

By the mid-'sixties the Ford range had evolved into one of the most progressive in the country, offering small and large cars, with several intermediate stages of luxury, performance and price: the 105E Anglia, the Cortinas, Corsairs and, at the top of the list, the Zephyrs and Zodiacs. The Mark II versions of the larger cars were replaced by engineer Ernie Page's Mark III in April 1962, and immediately impressed with their straightforward good looks, broad grille design and practical tail fins, which allowed the tail to be sighted easily when reversing. The Zephyr was available with either the 1703-cc engine of the Mark II or – as the Zephyr Six – with the 2553-cc unit originally used in the Mark II. But the new 211E 'four' also featured an all-synchromesh four-speed gearbox, with overdrive and automatic options. The Zephyr Four had a narrow oval grille with four concave vertical bars and single headlights, while the six-cylinder model had a full-width oblong grille incorporating the headlamp mountings. Both shells had broad rear quarter pillars while the Zodiac, with full-width grille incorporating dual headlight clusters, also featured very slim rear pillars. Four horizontal chrome bars were added to the tail, below the boot-lid.

The front detail modifications came in October 1962 when the interior trim of the 'Four' was improved, and increased rear seat space was provided on all models by increasing the track and modifying the rear bulkhead and wheel arches. Estate car versions of all three models, built by Abbott of Farnham, were also released. Then, in September 1963, the radiator grille of the 'Four' was lowered while the redesigned interior trim, including a 'cherrywood' fascia, was restyled. A floor change also became optional on the six-cylinder cars. Later interior paintwork was altered to match the trim offered, and cloth trim became optional on all models, together with heater and screen washers as standard fittings on the 'Four'. Comparable performance of the Zephyrs 4 and 6 showed maxima of 80 and 88 mph, while 0–50 mph times were about 15 and 12·5 sec respectively. Fuel consumption was fair at 23 mpg for the overworked 'Four', but the 'Six' was thirsty at only 16 mpg. Both models suffered from a lot of understeer. The Zodiac was much faster, topping 100 mph, getting from 0–50 mph in only 10 sec *and* managing 18 mpg.

In January 1965, Ford's first 'Executive' model appeared in the shape of the Executive Zodiac, featuring all normal extras as standard fittings (it was to be followed by the Corsair and Cortina versions). At the time the 'Four' was priced at £817 (manual), the 'Six' at £890 and the Zodiac at £1,029.

In February a single exhaust replaced the twin-pipe system on the Zodiac and in June some of the chrome moulding beneath the doors was removed from all models and amber flasher units were fitted in place of the white ones. In September the cloth trim option was removed, and then in January 1966, the Mark III series was discontinued, to be replaced by Fred Hart's V-engined Mark IV models.

These were announced in March 1966, large and square-cut with lots of room under the bonnet and inside, a short tail and a concave rear screen. The 3010E Zephyr Four and 3008E Zephyr Six differentiation was continued with the Corsair's V4 1996-cc engine in the cheapest version (£933 on introduction), and a new 2495-cc V6, with the same bore dimensions, in the 'Six' (priced initially at £1,005). Breaking with tradition, the 3012E Zodiac had yet another new engine, a six-cylinder unit with 72·42-mm bore giving 2994 cc. For the first time on a Ford live rear axles and disc/drum brake combinations were gone, independent suspension and disc brakes on all four wheels taking their place.

Radiator air intake was below the bumper on all models, the 'Four' having single headlamps, 'V4' insignia on bonnet and boot, an Aeroflow system, column change and bench seats (floor change, automatic and bucket seats were optional), while the 'Six' featured 'V6' insignia with overdrive and automatic transmission options. The Zodiac was generally similar, but had horizontal bars between twin headlights, and a fluted rear panel with full-width tail-light and reflector units. Fully reclining front seats and floor change were standard, with bench and column, overdrive and automatic options, while instrumentation was comprehensive and interior trim was in tough but attractive Vinyl. When it was introduced, the Zodiac's price was £1,220. In October the estate car versions were announced, and in September 1967 rear wheel camber was increased and steering ratio lowered on the two Zephyrs, while the Zodiac was revised with a star badge placed centrally in the grille, increased rear wheel camber, a raised motif on the bonnet, simplified Aeroflow controls and power-assisted steering. Larger wheels and radial tyres were also standardized. Prices were up to £999 (Four), £1,076 (Six) and £1,333 (Zodiac). Meanwhile the Executive influence, the production of a model with otherwise optional equipment as standard, had spread to the Mark IV, with the 3022E 2994-cc Ford Executive being released in October 1966. With automatic transmission, power-assisted steering and sun-roof as standard (although a manual with overdrive was available also), and walnut fascia, the Executive went through the same suspension mods as the rest of the range and was the most expensive of the Fords, at £1,567 on release. The Mark IV on the road was fast and comfortable, the Zodiac managing 103 mph, with acceleration from 0–50 mph in 7·5 sec and consumption of 19 mpg.

Meantime, the best-selling Anglia family had reached the end of its run, and was discontinued in November 1967. Replacing it was the Escort, the name being revived for a small new saloon with clean and aerodynamic lines, a marked waist upsweep over the rear wheels giving it an aggressive appearance. If anything, the shell was a little spartan in external appearance, but a choice of tastefully trimmed and attractive interiors was provided. The proven and popular Macpherson strut front and live axle semi-elliptic rear suspension system was retained in modified form in the new model and general production methods were greatly modernized. Six models were released, using three different engines, a new 1097-cc '1100' unit producing 53 bhp at 5,500 rpm, the small Cortina 1297-cc unit in 63 bhp at 5,000 rpm standard or 75 bhp at 5,400 rpm GT forms, and the Lotus-modified 1558-cc version, producing 115 bhp at 6,000 rpm. The 1100 was offered in Standard, De Luxe or Super trim forms, the 1300 Super shared identical trim with the more powerful GT, and then the potent Twin Cam stood alone at the upper end of the range.

The new model was longer, lower and wider than the Anglia, with more interior room (although rear seat head-room was limited, as was tail vision when reversing). The suspension was modified to include rack-and-pinion steering, for the first time on a Ford, and a link system took over from the anti-roll bar in locating the bottom ends of the front struts. Standard brakes on all but the GT and Twin Cam were 8-inch drums, the latter pair using servo-assisted front discs which were optional on all other models. Wide-rim 4½J wheels were also standard on the GT but optional for the others, while the Twin Cam housed 5½J rims in large flared wheel arches. The transmission system was designed in Cologne, featured an integral clutch and gearbox housing, offered closer ratios in GT form and had a remote gear-change with a single selector rod system as standard. The Twin Cam model, however, was considered too powerful for this unit, and used the normal close-ratio Corsair box instead. Great attention was paid in all models to noise and vibration damping, and the result was a class of small and nippy saloons, with a superb gear-change, light and direct steering, and a high degree of inborn stability, although side-winds could upset them rather. Maintenance requirements were cut to a minimum. Prices ranged from £604 for the basic 1100, £666 for the 1100 Super, £690 for the 1300 Super and £764 for the 1300 GT. The Twin Cam was priced at about £1,195, and against performance figures of 81 mph flat-out, and 0–50 mph in about 13 sec for the 1100, it achieved 112 mph and 6·4 sec 0–50. Estate car versions with the 1100 and 1300 engines appeared priced at £773 and £814 respectively, and an optional automatic transmission was offered for an extra £87, working well and robbing the cars of little power. But the crossflow engines were working really hard on overall gear ratios, which were fairly low, and engine and exhaust noise could intrude at speed.

In addition, a variant with a detuned type BDA version of Cosworth's Cortina-based four-valves-per-cylinder FVA Formula 2 racing engine was also announced, although it did not become generally available until 1970.

The big Zephyrs and Zodiacs were all new, while the Escorts featured some new mechanical parts but retained a largely conventional suspension set-up. Then in January 1969 Ford Europe Inc branched out into what was virtually the sports car market with a still largely conventional new car, not unlike a shrunken version of the American Mustang in appearance, and resurrecting the name of Capri. This in fact was the Ford 'Colt' project, a combined operation between Ford of Dagenham and Ford Germany. The result was a 'universal' motor-car, capable of accepting all engines in the two Ford ranges, and also offered with three optional trim packs, the 'X', 'L' and 'R'.

The Capri shell itself featured a low bonnet and roofline, with the radiator and engine mounted well back towards the bulkhead, and a roomy Escort-sized passenger compartment providing genuine accommodation for four people despite the steeply raked 'fastback' styling at the tail with its separate boot-lid and notched rear screen. A heavy styling ridge ran from the rectangular headlights back over the rear wheel arches to dip down behind them, and this effectively kept the Opel-Kadett-like upper body panels clean and free from mud. The wheelbase of the Corsair was combined with the track and length of the Cortina to place a wheel in each corner, and the Capri provided fast and controllable roll-free cornering ability with its usual combination of front struts, anti-roll bar and live axle with semi-elliptic leaf springs and radius arms, although wheel movement was more limited than previously. Disc/drum brakes were standard, with a brake servo on the 1600 GT model.

With the choice of seven engines, ranging in power output from 52, 64 and 82 bhp to 92, 123 and 144 bhp further up the range, the trim packs offered further individuality. The 'X' interior modifications of reclining front seats, an extremely comfortable rear bench seat (with separately formed squabs), twin horns, and reversing lamps, was offered along with the 'L' external badge, over-riders, dummy air scoops for the side panels, locking filler cap and bright metal side mouldings kit. Finally the 'R' pack was offered for the GT versions only, including 5-inch Rostyle sculptured road wheels, leather sports steering wheel, fog and spot lamps mounting in the grille and a map reading light. For the complete boy-racer, matt-black bonnet and tail panels were also available. Prices for this model example of 'customer engineering' with only the five smaller engines being released initially, ranged from £890 for the 1300 to £1,087 for the 2000GT, while a complete XLR package addition would cost over £79 more.

But the Capri, with its Escort-sized cabin, Escort-style suspension and rack-and-pinion steering, single rail selector gearboxes and powerful Corsair-sized brakes for all models except the 1300 (which used Cortina units) was a remarkable exercise, being offered with more options than any comparable car ever. Again it instantly began to sell well – Ford had put their finger once more on the pulse of the motor-buying public, and with this grand finale ended a decade of incredible development and huge commercial and competition success.

14 Gilbern

As the only Welsh-based motor manufacturer, Gilbern has a special claim to fame, bolstered by its production of occasional four-seat high-performance GT cars of a quite good standard of design and finish.

The company began when German-born Bernard Frieze, who had been working for a specialist glass-fibre body-builder, produced a complete 'special'. Giles Smith – whose family were in the butchery business in South Wales – was attracted by Frieze's car and between them they set out to build an improved model. Eventually, in 1959, they went into small-scale production with the Gilbern two-/four-seat coupé, the title being a combination of their Christian names. Originally operating from premises above one of the Smith slaughter-houses in Church Village, South Wales, the infant company produced both kit and assembled versions of their new car.

Using a boxy glass-fibre two-door body shell with a bulbous sloping roofline, the Gilbern GT was based on a robust tubular chassis frame.

Originally three engine/transmission packages were offered, a Shorrocks-supercharged 948-cc BMC A-Series Sprite unit, a 1558-cc MGA B-Series and a 1098-cc Coventry Climax mated to the MGA gearbox. The latter was dropped as the less sophisticated MG engine proved both more reliable and quicker! The kit included a fully trimmed body-shell to help the home builder to produce a professional-looking motor-car, and the tubular chassis frame itself carried the door, bonnet and boot-lid hinges to ensure their trueness. A coil-and-wishbone ifs system used A35 parts, and a BMC rear axle was used on coil spring/damper units, located by radius arms.

With the 1558-cc engine installed, the Gilbern was a vivid performer, since its all-up weight was over 2 cwt less than the standard MGA, which at the time was itself far from slow. Acceleration from 0–50 mph took 9·5 sec, and maximum speed was about 100 mph with some assistance, although the engine was revving easily all the time. As with most early glass-fibre kit cars, noise level was rather high, but on the Gilbern only at very high speed, and the well-instrumented and nicely appointed vehicle could seat two adults and two children quite comfortably, or the small rear seat would accept one 'transverse' adult. The 9-inch front disc brakes and 8-inch rear drums with optional servo-assistance provided quite powerful braking, and with a fair in-built degree of understeer the Gilbern was very quick and stable through fast corners, power being sufficient to kick the lightly laden tail round on tighter bends. But the early ones did seem to be lacking rather in torsional rigidity, and the otherwise comfortable suspension could be bottomed easily on rough roads. But this early GT was an excellent beginning for the company, and although such standards made it rather more expensive than some of the opposition, kits were available at £978, including wire wheels, disc brakes and a vacuum brake servo.

In 1960 just eleven cars left the Pontypridd works, including two early chassis/body structures which were supplied without engine and gearbox as Gilbern's original idea had been. However, thirty-three GTs were produced in 1961 and, with the 1622-cc MGA engine as standard, output rose to fifty-two in 1962. The works had moved to their present location up the valley in Llantwit Fardre, and in 1962 the well-known Welsh driver Tony Cottrell joined Messrs Smith and Frieze on the board and Gilbern's future began to look assured.

With the release of the 1798-cc MGB engine, this became standard in the renamed Gilbern 1800GT. The standard MGB gearbox was fitted, a Panhard rod improved back axle location, and among the listed extras were a Smith's fresh-air heater, radio, tool kit, fog and spot lamps, cigarette lighter and Laycock de Normanville overdrive on third and top gears. The usual MGB tuning parts were also available, and with a mildly tweaked unit installed, the 1800GT was capable of 112 mph in overdrive top, or around 108 mph direct drive. The 0–50 mph time was cut to just over 8 sec, and 90 mph came up in 29·7 sec from rest. The MGB engine was mounted slightly further back than previously in the square-tube chassis to improve weight distribution, and this provided a slight final oversteer tendency in an otherwise very stable machine. On smooth roads the Gilbern's handling was delightful, but on bumps its very firm suspension promoted hops and leaps which were quite uncomfortable for the occupants. All-round visibility was good apart from blind spots in the large rear quarter panels, and the domed plastic rear screen, which had been used from the car's inception, distorted rearward vision. But the quite spacious occasional four-seat cabin was trimmed very tastefully in black leather with carpet up to waist-level and white cloth above that, and was a good example to some other kit-car manufacturers.

In 1964 the Pontypridd concern sold 123 GTs, rising to 157 basically unchanged machines the following year. But a new model was on the way, for the handsomely 'boxy' look of the square-cut straight-waisted GT with its bulbous roof and square radiator intake was beginning to look its age. In 1966 Frieze and Smith produced a new model, turning to the compact new Ford 2994-cc V6 engine for motive power. It seems that they had never had direct supplies from BMC and this resulted in a partial change of allegiance. With an 8·9:1 cr and single Weber 40FA twin-choke carburettor, the 3-litre Vee unit produced 141 bhp net at 4,750 rpm, with 181·5 lb ft net peak torque at 3,000 rpm. The Ford four-speed all-synchromesh transmission was retained, with a 9-inch Borg & Beck diaphragm spring clutch, and this drove to a 3·9:1 hypoid bevel back axle. This power-train was fitted into a direct development of the earlier frame chassis, formed mainly from 1-inch 16 swg and 1¼-inch 14 swg square-section tube. Double tubes (one above the other) formed door sills and central backbone, and a mass of cross-braces between the paired tubes and around the scuttle and rear suspension gave added rigidity. The glass-fibre body on the GT had shown weaknesses and these were strengthened on the sleek and striking new body. Doors were again hung directly on the chassis frame, and an MGB back axle was used, sprung by coil-springs, with non-parallel, unequal length trailing arms and Panhard rod location. Independent front suspension was, again, a modified MGB system, and BMC rack-and-pinion steering simply had a longer rack tube to adapt to the new car's wider track. MGB 10¾-inch front disc brakes and 10-inch rear drums were used, with a dual Lockheed master cylinder and hydraulic system.

The new body shell featured a very slightly curved waistline in elevation, with a cut-off recessed tail transom and vertical nose with a wide tapering air intake retaining a little of the original model's square-cut character. Head-lights were slightly recessed into each wing and broad, flat bonnet, roof and boot gave a distinctive touch, the large glass area including steeply raked front and rear screens and slender pillars. Internally, trim and equipment was up to the usual high standard, and excellent Restall seats offered a wide range of adjustment for a comfortable driving position. Twin Herald-type fuel tanks mounted in the rear wings gave a 13-gallon long-range fuel capacity, and this new Gilbern, named the Genie, was a very attractive motor-car indeed.

At under 18 cwt, the Genie's 140 bhp shot it from 0–50 mph in only 6 sec and to 100 mph in 28 sec, with a maximum of around 120 mph. The interior was roomy, although a little mean on rear seat head-room, but was beautifully equipped and exceptionally well instrumented. In 1968, the price complete was £1,917, overdrive was an £89 extra, and in kit form a massive saving allowed for an easy assembly job at £1,447, with overdrive at only £69 – the kit's exemption from purchase tax extending to its extras.

The Genie's only shortcomings were the still uncompromising ride, but for the enthusiastic its characteristically taut feel and pretty neutral handling, with final oversteer if pushed really hard, were endearing qualities. Production forged ahead in small but increasing quantities, and in April 1968 Gilbern Cars Ltd were acquired by Ace Holdings Ltd of Cardiff. Founders Giles Smith and Bernard Frieze were retained as directors, and it was planned to raise production from the then-current two cars a week to five.

At the London Motor Show that year a further model was announced, this Genie-based Gilbern PI 130 having a Tecalemit-Jackson fuel-injected V6 with 165 bhp, and driving through a limited-slip differential. This PI was priced at £2,302 in spring 1969, compared with £2,046 for the basic Genie. Kits were priced at £1,749 and £1,549 respectively at this time, which was rather on the high side, but these motor-cars were easily assembled and offered performance and distinction of an unusually high order. Gilbern entered the 'seventies with the improved Invader model, closely based on these years with the V6 Genie series.

15 Ginetta

Four enthusiastic brothers, Bob, Douglas, Ivor and Trevor Walklett, founded this progressive and successful specialist sports car company. In the late 'fifties they were running an engineering concern in Woodbridge, Suffolk, and Ivor started the ball rolling by modifying an old Wolseley Hornet, both chassis and body, and finally writing-off this 'G1' model in his own drive.

A Lotus 6-like G2 'special' appeared in 1957 going into limited production and then the G3 model appeared, which really got Ginetta going as a constructor. This used a multi-tubular chassis frame and Ford 105E engine and gearbox, the whole being clothed in a heavily styled glass-fibre coupé shell. Introduced in 1960, this machine began to sell quite well, being light, easily handled, and well finished, unlike so many products of the then-booming specialist sports car 'industry'.

About sixty G3s had been produced by the time Ivor Walklett completed work on the G4 design – destined to become Ginetta's most successful model in both road and competition trim. Shown at the 1961 Racing Car Show, the G4 was very distinctive, with an exceedingly pretty and sleek-looking two-door two-seat coupé body. Headlights were cut back into the curving front wings, and a low waistline kicked-up over the rear wheels into gracefully formed spats, sloping down into a short and attractive tail. Coil-and-wishbone suspension was retained with a rigid rear axle, and with a variety of Ford engine/gearbox packages available the attractive G4 was to become Ginetta's best-seller, over 500 having been produced between 1961 and 1969. They were well built, both frame and glass-fibre shell being produced at the Ginetta works, and offered taut, sporting character, combined with a fair degree of refinement and figure-hugging comfort in their small two-seat cockpits. So well did demand for the G4 grow that large premises were acquired at Witham in Essex, Ginetta's base today.

In 1963 the G5 title made a brief appearance, using the 1498-cc Ford Cortina engine, but, externally unchanged from the G4, it soon reverted to this original classification. So far as road-cars were concerned – the company producing many varied and, with few exceptions, successful racing variants – the G4 bore the brunt of the demand for the duration of the period, but this was not for want of trying. A handsomely streamlined, chesty-looking G10 model appeared, using an American 271-bhp Ford V8 engine, with MGB doors and windscreen in a glass-fibre shell of their own high-quality production. This proved quite successful in competition, but was priced out of existence by the antagonistic attitude of the British insurance companies. So a standard 1798-cc MGB engine was introduced into the basic G10 chassis frame to compensate, a handsomely streamlined coupé roof being added to the basic below-waist shell to produce a high-performance coupé looking rather like a small Aston Martin. Ginetta suffered from inadequate supply of components from BMC, as had Gilbern, and the project had to be shelved.

So it was that the G4 pressed on as the only quantity production road-car to come from the Witham works until 1967, when the G14 backbone-chassised prototype road-car was projected. But this was shelved in favour of a simpler and cheaper tubular-framed G15 model, using Rootes Imp Sport mechanicals. The all-aluminium-alloy light weight four-cylinder engine had a capacity of 875 cc, with a 10:1 cr, and produced 55 bhp gross at 6,100 rpm, with twin Stromberg 125 CDS carburettors. A Laycock 6¼-inch diameter diaphragm clutch transmitted drive to the four-speed all-synchromesh gearbox, and this drove through standard Imp Sport-type drive shafts to the rear wheels, the engine being mid-mounted behind the G15's cockpit and ahead of the back axle line. Girling 9-inch front disc brakes and 8-inch rear drums were used, coil-and-wishbone ifs combining with the standard coil-sprung semi-trailing arm Imp suspension at the rear. The result was a sleek and tiny two-seater coupé, resembling a Lotus Elan but looking rather prettier and more delicate. It was fast, however, weighing just over 9 cwt, and having a maximum speed of around 100 mph, betraying its competition breeding in taut and predictable handling qualities.

The G15 was quite cheaply priced at around £1,000 – a Ginetta feature. The policy behind the new car was to offer an adequately trimmed, well-equipped, and nicely finished sports coupé for an attractive price, and demand for the G15 from its announcement in 1968 was considerable. The Walklett brothers looked like having their hands full in 1969, for, apart from aiming to produce some 200 G15s, they also had a full programme of sports and single-seater competition car development before them, including a Formula 1 racing car project scheduled to begin at the end of the year. Quietly and efficiently, Ginetta have grown in Lotus-like competition-cum-road-car production. This family business is now one of the most successful of Britain's smaller high-performance car manufacturers.

16 Gordon-Keeble

As manufacturers of high-performance luxury cars very much in the Lagonda, Bristol and AC idiom, this company had a rather chequered career. Under its Managing Director, Mr John S. Gordon, Peerless Cars Ltd produced a quality grand touring car, the Triumph TR-engined Peerless GT in small numbers in the late 'fifties. He resigned and sold his interests, and production of a slightly refined version was briefly taken up by Bernard Rodger Developments Ltd, but ceased by 1962. Meanwhile John Gordon had become interested in another project.

In March 1960 the Gordon GT appeared in prototype form. This car featured a two-door coupé body styled by Bertone in Italy. The chassis, designed by Jim Keeble, was a complex space-frame of electrically welded square-section tubes, with coil-and-wishbone ifs and a De Dion irs system located by parallel radius arms and a Watt linkage. Steering was by a cam-and-lever system, and Girling disc brakes were used all round, in handsome Dunlop pressed steel perforated disc wheels. The Bertone body was steel-panelled in this original form, and the interior was both extremely spacious and luxuriously appointed. The machine was propelled by a 4·6-litre Chevrolet Corvette V8 engine, and the original intention was to supply these in three standards of tune, ranging from the standard 233 bhp at 4,800 rpm package, through a sports 290 bhp at 6,250 rpm, to the full competition 360 bhp at 7,400 rpm form. A single dry-plate clutch was used, transmitting drive to a four-speed all-synchromesh gearbox with central floor change, and a chassis-mounted Salisbury final drive. Chevrolet 'Powerglide' automatic transmission was to be optional equipment, and at the time of the announcement the manufacturer was hoping to build a 16,000-square-foot factory to commence production that September.

This initial prototype proved a very exciting machine, with full, comfortable and spacious accommodation for four people and all their luggage, a true maximum speed of over 140 mph and acceleration from 0–100 mph in a furious 18·9 sec. But many factors delayed the project, and it was not until January 1964 that production of the vehicle, by then named the Gordon-Keeble GK1, got under way in the concern's new premises at Eastleigh Airport, Southampton. Mr George Wansbrough had become Company Chairman, and several modifications had been made to the original concept, the major one being that the Bertone-styled body shell was now being produced in glass-fibre by Williams & Pritchard, their moulds having been taken to the Eastleigh works. A 5356-cc Chevrolet engine was installed, and the announced price of the first model was incredibly low at £2,798.

The new 5·3-litre V8 was quiet, lazy and powerful, though not as 'rorty' a unit as was in fact available. Hydraulic tappets were retained, and with a single four-barrel progressive-choke Carter carburettor and 10·5:1 cr, it produced an easy 280 bhp net at 5,000 rpm, with 360 lb ft gross torque at 'three-two'. A GM 10·4-inch sdp clutch was used, mating to the high-geared all-synchromesh Warner manual gearbox. Girling discs were still used, with dual hydraulic circuits and servos; 11·38-inch diameter front and 11·06-inch rear. The coil-and-wishbone/De Dion all-independent suspension was also retained, now with Marles worm-and-wheel steering. This very opulently appointed and equipped car suffered only in minor details – the ventilation and heating systems on the early cars were rather weak and the same controls were either out of reach or inconvenient to operate. But otherwise this large but light machine, weighing around 28 cwt, was delightful.

It was quick and stable, only badly pot-holed roads upsetting its otherwise excellent ride and promoting an unpleasant sway and hop. The brakes were powerful, retarding well from the maximum speed of just under 140 mph, while acceleration from 0–50 mph took just 5 sec, the 100 mph mark was reached in under 17 sec, and 120 mph flashed up in 29 sec (it was indeed strange that a tortoise should be the Gordon-Keeble's insignia!). The big V8 was not exceptionally thirsty at about 14 mpg.

All-round finish was excellent, high-grade materials being used everywhere, and the Williams & Pritchard glass-fibre-work was of exceptional quality and really ripple-free. Once the mouldings had been made, hinged parts were offered-up and individually trimmed to give precise fit, and steel tubes were moulded-in to reinforce the whole structure. Then the resultant frame around the passenger compartment was filled with 1-inch thick sound and heat insulation, Plasticell rigid expanded polyurethane foam being used. On the floor Plasticell deadened vibration between the aluminium under-tray and fibre floor, and the aluminium was itself coated thickly with bitumastic sealer.

The electrically welded chassis frame included around 300 feet of small-bore 16.swg tubing, and the De Dion rear suspension was interesting in that the tube itself was of square-section, easing fitting and alignment of attachment brackets. A really striking feature was the amount of space inside the car, for full rear seat leg-room was available even with the front seats adjusted to their quite generous limit, there was plenty of head-room for the tallest drivers, and even luggage space was generous. The provision of so much headroom did, in fact, lead to criticism, as the seating positions were very low- and the driver had some difficulty in sighting over the long nose.

However, it soon became obvious that the low price was not realistic, and in February 1965 Gordon-Keeble raised the figure to £3,626. But again the manufacturers seem to have been rather too ambitious and, as had often been proved before, it is easy to become a motor manufacturer, but difficult to stay in the business. In May 1965 the concern went into voluntary liquidation, when only about eighty vehicles had been produced.

But the basic design and its execution had been of such a high standard that Harold Smith (Motors) Ltd, who were Rolls-Bentley specialists in London, stepped in, acquiring the assets of the original company, and production recommenced with a more realistic price tag of £3,989. In January 1966 wider 5-inch wheels were fitted, and in May the heating and ventilation systems were improved to remove the most serious cause of rare criticism of the GK1. Air ducts picked up cooling air from above the front wheel arches, whence it was fed into the passenger compartment through twin swivelling nozzles on the fascia. Independent driver/passenger ventilation control was provided, and at the same time a slightly longer gear lever, cranked towards the driver, brought this vital control much more easily to hand.

Under Harold Smith this excellent Anglo-American true 'Grand Tourer' continued in production until mid-1967, when a wealthy young American named De Bruyne (pronounced 'De Brooney'), acquired Gordon-Keeble. He set up a new company, the De Bruyne Motor Car Company Ltd, at Newmarket in Suffolk, and the handsome GK1, using the GM 5355-cc V8 engine, appeared at the New York Motor Show in April 1968 as the De Bruyne GT. Some body changes had been made, and the new price for the car was £4,250. At the same Show another model was announced, using the same engine but this time installed in a mid-engined two-seater coupé. This De Bruyne Grand Sport featured a steel platform chassis, coil-and-wishbone ifs and the De Dion rear suspension from the original car, and also had power-assisted rack-and-pinion steering, a ZF five-speed transmission and aggressively styled glass-fibre bodywork, the work of one Peter Fluck.

With these changes and the appearance of the new model, the story of Gordon-Keeble's decade of missed opportunity came to an end.

17 Hillman

As the principal Rootes Group 'marque' Hillman were concentrating on the medium-capacity saloon car market in 1960 with their assorted Minx variants and the Husky Estate. The first post-war Minx, which was basically identical to the model announced in 1940, was the Mark I, and this series was continued to Mk VIIIA (1951–6). In 1960 the Mark IIIA in a new numerical series was current. This was a four-door saloon, very much in the Minx tradition, with wrap-round rear screen and slight turn-over on the small tail fins. It used a 1494-cc four-cylinder ohv engine, with a Zenith W19 carburettor and produced 56·5 bhp gross at 4,400 rpm. This was mated to a four-speed gearbox with synchromesh on the upper three ratios (these being more closely spaced than previously). The almost universal coil-and-wishbone ifs system was used with a live axle on semi-elliptics at the rear. Lockheed drum brakes were fitted, two leading shoe-type at the front, and steering was by Burman recirculating ball. Standard, 'Special', De Luxe saloon, convertible and estate car variants were available, selling at £722, £764, £872 and £858 respectively. With the new close-ratio gearbox a floor change was standard, but Smith's 'Easidrive' three-speed automatic transmission was an optional extra. Maximum speed was about 81 mph, and with plenty of mid-range torque, the 1½-litre engine provided good top gear acceleration, giving a 0–50 mph time of some 15 sec.

The Husky Estate car available at this time used a 1390-cc four-cylinder engine of the type introduced into the Minx range in 1954. This produced a maximum of 51 bhp gross at 'four-four', used a Zenith VIG carburettor, and was mated to a lower-geared manual transmission similar to that of the Minx. The chunky van-like body used coil-and-wishbone ifs with a semi-elliptic rear end, smaller Lockheed drum brakes than the Minx, and lever instead of telescopic rear shock absorbers. The interior was spartan, but fairly roomy. The price was £659.

In March 1960 the Husky was given larger front and rear screens, a lower roof line with overhang, plated headlamp rims and hoods, and vertical grille bar styling, while, internally, a close-ratio gearbox was adopted. The new model was the Series II, and in August it was further modified by the adoption of a hypoid rear axle in place of the original spiral bevel unit.

In September the Minx Series IIIB appeared, the old Special model disappearing in favour of a more sensibly named 'Standard' version, using, in common with the De Luxe, convertible and estate models, a new Zenith 30VN carburettor, a hypoid back axle, improved air filter, a level plug in place of the gearbox dipstick, larger oil pump and a thinner front seat squab, providing more leg-room in the rear without limiting space in the front. The new hypoid final drive ratios were higher than those of the previous spiral bevels, slowing acceleration but increasing maximum and cruising speeds. The three-speed Easidrive automatic option still gave two-pedal control, using a Smith's magnetic transmission coupling. The saloons, convertible and Husky had a road speed of 16·3 mph per 1,000 rpm in top, in both manual and automatic trim, while the estate, using larger rear wheels, managed 16·5 mph. The Husky price was up to £674, but the others were unchanged. The automatic option, incidentally, cost over £124.

But in July 1961 the standard Minx was discontinued, the IIIB series being replaced by the new IIIC models. These used an enlarged 1592-cc version of the four-cylinder engine, were higher geared, and had detail changes to suspension and steering to reduce maintenance requirements. '1600' motifs replaced 'Minx' lettering on the front doors, this name being retained on the boot-lid, while chrome surrounds to the fuel filler and front quarter-lights were deleted. The bumpers were rounded instead of contoured, and a floor change was standard, although column-change could be specified on export models (the Smith's automatic transmission was still available). With the new gear ratios speed per 1,000 rpm in top was up to 17·2 mph, and prices for all models were increased.

The 1961 Motor Show saw the introduction of the completely new Super Minx Mark I. This unitary construction shell offered more passenger space, the wheelbase having been increased by 5 inches from that of the Minx, although overall length and width were only up by 3 inches and 1½ inches. The coil-and-wishbone ifs and semi-elliptic rear of the Minx IIIC were retained, while the 1592-cc engine was fitted with a Zenith 32VN carburettor, and now produced 62 bhp at 4,800 rpm, but much improved acceleration. The new body was a stylish combination of straight horizontal lines and side and roof panel curves, with two hooded headlamps flanking a constant-depth full-width grille, wrap-round front and rear screens, and Rootes' still-attractive small and unobtrusive tail fins. The Super Minx was priced at £854, cheaper than both Minx estate and convertible models, and many were surprised to find a particularly well-behaved back axle and controlled roll giving very good handling qualities. Steering was heavy, but an 82 mph top speed, 14-sec 0–50 mph time and 25 mpg economy were fairly respectable.

In January 1962 the Super Minx Estate was first produced, to be followed in March by the convertible. These were announced to the public in May and

June, at which time the comparable Minx models were discontinued. In September the Mark I Super Minx itself was deleted, to be replaced by the Mark II saloon, convertible and estate range. Major changes were the elimination of all grease nipples, the fitting of 10·3-inch Lockheed disc brakes on the front wheels, a relocated petrol tank giving increased boot space and the replacement of the Smith's automatic option by a Borg-Warner Model 35 unit. Alterations to the engine's timing and fitting a Solex 33 PSEI carburettor produced 58 bhp (net) at 4,400 rpm coupled with increased torque allowing the high-ratio top gear to be used giving a top gear speed per 1,000 rpm of 17·2 mph. Estate car ratios were unchanged. New design individual front seats replaced the bench of the Mark I (these featured rubber-diaphragm contour moulding with a spring sub-frame for the cushions). A central locking handle appeared on the boot-lid, and the new model, despite an engine slightly down on peak power, was smoother, quicker, and more economical than before.

Throughout this period development had been going ahead with a new small-capacity family saloon, to combine roomy interior accommodation with compact external dimensions in BMC Mini vein. The result was the rear-engined Imp saloon, finally announced in May 1963. The rear engine layout was chosen since it was basically cheaper than the front-wheel drive alternative (which has to incorporate constant velocity universal joints to allow steering movement), it concentrated weight over the driven wheels and allowed lighter steering. In addition it provided quieter running; at least for the front-seat passengers. In order to achieve good handling characteristics it was decided to produce a lightweight engine/transmission package, and this was feasible through extensive use of light alloys (a 65,000-square feet aluminium die-casting plant being established at Rootes' new Linwood factory near Edinburgh to produce the units). In fact, the resulting 875-cc four-cylinder units owed a lot to the 741-cc Coventry Climax FWM. This well-oversquare, single overhead camshaft engine had an all-up weight of only 170 lb, the four-speed all-synchromesh gearbox adding a further 66 lb. An automatic choke and Dunlop pneumatic throttle were provided on the special Solex B30 PIHT carburettor used, and output was 39 bhp (net) at 5,000 rpm.

These mechanicals were mounted in the rear of a light, angular two-door shell, box-section door sills and the transmission tunnel contributing to its stiffness. Curved box-section wishbones with very closely spaced central pivots gave swing-axle front-suspension geometry with co-axial coil spring damper units picking up in the scuttle structure, while at the rear semi-trailing fabricated wishbones were sprung by coil springs and damped by remotely mounted telescopic dampers. Rack-and-pinion steering was used with 12-inch 4J wheels all round.

Accommodation was fairly spacious for such a small package, with boot space in the nose and a wide-opening rear window giving access to a luggage compartment behind the rear seat and above the inclined engine with its forward-facing gearbox. Heating and ventilating systems were standard in De Luxe models, and safety-belt mountings were built-in along with a zone-toughened windscreen as standard.

The result was an unusual-looking motor-car, with a top speed of just under 80 mph and a 0–50 mph time of 15 sec, combined with a fuel consumption

of some 40 mpg. Its rear engine gave rise to some instability in cross-winds, but it had neutral handling characteristics which allowed controllable understeer or oversteer to be induced virtually at will. The steering was very light but had a lot of castor return, while ride was good for such an inexpensive motor-car and the performance offered by the very mildly tuned standard engine was perfectly adequate. (There was plenty more to come with tuning.) The standard and De Luxe models were priced at £508 and £532 respectively and had a lot to offer for such an economical figure.

In August 1963 both the Husky Series II and Minx Series IIIC models were discontinued, being replaced by Series III and V versions respectively. The new Husky had no greasing points, a lower bonnet line, redesigned fascia with full-width parcels shelf and a combined ignition/starter switch, while a horizontal bar grille incorporating side lights and indicators was adopted.

The Minx Series V De Luxe had a restyled shell with squared roofline, rounded rear wings replacing the vestigial fins of the earlier models, and a larger windscreen with squared-off surround. A grille of five horizontal bars was fitted, with a central badge, and 'Minx' lettering reappeared on the sides in place of the '1600' insignia. Disc brakes were restored at the front. Borg-Warner automatic transmission was optional, and the prices of the two revised models – the Husky and the Minx – were only £587 and £635 respectively. The 1390-cc Husky was good for 71 mph, and 0–50 mph in 16 sec, but with only about 26 mpg; the Minx was slower than the Imp (78 mph maximum and 0–50 mph in 16 sec) while consumption stood at about 28 mpg.

In November the Super Minx axle ratio was changed to give 16·2 mph per 1,000 rpm in top, and in June 1964 the Super Minx convertible was discontinued, to be followed in September by the Mark II saloon and estate models, both being replaced by Mark III versions. These had a sharper roof-line, deeper and wider windscreen, wide raked rear screen and reclining front seats. The fascia was black-trimmed on top with wood veneer underneath and the estate car also had longitudinal roof-ribbing, in place of the transverse style used previously. These new Mark III models were priced at £769 for the saloon and £799 for the estate car, and more powerful engines much improved performance, the saloon touching 82 mph, getting from 0–60 mph in 13 sec and combining this performance with a high degree of comfort, good looks and an overall fuel consumption of about 24 mpg.

At the same time the Husky and Minx had all-synchromesh gearboxes fitted, while the Husky also had a diaphragm-spring clutch as used on the Imps from their inception, and an anti-roll bar on the front suspension. The instruments were given vertical markings, while padded sun visors and an organ-type accelerator pedal were added. The Minx also had screen washers standardized and the vertically annotated instruments added.

In September the following year the basic Imp model was discontinued as further variants under Rootes' other marque names appeared, and the Mark II De Luxe and Super saloons were introduced. The De Luxe version had rear ashtrays, leathercloth parcel shelf padding, underseal, a slightly larger diaphragm-spring clutch and larger valves, while the Super featured a mock grille between the headlamps, contoured rear seats, padded arm-rests, twin-tone horns, wheel trims and chrome rubbing strips.

In the same month the Minx was revamped with a new five main bearing

1725-cc engine, which also appeared in the Super. In these new Series VI and Mark IV forms, the Minx and Super Minx offered further refinement now allied to a smooth and willing engine. The 1725-cc unit, with a Zenith 34IV carburettor, and cr of 8·4:1, produced 65 bhp net at 4,800 rpm, and was mated with an all-synchromesh gearbox via a Borg & Beck 7½-inch ds clutch. Mixed disc/drum and ifs/live rear axle systems were retained, and the new models were priced at £660 Minx saloon, £805 Super Minx saloon, and £845 Super Minx estate car.

In December 1965 the Husky utility was discontinued, and in August 1966 the Super Minx saloon followed to be replaced by the all-new Hunter Mark I. The Minx family had established a reputation for solidly built family cars of comfortable but sluggish character and generally rather dull performance and only average economy. The new Hunter was lighter, had more power, burned less fuel and yet was just as comfortable and reassuringly 'solid' as the earlier machines.

With an aluminium-alloy head, a cr of 9·2:1 and a Zenith Stromberg 150CDS carburettor, the 1725-cc engine now produced 74 bhp net at 5,000 rpm, combined with an impressive 102 lb ft torque (compared to the Super Minx's 91·4 lb ft). Code-named *Arrow*, the Hunter project had produced a car with a lightweight body, many pounds having been saved by adopting strut-type ifs to eliminate the need for a heavy cross-member, and since a convertible model was not envisaged, the additional in-built stiffening of the Super Minx was not needed in the Hunter. End boxes were lightly constructed to absorb crash damage and impact forces, while the double box-section pillars and strong floor pan gave a shell torsionally stiffer than that of the Minx, yet weighing 155 lb less. The square-cut styling was obviously in the Rootes lineage, yet the new car was much cleaner and sleeker than the Minx. Use of alloy in the engine saved a further 33 lb, and to provide room for the side-mounted carburettor between the bulging Macpherson strut-mounting wings, the engine was inclined at 10 degrees to the right. A leaf-spring rear axle was retained, but spring rates were down with the lighter car, and 106 lb were saved in the suspension alone. In view of the car's lighter weight smaller 9·6-inch Lockheed disc brakes were fitted at the front while self-adjusting rear drums were standard. Transmission was unchanged, and both Laycock de Normanville overdrive (with a 3·9:1 back axle) or Borg-Warner Model 35 (with the standard manual 3·70:1 axle ratio) were optional.

Maximum speed was a lively 92 mph, and the 0–50 mph time was cut to 9·3 sec. Better still, fuel consumption was as good as 32 mpg overall. Gone was the understeering slushy feel of the old Minx, for the Hunter could be put into a power-induced tail-slide more or less at will, and with light and responsive steering was easily controlled. Body roll was well controlled, but without a servo the brakes were rather heavy and dead, though sufficiently powerful for normal motoring.

Internally, reclining front seats and a bench rear were deep and comfortable, while a very efficient fresh-air heating and ventilation system included omni-directional fascia vents. Opening quarter-lights were still retained, surprisingly, and contributed to rather high wind noise level at speed. But the new car, a vast improvement over its forerunners, was inexpensive at £838.

In November 1966 the first 'New Minx' was produced, to be announced in

January the following year. Using a similar shell to the Hunter, the Minx was powered by a 1496-cc four-cylinder ohv engine, using a Zenith 150CDS carburettor and, with a cr of 8·4:1, producing 60 bhp net at 4,800 rpm. Drive was taken via a 7½-inch Borg & Beck clutch to a four-speed all-synchro gearbox, and Borg-Warner Model 35 three-speed automatic transmission was optional. With rather more austere trim than the Hunter, front bucket seats and heater as standard, the new Minx was priced at £752. It had a top speed of 83 mph, a 0–50 mph time of under 12 sec and was reasonably economical at 30 mpg. An Estate version followed in April, and this sold for £868.

The same month the new Imp-based Husky Estate appeared, while in January a more exciting version of the Imp, the low-roofline Californian, had made its bow. This immediately made the standard models look high and antiquated, although in fact the roof was only 1½ inches lower. Front and rear screens were more steeply raked, the rear one now being fixed, while the steering column was lowered and reclining front seats were standardized. In addition the rear bench seat had separately folding squabs to form extra luggage space. In other details the car was pure Super Imp. The 875-cc 39 bhp engine was retained, but the front suspension pivot point was lowered by ¾ inch, reducing front wheel positive camber by one degree, and reducing understeer due to weight transfer. Maximum speed was 81 mph, 0–50 mph time was about 15 sec and consumption was still an excellent 35 mpg. The Californian was stylish, comfortable, handled better than the earlier Imps and was a very attractive small family car buy. The car was priced at £647.

From May front wheel camber was decreased on the Standard and Super Imp saloons, with consequent reduction in tyre-scrubbing understeer. In March the Minx Series VI had been discontinued, and in April the Super Minx Estate was deleted from the list.

In May 1968 servo-assisted brakes became optional on the New Minx and Hunter models, removing a source of constant criticism. This was followed by the introduction of a Minx De Luxe model, half-way between the standard car and the Hunter II in terms of trim and equipment but retaining the same engine. The existing Hillman Estate became the Minx Estate, still with the short-stroke 1496-cc engine but having the 1725-cc unit as an option with automatic or manual transmission. The Imp range was revised with a more luxurious interior and full-width instrument panel.

With these two basic ranges, the small Imp and the medium-sized Hunter models and their variants, the Hillman section of the Rootes Group went into the last year of the 'sixties.

During this period, however, the group suffered financial problems, and on 17 January 1967 it was announced that Rootes Motors Ltd and the American Chrysler Corporation had agreed to become closely linked. Chrysler were to make available £20 million for Rootes' use, £10 million of this being urgently required working capital. Under the same agreement Chrysler would come to hold some two-thirds of the total equity share capital and votes – yet another huge firm in the British industry had fallen under strong American influence.

18 Humber

Solid, dependable and, for their price, luxurious, the Humber range rather mirrored the Singer division of the Rootes Group in its smaller-sized saloons, while the bigger limousine-type machinery had a heavy, reliable and dignified appeal all of its own.

At the start of the decade the company were building the big Hawk and Super Snipe models in not very large quantities. For 1960 the Super Snipe's six-cylinder engine was bored out to 2965 cc from 2651 cc, the resultant oversquare engine offering increased maximum power and torque. This Series II unit used a Zenith 42WIA carburettor, had a cr of 8:1 and produced a very healthy 121 bhp net at 4,800 rpm. Drive was taken via a 9-inch sdp Borg & Beck clutch to a three-speed gearbox (with synchromesh on all but first yet again), with Laycock de Normanville overdrive and Borg-Warner fully automatic optional equipment. A divided Hardy Spicer open prop-shaft drove through a hypoid back axle, and robust coil-and-wishbone ifs with a semi-elliptic sprung live rear axle were used. Front drum brakes were replaced by 11¾-inch diameter Girling discs, 11-inch drums being retained at the rear, while several detail trim and equipment changes were also made for 1960. Three variants were offered, the basic ton-and-a-half saloon, a touring limousine in what was later to be described as 'executive' form, and a big Estate. The obviously Rootes Group styling, with curved roof line, hooded headlamps and a broad tapering flash of contrasting colour along the body side was quite attractive in a heavy way, and prices were set at £1,453 (saloon), £1,594 (limousine) and £1,701 (Estate). Handling was rather willowy, but top speed was about 95 mph, acceleration from 0–50 mph took 12 sec and fuel consumption was about 25 mpg.

· The Series IA Hawk introduced at the same time used the same basic four-door body shell, but this time with a 2267-cc engine, with a Zenith 36 SIA carburettor, having a low cr of 7·5:1 and producing 73 bhp net at 4,400 rpm. In view of this unit's restricted torque output a four-speed gearbox with synchromesh on the upper three ratios was standard, with the same optional transmissions as the Super Snipe. With a rather lower performance potential and lighter all-up weight, Lockheed drum brakes were retained all round on the Hawk, 11-inch diameter fronts and 10-inch rears, and three variants comparable with the Snipe were offered at £1,191, £1,304 and £1,410 respectively.

October 1960 saw further changes, however, with disc brakes appearing on the Hawk Series II and a further modified Super Snipe Series III being released. In particular the Snipe was something of a British trend-setter in featuring twin-headlamp styling. The idea was to remove the compromise arrangement whereby one reflector had to produce both a concentrated long-range light beam and non-dazzle dipped illumination. One light in each twin-set had a single-filament long-range beam, while the other with twin filaments produced satisfactory dipped beams and a fan-shaped 'splash' to supplement the long-range lamps. To accommodate these small-diameter light units the wing styling had to be changed, broadening the pressings and accommodating both lamps under a single hood. A wrap-round grille was adopted, incorporating mounts for the side lights and indicators, while for the first time the Snipe mascot was dropped. The forward overhang was increased to make room for optional air-conditioning equipment when specified, and the contrasting side flash was gone, replaced by a bright metal strip.

Engine modifications were concentrated on increasing life and refining its unchanged performance, heavy-duty steel-backed lead-indium bearings being used in all but the rear main, while oil gallery sizes were increased, and minor changes incorporated to ease fitting of optional equipment. Minor synchro-mesh and transmission control improvements were also made. In order to improve these big cars' stodgy handling, suspension changes included stiffer and thicker front coil springs, and wider rear leaves to increase lateral control. This increased roll-resistance markedly, and so a more slender front anti-roll bar was fitted. The result was much more manageable handling, reducing the effect of the model's large proportions.

Finally, passenger space was improved, extra equipment added internally, and the front bench seat was totally redesigned to provide a greater range of adjustment and a better driving position. The Hawk meanwhile was un-changed in appearance, but had Snipe-type servo-assisted Girling disc brakes at the front, an improved and more robust gearbox, and similar suspension changes added. Minor interior trim changes were made and the six dignified Super Snipe and Hawk models soldiered on into 1961.

Change came in July 1962, when the Series III Hawk saloon, touring limousine and Estate models appeared. With a restyled rear window, wind-screen surround and guttering, a 16- (instead of 12½-) gallon fuel tank and overdrive available on third gear as well as top, the new Mark IIIs produced 73 bhp at 'four-four' from their 2·2-litre engines.

In August the Super Snipe Series IV appeared with improved lightened steering, restyled rear screen, chromed roof gutters and tail fins, hinged rear door quarter-lights and further improved interior trim. The 'six' now produced 124 bhp at 5,000 rpm, while torque figures of 160 lb ft net at 2,600 rpm were quoted. Still retaining its standard three-speed gearbox, the Snipe, like the Hawk, required a keen observer to note the external differences from the previous year's releases. But the soft suspension still 'floated', even at low speeds, the car cornered sluggishly and was genuinely best for dignified transport at dignified speed.

Then, in January 1963, a third model joined the range. Based on the shell from the Super Minx/Singer Vogue, this was the Humber Sceptre Mark I, featuring a small grille with vertical bars, twin headlamps, sidelight/indicator units in horizontally barred side grilles, and rear fins moulding into Vees on the tail around the vertical rear light clusters. Servo-assisted front disc brakes were fitted as standard, and a close-ratio four-speed gearbox with self-cancelling overdrive on third and top was also used. This was a brisk saloon, reaching 92 mph, and accelerating from 0–50 mph in under 13 sec. In July a single Solex twin-choke compound carburettor replaced the twin Zeniths used previously.

September 1964 saw a new all-synchromesh gearbox fitted in the Sceptre, together with an adjustable steering column, fully reclining front seats, dimmable warning lamps and a lockable fuel filler cap. At the same time a new Series IV Hawk model appeared, in saloon and touring limousine trim. This featured Rootes' fashionable sharper roofline, a deeper and wider windscreen, full-width steeply sloping rear screen, rubber-insert over-riders, three separate circular rear lights on either side and 'Hawk' in script appearing on the boot-lid in place of the previous 'Humber' capital lettering. A four-speed all-synchro gearbox was adopted, with a Borg & Beck diaphragm spring clutch, optional Laycock de Normanville overdrive, and an unusual modification in the provision of a rear anti-roll bar and dual-rated leaf-springs. Vertically annotated instruments were fitted in common with other Rootes models, and at the same time the Series IV Estate appeared with unchanged styling, no rear anti-roll bar, but all other modifications incorporated.

The Super Snipe meanwhile was released in Series V form with standard power-assisted steering, the restyled body shell, 'Super Snipe' script lettering on the boot-lid, hooded triple rear lights, chrome door frame surrounds and several other detail changes. Twin Zenith Stromberg 17SCD carburettors were fitted, power output from the 8:1 cr six-cylinder engine being up to 128·5 bhp net at 5,000 rpm, with 167 lb ft torque at 2,600 rpm. Again, a diaphragm clutch was fitted, while synchromesh was still lacking on the first of the three speeds. Borg-Warner automatic transmission was still optional, as was Laycock overdrive, and prices for these three models stood at £998 (Sceptre saloon), £1,512 (Super Snipe saloon) and £1,095 (Hawk saloon).

But a new model had appeared at the head of the range, the Humber Imperial. This used the same basic Hawk/Super Snipe body shell, but externally was distinguishable by its black leathercloth roof covering and matching fog and spot lights mounted on the nose as standard. But the Imperial was much more luxuriously equipped than the Super Snipe, with fully reclining front seats, separately controllable heating systems, twin-speaker standard radio, an alternator and a new four-speed all-synchromesh gearbox as a major mechanical improvement. A thicker front anti-roll bar was used to improve ride and handling, while the rubber front suspension cross-member mountings were improved to transmit less road noise. Hydro-steer power-assisted steering was standard, as on the Super Snipe, while the Imperial also used Selectaride driver-adjustable rear shock absorbers. Price of the new model stood at £1,796.

September 1965 found the Mark II Sceptre being introduced, using the five main bearing 1725-cc engine common to other medium-size Rootes saloons, and appropriate 'Rootes 1725' insignia appeared on the front wing and boot-lid. An alternator was standard, together with self-adjusting rear brakes and such refinements as a courtesy boot light. Automatic transmission was an optional extra.

At the same time the Hawk's automatic option was reintroduced for the home market. Until then it had only been offered on export models, and in this form the Hawk/Super Snipe/Imperial range continued until June 1967, when the Imperial saloon and limousine, and the Super Snipe saloon, limousine and Estate versions were all discontinued. The three Hawk models survived until October, when the saloon and limousine models were deleted, and then in January 1968 the Hawk Estate was also discontinued. There were to be no more big Humbers.

Only the Sceptre survived to continue the Humber name, and in September 1967 the Mark II model was deleted in favour of a new version using the attractive and lightweight Hillman Hunter shell. 'Humber' lettering appeared in capitals on the boot and bonnet, while the narrow Humber grille of nine horizontal bars and a centre badge was flanked by twin headlamps, with sidelight/indicator units below a wrap-round front bumper. Indicator repeaters were mounted on the wing, with chrome beading around the wheel arches and along the body sills. The roof was covered in black vinyl, and a matt tail panel carried horizontal rear light clusters. The standard specification was very comlete, including twin reversing lights, reclining front bucket seats and individually-formed rear seats.

With twin Zenith 150 CDS carburettors, the Humber's 1725-cc engine produced a useful 88 bhp net at 5,200 rpm, and the four-speed all-synchromesh gearbox was driven from a 7½-inch Borg & Beck diaphragm clutch. Overdrive was standard on third and top, with Borg-Warner 35 automatic optional, and the new Sceptre, with its servo-assisted 9·6-inch diameter front discs and 9-inch diameter rear drums, was very well finished, thoughtfully and tastefully furnished, and was a thoroughly pleasant Rootes medium-sized luxury saloon.

As the sole surviving Humber model, the Sceptre was a very attractive machine, offering good performance and a very high standard of comfort and finish for £1,259. This 1969 model marked the end of the decade for Rootes' Humber division, a decade during which the true Humber models had disappeared, allowing the marque to continue in terms of the badge alone, even if the traditions of solid, dependable and comfortable transport were allowed to survive.

19 Jaguar

The name of Jaguar has a very special place in the hearts of all competition enthusiasts, for five outright wins in the Le Mans 24-Hours Race only head the list of the marque's racing successes. Their famous XK engine formed the firm foundation upon which these victories were achieved, and its road-going applications have been motor-cars renowned for their incredible value for money, performance, handling and finish.

In 1960 the Coventry company were offering six basic models. These were the 2·4-, 3·4- and 3·8-litre Mark II saloons, the big 3·8-litre Mark IX limousine and the sporting 3·4- and 3·8-litre XK 150 machines.

The Mark II body style was introduced in October 1959, the classical attraction of the curved roof and sloping nose with its vertical oval grille and the tapered tail being as for the Mark I. But visibility had been much improved with larger windows, a larger rear screen and more slender roof pillars. Disc brakes had been introduced on all four wheels, while a wider track rear axle, semi-recessed fog lamps in the nose and small faired sidelights on top of the wings had also been added.

The 2·4-litre engine was a 2483-cc version of William Heynes's famous six-cylinder XK design, featuring twin chain-driven overhead camshafts in a light alloy cylinder head. Carburation was by two SU HD8s, and with a compression ratio of 8:1 the oversquare engine produced 120 bhp. Both automatic and manual transmission models were available.

The 3·4-litre car was essentially similar to the smaller-engined Mark II, apart from external '3·4' badges and better performance, 210 bhp coming from the long-stroke 3442-cc power plant. The 3·8 was bored and stroked to 3781 cc, producing 220 bhp and providing the Mark II saloon with really vivid performance.

Design of these models had been in the hands of Sir William Lyons himself – the artist-engineer company founder – engineer William Heynes and Mr C. Bailey, and interior appointment and instrumentation of the Mark II saloons was quite lavish, with great use made of wood panelling and veneer, and deep and plush seats and carpets. Yet prices were low for the performance and comfort thus provided. The 2·4 with overdrive was priced at £1,589 in October 1959, the 3·4 at £1,732 and the 3·8 at £1,843. Acceleration from 0–50 mph took just over 10 sec in the 2·4, or 9 sec in a 3·4, while maxima were 104 and 120 mph respectively. Consumption stood at 16–24 mpg for the class.

The big Mark IX, using the 3·8-litre engine, had been introduced in October 1958, using a shell similar to that of the earlier Jaguar limousines, with huge curved separate front wings, a tapered bonnet with a rectangular grille, and large spats around the rear wheels. This was a really big and heavy car with disc brakes and power-assisted steering as standard. Automatic transmission or overdrive on the standard four-speed manual gearbox were options and the interior was most luxuriously equipped. Even so, price was only just over £2,000 for these very ponderous-looking and ponderously dimensioned vehicles – although this appearance belied their performance. ·

Jaguar's original XK120 sports car had appeared in 1948, and in 1960 the same basic recipe was soldiering on in the form of the XK150 models. These cars were available with both 3·4- and 3·8-litre engines installed, while fixed and drop-head coupés, a two-seater roadster and the high-performance S-type were also offered. In 1960, overdrive was standard on all models, while automatic transmission and a limited-slip differential were optional extras. Torsion bar independent front suspension was standard on all models, with a live axle on half-elliptic springs at the rear and rack-and-pinion steering. The 3·4-litre engine produced 210 bhp in standard tune, while with the high compression 9:1 S-type cylinder head, and triple SU HD8 carburettors, output was raised to 250 bhp at 5,500 rpm. The 3·8 unit in normal tune offered 220 bhp at 'five-five' rising to 265 bhp at the same engine speed in the S-version. Prices for these XK150s in 1960 ranged from £1,665 for the 3·4 FHC and two-seater roadster, to £2,204 for the 3·8 'S' DHC. Once again this was very good value for such fast and furious machinery, the 3·8 XK150 S fulfilling its title by exceeding 150 mph flat-out.

Change was imminent, however, and the design team of Lyons, Heynes and

Bailey were directing the development of two very advanced new models, the Mark X limousine, to replace the ponderous and now ancient-looking Mark IX, and the E-Type.

In March 1961 the 3·8-litre E-Type Jaguar was introduced for export only, in open two-seater and fixed-head coupé styling of quite breathtaking balance and beauty. With fluent yet aggressive lines, its faired-in headlamps, thrust-forward radiator air intake and louvred bonnet, with 'power bulge' to clear the XK engine's head, breathed pure 'sports car'. The two-door body was a fully stressed steel monocoque, carrying torsion bar ifs and introducing twin coil-spring irs too. Dunlop servo-assisted disc brakes were fitted all round, and with an all-up weight of only 22 cwt, the Jaguar E was given stunning performance by its 265 bhp, triple SU HD8-carburetted 3·8-litre engine. A limited-slip differential was also standard equipment, and home orders flooded in upon the new model's release in July. Then in October came the announcement of the new Mark X, just as advanced as its sporting sister model, with completely new styling, a centre section and roofline reminiscent of the Mark II saloons blending in with a long and shapely nose incorporating dual headlamps, and with a lengthy and commodious tail. It was longer, wider and much lower than the preceding Mark IX, and of true monocoque construction.

Strength was provided by the pressed steel sills of double-box section, running into a fully triangulated box structure fore and aft, including the wheel arch and wing pressings. The transmission tunnel also gave added structural strength, and transverse box sections in the form of the scuttle, bulkhead and rear seat pan gave transverse rigidity. This enabled the roof pillars to be kept slim and light, and all-round visibility in the new car was excellent. Coil spring ifs was introduced in this model, the assemblies being slung on a forged cross-member rubber-mounted on the monocoque for maximum insulation from road noise and vibration. Independent rear suspension followed that of the E-Type very closely, with universally jointed drive shafts acting as upper lateral location members, with forward-facing steel radius arms. Twin coil spring/damper units were mounted on either side, and the whole assembly was supported in a gigantic steel bridge, again rubber-mounted to the monocoque. A Powr-Lok limited-slip differential was standard, while the servo-assisted Dunlop rear disc brakes were mounted inboard on either side of the diff housing. Separate hydraulic systems served front and rear discs, Burman power-assisted steering was standard, and with the 3·8-litre S-type engine installed the new limousine had a maximum of 120 mph, 0–60 mph acceleration in about 10 sec and a fuel consumption of about 18 mpg. All this was being offered for £2,392, while Laycock de Normanville overdrive for the manual version or full automatic transmission were optional extras.

In June 1962 heel wells and seat recesses in the E-Type increased leg-room, and in September 1963 Jaguar's next development appeared with the release of the Series S saloons. These were to provide something of a half-way house between the accepted Mark II cars and the new Mark X, featuring the irs of the later model. The body styling was altered to incorporate a Mark X-style flattened tail and lower roof, while the nose remained Mark II apart from a heavier grille surround, cowls over the head and fog lamps, shallow section bumpers and elongated sidelights incorporating turn indicators. The new model had a wheelbase 1⅜ inches longer than the Mark II, a slightly wider track and was some 3½ cwt heavier. Price on announcement was £1,669 for the 3·4-litre version, or £1,759 for the 3·8. Twin SU HD6 carburettors were standard, while a cr of 8:1 was standard with optional 7:1 and 9:1 heads. Power outputs were 210 bhp for the 3·4 and 220 bhp for the 3·8, and the Jaguar S-types were attractive hybrids, combining the fairly compact size and performance of the popular Mark IIs with the refinement and ride of the sophisticated Mark X.

But throughout this period one major criticism had been made of the Jaguars, and this concerned their standard manual Moss gearbox. It was a four-speed unit with synchromesh on only the upper three ratios and this was slow, heavy and sometimes unpredictable – spoiling the otherwise extremely sporting E-Types for example. So, in October 1964 a new transmission appeared, mated to a bored-out 4235-cc version of the famous XK engine. The new manual gearbox featured baulk-ring synchromesh on all four forward speeds and was a huge improvement over that retained for so long. Two new 4·2-litre models were announced using this manual transmission, the 4·2-litre E-Type and the 4·2-litre Mark X.

Both were unchanged in major styling features, but the E had an alternator as standard, a redesigned exhaust system with aluminized silencers – still rather vulnerable on bumpy roads – a copper full-flow radiator of tube and corrugation construction and a new type of brake servo for its four-wheel discs. Open two-seater and fixed-head coupé models in both left- and right-hand drive forms were continued. The new Mark X, meanwhile, also had an alternator standardized, with aluminized exhausts, redesigned radiator and water impeller, a new type of servo and increased brake pad area. An improved heating system was also incorporated, with independent controls for each side of the wide car.

The all-synchromesh gearbox was introduced as an option in the S-type cars at the same time, to become standard in March 1965. By June the new transmission was being fitted in the three Mark II saloon car models as well, to complete the range. In October more robust silencers with aluminized anti-rust finish were fitted to the Mark IIs, together with more powerful headlamps. A new-type tougher windscreen was fitted to the Mark IIs and the S-types, while the latter models also had larger brake servos and improved design front seat cushions added. The old 3·8-litre Mark X was discontinued, the newer 4·2-litre Mark X had full air-conditioning offered as an option, and the 3·8-litre E-Type was also deleted, production concentrating on the 4·2.

Further development came in March 1966 with the announcement of the 'stretched' E-Type 2+2, with 9 inches added to the wheelbase to make room for two occasional rear seats under a raised coupé roofline. With a much larger windscreen the 2+2 just didn't look right, losing the balance between low waist and low roof apparent in the two-seater models. But for the enthusiast with a small family the car was ideal, and the plushly upholstered rear seat's squab would move forward to increase luggage space, still accessible through the wide-opening tail-gate. A lockable glove box was provided together with a full-width parcels shelf below the fascia, and automatic transmission was an option. Price for this high-performance 'four-seater' was £2,245.

Then, in August 1966, there appeared the next step in the hybridization scheme, the Jaguar 420. This was virtually the all-independent S-type shell with the dual headlamp nose of the Mark X grafted on, retaining the four-door centre section in near-original Mark II style. Powered by a 245 bhp 4·2-litre XK engine, the 420 was available with either Borg-Warner Model 8 dual range automatic transmission or the nice new all-synchro manual box. Overdrive was a further option on the manual model, and other features included a limited-slip differential, self-adjusting, twin-circuit disc brakes on all four wheels, recirculating-ball steering (Jaguar-Bendix 'Varamatic' power assistance optional), an alternator, pre-engaged starter and even a transistorized clock. The 420 was a full five-seater with Connolly Hide leather upholstery, reclining front seats, folding arm-rests front and rear, and variable-control heating to front and rear compartments. Yet the new saloon was priced at only £1,930, had a top speed of about 115 mph, would get from 0–50 mph in only 7 sec, and still do about 16 mpg in the process.

In September 1966 the 2·4-, 3·4- and 3·8-litre Mark IIs were all revised, losing their standard fog lamps, and having tufted carpets replace the pile used previously. Ambla replaced leather upholstery, although the previous specification was still available at extra cost. Standard manual and overdrive versions of the 2·4 were continued, but the model's automatic option was deleted. With these deletions standard prices were considerably reduced.

Then in October, the Mark X was superseded by the 420G in saloon and limousine form, the latter having a modified front bench seat to increase rear leg-room. The 420G was distinguishable by its full-length chrome side strips, and a heavier vertical bar down the centre of the grille. Repeater flashers were fitted to the front wings. Fuel capacity in twin tanks mounted within the rear wings was 20 gallons, compared with the 420 model's 14, and boot space was larger at 27 cubic feet compared with the 420's 19. 'Varamatic' power steering was standard, of course, and with triple SU HD8s, the 420G's engine produced the full 265 bhp. Weight, at 35¾ cwt, amply demonstrated the difference between this machine and the 30·7-cwt 420. The price was £2,238.

With this new classification style, '420' replacing '4·2 litre', the Mark IIs were at odds with the rest of the range, apart from the exceptional E-Type, and in September 1967 things were rationalized. The 2·4-litre model became the Jaguar 240, with suitable insignia on the tail, slim bumpers, a reintroduced automatic option and a revised cylinder head and dual exhaust system with twin SU HD6s pushing power output up to 133 bhp from 120. The new car cost just over £1,300, while the less-radically altered 340 (née 3·4 Mark II), was priced at just over £1,550. But even the 240 was good for 105 mph, and would get from 0–50 mph in 8 sec in considerable comfort, and the 340 was therefore deleted in 1968.

That same month of September saw the 3·4- and 3·8-litre S-types undergo the trim revisions previously made on the Mark IIs, and so the 240, 3·4S, 3·8S, 420 and 420G entered the last two years of the decade. No major changes had been made to the 4·2 E-Types at all, but one further saloon model was to join the range, the Jaguar XJ6. Introduced in September 1968, amidst a blaze of publicity, the XJ6 was the first completely new Jaguar model to appear since the Mark X. It was designed in fact around a new range of Vee-engines, to be announced for the 1970 or 1971 models, the size of the engine compartment alone suggesting some cylinder configuration other than in-line. However, initial introduction was made with the usual XK variants installed, in this case in 2·8- and 4·2- litre forms.

The monocoque was similar to that of the Mark X although two extra-large section cross-members under the front seats and forward of the rear-seat pan added considerably to torsional strength. Again most of the car's 'twist-resistance' came from beneath the waistline, while carefully tapered centre door pillars gave rigidity to the roof panel – otherwise slender pillars all round giving a large glass area and first-class all-round visibility. The passenger compartment in this monocoque structure was extremely strong, while both end-boxes were designed to be more easily crushed in the event of an accident, and were thus impact-absorbent in defence of the occupants.

A new ifs system featured shock absorbers mounted independent of the coil springs and anti-dive geometry to prevent the car dropping its nose under heavy braking. The whole system was mounted on a fabricated sub-frame, rubber-mounted to the monocoque and also carrying the front of the engine – a new departure eliminating a great deal of engine vibration transmission to the passenger compartment. The rubber-damped engine mass also cut road noise and Dunlop, who specially developed VR SP Sport tyres for the car, were able to concentrate on adhesion rather than low road noise levels. The well-proven E-Type/Mark X rear suspension system was perpetuated in the XJ6, slung in a pressed-steel subframe attached through rubber insulators in a transverse tunnel behind the rear seats. Steering was new, with the latest Adwest power-assisted rack-and-pinion system providing light steering yet with plenty of feel and feed-in, safety features including collapsible steering links and a Saginaw wire mesh collapsible sleeve in the column. Safety features largely characterized the whole car, with ergonomically designed seats and controls, a distinct lack of dangerous interior protrusions and of course the basic prerequisites in a really safe car of plenty of power, superb brakes (Girling discs all round with tandem hydraulic circuits) and really controllable handling characteristics.

The new 2·8-litre engine was almost square in its 83 mm × 86 mm dimensions, and produced 180 bhp at 6,000 rpm. This was very close to the old 3·4 unit, yet was just below the capacity limit at which certain European states impose stringent surcharges. The 4·2-litre variant on the other hand featured a new head-stud anchorage which effectively reduced distortion and head gasket failures. Cooling and lubrication systems were also revised and improved, and a choice of manual gearboxes with or without overdrive and Borg-Warner automatic transmissions was available. With the 2·8-litre engine a Type 35 automatic was offered, the Model 8 being available for the more powerful 4·2. The result of all this was a motor-car which had incredibly high cornering powers, and such a combination of speed and controllability, careful execution and deep design thought as to be immensely safe. The styling was very much in the Jaguar style, fluid and handsome, and the XJ6 was the first of the breed to have horizontal radiator grille bars in its rectangular intake. A fashionable 'kick' in the waistline just ahead of the rear wheel arch gave the shell great character, and although still swamped with export-only orders at the time of writing, the XJ6 offered remarkable home market value at from £1,797 for the basic 2·8 model to £2,254 for the 4·2.

In October modifications to the Jaguar E models were also announced, body changes having originally been made to comply with US Federal safety regulations now being standardized for the rest of the world. In basics the three-model range – two-seat roadster, two-seat coupé and 2+2 coupé – continued, but their smooth good looks were spoiled with exposed podded unfaired headlights, brought forward 4½ inches in their tunnels from the original 1961 position, 1½ inches ahead of the 1967 advance. The lower-powered controlled-emission engine remained purely for the American market, but a 68 per cent increase was made in radiator air intake area to keep it cool, with a full-width front bumper bar across its middle. Sidelights were much larger front and rear, with reflectors ahead of the front wheels on either side. At the tail very large tail-lamp clusters had to be fitted to suit the new regulations, mounted on a vertical full-width panel cut-back into that beautiful pointed tail – which was now completely spoiled. In the cockpit, rocker-switches were fitted in view of the new regulations, and the 2+2 also had a more raked windscreen fitted with two wipers in place of the original three. Adwest Pow-a-Rak steering was available as an optional system, a Saginaw collapsible cage appeared in the steering column and further optional equipment included chromed pressed-steel disc wheels. Demand was as high as ever, however, and production was extended to the full to supply the continuing demand.

And so Jaguar cars came to the end of the decade, all set for the introduction of a new Vee-engine range to replace the quite remarkably successful XK six-cylinder in-line unit. Ranging from the 240, through the XJ6 series, to the 420G and the E-Types, Jaguar offered luxurious high-performance cars at really inexpensive prices, true to their long-standing tradition of 'Grace, Space, Pace'.

In 1966 it had been announced that the British Motor Corporation and Jaguar Cars Ltd intended to merge, and as a result British Motor Holdings Ltd was formed officially on 14 December 1966. This was followed by the merger with British Leyland to form the gigantic British Leyland Motor Corporation, yet Jaguar, of all the member companies, seems the one least likely to lose its identity.

20 Jensen

Formed by brothers Alan and Richard Jensen in West Bromwich in 1931, this company entered the 'sixties essentially as a contract body builder for other manufacturers. The cycle had started before World War II with sports bodies for Austin and Standard; during the war the company worked on military fire engine contracts, and afterwards undertook the production of aluminium-bodied pantechnicons as a major line of business. But the company's principal post-war business was for BMC, the West Bromwich works producing large numbers of A40, Gypsy and Estate A95 and A105 bodies, and more than 90,000 Austin-Healeys. In the late 'fifties a new plant was opened for the assembly of the Volvo P1800 as well, yet throughout this period small-quantity production of the company's own cars continued.

In October 1953 a striking four-seater named the Jensen 541 had been announced, and during the following year its original steel body construction was abandoned in favour of glass-reinforced plastic. In 1960 this basic 541 was still in production in 541R guise. The rounded but sleek and purposeful-looking glass-fibre body was mounted on an exceptionally robust frame, formed from 5-inch diameter 14-gauge side tubes braced with both pressings and cross-members to combine frame and platform design. Coil-and-wishbone ifs and a semi-elliptic live rear axle were used with Armstrong shock absorbers (piston-type at the front and telescopic at the rear) with servo-assisted Dunlop disc brakes all round. Steering was by rack-and-pinion and the car was powered by an Austin long-stroke six-cylinder engine of 3993-cc, using push-rod ohv, and three SU HD6 carburettors. The power output was unspecified, but was around 130 bhp. A four-speed gearbox with overdrive on top was standard. Unusual features were the front-hinged nose of the car which opened to completely expose the engine, and a controlled shutter in the air intake for limiting air-flow over the radiator. Price was £2,706, and for this Jensen offered a very individual and unusual motor-car, with high-performance potential and considerable interior comfort.

But only about 225 541R models were ever built, following the original 200 541s (the first saloon cars to use disc brakes all round), and the 'R' was replaced by the 541S in October 1960. The new model was extensively revised – 4 inches wider, with nearly $1\frac{1}{2}$ inches more head-room front and rear – while luggage space was also improved and the Rolls-Royce version of the GM Hydra-Matic automatic transmission was standard. Seat belts were also standardized (and many other items usually available only as extras were standard in the Jensen), making this the first British car so equipped. The three-carburettor, 4-litre BMC engine was retained, but a rod accelerator linkage provided more precise control than the original cables. A Powr-Lok limited-slip differential was standard with the Hydra-Matic transmission and optional with the normal manual gearbox, and the all-round Dunlop disc brakes ingeniously used the left-hand chassis side tube as a servo vacuum reservoir. The chassis was wider and longer than that of the 541R unit, while other notable changes included even more luxurious interior fittings and a normal air intake in the nose using a driver-controlled blind in place of the earlier vane. Another aperture let into the top of the nose supplied cold air to the engine, while extractor ducts low down on either side aft of the front wheel arches let the engine bay 'breathe'. As before the body was of glass-fibre, apart from the aluminium-panelled doors. Naturally the new 541S was more expensive, being priced at £3,195 (automatic transmission) and £3,096 (to special order only) in manual form. Chassis numbers were prefixed '100' for the automatics and '102' for the manual variants.

From August 1961 electric rear window demisters were fitted, and in November a thermostatically controlled electric fan replaced the engine-driven one. Production was running at 'one and a bit' per week; the manual model was discontinued in March 1962, the automatic outliving it by over a year to be finally deleted from the list in September 1963. Only about 110 examples of the 541S were produced.

By the time production ceased, the replacement C-V8 had already appeared, being announced in October 1962. The allure of the large-capacity American V8 engine with its easy, smooth torque and power output, had attracted Jensen just as it had attracted Bristol, and they chose a 5916-cc Chrysler V8 producing 305 bhp gross and dropped it into a body very similar to the basic type 541 shell. Still in glass-fibre, still beautifully finished and lavishly equipped, the C-V8 used another version of the massive tubular and boxed pressing chassis structure, retaining coil-and-wishbone ifs with a live rear axle on semi-elliptics and mating the Chrysler engine to a Torqueflite transmission from the same manufacturer. This had an over-riding manual and kick-down control and with the Powr-Lok limited-slip differential, rack-and-pinion steering and Dunlop servo discs all round their new 140-mph car was extremely safe and controllable. Chrysler three-speed all-synchromesh manual transmission was available to special order, while among the standard equipment were reclining front seats, a Motorola radio with twin speakers and a roof-concealed aerial, laminated glass throughout, safety belts, a fascia-controlled filler cap and even a fire extinguisher. Price was £3,392 – good value in terms of performance, individuality, luxury and fittings. Top speed was a true 136 mph, 0–50 time under 6 sec, and fuel consumption about 16 mpg.

About seventy Mark Is were produced before a Mark II version appeared in the following year. In this, sidelights were combined with flash indication below the headlamps; a lockable button replaced the chrome handle on the bonnet, and a smooth boot-lid was fitted. Selectaride rear dampers were also standardized.

Then, in January 1964, the 5916-cc engine was discontinued, and a big-bore 6276-cc engine replaced it. In July the integral radio aerial was replaced by an external one, and in November new door locks, handles, and rear screen demister controls were fitted and a chrome bead base added around the filler cap. In July 1965 the Mark II was discontinued after some 250 had been built. For its price of £3,491, the Mark II's 0–50 mph time of under 6 sec, its consumption of over 16 mpg and top speed of close on 140 mph were very attractive.

The new Mark III had equal-size headlamps with no chrome surround to their unfaired recess, while other additions were new section bumpers with overriders, separate round flashers, a dual braking system, redesigned fascia with face-level vents, spring-loaded boot hinges and the name on the boot-lid.

But in October 1965 came really sensational news: Jensen had produced a four-wheel drive road car. Major A. P. R. Rolt, Managing Director of Harry Ferguson Research Limited had caught the Jensen brothers' attention with his company's four-wheel drive system, incorporating Dunlop Maxaret anti-lock braking devices. A prototype vehicle was shown to the public in October 1965, and reaction was immensely enthusiastic. The new model, christened the FF or 'Ferguson Formula', used the existing C-V8 shell with the 330-bhp 6·2-litre Chrysler engine with its Torqueflite transmission offset

78

in a modified chassis. A two-piece front prop shaft ran from a central controlled differential and transfer drive to an off-set Salisbury differential
driving the front wheels through universally jointed half shafts. At the rear the
existing system was used, but without the Powr-Lok limited-slip differential,
which was no longer thought necessary. The re-located mechanical masses in
the car's forepart necessitated redesign of the ifs system, dual coil spring
damper units being used on either side, with the drive shafts rotating between
them. The Ferguson system was designed on a drive-sharing principle making
wheel-spin virtually impossible, even with each wheel on a different type of
surface and adhesion and traction set very high new standards.

The Maxaret braking system fitted, sensed impending brake locking and
operated on the servo reducing its assistance or – *in extremis* – relieving
pressure on the brake pads until adhesion was restored. A weight increase of
about 3 cwt cut top speed to about 117 mph (at 4,600 rpm) but the FF more
than made up for any loss on the straights through corners and in inclement
conditions. Price was £5,249.

So enthusiastic was the reception of the FF that C-V8 sales seemed
threatened. Work had, in fact, commenced on the car in 1962, shortly after
Ferguson's system had been proved beyond doubt in a 1½-litre Climax
front-engined Grand Prix car run for the organization by Rob Walker. In
view of the threat to the C-V8 a major redesign was decided upon, and the
Italian coach-builder Vignale was commissioned to design and construct a
batch of pre-production cars. These were shown at Earl's Court in 1966,
having been styled and built very quickly. The new body was handsome,
angular and aggressive, with a huge wrap-round rear screen, and twin side-by-
side headlamps with oblong side/flashers beneath them, recessed into an
imposing horizontally barred grille. Still using the 6·3-litre Chrysler engines
and Torqueflite transmission the new cars revived the Jensen Interceptor title
of the 'fifties and introduced the FF in production form.

The FF differed from the Interceptor bodily in having a brushed metal
roof pan, 'FF' insignia beside the rear number plate and on the grille, and a
bonnet scoop. The Interceptor had single extracter vents behind the front wheel
arches, while the FF had two. To incorporate the FF's additional equipment
the wheelbase was extended (by 4 inches), and overall the car was 3 inches
longer. Otherwise the Vignale shells looked very similar to the casual observer.

Prices at the time of their introduction were £3,743 for the Interceptor and
£5,340 for the FF. The Interceptor had a beautifully smooth and powerful
combination of engine and transmission, immensely comfortable armchair-
type seats (though it was short of rear seat leg-room), and handling which was
stable enough – combined with direct and responsive steering – to allow full
wheel-spinning use of its 325 bhp. Some of the controls were rather complex,
unnecessarily so, but with a maximum speed of just under 140 mph, and a
0–50 mph time of as little as 5·5 sec this car, weighing over 1½ tons, was an
extremely exhilarating and well-balanced machine to drive.

The FF was an outstanding example of sophisticated automotive engineering, and while 3 cwt heavier than its sister car, still had a maximum speed
of 130 mph, and achieved essentially the same 0–50 mph time with no drama
whatsoever. Acceleration on lock was instant and completely free of wheel-
spin, while in the wet or on icy surfaces the car's 'safety quotient' was

79

remarkably high with its Maxaret anti-lock braking system. This could have been improved by ironing out some of the suspension 'bounce' incurred in heavy braking from high speed, but basically the system succeeded in what it set out to do. Interior accommodation was quite up to the Interceptor's high standards. Fuel consumption on the two new Jensens was about 13 mpg, so the 16-gallon fuel capacity was by no means over-generous.

In October 1967 the excellent Adwest power-assisted steering system became optional on both cars (this gave a standard of feel and control superior to most similar systems and soon to become such a feature of the Jaguar XJ6 series). In January 1968 quartz iodine headlamps and an electrically operated radio aerial were standardized, but meanwhile production difficulties dogged the new models, and soon the West Bromwich company were faced with considerable financial problems. With the end of the Volvo contract in 1963, Jensen had undertaken Sunbeam Tiger production for Rootes and between 1964 and 1967 they built several hundred of these Ford-powered machines for export to the United States. On January 1 1968, the new US Federal safety regulations were produced and in order to meet these both Austin-Healey and Sunbeam products would have had to have been extensively modified. Therefore both parent manufacturers decided to discontinue the models concerned, and Jensen were suddenly faced with a total loss of contract production work. The controlling Norcros Group consequently called in Mr Carl F. Duerr, an American management consultant, to streamline the company, and under his guiding hand as Managing Director, Jensen have remained alive to the end of the decade with their big and beautiful Interceptor and FF models in full production and selling well. The company now has a very special place among today's small surviving band of quality car manufacturers, with their extremely advanced and sophisticated machines.

21 Lagonda

Wilbur Gunn, an engineer, spent his early life at Lagonda Creek, Springfield, Ohio, and in 1898 he produced a single-cylinder motorcycle, building it on the lawn of his house at Staines, where later the original Lagonda factory was to appear. He developed a tricar range in 1904 and from then on advanced and speedy Lagonda cars were produced, including the V12 in 1937 and an all-independently suspended 2·6-litre twin ohc model after the war. David Brown acquired both Aston Martin and Lagonda in 1947, and Lagonda production of 3-litre sports saloon and drop-head models continued until 1958, when it was ceased in order to concentrate on the combine's extensive Aston Martin competition programme and on design of the new Lagonda Rapide.

The new model was released, and was very well received, at the 1961 Paris Motor Show. The body was long, sleek and graceful, with a distinctive grille divided by one central bar and tapering side grilles with horizontal bars. The shell was English-built to an Italian design by Superleggera Touring of Milan. It was a full four-door five-seater in magnesium-aluminium panelling over tubular steel frames, the whole being built up on a steel platform chassis, and rust-proofed, under-sealed and insulated. Luxurious accommodation for five people was provided, giving reclining front seats, and a bench rear with fold-down centre arm-rest. Upholstery throughout was top-quality hide and pile carpeting was used. A lockable glove box and rear picnic tables were standard equipment. Instrumentation included a speedometer, tachometer, oil pressure, fuel, ammeter and water temperature gauges and an electric clock, a radio with electrically operated aerial, a map reading light, complete heating and demisting system (including rear screen demist) and even electrically operated door windows. The boot was also exceptionally large and roomy.

A typically Aston Martin-Lagonda six-cylinder twin ohc engine was used, bored out to 3995 cc and, with two Solex twin-choke carburettors and an 8·25:1 cr, producing 236 bhp at 5,000 rpm. The cylinder block was cast in aluminium alloy with centrifugally cast chrome vanadium iron wet liners, and a seven main bearing crankshaft featured a bonded rubber vibration damper. The cylinder head was also in aluminium alloy, with hemispherical combustion chambers, flow-tested ports and large-diameter inclined valves. The camshafts were driven by two-stage Duplex roller chains with manually adjusted tensioners. A three-speed automatic transmission was standard, with an intermediate hold control mounted on the steering column, while four-speed all-synchromesh manual gearbox with floor-mounted gear-change was also available to order. Drive was transmitted through a needle roller-bearing divided prop-shaft to a frame-mounted hypoid final drive.

Suspension was independent all round, with a coil-and-wishbone system at the front and a De Dion axle at the rear mounted on parallel trailing links and under transverse Watt linkage control. Transverse torsion bars provided the springing medium, and large double-acting Armstrong shock absorbers were used. This De Dion location system had been widely used on the 2½-litre Grand Prix cars of 1954–60, including Aston Martin's own DBR4/250 machines, and was later to be adopted very successfully by the Rover 2000 saloon. Dunlop disc brakes were fitted all round, with dual hydraulic systems and servo-assistance.

The whole machine was extremely advanced and sophisticated in its design and engineering. It was priced at £5,251 and stood at the luxurious high-performance head of the David Brown range, but production was very limited, and when only fifty-five examples had been produced the model was discontinued in early 1964. At that time the selling price had dropped to £4,351, but Aston Martin expansion dictated its removal from the list. For what it was, the Lagonda Rapide was never over-priced, and if it is to be regarded as typifying the Lagonda motor-car one can only look forward to a revival of the marque.

22 Lotus

Of all British motor manufacturers, perhaps the most publicized in relation to its size is Colin Chapman's brain-child, the Lotus Group. As manufacturers of advanced and sophisticated road cars, the company has gained world-wide acceptance and appeal, while as an efficient, trend-setting and supremely successful motor racing constructor and team, Lotus have been to the forefront of Grand Prix racing since 1962, and most other single-seater, sports and GT classes for some years previously.

At the start of the decade Lotus were still a very small concern, building competition sports and single-seater cars both for their own racing programme and to supply a large customer demand. But they did have one model which doubled as successful racing GT and fast, comfortable and controllable road transport – the revolutionary Lotus Type 14 Elite.

First projected in 1956, the prototype made its debut at the 1957 London Motor Show, but full production did not get underway for another two years. For such a small firm the production of a car requiring expensive steel pressings was unthinkable, and at the same time designer Chapman's originality of thought leant away from the simple metal space-frame idea with an easily formed glass-fibre body shell. Low weight was a major priority, for the new model was to double as road and track car, and so a chassis/body structure almost completely in glass-fibre was evolved. This consisted of three mouldings, a basic outer skin of particularly pretty and well-balanced styling, an inner 'tub' and a hefty undertray including robust wheel arch mouldings. A sheet-steel front suspension frame also provided jack points, while frame extensions bonded between the chassis elements offered door-hinge mountings and a windscreen hoop strengthening the superstructure and acting as an integral roll-over bar. The only other steel chassis parts were the bonded-in engine mountings and suspension pick-up points, and in this design Chapman proved the feasibility of long-lasting direct metal/glass-fibre joints.

A Coventry Climax FWE single ohc 1216-cc four-cylinder engine was fitted, with a single SU carburettor and producing a reliable 75 bhp at 6,100 rpm. This was mated via an 8-inch sdp clutch to a BMC B-Series gearbox, lacking synchromesh on bottom, and an open prop-shaft drove to a hypoid bevel differential mounted on the glass-fibre chassis structure. Suspension was all-independent, coil-and-wishbone at the front, with a rear system including a long combined coil spring/damper 'Chapman strut', and wheels located by the drive shafts and a single radius arm. Rack-and-pinion steering was fitted, and $9\frac{1}{2}$-inch Girling disc brakes were used all round, in the wheels at the front and inboard on either side of the final drive at the rear to reduce unsprung weight. Wire knock-off wheels were standard, and with the two-seat cockpit trimmed in functional elegance, the Elite was priced at £1,949 for 1960.

The Elite was an extremely attractive and quite fast sports coupé, endowed with hitherto undreamed-of handling qualities for a road-car. Although inclined to suffer on rough surfaces, the precise steering and legendary surefootedness of the Elite was matched by quite vivid performance, 0–50 mph acceleration occupying 8 sec, and maximum speed being about 112 mph. But fuel consumption was extremely good at some 34 mpg, and as competition successes began to accumulate, demand for the Elite from the *cognoscenti* grew.

In their Cheshunt works, Lotus were then building type 11 and 17 competition models and also the Lotus Seven, a very spartan two-seater sports model offering high performance in acute discomfort and, again, phenomenal handling abilities. The Lotus Seven was available with various engine/gearbox combinations, and with a light but strong tubular chassis, just enough room for two people, minimal consideration of comfort and weather protection and minimal overall dimensions, was very much a motor-car for an enthusiast of a particularly strong constitution.

In August 1960 the Elite's rear suspension layout was modified, with a twin radius-arm location for the rear wheels, in plan-form looking like a trailing reversed wishbone. This resisted toe-in on the wheels, a failing of the original cars, and greatly improved straight-running at speed.

Incorporating this modification, a new Series II model appeared in October that year, featuring Royalite door and tunnel trim, and a competition SE or Special Equipment variant was also made available, this using twin SU 1½-inch carburettors to boost power output to 83 bhp at 6,500 rpm. A very close-ratio German ZF all-synchro gearbox was fitted, so close in fact that about 45 mph in first was possible. Price of the SE was up to £2,118.

Both the Elite models and the Seven road-car were continued into 1961, and in October the Elite was offered in kit form for £1,299, a considerable saving in capital investment at least. A new, slightly more sophisticated and habitable Super Seven model was released, with the same basic structure but better-equipped cockpit, long flared glass-fibre wings replacing the bicycle-type on the standard model, and a Cosworth-tuned 1340-cc Ford Classic engine. This oversquare power unit, with a 9·5:1 cr and two twin-choke Weber carburettors, produced 85 bhp net at 6,000 rpm, and with a weight of only 8 cwt this little monster had a power/weight ratio of about 200 bhp/ton. Available in component form only, the Super Seven was priced at £599.

Into 1962, and in May a further Elite variant was introduced, the Super 95. A cold air duct appeared in the bonnet, long-range fuel tank was standard, and a brake servo reduced pedal pressures. With a 10:1 cr standard and twin SU carburettors, power output was raised to 80 bhp net at 'six-one' in standard trim. At £1,891, this was still a very quick and controllable road-car, a road-car for the enthusiast who liked a degree of refinement.

But for the man who loved performance and ultra-precise handling alone, a new version of the Super Seven was announced in the summer. Using the 1498-cc 118E Ford engine, but this time with only a single Weber and 8·3:1 cr, this producing 65 bhp net at 5,200 standard. The resultant motor-car was rather smoother and less temperamental than its forerunners, but for those who still liked lots of power in their projectiles a twin-Weber 1500 could be specified, producing fully 90 bhp. The new all-synchromesh Ford gearbox, sealed-beam headlamps (which were bracket-mounted and wobbled alarmingly at speed) and an electric engine cooling fan were all standard equipment, and the new model sold for £868 complete, or £645 in component form. This was expensive really for what one had materially, but for the performance and handling available was pretty good value. With the twin carburettor engine, acceleration was searingly fast, rushing from 0–50 mph in under 6 sec, the

100 mph mark passing in about 28 sec and top speed standing at just on 104 mph.

Now, while the Elite had proved a success despite the criticisms of many concerning its unorthodox but amazingly strong structure, production costs had soared, and in October a new convertible road model was produced, the type 26 Elan. Since the roof panel contributed a lot to the Elite's strength, a convertible could not possibly have been produced, and in the Elan Chapman used a new form of construction, with a fabricated steel backbone chassis, forking at front and rear to accept the engine and suspensions. A pretty, streamlined body sat like a saddle over this chassis, but contributed nothing to its strength. Comfort and refinement had been foremost in the Elan's design and its roomy little cockpit was notably habitable, the occupants sitting very low in best Lotus tradition, with the high transmission/backbone tunnel between them, a handsome well-instrumented fascia and the short streamlined bonnet ahead of them. A smallish boot occupied the Kamm-type cut-off tail, and again Lotus had produced a design study in balance. The Lotus twin-cam headed 1498-cc engine was fitted, as released for the type 28 Lotus-Cortina saloon, using a 9·5:1 cr and producing 100 bhp net at 5,700 rpm, with 102 lb ft net torque at 4,500 rpm. Novel features were the hydraulically operated pop-up headlights, which hid away under faired covers in the rounded nose, standing erect and revealed for use, while Rotoflex rubber drive-shaft couplings were used, giving a characteristic jerky take-off as they 'wound-up' under load. With a folding hood, the Elan was priced at £1,499 complete.

The Special Equipment and Super 95 model Elites were continued parallel with the Elan until January 1964, when both were discontinued, a total of only 988 ever being made. It was, and still is, a strikingly beautiful motor-car, and as an engineering exercise had been a great – if a rather expensive – success.

But meanwhile the Elan had been continued and developed, an optional glass-fibre hard-top being offered in May 1963 and new 1558-cc engines replacing the 1498s late in the year. With twin-choke Weber 40DCOE carburettors, this unit produced a smooth 105 mph at 5,500 rpm, and maximum torque was up to 108 lb ft at 4,000 rpm. Maximum speed was up to 112 mph, 0–50 mph time was just 7 sec and economy of about 25 mpg was reasonable. In this form, 'Elan 1600' flashes appeared on the front wings, and further development came in November 1964 when the Series 2 'Elan S2' model was announced. Several refinements had been made, including the addition of a full-width polished veneer fascia with lockable glove box, chrome instrument bezels, handbrake warning light, smaller pedals to give more foot space in the narrow well, quick-release fuel filler cap and rear lights merged into one oval unit (previously separate circular ones had been fitted). Large front brake calipers were used, and centre-lock wire wheels were an optional extra. 'S2' insignia appeared on this much-improved model, which was priced at £1,436.

A fixed-head coupé type 36 Elan model was announced in September 1965, basically similar to the convertible hard-top but with rather more attractive lines, rearward-extended boot-lid, boot-mounted battery, electrically wound windows, and generally greater refinement than hitherto. A 3·55:1 final drive ratio became optional for high-speed cruising, and in November a close-ratio gearbox was also offered.

1. AC's 428 Convertible originally appeared with a 427-cubic-inch American Ford V8 engine in 1965, the 428 unit being introduced in October 1966. Body by Frua, on an extended Cobra '427' chassis.

3. AC's Cobra 289 used a much-modified, but still identifiable, Ace body shell.

2. Cobra laid bare: the '289' chassis retained the simple twin-tube arrangement, but with 4-inch diameter main longerons and coil-springs all round. Note the fixed differential and universally-jointed drive shafts.

4. A brace of Aston Martins: the DB6 grand tourer and Volante Convertible in profile. The spoiler lip was claimed to give added stability at high speeds (as achieved on occasion at Le Mans but illegal on British roads), while the Volante's hood was power operated.

5. The DBS body shell was designed and developed by Aston's own engineers and

stylists. The base unit shown here carried pressed steel panelling and formed a really strong shell. Cross-bracing in the roof and doors is to prevent distortion before the panelling is attached.

6. Craftsmen at work in the body shop at Newport-Pagnell.

1

2

1. This Austin Mini Mk II demonstrates the styling changes made to the basic shell as the 'sixties drew to a close. The grille has lost its simple curved corners and larger rear lights have been added.

2. A 1959 original Morris Mini Minor displays the compact lines to become so familiar in the following decade. Not until 1969 did the external door hinges go, and then only on a small percentage of Mini models!

3. A late model Austin 1100 shows Mk II modifications with cut-back tail fins and ventilated wheels.

3

4

4. The basic Morris 1100 aroused tremendous interest when it appeared in September 1963. It borrowed the Mini's transverse engine mounting and added Alex Moulton's Hydrolastic interlinked fluid suspension system.

5. More capacity and more space was offered in this 1969 1300 Traveller. Its lineage is obvious and this compact yet roomy model was to prove quite popular.

6. Mark II modifications affected most of the old BMC range in their first year as British Leyland models. The revised 1800 looked less happy than most with its lengthened tail.

5

6

1. The Austin 1800 Mk I was introduced in October 1964, and impressed with its space but disappointed with its performance. Rally successes with cleverly modified machines did wonders for its sales.

2. An early-'sixties production-line scene in one of the BMC factories, with Farina saloons receiving final checks in the foreground and the faithful A35 vans and some of the last Metropolitans on the line in the background.

3. The first all-new model to appear under the British-Leyland Motor Corporation banner was this Austin Maxi, offering five doors, five seats and five forward gears.

5. The Austin 3-Litre saloon sounded like a throwback with its longitudinal engine mounting and 1800 centre-section. After extensive development it proved an astonishingly advanced and handleable large saloon.

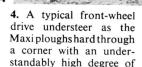

4. A typical front-wheel drive understeer as the Maxi ploughs hard through a corner with an understandably high degree of roll. Backing-off in this situation would bring the tail round and line the car up for the exit of the corner. (*Autocar*)

1. The essence of the British sports car industry, the Austin-Healey 3000 series was killed by US Federal Regulations. A large part of their production was contracted to Jensen Motors.

3. Bentley under pressure; the large and heavy Rolls-Bentley series performed amazingly well when really pushed hard.

2. Little brother: the Mk II Austin-Healey Sprite and MG Midget series were practical and sporting replacements for the 'Bug-eyed' Mk I Sprites but never attracted such genuine affection. Several saloon cars of the period had better performance.

4. Bentley's classical Vee'd radiator design graces the nose of this T-series vehicle with a two-door saloon body by H. J. Mulliner, Park Ward. Independent self-levelling suspension, disc brakes all-round, triplicated hydraulic systems and power steering made these models among the most advanced of the time.

5. Bond's Equipe GT4S was introduced in October 1964, replacing the original GT2+2 four-wheeler which appeared in May 1963.

6. The Bond 1300, using Triumph components once again with the new 1296-cc engine, made its debut in 1967. With its revised styling and better glass-fibre bodywork it was much improved.

1. Bristol's 409 was another development in the very small-quantity production series built by the company during the 'sixties. Advanced, fast and comfortable, the 5211-cc 409 automatic model was introduced in October 1965.

2. Daimler's Majestic Major saloon was widely used for formal travel, using one of the company's delightful light-alloy 4561-cc V8 engines. Twin heating systems and power steering were standard equipment in the eight-seater limousine model.

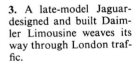

4. A Fairthorpe on trial at Goodwood on a Guild of Motoring Writers' Motor Show test day. Air-Vice Marshal Bennett's small concern produced a wealth of models but production of each was rather small.

3. A late-model Jaguar-designed and built Daimler Limousine weaves its way through London traffic.

1. Ford of Dagenham have come a long way since the utility saloons in the Anglia, Prefect and Popular range. The 103E Popular with its 1172-cc engine was replaced in January 1959.

2. The 100E Anglia was also discontinued in 1959 to make way for the 105E model. The body style continued until March 1961 with the new 997-cc 105E engine installed, and called the Prefect 107E.

3. Notch-back: the million-selling Ford Anglia series saw the beginning of a period of Ford racing and commercial success never approached in the 'fifties.

4. Anglia replacement: the Ford Escort series was introduced in January 1968 with this 1558cc Twin-Cam model at the head of the range.

5. Not a success; the Capri (illustrated) and Classic saloons were quickly replaced by the Cortina. This original Capri was introduced in September 1961, and ran until July 1964.

6. Biggest of the new Capri range is this 114-mph Capri 3000 GT XLR as shown at the 1969 London Motor Show. The 3-litre V6 engine made this a delightfully smooth and fast grand tourer.

7. The Classic was a grown-up Anglia which did not catch on. In original 1340-cc and later 1498-cc form, the two-and four-door saloon series ran from June 1961 to July 1963.

8. The Cortina was introduced in September 1962 in 1200 form and was produced with two- and four-door shells in standard and GT trim with 1200 and 1500 engines.

1

2

1. Civilized performance was offered by the new Mk II Lotus-Cortinas when they appeared in March 1967. Modified suspension, wide-rim wheels and brake servo helped make a very safe machine.

2. Cortina Estates sold in their thousands, and offered very good value for money in common with their sister models. The Mk II Estates were particularly attractive.

3

4

3. Ford's Corsair series offered slightly more space and comfort than the Cortinas. This 2000 De Luxe offered Aeroflow ventilation, two-speed wipers, servo disc brakes and wide-rim wheels as standard.

4. The Corsair 2000 Estate offered a fully-carpeted load space 6 ft 8 in long and had a freight capacity of 59·9 cubic feet.

5

6

5. The Mk III Zephyr and Zodiac series were fast and comfortable with six-cylinder engines but under-powered in four-cylinder form.

6. Largest of the range, the Mark IV Zephyrs and Zodiacs were comfortable and soft, but not very pleasant vehicles to drive. This all-independent monster is a Zephyr V6 De Luxe Estate.

7

8

7. and 8. Comparison in comfort: A Ford Prefect interior of 1959 and a Mk IV Executive Zodiac's cockpit ten years later.

1. Gilbern's two-door, four-seat Invader was fast but expensive. This Genie-based model took Gilbern into the 'seventies.

2. Blacksmith's job: this hefty but effective structure is the Gilbern Invader's chassis frame. Parallel radius arms and the transverse Panhard rod locating the rear suspension can be clearly seen.

3. Tiny and cramped, but selling well: Ginetta's Imp Sport-powered G15 was fast becoming a familiar sight on British roads as the decade closed.
(Autocar)

4. Spaceframe: the original Gordon GT chassis was the forerunner of those units used in the brilliantly-conceived and executed Gordon-Keeble GK1 series. *(Autocar)*

5. The Gordon-Keeble's handsome glass-fibre coachwork was built by Williams & Pritchard in works beside the Southampton factory. Contemporary road tests of the cars raved about its performance and handling, and could only fault instrument and control dispositions. *(Autocar)*

1. The Rootes Group's Hillman Minx saloons were delightfully solid, reliable and comfortable enough for the family motorist. This '1600' was introduced in August 1961.

2. and 3. A brace of Imps: Rootes' rear-engined baby sold well but had a long way to go to catch up on BMC/BLMC's Mini market. The Sunbeam Imp Sport was introduced in October 1966 with distinctive markings and a 55-bhp twin-Zenith carburated version of the 875-cc light-alloy engine.

4. The Humber saloons, estates and limousines were the largest and most expensive of Rootes' products. This is a 1964 Hawk Estate.

1. Jaguar have established a formidable reputation for 'Grace, Space, Pace'. Here their Mk X models are seen receiving a final polish.

2. The Coventry company dominated saloon car racing from its inception in the early 'fifties until the invasion of big American sedans in 1963. This is the Lindner/Nocker 3·8 Mk II on its way to winning the Nurburgring 6-Hours for the third year running, in 1963.

3. Competition bred the Jaguar E-Type and its successes were numerous in circuit races. Here reigning World Champion Graham Hill is on his way to a win at Silverstone in May 1963.

4. Rationalization in model names came during 1967, when this 2·4-litre became the 240, its companion 3·4 model became the 340 and the famous 3·8-litre Mk 2, sharing this body shell, was discontinued.

5. Ungainly changes in the body shape and overall length resulted in the swollen appearance of the E-Type 2+2 coupé. This Series II model also shows the ugly under-cut tail and protuberant headlights required to satisfy US Federal Regulations.

6. Sophistication reached a height in 1969 with this delightful XJ6 series of saloons, retaining the old faithful XK engine in 2·8-litre and 4·2-litre forms.

1. The Jensen 541S of 1960 hid a 4-litre Austin engine beneath its glass-fibre shell, and had automatic transmission and a Powr-Lok limited slip differential as standard. Manual transmissions were available to special order.

2. American Chrysler engines of 5916 cc were adopted in the Jensen C-V8 models introduced in October 1962. This Mk II version featured minor restyling and was eventually offered with a 6276-cc V8 engine from January 1964. The body was still glass-fibre.

3. Jensen suffered from many problems in the latter part of the 'sixties. However, its products were advanced and sophisticated, as this FF four-wheel drive model demonstrated to all who drove it.

4. Not until 1970 was another Lagonda model built, and then only a one-off four-door DBS, to replace this De Dion-axled Rapide of 1961.
(Autocar)

1

2

3

1. Colin Chapman's Lotus Elite specification was daring, but it worked amazingly well. Here the all-glass-fibre body shells near completion in the old works at Cheshunt.

2. The Elan replaced the Elite in October 1962, although quantity production of the pretty coupé continued in 1964. This is a late-model Elan SE with bulge in the bonnet to clear the 'smog-free' carburation system.

3. Effective simplicity: the Elan's fabricated backbone chassis was completely self-sufficient, the unstressed glass-fibre body shell sitting over it like a saddle. Little protection was offered to side-on impacts but the model's road-holding abilities became legendary.

4

5

6

4. The pretty Lotus Plus-2, starting life as an Elan Plus-2, was wider and longer than the original model and could carry two adults and two small children quickly and in comfort.

5. Spartan but fun: the Lotus 7 developed throughout the period to become better-equipped and better-made but never lost its inherently vintage characteristics, although its performance and handling were well in keeping with the other Lotus road models.

6. The Lotus Europa, or type 46, was the result of co-operation between Chapman and the French Renault concern. The mid-engined coupé had a backbone chassis similar to the Elan's and many proprietary parts appeared in its specification.

1

2

1. This original Marcos 'wooden wonder' led to the sophisticated and strikingly styled grand tourers built by this firm today. *(Autocar)*

2. The Adams brothers' aggressive styling made the Marcos series of grand touring cars very attractive indeed.

3. The Marcos Mini was not beautiful in everyone's eyes but it had great enthusiast appeal, however, and was an inexpensive way of building a distinctive small GT.

3

4

5

4. The MGA 1600 was an outstandingly successful export model for BMC, and breathed 'sports car' from every line.

5. MG's performance variants of saloon cars standard under other badge names are typified by this MG 1100. The distinctive grille and interior trim made a pleasant variation on the 1100 theme.

6. Typical of the age-old Morgan range is the Rover V8-engined Plus-8. The styling dates from between the wars, although the cast wheels and cockpit layout are modern.

6

1. Old Faithful: the Morris Minor typifies an age of motoring and continued through the 'sixties and its second million!

2. Reliant's first attempt at a four-wheel car for the home market was this Sabre sports car, announced in 1961 in four-cylinder form and developed in 1962 to accept a six-cylinder Ford engine. It was not a success.

4. The Scimitar appeared in September 1964, using an Ogle body shape originally devised for a Daimler sports coupé. Early models were cramped and rough but the go-ahead Tamworth firm developed it into an excellent and distinctive car.

3. The Reliant Rebel 700 saloon used the company's own ohv engine and its 70-mph speed (just) and 60 mpg made it a good, inexpensive runabout.

5. A new conception in space, pace and style was offered by the extremely attractive and well-selling Scimitar GTE.

1

2

1. Sacrilegious driving of the Rolls-Royce Silver Shadow revealed a remarkably high performance and cornering capability.

2. Rolls-Royce opulence is revealed in this interior shot from the early 'sixties.
(Autocar)

3. Rover's outstandingly successful and Internationally acclaimed 2000 model set new standards of sophistication in design when it appeared in October 1963.

3

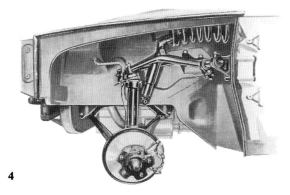

4

5

4. The 2000's front suspension system operated horizontal coil-springs by an unusual crank arrangement. One of the advantages offered was added resistance to frontal accident impacts.

5. The model's rear suspension featured co-axial coil-spring dampers, inboard disc brakes, semi-trailing-arm location and a De Dion axle tube to give parallel vertical wheel movement.

6. Body panels for the 2000 were hung on this base unit which has an immensely strong passenger area and resilient end boxes to absorb accident impacts.

6

1. Typical of the P4 Rover series models was this 95 as introduced in July 1962 and discontinued in July 1964. It used a 2625-cc engine.

2. The Rover 3-litre at speed displays a fair amount of roll and they felt like big and heavy cars. Front suspension was by torsion bars, and while the centre section was of modern unitary construction, a half-length sub-frame carried the engine and front suspension.

3. The light-alloy 3½-litre Rover V8 engine first appeared in a 3-litre type shell but it was later fitted in modified 2000 bodies to form the Rover 3500.

4. Rover's 3531-cc light alloy V8 engine as used in the 3·5 Automatic and 3500 was based on a discontinued American Chrysler unit. It was more compact and considerably lighter than the company's old 3-litre power units.

5. Twin carburettors distinguished the 2000TC model as introduced to the home market in October 1966. The P6 engine is a 1978-cc four-cylinder with exactly 'square' bore and stroke measurements of 85·7 mm × 85·7 mm.

1

2

3

4

5

6

7

7. Fitting a 4261-cc Ford V8 engine produced the original Tiger model, made available in the home market in March 1965. The car illustrated is a 4737-cc model, the Mk II, as introduced for export in January 1967.

1. Standard's four-cylinder model; the Ensign saloon of 1957–61.

2. The Standard Vanguard Six Estate was an attractive and well-equipped model for its time.

3. Styling for the later model Vanguards (as illustrated) was by the Italian Vignale concern.

4. The Vanguard's six-cylinder engine was later developed for the Triumph 2000 and GT6 models.

5. Sunbeam's Rapier saloons won numerous racing and rally awards to bolster their strong enthusiast appeal in the late 'fifties and early 'sixties.

6. The early Sunbeam Alpine sports cars had an advanced and complete specification so far as interior furnishings and equipment were concerned.

1. Triumph's long history of producing successful sports cars is typified by this TR3A.

2. Man's car; the TR4 series' road-holding was improved by the independent rear suspension system introduced in the TR4A, in March 1965. Export 4As continued with beam axles.

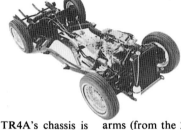

3. Massive engineering: the TR4's independent front and live axle rear suspension is shown in this shot, together with the massive tie-bar between the front spring mounts.

4. The TR4A's chassis is much more cluttered at the rear, with massive fabricated semi-trailing arms (from the 2000) and independent coil-springs picking-up on a transverse yoke.

5. The Spitfire 4 was a more attractive car than the competitive BMC models, but had an ultimate handling deficiency. Its 1147-cc engine produced 63 bhp giving a 93 mph maximum.

6. Logical development: the GT6 combined the Spitfire's attractive styling and a backbone chassis with the 2000 saloon's six-cylinder engine.

7. Late model Spitfires had much improved interior equipment and trimming, and, to meet legal bumper height minima in some export markets, had the front bar across the air intake.

8. Petrol-injected 2·5-litre engines were introduced in the TR5, externally similar to the 4A. Suspension improvements and re-styling resulted in this TR6 model as introduced in 1969.

18

1. Small saloon line-up: Triumph's Herald 1200 and 12/50 saloon, convertible and estate models.

2. The 1300 body-shell styled by Michelotti was a skilful miniaturization of the successful 2000 design. This TC model felt only marginally quicker than the standard version.

3. Triumph's Vitesse 2-litre Mk II was a much-improved version of this compact performance car, although it never quite fulfilled the promise one would expect from a 2-litre 'six'.

4. In the 'sixties Triumph established itself as a trim-conscious manufacturer. This 1300 interior, with wooden trim, ventilated upholstery, full instrumentation and adjustable steering column was typical.

5. The handsome and successful 2000 saloon.

6. Triumph were the first British marque to offer petrol injection as standard in a production car – the TR5 PI – and this engine was later fitted in the 2000 shell to form the 2500 PI saloon.

7. Production of early TVR glass-fibre body shells at Blackpool in 1960.

8. TVR's Tina convertible as it appeared at Geneva.

1. The 1969 Vixen S2 models still retained the distinctive body shape, now with the Manx tail typical of the later 'sixties and with attractive cast wheels.

2. Vauxhall's F-series Victors were discontinued in 1961. The American influence in the styling is obvious, as is the hazard presented by the wrap-round screen when the narrow door was open!

3. The Cresta and Velox PA models shared this body shell, but differed in their equipment. They ran from 1957 to 1962.

4. Vauxhall's VX 4/90 had luxury fittings and several performance options. The FBH and FCH series used 1508-cc engines from September 1961 to July 1963, and 1595-cc units from then until August 1967.

5. The FB Victor was a great improvement over the F-series models although its suspension was underdeveloped compared with some of its contemporaries.

6. Vauxhall introduced this handsome Viscount PCE model in June 1966. Its full specification included power steering, power-wound windows and an electrically-heated rear screen as standard.

7. The 1967 Victor 101 Super was yet another major restyling. The pronounced curves in the sides and windows gave more interior room and were claimed to increase the shell's stiffness.

8. Another styling change, late in 1967, resulted in the FD series shells as seen on this Victor 2000. These very attractive saloons won the Don Safety Trophy in 1967.

1

2

1. Vauxhall's first small car for many years, the Viva HA, was introduced in 1963.

2. The replacement, the Viva HB, was much improved, and its bodystyle with that kicked-up waistline proved the prototype of the FD Victors.

3

3. Wolseley's 1500 saloon shared its distinctive body shell with the performance Riley 1·5, although suspension systems differed. Interior space was limited.

4

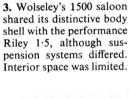

5

4. Typical of BMC badge-engineering was the Wolseley 6/110 Farina with its attractive frontal treatment and well-equipped interior.

5. Special or production car? Unipower's GT was the best-looking, and one of the best-selling, of the Mini-based enthusiast's cars. It was rear-engined, with rear-wheel drive.

6

6. The Vauxhall Viva GT was almost boy-racerish in original guise. For the 'seventies Vauxhall presented this less garish, and decidedly more attractive, model.

1. Jaguar's XJ6 set new standards in many respects, and its gentle roll-angle through fast corners is well illustrated here.

2. When a Jensen Inter-ceptor is pushed over the limit, it goes in a big way.
(Autocar)

1

2

3

3. The Vauxhall's soft suspension is well shown in this shot. Steering suffered from very low gearing and the back axle lacked adequate location for most of the 'sixties.

4. TVR at speed: the high scuttle line meant that forward vision over the lengthy bonnet was limited and the driving position was somewhat constricted by the rear-suspension tunnel immediately behind the seats.

4

5. An E-Type displays its sure-footedness out of a sharp right-hander as the Daimler SP250 on the right flexes, and opposite-lock is necessary to retain control.

5

1

2

1. and 2. Comparative cornering capabilities; the Midget corners in a stable understeering slide, while the Spitfire has reached its limit as understeer scrubs off speed, the tail rises and the swing-axle suspension jacks-up, up-edging the tyres and suddenly reducing tyre area on the road. Improved location in later Mark II GT6 and Vitesse models minimized the effect. (*Autocar*)

3

3. A GT6 Mk II with modified rear suspension giving near-vertical movement. The nearside rear wheel shows no tendency towards extreme positive camber as shown on the Spitfire.

4. Relative ultimate cornering characteristics, again demonstrated by *Autocar* staff testers, in a Cortina and Hillman Hunter.

5. Improved rear suspension system of the GT6 Mk II, showing the upper transverse leaf spring, radius arm and hefty lower location. The rubber doughnut compensates for changes in drive-shaft length as the wheel moves through its vertical arc.

4

5

1. MGB successes in all classes of racing were numerous during the 'sixties. This is the Enever/Poole car in the 1967 Nurburgring 1,000 Kms. It was driven to and from meetings on the road!

2. Racing Elans appeared in club events all over the world, and some stalwarts ran them in International endurance races; this is 53-year old Jack Holme racing in South Africa.

3. Rootes participated regularly at Le Mans in the early 'sixties, this Alpine winning the Index of Thermal Efficiency in the 1961 24-Hours. It averaged 91 mph over 2,194 miles; drivers were Peter Harper and Peter Procter.

Then, in January 1966 a Special Equipment sports/convertible appeared, with power output raised to 115 bhp, close-ratio gearbox, servo-assisted brakes, centre-lock wheels and repeater indicator lights all as standard. But in June the convertible models were discontinued, being replaced by a new drop-head coupé type 45 S3 model (subtle Lotus distinction), with fixed side-window frames, but otherwise generally similar. Both dhc and fhc SE models were also announced, using the 3·55 instead of 3·77:1 final drive ratio, with fitted carpets in cockpit and boot, inertia reel seat belts and a soft leather-rimmed steering wheel, the whole SE packet adding £163 to the basic price.

The new coupé shape contributed to improved performance, although the extra 10 bhp must also have helped somewhere. Top speed was now about 123 mph, while 0–50 mph times – even with the standard Ford gearbox ratios – were down to 6 sec, matching an E-Type Jaguar. Economy, however, was unimpaired and, with anything less than continual nine-tenths driving, improved. With the SE, extras included stiffer rear dampers to provide greater high-speed stability, and although this hardened the ride it was still very comfortable considering the enormous cornering power of the car. Cross-country journeys could be accomplished at very high average speeds in great safety and with a minimum of drama, the uncomplaining Elan just sitting on the road virtually irrespective of how it was flung into corners at seemingly impossible speeds.

Then, in December 1966, a new Lotus road-car was announced, aimed mainly at the European export market. This model, the type 46 Europa, was the first road-going mid-engined British coupé to go into production. Association with *Regie Renault* in France produced engine/transmission units as used in their R16 saloon; a five main bearing four-cylinder water-cooled engine mainly in light alloy. Capacity was 1470 cc, and for Lotus use cr was raised from 8·5 to 10·25:1, and a new high-lift camshaft adopted. A 28-mm double-choke Solex carburettor was also fitted, and power output rose from 58·5 bhp at 5,000 rpm to 78 bhp at 6,000 rpm. A final drive ratio of 3·56:1 was adopted, although gear ratios were otherwise standard, giving speeds through the gears at 6,500 rpm of 33 mph in first, 53 mph in second, and 80 mph in third, maximum speed being 115 mph.

This engine and transmission package was mounted behind the cockpit but ahead of the rear axle line in a similar steel backbone chassis to that of the Elan. This was a 'Y'-shaped member in 16 swg sheet steel, a front cross-member at 90 degrees to the car's longitudinal axis carrying the front coil-and-wishbone ifs made by Alford & Alder and as used in the Triumph Herald and Spitfire. At the rear a typically Chapman independent system of long radius arms and lower links forming ultra-wide based wishbones, with fixed-length Hooke-jointed drive shafts completing the wheel location, was fitted. Telescopic coil spring/damper units were used all round and the brake system included Girling 9¾-inch front discs with 8-inch rear drums.

The whole concoction was clothed in a streamlined but not particularly attractive glass-fibre two-door shell, styled by John Frayling, who had also produced the Elan revisions. It was interesting in using a Ford Anglia front bumper and a Cortina rear one and, with an Elan-like front-end merging into a high-sided tail with a small spoiler lip, the Europa was most distinctive. But entry to this low-built coupé wasn't easy, and a decorous exit for a mini-skirted girl almost impossible! Once ensconced, the Elan-like seating position and control disposition could hardly be faulted, but the slit rear window did not help vision in that quarter, particularly when attempting to reverse or sight oncoming traffic at difficult-angled road junctions. But purely as Lotus's latest design, and their first mid-engined coupé, this export-only machine had considerable attraction.

The Lotus 50, a 'stretched' and exceptionally attractive Elan Plus 2 model followed in June 1967. Here was Lotus's family transport, with two small rear seats for the children and plenty of luggage space for a family on the move. The new model again used a backbone chassis, with the wider, lower and sleeker body shell sitting astride the frame like a saddle, being rubber-mounted to it and taking no stress. It was 2 feet longer and 10 inches wider than the normal two-seat Elan, and some 3 cwt heavier, using the same twin-Weber 118 bhp engine. With the usual centrifugal ignition cut-out operating at around 'six-five', peak power was produced at 6,250 rpm, and gave the car a 118 mph maximum speed, combined with a 0–50 mph time of 6·8 sec. Fuel consumption was phenomenally good for a machine of such potential at around 30 mpg, and all the Lotus characteristics of precision, performance and delicacy of control were present in abundance. The rear occasional seats were rather small, but trim and interior appointment were of a high standard. This most attractive of Lotus products was priced at £2,113 on introduction. Then the Lotus Series 2 Europa (the type 54) appeared, with a detachable chassis, and Lotus were headed for the end of the decade. Electric windows and radio were offered as standard in the Plus 2 and in 1969 the Plus 2S appeared with some trim changes although retaining the 118 bhp engine. Elan S4s were available in Coupé and Coupé SE trim and the Europa S2 had become available on the home market at £1,667.

Twin Stromberg carburettors had been adopted on the Elan S4s by this time, 'de-smogging' them in compliance with the Californian regulations. In this state the 1558 cc engine produced 115 bhp at 6,000 rpm and externally the car had only a small bulge on the bonnet to betray this anti-emission equipment. With complete and thorough modifications to make all their cars comply with the new US Federal safety regulations the Lotus Group came to the end of a triumphant decade. For several years their production and sales *increases* had run at the rate of 40 per cent per annum, and they had developed from a small manufacturer of advanced high-performance specials to a quantity manufacturer of some of the best-mannered and attractive road-cars, and the most successful competition cars, available. For them it was a memorable decade indeed.

23 Marcos

In 1960 an astonishing newcomer appeared on the high-performance 'GT' market – the Marcos. Astonishing because its main structural members were made out of wood! At a time when originality was at a premium, Chapman producing his stressed glass-fibre Elite and others vying over the relative merits of metal space-frames, stressed skins and monocoques, the designers of the Marcos decided to produce a road-car of sufficient weight/stiffness ratio to double-up as a competition coupé. Jem Marsh, of Speedex 750 special fame, collaborated with aircraft engineer Frank Costin, and their car, and later their company, was given a combination of their own names.

The basis of the new car was Marine ply wooden sheet, laminated with a durable and extremely resistant phenol-based adhesive. Frame members were formed from spruce, the stressed parts of the structure being 3-mm thick mahogany or 1½-mm birch plies, choice depending on the local stresses involved. In view of its restriction to enthusiastic road or pure competition use, the new car was strictly a two-seater, with massive door sills and transmission tunnel forming boxed structural members. These three longerons were joined by a stressed plywood floor, further stiffening coming from a huge boxed scuttle bridge and a rear cockpit bulkhead-cum-rear roof structure. Most of the single-curvature body skinning was in ply, but double-curvatures as present in the nose and rear wings were moulded in glass-fibre. Wooden parts were joined with Aerolite 300 or 306 glue, while Araldite adhesive was used for plastic-wood jointings. The whole wooden structure was finally coated with Cuprinol preservative to prevent parasitic attack – making the Marcos the butt of many jokes: jokes which were to pale noticeably in the face of its future success.

As on the TVR models, Standard-Triumph Herald-type suspension units were used at the front with Girling 8-inch two-leading shoe drum brakes, while at the rear a live axle from the Standard 10 was located by a transverse Panhard rod and twin leading radius arms, picking up *behind* the axle line. Power came from a 997-cc 105E Ford engine using twin SU carburettors and special manifolding, with twin double-choke Webers as optional equipment. Also optional were a close-ratio gearbox, a 4·1 instead of 4·55:1 hypoid bevel final drive, front Girling disc brakes and cast magnesium road wheels. The first prototypes had featured a streamlined tubular front 'fuselage' with cycle-type front wings, but production models, built by Marsh's Monocoque Chassis and Body Company of Luton, used an all-enveloping nose section and were much more attractive. The cars were offered in component form, priced at £795 for a standard car. These kits came in big sections, and assembly was extremely simple and quick with only thirty-two nuts and bolts to be tightened.

For 1962 an improved model was produced, incorporating many changes. These began at the nose, with recessed faired-in headlights replacing the original podded fixtures, while a well-raked wrap-round windscreen and rear window were also used. Shallow opening windows appeared in the upwards-opening gull-wing doors, and the roof was much less domed than on the early production cars. Boot space was increased to about 10 cubic feet, and the 1340-cc 109E Ford engine could be specified instead of the 1-litre 105E unit. 'Forspeed' tuned versions were also available, and in this modified form the kit price was raised to £830. Weighing only 9¼ cwt complete, either engine produced a remarkably fast and accelerative motor-car.

Considerable competition success made the Ford-powered Marcos coupés very popular cars with the clubmen, and at the British Racing and

Sports Car Club's Racing Car Show in January 1964 a sleek new model was revealed. Styled by Dennis Adams, who had assisted Jem Marsh in running the production company at Luton, the new car was very low and long-looking, with twin headlamps under very raked and large transparent fairings, an air intake beneath the shark-like nose and steeply raked windscreen and rear window. Looking very much a 'wheel-at-each-corner' machine, the new Marcos, still retaining its stressed wooden monocoque chassis and glass-fibre body, was powered by a Volvo 1800 engine, this being the B18 five main bearing 1783-cc unit. Using two Stromberg 175 CD carburettors and a cr of 10:1, it produced 114 bhp gross at 5,800 rpm, with a peak 110 lb ft gross torque at 4,200 rpm. Drive was transmitted via an 8½-inch Borg & Beck diaphragm spring clutch to a Volvo four-speed all-synchromesh needle roller bearing gearbox, with Laycock de Normanville overdrive on top as standard. Unequal-length wishbones located the coil-spring ifs system, while at the rear a semi De Dion set-up appeared. Girling 9¼-inch diameter front discs and 9-inch rear drums provided powerful retardation, while rack-and-pinion steering was also standard. The new model's very low overall height (fractionally over 3 feet 6 inches) meant that the seats were very reclined, and therefore were fixed in position, the steering column and foot pedals being adjustable.

The car was light, fast and controllable, very attractively and purposefully styled, and showed a high standard of external and internal finish. Top speed was around 116 mph, while acceleration from 0–50 mph took just 6 sec. The Volvo engine consumed some 27 mpg making it reasonably economical in a GT car of such class. Vision was restricted over the long nose on humps, and manœuvring in town traffic was rather hit-and-miss, particularly in reverse when visibility was badly restricted. Wind noise level was extremely low. Although this was an expensive motor-car, at £1,854, Marcos sales increased and they continued to expand.

Late in 1965 modifications were made to the Marcos-Volvo's ventilation system, since a lot of engine compartment heat was being transferred to the cockpit, making long journeys extremely tiring. New vents were cut in the blue-tinted rear screen and in the bonnet, while prices were also cut to £1,429 in kit form, or £1,729 complete, increases in demand and production allowed the £265 reduction. This 1800IRS model with its semi-De Dion rear suspension was joined by the 1800L model employing the trusty old live axle with leading arms mounted to the chassis behind the axle line, and a transverse Panhard rod. An upper torque reaction link and coil-spring damper units completed the installation, while different rear brakes and smaller rim sizes were standard on the wire wheels. Initial price for this 1800L Volvo model was £1,309 kit or £1,584 assembled – the slight difference being reasonable for the kit still consisted of large and simply assembled components.

In January 1966 a new Marcos venture appeared at the Racing Car Show, this being an exceedingly ugly glass-fibre shell intended to accept Mini sub-frames with engine and suspension parts as the basis of an inexpensive and distinctive road or track GT. Known as the Mini-Marcos GT850, this shell was available in various stages of finish, starting at £645 which, again, was comparatively expensive.

There were also further developments in the high-performance medium-capacity GT class, and from their new home in Bradford-on-Avon, the company released a Ford Cortina 1500-engined version of the 1800. The original model was now being built for export only, and this new home-market version was priced at a more reasonable £1,612. With the decrease in price came a commensurate decrease in performance, however, for the 9:1 cr, twin Stromberg 150CD carburated 1499-cc engine's output was 85 bhp at 5,500 rpm, considerably down on the Volvo version. However, the car was still very light at 14½ cwt, and performed respectably. It used the all-synchromesh Ford gearbox, disc/drum braking system and similar suspension.

But with the 1500, Marcos tended towards the 'Sheep in Wolf's clothing' type of car – it was noisy, and lacked stability on bumps – and although available in kit form at a reasonable £1,295 could obviously do with more power. So, in January 1967 the Racing Car Show saw the introduction of a new model, still Ford-powered, but this time using a Chris Lawrence-tuned 1650-cc version of the four-cylinder engine. Front disc brake diameter was increased by ⅜-inch, and a sliding sun-roof was offered as standard. Rear suspension geometry was revised to overcome some of the bump steering experienced on the original system. The reclining driving position took a little getting used to, but the modified ventilation system was much improved, noise insulation was more effective and the car was very fast, stable and controllable. Cornering power was very high, and with 0–50 mph acceleration in a mere 6·6 sec, a near-120 mph maximum speed and fuel consumption of around 27 mpg this latest vastly improved model (selling at £1,860) was genuinely in the high-performance 'safety fast' bracket.

The Lawrence-Tune engine was bored out to make it even more oversquare, and a modified 10·5:1 cr cylinder head, a Solex PAIA 24/28 pressure compound carburettor and a high-lift camshaft were added to produce 120 bhp net at 5,400 rpm, peak torque of 126 lb ft net being produced at 3,500 rpm. The engine was extremely tractable, and the up-rated second gear Cortina transmission was delightfully quick, light and precise.

In late 1967 Marcos' 1600 appeared with the Heron-head Ford Crossflow engine installed, producing 95 bhp net at 5,500 rpm with 98 lb ft torque also at 'five-five'. The car was offered with attractive steel disc wheels, but either cast magnesium or spoked wheels were optional. At the same time a 1275-cc-engined Mini-Marcos appeared to supplement the basic 850GT model. This 1300 GT variant again used Mini sub-frames and mechanical parts, and now featured a full-width wooden fascia and generally improved interior trim. Rubber cone suspension still featured in the 850, while the new 1300 used the Hydrolastic system. Prices of the range at this time stood at £994 (850), £1,612 (1500) and £1,860 (1600) complete.

The two basic Marcos models, the ugly Mini-based machine and the lithe and aggressive-looking 15/1600, continued into 1968, but even with the latest Ford-engined versions performance still did not attain the level the constructors, and apparently some customers, thought was possible with such an aerodynamically clean shape. So, for 1969 a great development took place – a 3-litre Ford V6 engine was installed, which together with more refined interior trim and equipment resulted in one of the most pleasant Marcos products yet.

The compact V6 engine was little modified, having an 8·9:1 cr, Weber

40DFN-1 carburettor, and producing an easy 136 bhp net at 4,750 rpm. Maximum gross torque was 192·5 lb ft at 3,000 rpm, and this was sufficient – although mated to the 'low-performance' standard Ford Zodiac gear ratios – to punch the now much heavier 21 cwt-plus motor-car from 0–50 mph in under 6 sec, to 100 mph in under 21 sec and to a maximum of around 125 mph. Fuel consumption was still as low as 24 mpg, which was very good indeed. The heavier car handled even better than before – in a completely surefooted way it could be nosed and squirted through winding country lanes to maintain astonishing averages, while on the open road it cruised easily at the 70 mph limit and would unobtrusively break it. The ride was rather hard, but with other such sterling qualities was little noticed. The new 3-litre was available in component form at £1,770 or complete for £2,350. For a car which could outhandle a Jaguar E-Type (although it was not so fast), which had more individuality and – in a different way – similarly striking good looks, this was not exceptionally expensive.

Entering the 'seventies a new variant was introduced, using the 1996 cc V4 Ford engine, producing 93 bhp at 4,750 rpm, and with coil-and-wishbone ifs and coil-spring live rear axle. This 2-litre model joined the 3-litre, 1275 and 1600 in the 1970 Marcos range, and in this year the expensive wooden chassis construction was at last dropped in favour of a tubular frame. So Jem Marsh's company completed a decade's development. Since producing his Speedex 750 Austin-based specials in the 'fifties, both constructor and company had come a long way, in growing into one for Britain's most discerning manu-facturers with a sophisticated and genuinely unique range of high-performance motor-cars.

24 MG

If any British car company's name could be said to be synonymous with 'sports car', then it is this Abingdon-based division of the old British Motor Corporation.

The company were producing three models at the end of the 'fifties, the MGA Twin Cam, its rather more manageable MGA 1600 sister, and the MG Magnette saloon. In January 1959 a handsome fixed-head coupé version of the Twin Cam had joined its open sports two-seater companion, and in July that year the standard 1489-cc MGA had been replaced by the new 1588-cc '1600' model, again in both sports roadster and fixed-head coupé versions. This bored-out engine now had the same dimensions as the Twin Cam unit, but valve operation was by push-rods. A cr of 8·3:1 was used, and with twin S U HS4 carburettors the unit produced 79·5 bhp gross at 5,600 rpm. The four-speed gearbox had synchromesh on all but first, and an open Hardy Spicer prop-shaft took drive to a hypoid back axle. Coil-and-wishbone ifs – of course – was used, with semi-elliptic rear springs and Armstrong lever-type shock absorbers all round. Steering was by very direct and rather heavy rack-and-pinion, and disc road wheels were standard with wire wheels as optional equipment. In two-seat open form the sleek MGA, with its long curvilinear bonnet and front wings, dropping down past the cockpit to kick up into streamlined rear wings and a sloping tail, was priced at £940. The hard-top model, with its luggage-cum-tiny passenger space behind the front bucket seats, was selling at £1,026 and, as always, the MG sports cars were in huge demand all over the world.

The 1600 Twin Cam model, with an engine producing 108 bhp gross at 6,700 rpm, had a compression ratio of 9·9:1, twin SU H6 carburettors and increased coolant and engine oil capacities. It had Dunlop 11-inch disc brakes all round and was a little heavier than the push-rod models. Alternative final drive ratios were available and this was selling for £1,195 (sports) and £1,281 (coupé) in 1959.

The Magnette saloon, meanwhile, was available in Mark III Farina form, sharing a common body with other medium-capacity BMC saloons and powered by a version of the B-Series 1489-cc four-cylinder engine with twin SU HD4 carburettors. This unit produced 66·5 bhp gross at 5,200 rpm from a cr of 8·3:1, and was mated via a Borg & Beck sdp clutch to a four-speed gearbox. Again a Hardy Spicer open prop-shaft with a hypoid back axle was used, and powerful 9-inch Girling drum brakes were fitted on the coil-and-wishbone front and semi-elliptic rear suspension set-up. Cam-and-lever steering was used, and this tuned four-/five-seater appealed greatly to the family man with a sporting bent who could not afford a Jaguar or similar high-performance saloon. With its distinctive thrust-forward MG grille and well-equipped interior, the Magnette was selling at £1,012 in 1959, on announcement of the 1960 model.

But in June 1960 the powerful and really rather impracticable MGA Twin Cam was discontinued, and in its place the 1600 push-rod models were modified with sliding side screens on the coupé, while optional rear disc brakes and centre-lock disc wheels were offered. In May the Magnette engine was modified, with a changed combustion chamber design and new camshaft, and achieved a top speed of close on 90 mph and a 0–50 mph time of 13·5 sec.

Then, in March 1961 the MGA Mark I was discontinued in both open and coupé forms, and in June a new Mark II model appeared using a further bored-out but still undersquare engine of 1622 cc. Compression ratio was up to 9:1 and with twin SU H4 carburettors the unit produced a healthy 90 bhp net at 5,500 rpm, with 97 lb ft torque at 4,000 rpm. The disc/drum brake system was still standard, and externally 'Mk II' motifs appeared on the scuttle and boot-lid. The fascia was covered in leathercloth, and horizontal body-mounted tail lamps replaced the vertical wing-mounted fixtures of the Mark I models.

But more important news was of the release of a new MG Midget, this being a version of the AN6 Austin-Healey Sprite Mark II model. Using the same square-cut body shell as the Healey, the new Midget had the appropriate MG badge mounted on a thick central radiator grille slat, and used the same under-powered 948-cc A-series engine of the Sprite, producing 46·4 bhp net at 5,500 rpm, though with remarkable economy. Other details were as for the Sprite, and the model was priced on introduction at only £689.

In August that year the Magnette Mark IV was announced, using the 1622-cc engine in low-compression (8·3:1) form, producing 68 bhp at 5,000 rpm. It had front anti-roll and rear stabilizer bars, a new exhaust system with an additional silencer and automatic transmission as optional equipment. This model completely superseded the Mark III when the earlier type was discontinued in October, showing itself to have more refined handling and ride qualities, and still proving just as quick.

The New Year, 1962, was to be a busy one for MG. In June the GHN2 sports and GHD2 coupé MGAs were discontinued, and new rear springs fitted to the Magnettes, followed closely in July by the announcement of the new Series GHN3 MGB roadster. The integral construction body shell had lost a lot of the MGA's grace in having stiffly parallel lines with a large flat boot, pleasant tumblehome in the wings and doors and a large, gently curving bonnet, sloping down to a shallow and wide radiator grille. A modified B-Series engine was fitted, bored-out yet again (and still undersquare) to 1798 cc, and producing 95 bhp net at 5,400 rpm. Torque figures showed a peak of 110 lb ft at 3,000 rpm, power increase over the MGA being 5·6 per cent and torque increase no less than 13·4 per cent, while in fundamental aspects the suspension, steering and brakes were similar to the earlier model. There was more room in the cockpit, however, and the driving position was much improved, the MGA driver having an over-large steering wheel thrust forward hard up against his chest. Top speed was 107 mph, 0–50 time under 10 sec and consumption about 25 mpg, while handling was the usual pleasant BMC combination of solidity and precision.

October that year saw the release of the MG 1100, a high-performance version of the recently announced Morris 1100 model. This used the same two- and four-door body shells as the Morris (the two-door was for export only) but with a broad, and almost square, representation of the MG grille grafted on to the front end. The transversely mounted front engine, driving direct to the front wheels, was offered with optional 8·9 or 8·2:1 crs, with twin SU HS2 carburettors, producing a smooth and fairly quiet 52 bhp at 5,500 rpm. Maximum torque was 61 lb ft net at 2,750 rpm, and this was sufficient to give this comfortable and nicely trimmed motor-car a maximum speed of 87 mph, and a 0–50 mph time of under 15 sec. Not a great improvement over the standard 1100, but still a measurable and – more important – obvious one to the driver. Fuel consumption, too, was unaffected at about 30 mpg.

That same month the Series G/AN1 Midget was discontinued, being replaced by the 1098-cc G/AN2 machine. This featured Lockheed front disc brakes as standard, carpets in place of rubber mats, baulk-ring synchromesh on the upper three gear ratios and wire wheels with knock-on hub caps as optional extras. The 1098-cc engine now produced 55 bhp giving the Midget a more sports car-like performance with a top speed of over 90 mph, a 0–50 mph time of under 10 sec and fuel consumption in the order of 30 mpg. That same October the Magnette saloon was modified with a duotone paint finish, screen washers and 'rimbellishers' as standard.

In December 1962 the 1100 was modified after very few had been produced, with a thinner front seat squab to increase rear passenger leg-room. January saw a walnut fascia also adopted as standard in the 1100, and in April 1963 thin felt slides and compression springs improved the sealing and action on the Midget's side screens. The MGB's rear springs were modified in May, and in June a starkly handsome glass-fibre hard-top became an optional extra for the big-engined sports car.

February 1964 saw a new remote gear-change fitted in the 1100, and in March the G/AN2 Mark I Midget was discontinued, to be replaced by the G/AN3 Mark II model. Again mirroring Sprite development, the new Midget had a curved windscreen, lockable doors with externally operated press-button handles, and fully winding side windows with hinged quarter lights. Tachometer and speedo were binnacle-mounted directly ahead of the driver and supplementary instruments were sited on the fascia centre.

In September a diaphragm spring clutch and improved heating system appeared as standard with crushable sun visors and plastic-framed mirror on the new 1965 model 1100s, while a clean closed-circuit breathing system was adopted for the MGB, with a five-main-bearing crankshaft as used in the then brand-new 1800 saloon. An electric tachometer replaced the original mechanical instrument, a new type of fuel gauge was fitted and an oil cooler became standard equipment. In the following month the 1965 Magnette appeared with a modified steering mounting, greaseless prop-shaft and the crushable sun visor and plastic-framed mirror safety features. Prices of the range at this time ran from £624 for the Midget, through £714 for the four-door 1100, to £847 and £893 for the MGB and Magnette respectively.

In March 1965 12-gallon fuel tanks were specified as standard on the MGB, followed in May by the appearance of greaseless prop-shafts on the Midgets. In June a similar modification was made to the 'B', and in October a new Series G/HD3 MGB GT fixed-head coupé appeared. The standard body shell was used from the waist down, and on to this was grafted a handsome 'lid' sloping forward from the extreme tail to reach its full height just above the rear wheels, then running forward to the screen. A large upwards-opening tail-gate on concealed hinges contained the raked screen, and large quarter windows gave reasonable all-round vision. Behind the normal bucket front seats was a folding bench, and in the tail of the car a useful flat luggage space was provided, the spare wheel and tool kit being carried below its floor. Leather upholstery was used, and total price for this attractive 'Grand Touring' car was £998 on release. A new quiet back axle tube design was adopted; and the GT could top 107 mph, accelerate from 0–50 mph in under 9 sec, and still returned about 25–7 mpg.

Otherwise the range was largely unchanged for 1966, and in May that year reclining front seats were offered as optional equipment for the pleasant little 1100 saloon. In October the Series G/AN4 Mark III Midget was released in the Motor Show season, using the 1275-cc engine which also appears in the Sprite Mark IV. The folding hood was a non-removable integral fitting, separate brake and clutch master cylinders were used and a 6¼-inch diaphragm clutch was standard.

From April 1967 reversing lamps became standard MGB equipment, on both roadster and GT models, and in October 1967 a spate of changes and additions appeared. The 1275 Midget continued unchanged, but, in keeping with the other fwd BMC saloons, a new Mark II 1100 was announced with cut-back tail fins, larger rear lights, repeater indicators on front wings, restyled seats and interior trim and the necessary 'Mk II' insignia on the tail. From June a 1275-cc engine had been optional equipment, and at this time a separate '1300' model using the engine as standard was announced. In two- and four-door, manual and AP automatic trim, the new 1300 shared the 1100 body shell, but used the standard single SU HS4-carburated 1275-cc engine producing 58 bhp net at 5,250 rpm. The new MG saloon, for a change, did *not* have a higher-performance engine.

Another re-engined machine was the MGC, a hybrid vehicle based on the MGB using a much-modified 2912-cc C-Series engine from the soon-to-be-discontinued Austin-Healey 3000. Known as the ADO52 design, the 'C' was available in open roadster and GT forms with either four-speed manual or Borg-Warner 35 automatic transmission. Although the shell looked identical to the 'B' apart from a rather ungainly rectangular bulge in the bonnet, a new floor pan had been built, providing a triangular structure to accept the new torsion bars for the non-coil ifs system. It seems that the increased length of the six-cylinder engine caused the old coil-spring ifs to be dropped in favour of torsion bars, and the front anti-roll bar, standard on all MGB GTs, appeared in heavier form on the C's front end. The new all-synchromesh gearbox had a low first gear compared with the standard close-ratio Healey transmission, but a high back axle ratio was used to give easy high-speed cruising capabilities. MGB rack-and-pinion steering was retained, but Girling servo-assisted brakes were adopted as standard; $11\frac{1}{16}$-inch diameter discs front and 9-inch drums rear.

The 3-litre engine had the same dimensions as the Healey 3000, but otherwise the bottom end had been altered with seven main bearings, and power output was the same, if a little more smoothly delivered, at 150 bhp gross at 5,250 rpm. Twin SU HS6 carburettors supplied the mixture, and the 22-cwt car had a top speed of about 118 mph, getting from 0–50 mph in only 7·6 sec (a slightly disappointing figure) and returning about 22 mpg average. But there was something rather soft and sluggish about the car; it lacked the harsh sportiness of the big Healey and also the precision of the competitive TR5, and it seemed a mistake not to have restyled the model completely, for it looked rather like a 'messed-about' MGB with no real character of its own. But it was very reasonably priced at £1,102, and offered fast and comfortable transport.

The MGB was itself revised that October, automatic transmission being offered for the first time as optional equipment, a new floor-pan with a larger transmission hump having to be adopted to house it. A new all-synchromesh four-speed gearbox was also adopted (at last), and the quiet tubed axle standardized on the GTs when they were released also appeared on the roadster. Prices were up to £948 for the sports and £1,093 for the GT. The roadster MGC was most certainly not over-expensive.

Meanwhile the big old Magnette saloon had been soldiering on quietly, and in April 1968 it was finally discontinued. In March the 1100 had also been deleted, and April saw the four-door MG 1300 discontinued in favour of the rather lighter two-door model, which was now offered for the home market.

But for 1969, new 1300 Mark II models were announced in October 1968, the MG variant having only two doors, but very attractive figured walnut fascia panels, with three large circular instruments, a speedometer, tachometer, and combined oil pressure, water temperature and fuel gauge display. Rocker switches replaced the good BMC toggle types used previously, and a handsome three-spoked leather-rimmed steering wheel was fitted. The seats had been redesigned, were much more comfortable and were trimmed in Ambla.

But it was in the engine bay where the important changes were made, with Cooper S-type modifications in the form of a twin SU HS2 carburettor set-up. The cr was up to 9·75:1 from 8·8 and larger porting helped to produce 70 bhp net at 6,000 rpm. Torque was up from 69 lb ft at 3,500 rpm to 77 lb ft at 3,000, and a stiffer crankshaft was used in a considerably strengthened block to accommodate these increases without complaint. The excellent AP automatic transmission with full manual over-ride was still optional equipment, and with these modifications the Mark II models showed a maximum speed of 95 mph, accelerated from 0–50 in under 10 sec and were still fairly economical, managing about 28–30 mpg.

And so MG came to the end of the decade, their sporting saloon tradition having been revived after a short relapse to run side-by-side with their traditional sports car line. With the MGB and MGB GT models the company had followed the general trend towards refinement and habitability so prevalent among the ever-developing British sports car industry, and while the MGB was an undoubted hit, its larger-engined sister model was something of a hybrid, unfortunately behaved as such, and was to be quite short-lived.

25 Morgan

'Tradition' plays a big part in this company's design thinking, and also in the attitude of its many home and export customers. Morgan cars epitomize the true sports car spirit, in a tough and spartan way are tremendous fun to drive and have a certain aura unequalled by their mass-produced contemporaries.

A new Morgan 4/4 Series 2 model was released for 1960. This was closely based on the original 1172-cc side-valve Ford-engined sports car, but had a widened body, covering the hitherto separate running boards and rear wings, and providing extra room – some 5 inches – in the cockpit. Optional 7:1 or 8·2:1 compression ratios were available, and the four-cylinder undersquare power unit used a single Solex downdraught carburettor in standard form, or twin SU HS2s in competition trim. Power output was 36 bhp gross at 4,400 rpm in standard trim, or 40 bhp at 5,100 rpm in competition form, and this was transmitted via an 8-inch sdp clutch to a Ford three-speed gearbox without synchromesh on bottom. A Hardy Spicer open propeller shaft was used, driving to a hypoid bevel back axle.

These mechanicals were mounted in a low, underslung Z-section chassis frame similar to that of the more potent Plus 4 model, using a version of

Morgan's vertical coil sliding pillar ifs system as originally patented in 1912, including a lubrication system operated by a button on the dash-panel, which the driver had to operate every 300 miles or so to keep his suspension suspending. Semi-elliptic rear springs located and suspended the rigid axle, the 4/4 had powerful 9-inch Girling brakes all round (two-leading-shoe type at the front) cam-and-peg steering and optional bolt-on disc or centre-lock wire wheels. It was priced at only £706 standard or £780 in competition trim.

The Plus 4 model, on the other hand, was much more potent, using a 1991-cc Triumph TR engine. This had an 8·5:1 cr, twin SU H6 carburettors and produced a maximum of 100 bhp gross at 5,000 rpm. The engine was harsh and rather noisy but powerful. It drove via a 9-inch Borg & Beck sdp clutch to a four-speed, non-synchromesh bottom, gearbox, thence by Hardy Spicer open propeller shaft to a hypoid bevel rear axle. The same chassis frame as the 4/4 was used, and the same brakes and steering gear in standard trim. Two-seater, four-seater and drop-head coupé models were all available, prices running from £914 to £936 and £982 respectively.

At the same time, a BMC B-Series engined Morgan 1500 model was available for export, having been introduced in Series 4 form in January 1959 in fixed-head coupé and convertible versions. It became available in Britain in July 1960.

September that year saw the underpowered side-valve 4/4s discontinued in favour of re-engined models using the new 105E Anglia 997-cc ohv unit. The Series III machine used standard-trim engines, producing a peak of 39 bhp net at 5,000 rpm, mated to the standard Ford clutch/gearbox assembly (the overall ratios in conjunction with the Morgan's 4·4:1 rear axle were rather higher than those of the Anglia saloon). A simple remote gear-change system was adopted, proving completely at home on this good gearbox, and only slight modification had to be made to the Z-section chassis frame to fit in the new transmission. The new gear-change was unusual in sliding horizontally in and out under the dash, twisting to change across the gate. Modifications also resulted in a wider scuttle structure, which increased foot-room in the cockpit, and improved steering by Cam Gears featured a variable ratio steering box and shorter drop arm to give lighter steering, although this felt no less direct. A new central switch panel appeared on the functional fascia, and flashing indicators were now standard throughout the range. The single 997-cc 4/4 model was priced at £737.

Similar steering and switch panel modifications were made to the three Plus 4 models, although 11-inch diameter Girling disc brakes now became standard on the front instead of being optional equipment.

In November the convertible 1500s were discontinued, and in April 1961 the 1500s disappeared altogether with the deletion of the coupé models. That March a Plus 4 Super Sports version had been announced using twin double-choke Weber carburettors, a four-branch exhaust manifold and wire wheels as standard, while October found the 4/4 Series III Tourer discontinued, to be replaced by a new Series IV model using the latest 1340-cc Ford 109E engine as used in the Classic saloon. With a Zenith 32VN carburettor and 8·5:1 cr, the Morgan's new engine produced 54 bhp net at 4,900 rpm, with peak torque of 74 lb ft at 2,500 rpm. The Ford four-speed gearbox, 'remoted' by Morgan, was used again, with a 7¼-inch sdp clutch, and to contain the latest model's 90 mph top speed 11-inch Girling discs were standardized at the front, with 9-inch rear drums. Bishop cam-type steering was adopted but otherwise this much-improved car was little changed and price had only increased marginally to £774, making it the cheapest, yet one of the most individual, over 1-litre British sports cars. That October the Plus 4 and its 115 bhp Lawrence-tuned Super Sports variant continued largely without change, but the coupé had visibility improved with a deeper windscreen and larger side windows.

The Morgan 4/4 was very popular, sharing most features with its 2-litre sister-model, but with its smaller, lower engine, a sleeker bonnet and scuttle line some 3 inches lower than the TR-powered version were possible. Smaller tyres were used, and the 4/4 was some 2½ cwt lighter overall. It would accelerate from 0–50 mph in well under 12 sec, and had a true top-speed of about 85 mph, fuel consumption being quite good at about 30 mpg. The driving position was rather cramped for a tall driver, and there was little spare footroom among the pedals. But the direct and positive steering, and the vintage attributes of solid springs and dampers and a slightly flexible chassis allowed really fast cornering with very little roll and a lot of warning before a gradual oversteering slide began in earnest. Rough surfaces could give both car and passengers a hard time, but Morgan enthusiasts were – and still are – entirely oblivious to such 'shortcomings'; this also being true of the car's minimal 'weather protection'. The 4/4 was, above all else, a pleasure machine for the young at heart; it was spritely, and it was economical.

The 2138-cc Triumph TR4 engine was adopted in the Plus Fours from July 1962, the early 1991-cc unit continuing as optional equipment. The new engine produced 105 bhp at 4,750 rpm and was available in two-seat tourer and coupé, and four-seat tourer form. Chassis and shells which were – as ever – hardly altered. But a new Plus 4 Super Sports model was produced in October, having a lower and rather more sleek body as in the 4/4, giving reduced frontal area and weight. Tuned 2·2- or 2-litre engines were again available, in this instance producing some 120 bhp at 5,500 rpm.

In January 1963 a new Series V 4/4 was released, using the latest Ford 1498-cc engine with 8·3:1 cr and a Zenith carburettor, producing a smooth and willing 59·5 bhp net at 4,600 rpm. This was mated to the new all-synchromesh Ford gearbox and endowed the 13-cwt tourer with much more vivid performance than hitherto. Price, however, was down to only £683 in standard form, and as usual the huge brakes, direct steering and predictable handling made this very much a driver's sports car.

More was to come, for in September the 1498-cc GT engine was adopted with twin-choke Weber DCD1 carburettor, 9:1 cr and a four-branch exhaust manifold, producing 78 bhp at 5,200 rpm and peak torque of 91 lb ft net at 3,600 rpm. This was an enormous improvement, yet the GT-engined 4/4 Competition model was still very cheaply priced at only £755.

The Plus 4 coupé two-seater was built only to special order from January, and in October a very new model was announced, the Morgan Plus 4 Plus. With this machine the Malvern company went 'modern', producing a glassfibre bodied fixed-head coupé with lines reminiscent of the Lotus Elite. The new body was in glass-fibre as opposed to the traditional metal panelling over ash frames, and sloped down at the nose, headlamps being thrust forward on streamlined wings and flanking a narrow vertical central grille with small horizontally barred intakes on either side. A moulding in the bonnet reproduced the classic tapering bonnet line of the 'proper' Morgans, and the bulbous roofline presented an almost elliptical profile. The 2138-cc TR engine was used, with 9:1 cr and twin Stromberg CD carburettors producing 105 bhp net at 4,750 rpm with 128·3 lb ft torque at 3,350 rpm. A Borg & Beck 9-inch sdp clutch transmitted drive to the Triumph gearbox, which still had a non-synchromesh bottom gear. Weight was 16¼ cwt and, priced at £1,275, very few Plus 4 Plus models were to be built. The rest of the Plus 4 range was largely unchanged, two- and four-seater tourers and the Super Sports being available at £816, £834 and £1,118 respectively at this point.

In January 1964 the 4/4 with 1340-cc engine became available to special order only, and in February adjustable bucket seats were standardized on the alien-looking Plus 4 Plus. In October the Plus 4 two-seat coupé was reintroduced for general sale, and then in February 1965 the 1340-cc 4/4 was finally discontinued completely.

October that year saw the announcement of a new Plus 4 Competition model, with the lower 4/4-type body styling, four-branch exhaust manifold, wire wheels, big tyres and adjustable rear shockers as standard. Twin Weber carburettors were fitted to the 2138-cc engine, power output increasing to 112 bhp net at 5,200 rpm while gross torque figure stood at 132·5 lb ft net at 3,000 rpm.

At this time the 4/4 Series V standard and Competition models differed in having Zenith 33 VN and single Weber DCD22 carburettors respectively, producing 65 bhp net at 'four-eight' and 83·5 bhp at 'five-two' from later 1499·9-cc Ford engines. There were now eight models in the range.

In November 1966, Morgan discontinued the Plus 4 Competition model and the hardly successful Plus 4 Plus. The bonnet line of the two-seater tourer Plus 4 was lowered in conformity with the rest of the range in December. Without major changes the range continued in production at the Pickersleigh Road works, much of the output being exported. In January 1968 the 4/4 Series V models were discontinued, to be replaced by new tourer and Competition '1600' cars, using the latest Ford Crossflow 1599-cc engines. In standard form this unit used a 9:1 cr and a Zenith single-choke downdraught carburettor, producing 74 bhp gross at 4,750 rpm. On the Competition and four-seater models the higher-rated GT engine was fitted, with 9·2:1 cr and twin-choke Weber carburettor, producing 95·5 bhp gross at 5,500 rpm, and 103·5 lb ft torque at 3,600 rpm.

The advent of America's Federal Safety Regulations in 1968 effectively precluded Peter Morgan's products from his major export market, and rather than lose his ranges' traditional character he directed his attention very successfully to less fussy regions – production of the basic TR-engined Plus 4s continuing unabated at Pickersleigh Road. Then in late 1968 the most startling machine was announced – Morgan followed the AC and Sunbeam lead in fitting a V8 engine into an existing sports car design.

This new model, the Morgan Plus 8, used the smooth and light aluminium Rover V8 engine from the 3·5-litre and Three-Thousand-Five saloons. This compact engine was very closely comparable to the 2·2-litre TR unit already being used, and few major changes to the structure were needed to accommodate it. The Moss gearbox of the Triumph-engined cars was retained, driven through a 9½-inch Borg & Beck sdp clutch from the 10·5:1 cr, 3528-cc engine. This unit, with twin SU HS6 carburettors, produced 185 bhp gross at 5,200 rpm, and 226 lb ft peak torque at 3,000 rpm.

The Z-section chassis frame was retained, but extra stiffening appeared in the form of strongly gusseted cross-members, and steel replaced wood in the floor panel. Sliding pillar coil spring ifs was retained with the leaf-spring suspended rear axle, but the angularity of the rear springs was altered to give improved location and wheel movement was increased slightly to improve the ride. New cast-alloy 5½-inch road wheels were fitted, but, remarkably, the low-bonnet 4/4 profile was still retained. Removable hood and side screens were still much in evidence and other innovations (with an eye to the American requirements) included recessed rocker switches, lockable steering column and deep and comfortable Restall bucket seats.

With the generous torque of the Rover V8, the new model was extremely tractable, and extremely fast through the gears, 0–50 mph time being 5 sec and 0–100 mph taking a mere 19 sec, at which speed its antique shape was rather against it. Maximum speed was a good 125 mph, excellent for a £1,475 motor-car. It retained the classic Morgan 'hair-shirt' tendencies to leak in rain, clatter and clang and skip from peak to peak on bumpy surfaces; to be at all happy, passengers had to be as enthusiastic as the driver! But on smooth surfaces the limited-slip differential provided tremendous traction, and with a strong basic understeer tendency an opened throttle was sufficient to kick the quite controllable tail out of line. In the wet lurid oversteers could be induced at will, and apart from rather unpleasant chassis-twisting lurches when high cornering forces were experienced, the Plus 8 was genuinely the ultimate in 'Morganism'.

With this V8-engined machine at the head of the TR-engined Plus 4 and Ford 1600 4/4 ranges, Morgans at the end of the decade were very similar in many respects to those at the end of the 'fifties. But ask any Morgan owner what it is that makes such an antiquated machine attractive in this day and age, then stand back, and listen to him for an hour or two. Owning and driving a Morgan is almost synonymous with being the ultimate motoring enthusiast, for, above all else, they're fun.

26 Morris

As, with Austin, a major element of the British Motor Corporation, the Oxford company developed a large and popular range of small- and medium-sized saloon cars throughout the 'fifties, and moved into the sixties sharing many of these with BMC's other partner concerns.

The Morris range in 1959 was headed by the immensely successful Minor model, now in 948-cc form, and supported by the new Morris Mini, with the three medium-sized family saloons, the Cowley 1500, Oxford and Oxford Farina ranged alongside.

The Morris Minor 1000 was introduced in 1956, the 948-cc A-Series engine at last giving an excellent shell and suspension system the power it deserved to make it quick and interesting transport in comparison to the rather underpowered and turgid form in which it had originally appeared. The undersquare engine produced 37 bhp gross at 4,800 rpm, drive being transmitted through a nicely spaced four-speed gearbox and Hardy Spicer prop shaft to the hypoid back axle. Independent front suspension was by a well-controlled torsion bar system, while at the rear a semi-elliptic leaf-sprung axle was used. With rack-and-pinion steering these rather simple but nicely finished little two- and four-door saloons were surprisingly quick and controllable through corners although hardly in the sporting class in a straight line.

August 1959 saw the release of Alec Issigonis's startling new small saloon series, the ADO15 Austin Seven and Morris Mini. With their transverse 848-cc A-Series engines using single SU HS2 carburettors, and driving to the front wheels through a simple system of helical spur gears and double-jointed drive shafts, the Minis set new standards of packaging for a small family saloon. With their Alex Moulton-developed rubber cone suspension system they were also incredibly quick and controllable through the corners. By common consent the direct gearlever was rather too long and the change rather slow, but as already described in the Austin chapter, the Mini was all set to sell a million.

Further up the scale, the standard 1498-cc B-Series-engined Cowley 1500 saloon was discontinued in March 1959, while the big, bulbous Oxford saloon Series III and Traveller Series IV – using the same engine – were also removed, the saloon being deleted at the same time as the Cowley, and the Traveller continuing until April 1960. This Series IV model produced 55 bhp gross at 4,400 rpm, and offered reasonable economy and performance for a large 22¾-cwt Estate. Again a torsion bar ifs system was used, with a live axle on semi-elliptics at the rear, and the model was unusual in having rack-and-pinion steering. This was very direct and imparted a great feeling of control to the driver, unusual in a car of such proportions at that time. The Traveller was priced at £943 and was in considerable demand until its deletion.

Only one of the medium-sized Morris saloons continued seriously into the 'sixties. This was the Farina-styled Oxford, sharing its square-cut handsome body shell, with prominent tail fins, with the other BMC marques. This Oxford Series V was introduced in March 1959, replacing the original Cowley and Oxford saloons, and using – once more – the 1489-cc 55 bhp B-Series engine. A heavy flywheel made the engine very smooth at low road speeds, pulling away from 10 mph in top gear without serious complaint. The standard four-speed gearbox with synchromesh on top three ratios was fitted, and coil-and-wishbone ifs replaced the torsion bars used hitherto. The effect was roughly identical, but torsion bar installations do tend to transmit more road noise than a good coil system. The semi-elliptic live rear axle was, of course, retained, and cam-and-lever steering replaced the direct rack-and-pinion system of the earlier cars. The new Oxford was attractively and practically trimmed and equipped, and entered the lists at £943 – quite expensive for a 1500-cc saloon, but it was a large, roomy and comfortable one.

So Morris entered the 'sixties, with the Minis, saloon, convertible and Traveller Minor 1000 models, the Series IV Oxford Traveller and the new Series V Farina Oxford saloon. In February 1960 the Minis received improved interior trim, padding on each side of the central instrument cluster and in the door and side panels, improved window catches and modified telescopic dampers. March saw a new twin-bulb rear number plate lamp standardized on the Farina Oxford, and May found modified combustion chambers and new camshafts appearing in the B-Series engines. In September, two new Travellers were announced, the long wheelbase Mini version, basically identical to the Austin variant, and the new Series V Farina model. The Mini Traveller offered 35½ cubic feet of luggage space, while the Oxford was ingeniously designed with multi-purpose rear seats. These would fold flat to give extended luggage area as in the normal Traveller or Estate, remain raised normally to give four-/five-seat saloon accommodation, and finally fold back to form two bunks with built-in head-rests. Standard and De Luxe Mini, Minor and Oxford models were now available, and the two new Travellers were priced at £623 (Mini) and £929 (Oxford).

In June 1961 the Super Mini was first put into production, being released in September with better trim and sound-proofing than the standard and De Luxe models, and with lever-type interior door handles replacing the 'string' used on the rather crude original vehicles. An oval instrument nacelle carried three circular instruments and duotone paint finish was standard. Meanwhile, in August, the basic and De Luxe models had had plated grilles fitted, in place of painted ones, with a 16-blade fan, and a new Series VI Farina Oxford had also appeared.

This Series VI machine used the 1622-cc version 'B' engine, with either 8·3 or 7·2:1 cr producing an optional 60 or 55 bhp net respectively at 4,500 rpm. The four-speed, non-synchromesh bottom, manual gearbox was retained as standard but with higher gear ratios installed, and Borg-Warner automatic transmission became an optional extra. Anti-roll bars were fitted front and rear to improve the ride, and slight spring changes reduced the car's height. Track and wheelbase were also slightly increased. A new grille curved under the headlamps to incorporate round sidelight/indicator units, and on the saloon the rear wing line was lowered with cut-back fin-tips improving and smoothing the shell's handsome appearance. In October the Minor range appeared with flashing indicators in place of the old-fashioned and ineffective semaphore type – the Minor having been one of the last vehicles to retain them – screen washers became standard on De Luxe models, and the glove boxes were left uncovered, with no lids. That same month the Series V Oxford saloon and Traveller were discontinued, to be replaced by the Series VI models. The Mini-Cooper also appeared, as described in the Austin chapter, with a twin-carburettor, long-stroke 997-cc engine producing 55 bhp at 6,000 rpm and fitting 7-inch diameter Lockheed front disc brakes in place of the original drums.

A 1489-cc diesel engine using the old B-Series bottom end and a 23:1 cr head, was dropped into the Series VI Oxford saloon in March 1962 to produce economical, if leisurely, transport. Top speed was 68 mph, and 0–50 time 24 sec! Vynide replaced cloth upholstery in the basic Mini saloon at the same time. In June new rear springs appeared on the Series VI petrol Oxford saloons, and August saw the announcement of the new 'Super-Min', the Morris 1100.

This ADO16 project emerged in two- and four-door forms, the shell being plain and squarish, but with a handsome forward rake to the rear screen, broad quarter pillars and a lot of glass area. The new A-Series engine variant, of 1098 cc, was slightly larger in both bore and stroke than the ADO50 Cooper design, used a single carburettor and, with a cr of 8·5:1, produced 48 bhp net at 5,100 rpm. An alternative 7·5:1 low-compression head was available, and an interesting feature was the provision of a vibration damper on the crankshaft nose, deemed necessary due to the overhung flywheel position. As on the Minis, a side-mounted radiator had air drawn through it by a 16-blade pusher fan, running at 1·2 times engine speed and expelling through the left-hand wheel arch. Transmission was similar to the Mini, with a sump transmission driven by clutch-engaged spur gears from the crankshaft. Baulk-ring synchromesh on all but bottom offered lighter and more efficient engagement than the constant-load synchromesh type used in the ADO15 design, and a pleasantly short remote gear-change, similar to that of the Cooper, was fitted, although a rubber sandwich piece was included to prevent the maddening rattle so prevalent in the Coopers.

As on the Mini, front and rear sub-frames carried the power/transmission/ front suspension package and the rear suspension, but here the 1100 broke new ground in using a Moulton Developments' patented Hydrolastic suspension system. In effect front-wheel location was by upper links and wide-based lower wishbones (formed by a single link and a forward-mounting torque arm), while at the rear, independent fabricated trailing arms with a conventional anti-roll bar and twin anti-pitch bars carried the road wheels. The Hydrolastic system consisted of four displacer units on each wheel, interconnected front to rear on the same side so that a self-levelling characteristic was built in. To resist pitch, deflection of a front wheel would cause the rear wheel on that side to be pumped down, effectively maintaining level ride in the car over bumpy surfaces. The fluid used also gave self-damping properties, consisting of 49 per cent water, 49 per cent methyl-alcohol anti-freeze, 1 per cent rust inhibitor and 1 per cent distasteful dye as demanded by law.

The drawback of this system was that suspension deflections set up by power- or brake-induced attitude changes of the car itself tended to be magnified. Thus, dropping the clutch for a quick getaway caused the tail to drop under weight transfer, pumping fluid to the front suspension units and so forcing the nose even higher. Under braking the same thing happened, only in reverse, the tail pumping into the air, but apart from this the 1100 produced excellent ride comfort, control and adhesion in all conditions on all types of surface. Built-in stability modifications resulted in cornering attitudes less dictated by throttle-on or throttle-off than the Mini, in which backing off in a corner promoted instant oversteer, and generally the roomy but still compact

1100 was more refined and civilized, but less swerveable. In basic and De Luxe finish, 1100 prices on announcement ranged from £661 (two-door) to £695 (four-door De Luxe).

At that time some 400,000 Minis had already been produced, and the new 1100, with its top speed of 80 mph, 0–50 mph time of about 15 sec and 32 mpg economy was an attractive buy for someone taken by Issigonis's advanced specification combined with BMC's traditional reliability and good finish.

The Minor series also came in for change at this time, with the new 1098-cc engine replacing the 948-cc unit, baulk-ring synchromesh appearing on the upper three gear ratios and higher gearing being used to produce an effortlessly economical (36 mpg) and reasonably quick (78 mph) motor-car. An all-metal Mini Traveller was announced for the home market, and the Mini De Luxe and Super separate models were discontinued, to be replaced by a Super De Luxe variant featuring the oval instrument panel with revised fittings and trim. Some Minis were, from this time, also fitted with the more effective baulk-ring synchromesh system.

A new Cooper model, the 1071-cc 'S' appeared in March 1963, with an output of 68 bhp net at 5,700 rpm and maximum torque of 62 lb ft at 4,500 rpm. Lockheed 7½-inch diameter disc brakes were used at the front, with the normal 7-inch drums at the rear, and a close-ratio gearbox with alternative final drive ratio was also made available. Improved heaters appeared throughout the Mini range at this time. In May improved sliding window catches were fitted to the Minis, and in July balanced brake drums were introduced on the Farina Oxfords. September saw new telescopic dampers on the 997 Coopers, and in October the new 1100 Minors were modified with longer windscreen wiper blades operating in tandem, combined side and amber indicator lights, and near-side door locks on the two-door models. The 1100 saloons also had their screen washer bottles and jets repositioned, and so the relatively unchanged Morris range entered 1964.

But this was to be a year of change, beginning in January, when the 997-cc Cooper engine was discontinued, to be replaced by a bigger-bore, shorter-stroke 998-cc unit. In March the 1071-cc 'S' was discontinued, to be replaced in April by the potent 1275 'S' version described under the Austin heading earlier in this volume. Then, in September, the 1965 models began to appear, a major innovation being the use of Hydrolastic suspension on all Mini saloons, replacing the sporty, hard and uncompromising rubber cone-type of the original vehicles. The starter was combined with the ignition switch, and courtesy lights, oil filter warning light, crushable sun visor, plastic-framed mirror, a modified gearbox, diaphragm clutch and two leading shoe front brakes were adopted on the 850 range. On the 998 Coopers the rubber block remote gearlever insert from the 1100 was at last adopted, to kill chatter, and the sun visors and plastic-framed mirror were adopted as was universal in the BMC ranges. The Minor 1000, although now using an 1100-cc engine, was similarly modified and further refined inside – such as having lids fitted to the glove boxes – and a two-spoke steering wheel was standardized with the visors and driving mirror modifications. The 1100 itself received a diaphragm spring clutch, visors and mirror, while both petrol and diesel Oxfords were modified with greaseless prop-shafts, modified steering mounting and the other standard changes.

In January 1965 the 970 'S' Cooper was discontinued, and in March the heater system became standard on the 1100 De Luxe. Motor Show time in October found the AP automatic transmission system with full manual over-ride adopted in the 850 Minis and 1100s, and at the start of the new year, safety bosses appeared on the external door handles in the Mini ranges. January 1966 also found twin fuel tanks and an oil cooler standardized on the 1275 'S' Cooper.

March that year saw new model releases in the shape of the two-door 1100 Traveller and Mark I Morris 1800, this big spacious saloon being available in standard or De Luxe trim, and differing from the Austin model only in having a large circular 'Morris' badge in the centre of a six-horizontal-bar grille. In May reclining front seats became an optional extra on the 1100 saloons, and so the range continued into 1967.

In October the Mark II Minis appeared with external trim and equipment changes as for the Austin models, the Mark II 1100s following suit. A Mini 998-cc '1000' model similar to the Austin version was released, together with a 1275-cc-engined '1300', exactly as for the Austin model and again using the revised 1100 shell. 1300 figures included an 87 mph maximum, 12-sec 0–50 time and about 28–30 mpg consumption. In May the 1800 had already been modified with walnut veneer on the fascia, centre console and door cappings, Ambla upholstery instead of hide on the De Luxe, restyled heater controls and pile carpeting throughout. Power-assisted steering became optional in September, and then in March 1968 the 1800 Mark II was introduced, with a grille of four horizontal bars, large sidelight/indicator units, and rear wings extending aft to form fins incorporating vertical rear light clusters and carrying '1800 Mk II' insignia. Rocker switches replaced toggles, and flush-fitting door handles appeared inside. Engine power was raised, and larger wheels were fitted too.

In March 1968 the Morris 1100 Super De Luxe two- and De Luxe four-door saloons were discontinued, leaving the De Luxe two-door, Super de Luxe four-door and Traveller models to continue. Both De Luxe 1300s were deleted, the remaining Super De Luxe two- and four-door models and the Travellers continuing alone.

For 1969 the basic range was largely unchanged apart from the new 1800S saloon version, which had a lot of MGB about the engine, a new cylinder head, new inlet and exhaust manifolding, cr up to 9·5:1 from 9·0:1 and twin inclined S U H S6 carburettors. This unit produced 95·5 bhp at 5,700 rpm, and maximum speed was up to over 100 mph, with a 0–50 mph time of under 10 sec. Disc brakes of 9·7 inches diameter replaced 9·59-inch front units, and latest-type 'three pot' calipers from the Austin 3-litre were used, allowing greater pad area in the space available. There was no automatic option with this model, wh‚h was inexpensive at £1,056 for high performance comfort and space.

So Morris came to the end of the decade, offering a huge range (though lopped in early 1968 in a rationalization move) of seven Minis, two 1100s, three 1300s, no less than eight Minor 1000s, four Oxfords and the brace of 1800s. The Morris split personality of sophisticated and advanced transverse-engined front-wheel drive vehicles on one hand, and the completely conventional and traditional Minor 1000s and Farina Oxfords on the other, was more marked than ever before, but as part of the new BLMC combine continued success seems assured.

27 Reliant

Reliant grew immensely in stature during the 'sixties, progressing from the manufacture of three-wheeled economy cars (all powered by the company's own delightfully engineered little four-cylinder engines) to the production of high-performance GT-type cars of high-quality finish and considerable charm. Reliant were formed in 1935, building metal-shell three-wheelers initially and changing to glass-fibre construction in 1956 with the Reliant Mark III model. They are today the biggest user of automotive glass-fibre in Europe, and offer the largest range of glass-reinforced bodies in the world.

Typical of their original three-wheeled products were the Regal Mark V and Regal Mark VI saloons, built between 1959 and 1961. Designed by D. J. Page and F. R. Heathcote, these little three-wheelers weighed less than 8 cwt and were powered by a 747-cc side-valve engine, producing 17·5 bhp at 4,000 rpm, which was virtually a licence-built Austin 7 unit. Compression ratio was a modest 5·7:1 and the engine would almost literally run on anything one cared to put in it! Three forward speeds and one reverse were standard, and in 1962 these two models were replaced by the Regal 3/25 still clothed in an angular but practical glass-fibre body of very high finish. The engine of the 3/25 was an all-alloy 598-cc four-cylinder unit this time with push-rod operated ohv and a 7·8:1 cr, and it produced 24·2 bhp at 5,250 rpm. Four forward speeds and reverse were standard, and the average price, including seat belts in the specification, was £547. K. Wood had joined Messrs Page and Heathcote in the design of the 3/25, and in 1963 this same trio produced a van version, costing £441 with a passenger seat.

The three-wheeled Regal was extremely successful in its class, and not until August 1968 was it replaced by the 3/30 saloon. Capacity was up to 700 cc, and cr slightly down to 7·5:1, but a healthy 29 bhp were produced at 5,000 rpm.

But in March 1961 the company's second four-wheeler (the first having been the Sussita model designed in 1958 and built in Israel by Autocars Ltd of Haifa) was announced for export only as the Israeli 'Sabra'. This car, anglicized as the Sabre 4, used the Ford Consul 1703-cc engine fitted with a modified cylinder head, larger valves, stronger valve springs and twin SU carburettors, producing 73 bhp at 4,400 rpm. This was mounted in an immensely strong box-section chassis using a strange suspension system and featuring a rather bizarre glass-fibre body with massive protruding over-rider horns. The front wheels were carried on tubular leading arms pivoted at

$38\frac{1}{2}$ degrees to the frame's longitudinal axis and suspended on coil-springs as was the rigid rear axle system. A sports soft-top or detachable hard-top were available, and this decidedly ugly-looking machine was priced at just under £1,000. Design was by the three-wheeler team, joined by C. Fine-Thompson.

In June 1962 a fixed-head coupé GT version was first built, being released in October. This featured a steeply raked roofline to the rear and a sawn-off tail design. Also announced in October was the new Sabre 6 model, using a Ford Zephyr Six engine of 2553 cc, and being clad in a rather more attractive version of the basic bodywork, with shorter bonnet, minus the air scoop, and with a wider grille divided by a single vertical bar. The rear wheel arches were rounded off and twin exhaust pipes were used. This new model was introduced at £1,016, and four- and six-cylinder variants ran side by side until the smaller model was discontinued in December 1963. Late models had featured a similar bonnet and grille to the Sabre 6, but in the 1964 version of the $2\frac{1}{2}$-litre car, which continued in production until September 1964, wishbone front suspension replaced the unconventional leading arms. The model was quite sporty, topping 109 mph, accelerating from 0–50 mph in 7·2 sec and still managing about 26 mpg.

That September two new models were announced, the first a tiny two-door four-seat saloon somewhat similar to a Mini in appearance but with the 598-cc ohv three-wheeler engine in the front driving to the rear wheels. This FW4 Reliant Rebel, with an engine producing 28 bhp at 5,250 rpm, was the work of Messrs Page, Heathcote and Wood and provided the basis of a good, inexpensive and economical little car. Only a few were produced before January 1965 when the FW4A version appeared with improved trim, fewer bars on the radiator grille, and 5-inch diameter round-dial instrument clusters. Top speed was about 64 mph, and 0–50 mph 'acceleration' occupied 21 sec. Fuel consumption, however, was a good 50 mpg.

The second model was the replacement of the unattractive Sabres, this being the much more conservative and handsomely styled SE4 Scimitar GT, engineered by Page and Heathcote and with body designed by David Ogle Ltd. This was very similar to an earlier Daimler SP250-based design study produced by Ogle, a high-waisted glass-fibre shell which was clean and attractive, if rather narrow, with dual headlamps sunk into the knife-edged nose. Wire wheels were standard. Again a box-section chassis was used, mounting the 2553-cc Ford Zephyr Six engine in the front, with a triple SU carburettor system and producing 120 bhp at 5,000 rpm. An all-synchromesh four-speed gearbox was standard with a German ZF unit as an optional extra. Maxima were 112 mph flat-out and 7·3 sec 0–50 mph, while consumption was about 26 mpg. However, road experience with one of the new cars showed that while its engine was powerful it was noisy and intractable, while interior finish still left something to be desired and rear seat leg-room was laughable. Handling was not at all bad for such a big car with a long and heavy front-mounted engine, but in September 1965 new-type rear suspension with trailing arms was fitted. On release the Scimitar GT was priced at £1,379.

In October 1966 the straight-six 2553-cc-engined model was discontinued and replaced in the Series SE4A version using the newly released Ford Zodiac 2994-cc V6 engine. This was a short and compact unit which helped weight distribution a great deal and the new Scimitar, the work of D. J. Page and B. F. Cottier, was very much more refined than its predecessor. Additional cross-bracing was provided in the chassis, a black padded fascia was used, disc wheels replaced the heavier wire ones and a fresh-air system with variable vents was also incorporated. The ZF gearbox option was no longer available. With an engine giving 144 bhp at 4,750 rpm this new SE4A Scimitar had an excellent performance and was not expensive (£1,516 on announcement).

Reliant's association with Autocars of Haifa led to their partnership with another Middle Eastern manufacturer, Otosan of Istanbul, in December 1966. For Otosan they designed and built base units for a five-seater two-door glass-fibre saloon, not unlike a Ford Escort in appearance, named the Anadol. Using 1200- and later 1300-cc Ford engines, half of the Anadol's components were provided from the UK, Otosan building up production to about 4,000 Anadols per year in 1968. Meanwhile special TW9 three-wheeler pick-ups were also being sold to Greece – for a smallish company Reliant's export and enterprise record is excellent.

August 1967 saw further additions and alterations to the four-wheeled range with the introduction of the further refined SE4B Scimitar 3-litre and its SE4C Scimitar sister fitted with a 2495-cc V6 engine. Similar externally, the 2½-litre model could be distinguished by its '2·5 litre' insignia on the rear. In this form the car had 118·5 bhp at 4,500 rpm, giving it a top speed of 113 mph, 0–50 mph acceleration in 8 sec and some 28 mpg. (The price on announcement was £1,450.)

In October the Rebel was modified to accept the company's own delightful little 701-cc engine (in this FW4B form having 31 bhp at 5,000 rpm), and in December the FW4BEZ Rebel Estate version was announced using the same engine, but with a side-hinged single rear door latched on to the tail of the barely modified basic two-door shell. Prices of the two new Rebels were £609 and £640 respectively, and while obviously built to this price they proved remarkably good cars. They were very manœuvrable and the tiny engine was very accessible and economical; while trim was rather spartan and the seats shallow, the basic design proved surprisingly practicable. J. R. Crossthwaite, B. F. Cottier and K. Wood were responsible for the design changes. With the larger engine top speed was up to 70 mph, 0–50 mph time down to 17 sec and fuel consumption down slightly to 45 mpg. Production of the 598-cc Rebel ceased in January 1968.

In October 1968 the 1969 Scimitar 'Estate', the SE5 Series GTE, was announced. Still using the 144 bhp Ford Zodiac V6 unit, the GTE was immediately hailed as the best-conceived, most attractive and most refined Reliant yet. The body mouldings, in glass-fibre of course, were to an extremely high standard of finish, and interior fittings and appearance were first rate. Price initially was £1,759, later rising to £1,926, including overdrive, radio and seat belts as standard. Performance was very good at 114 mph flat-out, only 7·8 sec 0–50 mph and about 25 mpg.

Reliant have carved for themselves quite a reputation for good quality performance cars with just that important touch of individuality. Learning by their mistakes in the four-wheel field, and with the invaluable assistance of David Ogle Ltd, their design team eventually evolved some extremely good GT models.

During the period, the Tamworth company had also grown to be the biggest single producer of glass-fibre body shells in Europe (in 1967 some 350 sets were being made per week). In 1960 3,000 vehicles were built by Reliant. In 1968 the figure was over 16,000, and in 1969, with the take-over of the Bond concern, the company completed ten years of constant, and very successful, development.

28 Riley

In this decade Riley became merely a name on fast, well-equipped versions of the basic BMC saloon models, part of the flood of Mini and 1100 transverse-engined fwd vehicles which appeared after 1961.

In 1959 the handsome One-Point-Five saloon had been upholding the Riley competition tradition in saloon car racing for some years. This car was really a 'two-seater', with very limited rear-seat room and it was also very much a 'sporting' model, with a quick four-speed gearbox (synchromesh on the top three), torsion-bar ifs and a well-controlled semi-elliptic rear axle. Large 9-inch two leading shoe and 8-inch rear drum brakes were used. The B-series 1498-cc engine used twin SU H4 carburettors, had an 8·3:1 cr and produced 68 bhp gross at 5,400 rpm. Cornering power was high, but the ride was rough and choppy, the rack-and-pinion steering transmitting a considerable amount of shock – sportiness bringing harshness in its wake. Top speed was about 85 mph and the 0–50 mph time was 12 sec, but fuel consumption was not very good at about 25 mpg.

Riley's Farina-styled saloon was the 4/Sixty-Eight model, as conventional as others of that ilk but in this instance with very attractive burr walnut veneer on the instrument panel and door cappings, full instrumentation (including matching speedometer and tachometer) and thick pile carpeting on the floors. The engine was also tuned, with twin SU HD4 carburettors, and produced 66·5 bhp gross at 5,200 rpm. Although not comparing with the small One-Point-Five, the 4/Sixty-Eight was well ahead of its Farina competitors in performance and on a par with the Wolseley model in trim. Prices of these two Riley models as announced for 1960 were £815 and £1,028 respectively.

Modifications in May 1960 cleaned up the One-Point-Five shell, with interior hinges for boot and bonnet replacing external chrome ones, while the engine was given a new camshaft and reshaped combustion chambers. This revised engine also appeared in the 4/Sixty-Eight, producing a net maximum of 63·5 bhp at 5,000 rpm with peak torque of 82 lb ft at 'two-five'. SU H4 carburettors were used on the smaller car, with PDs on the big Farina saloon, which was also lower geared than the sprightly yet quite long-legged One-Point-Five. In September the 4/Sixty-Eight was joined by – and in the following month superseded by – the new, larger-engined 4/Seventy-Two model. This new car used a 1622-cc single carburettor unit, with an enlarged bore and slight suspension modifications, including a front anti-roll bar and rear stabilizer. Power was up to 68 bhp net at 5,000 rpm, and torque was also increased to 88 lb ft at 'two-five'. Automatic transmission was optional, and even in this form the 4/Seventy-Two returned a top speed of 86 mph, a 0–50 mph time of 13·5 sec and economy of about 25 mpg.

Also making its debut at the October Motor Shows was a Riley Mini variant, the Elf Mark I. This differed from the basic cars in having an extended boot with tiny tail fins and the traditional vertical Riley radiator grille grafted on to the restyled nose. Wooden veneer was an interior refinement, and with the standard 34 bhp 848-cc transverse engine, front-wheel drive and four-speed gearbox with its weak synchromesh, the new Elf was offered at £693. This was the most expensive Mini variant on the market at the time, its high-quality upholstery in a mixture of leather-substitute and soft pile cloth and better sound-proofing making for quite opulent and eminently practicable town transport.

June 1962 saw the Farina saloon rear spring modifications incorporated on the 4/Seventy-Two, and in October duotone paintwork and screen washers became standard. At the same time the One-Point-Five engine was given a new crankshaft, and some Elfs began to appear with the effective 1100-type baulk-ring synchromesh, still on the upper three ratios only, and genuine leather replaced leather cloth on wearing parts of the seats. The Mark I Elf was then discontinued in November, the Mark II being released in January 1963 with the 998-cc engine, in this instance with an 8·3:1 cr, single SU HS2 carburettor and producing 38 bhp net at 5,250 rpm, with peak torque of 52 lb ft net at 2,700 rpm. Two-leading-shoe front drum brakes were also fitted, and in May the improved Mini range window catches also appeared. Top speed rose from around 72 to 76 mph, and flexibility was much improved. New telescopic dampers were added in September, and a year later Hydrolastic suspension, a diaphragm clutch, combined starter/ignition switch, crushable visors and a plastic-framed driving mirror were all standardized on the Elf. The 4/Seventy-Two gained the Farina modifications of an altered steering mount, greaseless propeller shaft, and 'safety' visors and mirror. In November the safety features appeared on the One-Point-Five as well.

The 1100 models in the BMC ranges were steadily gaining popularity, and it was almost inevitable that a Riley variant should appear; hence in September 1965 the Series R/AS1 Kestrel. The 1098-cc transverse engine was available with optional 8·9:1 or 8·1:1 compression, and used twin SU HS2 carburettors to produce 55 bhp net at 5,500 rpm. Maximum torque was 61 lb ft net at 2,750 rpm and, principally distinguished by the Riley grille, this was a most attractive little luxury car with a useful performance edge over the standard 1100s. Walnut veneer appeared in the interior, and extra instrumentation included a tachometer. On release, the Kestrel was priced at £781.

That year was one of change, and in April the rather dated One-Point-Five had been discontinued. The car had disappeared from the circuits two years before, and as a nicely appointed, quick and manoeuvrable medium saloon was now being challenged hard by the more modern products of the opposition.

The Elf, Kestrel, and 4/Seventy-Two continued into 1966, optional reclining front seats being offered for the Kestrel in May, and a new Mark III Elf being announced in October. This was a considerably revised and cleaned-up motor-car, the ugly external door hinges being replaced by concealed ones, with standard push-button door handles and winding windows, reshaped door panniers, fresh-air ventilation and a remote gear-change.

Without other major alterations the Riley range continued into 1967. For the Motor Show in October a new Kestrel 1300 was announced, with the all-synchromesh gearbox and more robust brakes, available in standard four-door manual or AP automatic transmission trim.

A Mark II Kestrel 1100 was also announced at this time, with the tail fins cut back and larger tail-light clusters and with the AP automatic transmission optionally available. But this model had a very short life, being discontinued in January the following year. The faithful old 4/Seventy-Two still soldiered on at the head of the range, the only conventional – or traditional – Riley still to survive.

Finally, the 1969 Riley 1300 was given an attractive figured walnut fascia, rocker switches in place of the old toggles and trim generally similar to the parallel MG model. A new Cooper S-based twin carburettor engine was also fitted, with a high-compression head (9·75:1), twin SU HS2 carburettors and larger ports, raising power output to 70 bhp net at 6,000 rpm. Torque rose from 69 to 77 lb ft, 500 rpm lower in the range, and to cope with these increases the crankcase was stiffened and a specially hardened crankshaft was fitted. Full exhaust emission control was built-in, and a close-ratio gearbox was fitted. With these alterations top speed rose to about 90 mph, and 0–50 mph acceleration time was down to 9·1 sec, while economy was largely unimpaired.

The three Elf, Kestrel and 4/Seventy-Two models were now the only cars left carrying the once-proud Riley badge, and in mid-1969 it was decided to phase out production of the cars before the end of the year. So the Riley marque, the 'genuine' versions of which ceased in 1938, finally came to the end of the line.

29 Rolls-Royce

This Crewe-based motor company have a name synonymous with all that is best in luxury car engineering – combining opulence, silence and supreme comfort with considerable performance and, in later years, handling ability. The products of their talented and dedicated team of designers, under the technical directorship of Harry Grylls, Chief Engineer John Hollings, and his assistant J. G. McGraith Fisher, have already been described in some detail in the Bentley chapter. In particular the T-series version of the Rolls-Royce Silver Shadow is described in full there.

However, in 1959 their Silver Cloud II model had appeared with the larger

6230-cc V8 light-alloy engine installed and was available in bare chassis form to selected coach-buildings with standard or long-wheelbase trim. These bare chassis with mechanical and suspension parts fitted were priced at £2,985 and £3,045 each, and with painstaking care Park Ward, H. J. Mulliner and James Young built their own interpretations of the ultimate in luxury transport on these foundations. Rolls' own Silver Cloud II four-door saloon was the least expensive (one cannot say cheapest!) at £5,802, Park Ward producing a long wheelbase saloon with chauffeur division at £7,077. Mulliner's convertible coupé was an attractive buy for the wealthy sub-tropical resident at £7,601, while James Young's interpretation of a long-wheelbase divided saloon was priced at £8,451.

In almost utter silence the Silver Cloud II was surprisingly quick, reaching 50 mph in 7·9 sec, and having a maximum speed of about 114 mph. Fuel consumption was limited at around 12 mpg, but if you could afford a Rolls, you needn't worry about running costs. The automatic transmission ratios were widely spaced, and selected jerkily unless the driver was very careful, the only real criticism possible. The transmission had been designed originally in America twenty years before, and was beginning to feel dated. It lacked a torque converter, and so with no multiplication of effort was sadly lacking in mid-ratio acceleration.

With the classical vertically slotted radiator the dignified ponderousness of the Rolls-Royce was utterly in keeping with the large commercial concern or wealthy private individual clientele. Heading the range was a very long wheelbase (12 feet) Phantom V model, otherwise similar mechanically to the Silver Cloud and S-series Bentleys. A bare chassis was priced at £3,130, and variants included seven-passenger limousines by Park Ward and James Young (the former being the most expensive available at £9,989) and touring limousines from Mulliner and Young.

During the early part of the 'sixties modifications were made step by step, map-reading lights, combined flasher and headlamp flick switches, revised rear lamp styling, handbrake warning lights, improved hosing and rear seat passenger foot-rests being among the additions. In October 1962 the Phantom V's engine had the compression ratio increased, twin headlamps added, and so on, the Bentley S3-type changes also being incorporated into the Silver Cloud III range. The big Phantom V suffered transmission defects too, yet despite weighing 51 cwt, 0–50 time was under 10 sec, and top speed was 101 mph. In October 1963 Rolls' wholly-owned subsidiaries H. J. Mulliner and Park Ward combined, and in March 1964 minor styling changes incorporated 'RR' monograms on the headlight fairings with four-door models, and on the flat headlight surround on two-door ones. Similar insignia were adopted on the Phantom V and at the same time the 2-inch carburettors were adopted. May saw wider wheel rims adopted as standard on the basic saloon, long-wheelbase standard and James Young Silver Cloud models.

But in 1965 the delightfully attractive Silver Shadow was on the way, and that October the 'Clouds' were discontinued, production of the Phantom V continuing in small numbers for specialist limousine orders.

The new Silver Shadow received a mixed response, loved by the motoring press and by those who put aesthetics and engineering sophistication before status-symbol appearance and dignified antiquity. In particular the changed proportions of the traditional radiator, which was now considerably more shallow than hitherto, brought broadsides from the 'old brigade'. But quite how anyone could seriously challenge the attraction of stylist Blatchford's beautifully balanced new shell I fail to comprehend. Early defects were a high degree of roll – later limited by suspension stiffening – and although the steering was rather slow, adhesion was incredibly high. Acceleration times included 7·8 sec 0–50 mph, and top speed was a whispering 118 mph.

New prices on introduction were £6,556 for the basic model, and as this most advanced of all Rolls-Royces developed, two-door James Young and Mulliner versions were introduced in early 1966. The James Young model was deleted during 1967, however, and so the standard and Mulliner, Park Ward models continued toward the end of the decade. In spring 1969, current Rolls-Royce prices stood at £7,959 (standard saloon), and £10, 643 (Mulliner, Park Ward model).

But at the end of 1968 a new Phantom VI model had appeared, bodied by Mulliner, Park Ward, and again with separate chassis, leaf-sprung rear axle, and enormous dimensions. Nearly 20 feet long and weighing well over 2½ tons, the Phantom VI was the most expensive of Rolls-Bentley products, at £13,123.

The four-speed fluid coupling automatic transmission of the Silver Shadow had been replaced by a much more modern conception, using three well-chosen ratios and an effort-multiplying torque converter. This transmission, basically a GM400 unit, had been fitted to all left-hand drive export models from late 1965, since the Shadow's inception in fact, and the new transmission proved extremely smooth, featuring a much-improved kick-down acceleration. The 0–50 mph time was reduced from just under 8 sec, to just over 7 sec with the GM400, and 100 mph came up in around 32 sec, over 3 sec quicker than before. Surprisingly, the Silver Shadow also proved slightly more economical with this four-speed drive, returning about 11 mpg, 1 mpg better than previously. Now the 'world's best motor-car' really was almost faultless.

30 Rover

The Rover Company Ltd entered the 'sixties with a firmly founded reputation for smooth, quiet and virtually indestructible motor-cars. High standards of workmanship were evident in the firmly 'British' solidity of the Rover models' coachwork, the attention paid to vibration- and sound-proofing, to the shell's anti-corrosive properties and also to comprehensively equipping the interiors for maximum comfort and habitability. The 'old English upright Rover' had become as much a symbol of staid middle-class affluence as the Rolls-Royce had become the transport of aristocracy and the super-rich.

In October 1949 the first P4 Series vehicle, the Rover 75, had been announced, and ten years later this same basic body style was still in production

ROVER

for the '60', '75', '90' and '105' models. In July 1959 they were all discontinued, but the style lived on in the '80' and '100' versions.

The '80' used a shell virtually identical to that of the extinct '75', and was powered by a four-cylinder 2286-cc 77 bhp engine. Valve gear included an overhead inlet controlled by roller cam followers and push-rod-operated rockers, while exhaust valves were inclined on one side and operated by roller cam followers bearing directly on them. Front 10¾-inch disc brakes were standard with powerful 11-inch drums at the rear, the system also having servo-assistance as standard. Overdrive on top was optional for the four-speed gearbox and another forward-looking feature was the combined ignition and starter switch.

The Rover '100' P4 featured a six-cylinder 2625-cc engine in the shell used previously by the '90', had 104 bhp to push it along and otherwise had similar features to the twin '80' model.

Entirely separate from these P4s was the P5 3-litre Mark I, the deep-chested, much less bulbous five-seat saloon introduced in September 1958. This big saloon was offered in both manual and automatic transmission forms, and was distinctive in that it had a forward sub-chassis carrying the suspension, engine and auxiliaries combined with a unitary construction steel body. Laminated torsion bar ifs was used and the 2995-cc six-cylinder engine produced 115 bhp at 4,500 rpm. Front disc brakes were fitted as standard in this model from July 1959 onwards, and in January 1960 interior trim was altered, upholstery having vertical instead of transverse flutes and oblong interior lights replacing round units. Twin rear ashtrays and coat hooks were also added. Although big and heavy, the 3-litre was far from slow, having a top speed of about 103 mph in coupé form and even getting from 0–50 mph in 13 sec with automatic transmission. In February 1960 the 3-litre had fresh-air controls, fascia frame, glove-box lid and door casings revised, while stainless steel sensibly replaced chrome strip around the windows and in the roof gutters. In March, the prism reflectors above the sidelights on the '80' and '100' were also deleted. The two P4s then had their steering ratio lowered and the 3-litre-shaped gearlever installed, and in May 1960 the manual P5 had overdrive standardized on top although it could still be ordered without. In October power-assisted steering was made yet another optional extra and in June 1961 the P4s lost their '80' and '100' designation and both became known simply as 'Mark IVs', although they were unchanged.

In September the 3-litre P5 was fitted with new wheel trims, quarter-lights, twin ashtrays beneath the parcels shelf and an additional SU petrol pump for use in emergencies operated by a fascia switch. A similar emergency pump was fitted to the six-cylinder (ex '100') Mark IV, together with twin ashtrays in the rear of the front seat squab while the four-cylinder (ex '80') Mark IV had only the latter alteration made.

But in May 1962 the 2½-year-old '80' was discontinued after 5,900 had been produced and then, in July, the better-selling '100' also ended its run at 16,621. The 3-litre Mark IA was also discontinued, and the replacement models released at the same time. The '95' replaced the '80', featuring the six-cylinder 2625-cc '100' engine while the '110' replaced the '100' using a similar power unit but this time producing 123 bhp at 5,000 rpm compared with the '95's' 102 at 4,750. It also lacked an overdrive kick-down, while the '95' itself had the overdrive option removed. The 110 model would just touch

113

100 mph, had a 0–50 mph time of under 12 sec, and the Mark II 3-litre was improved with more power, a close-ratio gearbox with floor-mounted gear-lever, though no kick-down switch linked to the overdrive mechanism and no reservoir for the servo vacuum brake system. Sealed-beam headlamps were fitted as standard and a flasher was incorporated in the indicator stalk. Power steering and two-speed heater fan were also standardized, along with Road Speed tyres and generally improved seating and interior trim. A lowered roofline version, the 3-litre Coupé was also introduced at this time, giving the car a sleeker and rather more attractive appearance without expending any of the traditional Rover air of dignity.

During their production run, which ceased on 27 May 1964, the two final P4 Series variants, the '95' and '110' were produced in relatively small quantity, only 3,680 and 4,612 respectively being built. The fourteen-year-old Series was finally abandoned with a total of 130,342 units having been produced. The only major modifications during the final models' two-year run was made in February 1964, when the '95' received a new main wiring harness and its six-cylinder engine a larger diameter crankshaft.

Meanwhile the Mark II 3-litre models had had lower ratio steering and a hydraulic steering damper fitted in October 1962, but in October 1963 Rover's long-awaited new car appeared.

In 1962 the north site at Solihull had been extended by some 266,000 square feet in preparation for the new model, and the Rover Engineering Department had spent six years working on it, pre-production units appearing in 1963 preceded by fifteen early prototypes. These cars were styled loosely after the T4 Rover Gas Turbine saloon, and carried 'Talago' insignia to hide their identity, this name being derived from the initials of Mr T. A. L. Gawronski, the project engineer responsible for programme planning and production. £10·6 million had been invested in the new car and on its announcement, as the Rover 2000, the motoring press greeted it with open arms, it being immediately voted 'Car of the Year'.

The basis of the new car was a strong welded steel base unit carrying the mechanical parts and providing mountings for the body panels. In case of damage, both base unit and panelling were jig drilled to ease repair by replacement. The shell was all steel apart from aluminium alloy bonnet and boot-lid and the shell's underside was painted in a slipper bath, then coated with anti-corrosive sealer. All mating body panels were also treated with zinc dust primer. Hung on the base unit was a sophisticated suspension system, incorporating double wishbone ifs with anti-dive characteristics built in, sprung via a linkage by horizontal coil springs bearing on the front bulkhead. At the rear a De Dion sliding-tube was employed similar to that so universal among the 2½-litre Formula 1 cars of the 'fifties, located by Watt linkages and sprung on coils, Gydraulic telescopic shock-absorbers were used all round, while Marles worm-and-roller steering was direct and positive and braking powerful with servo-assisted Dunlop discs all round. The engine was a 'square' four-cylinder 1978-cc unit with single ohc producing 99 bhp at 5,000 rpm.

Inside, the new 2000 upheld all the best traditions of Rover comfort and space while safety features were numerous – collapsible steering column, extensive crash-padding and general reduction of all dangerous projections being much in evidence.

This new Rover P6 2000 was an immediate sales success, orders pouring in from all parts of the world. Maximum speed was 104 mph, while 0–50 mph time was only 10 sec. In addition 24 mpg from the 2-litre engine was reasonable. In August 1964 Butyl rubber bushes were added to the rear suspension bottom links, and front suspension was fitted with nine-coil 17½-inch springs in place of the original eight-coil 16½-inch ones. A new horizontal mounting bracket for the spare wheel, limiting boot space rather, was also included. In October noise level was further reduced by redesigning the front and centre exhaust pipes, while the wipers were given a larger sweep area and a courtesy light was added to the interior mirror.

In January 1966 'shepherd's crook' petrol reserve, choke and heater controls were fitted and in February appearances changed with reversing lamps in unit with the tail/stop clusters in place of reflectors, these moving to the boot-lid. Map reading lights at either end of the parcel shelf were also deleted. In August Girling discs replaced the original Dunlop fittings and the bonnet release was modified with the control in the soft glove box above the driver's legs. In October 1966 an automatic optional model was announced, using the Type 35 Borg-Warner transmission – of course – with either fully automatic or alternative manual intermediate control. The control lever was mounted on the central console, and had an illuminated indicator. A transmission oil cooler was mounted in the radiator.

At the same time, the home market Rover 2000TC was introduced, using two SU HS8 carburettors mounted on a special 10:1 cr aluminium alloy head. Power output was up to 124 bhp at 5,500 rpm, oil cooler and tachometer were standard. Wire wheels were an optional extra, and 'TC' badges on bonnet, front wings and console distinguished it externally, while export models also featured sculptured road wheels and more extensive chrome-strip trim. The TC could touch 109 mph flat-out, rush from 0–50 mph in only 8·5 sec and consumed no more fuel than the standard 2000. With more power its excellent handling capabilities could be exploited to the full.

With the TC's introduction, the basic model was dubbed the SC (single carburettor) and the three models ran concurrently, priced at £1,357 (SC), £1,567 (automatic) and £1,535 (TC), in 1967. April 1968 saw further modifications made, with a clear plastic fluid reservoir, bar front-seat adjustment levers and other minor changes being made to comply with export specifications and local legal requirements. In October 1968 a new roller-bearing gearbox was standardized along with cross-flow radiators, and total Rover 2000 production to the time of writing (7 February 1969) stood at 125,526 – the company's huge investment and advanced engineering policy had been paying off.

But while the beautifully styled, extremely well-engineered and safe 2000s were attracting many new buyers to the Rover camp, the P5 3-litre had been soldiering on in the old staid, but fairly quick, comfortable and indestructible Solihull fashion. In February 1964 the fascia design had been revised, with larger speedometer numerals, and yellow minimum oil marking, while blanking plates were added to the rear over-riders. The 2995-cc engine had a larger diameter crankshaft fitted, together with a replacement rear silencer of 'long-life' aluminium-coated steel, front suspension ball joints were sealed for life and variable-speed windscreen wipers were also introduced.

In August power-assisted steering was standardized on the saloon, and then in September 1965, the 3-litre Mark III was announced. Using basically the same shell as the earlier cars, this model featured a larger radiator badge, full-length steel side strips ending in three dots and 'Mark III' flashes on front wings and boot-lid. The front seats were restyled and individual rear seats in 2000-style added. A clock was let into the passenger's side of the fascia.

For a short while the Marks II and III ran concurrently, and then in January 1966 the former was discontinued, Mark III automatic and manual saloons and coupés completely replacing it. Finally in August 1967, the Mark III 3-litres were discontinued to be replaced by the P5B V8-engined 3½-litre class, but a grand total of 48,548 P5 3-litres had been made when production ceased.

The replacement P5B followed the growing fashion of fitting smooth and torquey American V8 engines into British-made chassis and shells, and for the purpose Rover chose a GM-based ohv all-aluminium lightweight unit of 3528-cc, producing 184 bhp at 5,200 rpm. More important was the torque rating of 226 lb ft at 3,000 rpm, for this allowed a Borg-Warner 35 automatic transmission to be specified as standard with no manual option. The engine was short and compact, with a very stiff crankshaft running in five main bearings. Twin SU carburettors were mounted on a separate aluminium alloy inlet manifold, while self-adjusting hydraulic tappets made this a very quiet and smooth unit. Worm-and-peg power-assisted steering was used, while the laminated torsion bar ifs, semi-elliptic rigid axle rear, and front disc/rear drum servo-assisted brake system made this a well-handling and very secure-feeling motor-car. The body shell itself was in welded steel while a separate welded forward chassis unit carried engine, transmission, front suspension and steering in standard P5 fashion and was rubber-mounted at six points to the integral shell, giving first-rate noise and vibration insulation. Top speed was 110 mph, 0–50 mph acceleration occupied only 8 sec, and yet the V8 was not uneconomical at 18 mpg. This Rover 3½-litre was offered in traditional saloon form or in the rather more attractive, though no less dignified-looking, coupé style and prices on introduction stood at £2,174 and £2,270 respectively.

The next obvious step was to put this silent and powerful V8 into a 2000 shell, and in April 1968 the hybrid Three-Thousand-Five model was released. Again automatic transmission was standard, and only external differences from the 2000 were a thrust-forward radiator air intake beneath the front bumper, '3500' badges on radiator grille, wings and boot-lid and 'V8' insignia on bonnet and boot. Larger section tyres were standardized ($185HR \times 14$ replacing the 2000's $165SR \times 14$ size) while rubber-faced over-riders and a polished finisher on the bonnet front edge were also added.

Current price at time of writing is £1,830 which seems very cheap compared with the £2,270 for the V8-engined 'tank' that is its sister model, and to 7 February 1969, no less than 6,310 units had already left the Rover works.

During the decade many changes had come to Rover. With the 2000 and their racing gas-turbine cars built in conjunction with BRM and performing very creditably in the Le Mans 24 Hours Race the company emerged as one of the most sophisticated and advanced – in an engineering sense – among the British industry. In 1965 the merger with Alvis had taken place, the Solihull company buying the whole of the other's share capital. The Land-Rover utility range, instituted in 1948, passed the 500,000 production mark on 1 April 1965, having earned more than £230,000,000 in foreign exchange in the interim period, and in 1966 Rover won the Queen's Award to Industry for their sustained and substantial increases in exports over the previous three years. In June the AA Gold Medal was awarded to the company for 'The high degree of inherent safety incorporated in the design and construction of the Rover 2000 car', and then in December 1966 a take-over offer was made by the British Leyland Motor Corporation for the combined Rover/Alvis organization. This was finalized in March 1967 and Rover became a wholly-owned subsidiary of the Group. But there has been no sign of the Rover car losing its identity in an orgy of 'badge engineering', and it stands today as a unique example of prestige design and engineering in a quantity-produced motor-car.

31 Singer

Sir William Rootes served his apprenticeship at Singers, and it seems that when the company ran into financial crises in 1956 his motor manufacturing group stepped in to prevent the marque from disappearing into limbo, like so many before it. Since that time the Singer badge has appeared on the more refined and luxurious medium-sized models in the Rootes range.

In 1960 the Minx-based Gazelle was the only Singer being produced, in Series IIIA form at the time. Its 1494-cc engine had been fitted with twin Solex 32PBIS downdraught carburettors mounted on the special induction manifold originally developed for the model's sister car, the Sunbeam Rapier. Compression ratio was 8·5:1 and maximum power was 64 bhp at 4,600 rpm. Smoothness was a keynote of the Singer design, and in order to achieve such a throttle action a special linkage was designed for it in addition to a large throttle pedal pad. The standard Rootes four-speed gearbox had synchromesh on the upper three ratios, and for the 1960 models these were a new close-ratio cluster. Coil-and-wishbone ifs with a semi-elliptic rear end was, of course, standard, with 9-inch Lockheed drum brakes all round and Burman recirculating ball steering, while optional extras included overdrive and Smith's Easidrive automatic transmission. At this time the Gazelle and the Minx were the only 1½-litre cars available with fully automatic transmission, and saloon, convertible and estate car versions were available, with prices standing at £848, £943 and £957 respectively. The saloon's maximum speed was about 82 mph, and with a 0–50 mph time of 16·4 sec and economy of about 28–30 mpg the well-appointed Gazelle was an attractive buy.

In September 1960 the Series IIIB Gazelle was released, using a hypoid final drive in place of the earlier spiral bevel unit, and a single Solex 32PBIS carburettor replaced the previous twin unit arrangement. Power was down to

62 bhp at 4,500 rpm, and detail improvements had been made to the gearbox, a floor change being standardized although column change was optional. Overdrive and automatic options were retained and the pretty and well-finished Singers continued to sell steadily.

Then, in July 1961 a new model was produced, officially entitled the Singer Vogue and soon to be known affectionately, and inaccurately, as the 'Vague'. The new model used the larger body soon to become familiar in the Hillman Super Minx, and, although only 1¾ inches wider than the Gazelle shell, it offered much-increased accommodation with its 5-inch greater wheelbase, 2½-inch greater front track and 13-inch in place of 15-inch wheels. The roofline was lowered by 1¾ inches, and with the same high standard of trim (for a medium-capacity car in this price range), a large glass area, and good looks, the new Vogue was offered with either the four-speed manual or three-speed automatic transmissions. The 1592-cc engine, with a Solex 32PBIS carburettor, produced 62 bhp net (66·25 bhp gross) at 4,800 rpm, and the new model was priced at £956 in standard form, automatic costing an extra £128 and Laycock de Normanville overdrive, £61.

In February 1962 the Gazelle convertible was discontinued, followed in March by the Estate version. In May a new Vogue Estate appeared, and September saw the discontinuation of the Vogue Mark I, a Mark II version having been produced in August in both saloon and Estate car trim. Similar changes to the Hillman Super Minx had been made, improving hill-climbing and acceleration, while grease points had been removed, front disc brakes standardized and Borg-Warner automatic transmission specified as optional in place of the Smith's Easidrive. Unlike the Minx models, the Singers had three transmission options – fully automatic, manual overdrive and floor or column manual change. Externally the Vogue had lost its chrome bonnet strip, and had amber front indicators, individual front seats, twin reversing lamps and two-speed wipers as standard.

August 1963 saw the final Gazelle IIIC produced, being replaced by the front disc brake Series V model in September. Wider rear doors with fixed rear quarter-lights, the Minx shell's squared roofline and larger, more square windscreen and a redesigned fascia were all incorporated, the finless rear wings carrying vertical tail-light units. The new model's designation appeared on the rear wings and with Borg-Warner automatic transmission available the Series V Gazelle was introduced at £723. The Vogue was priced at £828 at that time.

In September 1964 the Minx modifications of an all-synchromesh gearbox, diaphragm clutch, fully reclining front seats and vertically annotated instruments were included in the Gazelle and a floor-mounted control lever was standardized for automatic versions. At the same time the Mark II Vogue was discontinued, and the following month, at the Earl's Court Motor Show, there appeared both the new Series III Vogue and a Super Imp variant, the Singer Chamois. The new Vogue had the sharper roofline of the Super Minx with a deeper and wider windscreen, wide sloping rear window, reclining front seats, floor automatic control lever and combined door-arm-rest-cum-pulls on the saloon. The Estate had the longitudinal instead of transverse roof ribs of the Super Minx model.

The new Chamois used the standard Imp shell but was more refined and better trimmed, carrying a dummy plated grille of horizontal bars, twin chrome side mouldings and five chrome rubbing strips on top of the engine cover. Heater, overriders, slotted wheel trims, arm-rests, water temperature and oil pressure gauges were all standard, while wood veneer appeared on the fascia and door cappings surmounted by deep crash-padded rolls. Retaining the standard 39 bhp engine, the Singer Chamois was released at £582.

In September 1965 a Mark II Chamois was announced, following a change from automatic to manual choke in May. The new model added padded front and rear parcels shelves, contoured rear seats and larger valves. Mark II plaques appeared on the doors, and price was up by only £8.

At the same time the 1725-cc five main bearing Rootes engine appeared in the Gazelle Series VI and Vogue Series IV machines. The former had a squatter grille flanked by three horizontal bars with rectangular side light/indicator units, locking buttons for vent windows, self-adjusting rear drum brakes and the nicely angled gearlever of the Minx models. The Vogue used a twin-choke Solex 32PAIS carburettor, however, with a cr of 9·2:1 as on the Sunbeam Rapier, while the Gazelle packed a single Zenith 34 IV downdraught carburettor and a cr of 8·4:1. The units produced 85 bhp at 5,500 rpm and 65 bhp at 4,800 rpm respectively. Gearbox ratios were alike on the saloons, only the Vogue Estate being lower geared, and price labels read £757 (Gazelle) and £896 (Vogue saloon).

But in August 1966 the first new-model Vogues began to roll off the production lines, using the standard Minx/Hunter shell and released to the public in October. The new Vogue was distinguishable by its horizontally barred grille incorporating a raised centre section and rectangular headlamps, chrome side strip and appropriate 'Singer' and 'Vogue' lettering. Ventilated Amblair upholstery was used, together with a full-flow ventilation system using rear pillar extractors. The 1725-cc engine was fitted with a Zenith Stromberg 150CDS carburettor. It had a cr of 9·2:1, produced a maximum of 80 bhp gross at 5,000 rpm, and a hefty torque figure of 103 lb ft gross at 3,000 rpm. The all-synchromesh gearbox was used with overdrive on third and top or Borg-Warner 35 automatic transmission options. The price was £911, and meanwhile the Vogue IV Estate was continued, using Solex 32PAIS carburation and producing 91 bhp gross at 'five-five'. This was a remarkably sprightly and economical motor-car for its class, having a maximum speed of about 90 mph, a 0–50 mph time of only 12 sec and returning some 25 mpg.

The Chamois Sport was introduced at the same time with the Sunbeam model's 55 bhp twin Zenith-carburetted engine, bearing suitable 'Sport' badges on the doors and engine compartment. Reclining front seats were standardized, a brake servo added and louvres cut into the engine cover, and the Sport and standard Chamois models ran concurrently. In November the new Gazelle model, again using the Hunter shell, appeared in automatic form only, using the 1725 engine, and Borg-Warner 35 transmission with a central console-mounted control lever. A 1496-cc manual version followed in December, using an all-synchromesh manual gearbox and, with Zenith 150CDS carburation the new Gazelle had 60 bhp net at 4,800 rpm. This was not enough to produce scintillating performance, but it was perfectly sufficient for a comfortable, docile and pleasantly refined family saloon.

In March the following year the old-type Gazelle was discontinued, and in April the Chamois coupé was announced, based on the Hillman Californian fastback Imp, together with a new Hunter-based Vogue Estate, replacing the Series IV Estate. The new Chamois was luxuriously appointed, and joined the Sport model at £665, although it retained the standard 39 bhp engine. The standard Chamois Mark II saloon was selling for only £619 at that time and at these prices the Singer 'Imps' were decidedly attractive buys.

In May the saloon was modified with zero front wheel camber, while the Sport also had this modification in addition to removal of the brake servo from boot to engine compartment. In August it was announced that all models, the three Chamois, two Gazelles and two Vogues, were to continue into 1968 unchanged and then in May 1968 servo-assisted brakes were made optional on the auto and manual Gazelles, and the Vogue models.

For 1969 the range was continued, although prices were up to £705 (Chamois II), £748 (Chamois coupé), £785 (Chamois Sport) – all of which now featured twin headlamps, new seats and more elaborate fascia designs – £937 (Gazelle) and £1,047 (Vogue V saloon). The Vogue Estate was the most expensive model in the range at £1,176 but at this time the Singer marque was in a healthier state than at any time since its incorporation into the Rootes Group. But it was only an example of badge engineering, with no purely Singer models being produced and early in 1970 the range was discontinued in a Chrysler rationalization move.

32 Standard

In 1959 the Standard range consisted of pleasantly solid and attractive saloons. The well-known Eight with its tiny 803-cc engine had been discontinued in July, and so the 948-cc Ten Companion Estate, 1670-cc Ensign and 2088-cc Vanguard saloon models flew the banner into the 'sixties.

The chunky 1-litre model used a four-cylinder push-rod ohv engine in orthodox style, fitted with a single Solex downdraught carburettor and, with an 8:1 cr, producing 37 bhp gross at 5,000 rpm. Transmission included a small 6¼-inch Borg & Beck sdp clutch, and a four-speed gearbox with synchromesh on the upper three ratios. Surprisingly, for a car of such a lowly class, Laycock de Normanville overdrive was optional on top, third and second gears, and there was also a two-pedal version available with Standrive automatic clutch operation, gear selection still being controlled by a central lever. A Hardy Spicer open prop-shaft and hypoid bevel final drive were used, while an unremarkable coil-and-wishbone ifs/semi-elliptic rigid axle rear suspension system was employed. Girling 7-inch drum brakes were fitted, with two leading shoe units at the front, and the steering was Burman or Cam Gears worm-and-nut. The little Companion had a surprisingly complete specification, and sold at £702.

More adventurous was the big Ensign saloon, with an undersquare 1·7-litre engine offered with optional compression ratios of 8:1 or 7:1. This, too, used a Solex downdraught carburettor and produced a gross maximum of 60 bhp at 4,000 rpm. An 8-inch clutch was fitted to cope with this extra power, and higher ratios were used in the four-speed semi-synchromesh gearbox. Nine-inch Lockheed drum brakes were featured, again with the powerful two leading shoe front design, suspension was similar to the Ten, and Burman recirculating ball steering was standard. For £849 this Ensign model, using the medium-sized engine in the large Vignale-styled shell of the Vanguard, offered economical and roomy transport for those who could not aspire to its bigger-engined brother.

At the top of the range stood the Vignale-styled Vanguard, the flowing-line version which had replaced the Phase III car in manual and automatic form in October 1958. The Phase III Estate had been continued, however, and all these variants were powered by a four-cylinder undersquare unit of 2088 cc. With a 7·5:1 cr, and single Solex downdraught carburettor this engine produced only 68 bhp gross at 4,200 rpm. A 9-inch clutch was fitted, and both four-speed and three-speed column-change gearboxes were available, neither with a synchromesh bottom gear. Laycock overdrive was again available on the upper ratios, or an optional full Borg-Warner automatic transmission could be specified. Drum brakes of 10-inch diameter were standard, as was the coil-and-wishbone ifs/semi-elliptic live rear axle suspension. Steering was again by Burman recirculating ball. Prices were £985 for the Vignale saloon and £1,092 for the Phase III Estate.

In January 1960 heater and screen washers were standardized on the Ten, and in September a Mark II Ensign appeared, using longer rear road springs. Then Standard-Triumph released a new six-cylinder Vanguard in October, this using a 1998-cc engine owing more to the Triumph side of the business than to Standard. The original wet liners of the 'four' were discarded in this design, pistons operating directly in the block as with the Herald model. The wet-liner engine had been designed back in the 'forties when cylinder wear was very much a problem, and in the light of modern knowledge their removal saved time, money, weight and size, the new 'six' being only marginally larger overall than the 'four', and amazingly ½ cwt lighter! An 8·0:1 cr was adopted, and with many interesting detail features the new engine used twin Solex B-32 PIH downdraught carburettors. Power output was 80 bhp net at 4,500 rpm, with a peak of 107·5 lb ft torque at 'two-five'.

Externally, the new model was virtually identical to the four-cylinder, but the interior was improved with more luxurious trim and fittings, and three-speed, four-speed, overdrive, manual and Borg-Warner fully automatic transmission options were all offered. An Estate in the Vignale basic style was also available, and prices stood at £1,021, and £1,134 respectively. Top speed was found to be just on 90 mph, an improvement over the four-cylinder model of some 8 mph, while 0–50 mph time was cut back from about 14 sec to under 12. Noise level was commendably low, although so was the ratio of the heavy steering. The 10-inch brakes were powerful and with reduced weight, handling was greatly improved, much of the understeer of the four-cylinder being removed. The interior was comfortable and quite plush without being opulent, and practical without being spartan – the happy compromise that all manufacturers in this class strove for and so few achieved. Fuel consumption was none too impressive at about 24 mpg, but for swift and smooth transport Standard's biggish saloon was very attractive.

From November Burman recirculating-ball steering appeared in the continuing four-cylinder Vanguard, a flush-fitting scuttle air intake replaced the earlier hooded type and longer rear springs were adopted to improve the ride. Four-speed floor-change transmission was standardized, with three-speed and column change to order. The flush intake also appeared on the Ensign.

In January 1961 production of the six-cylinder Estate and automatic saloon commenced. That same month the Ten Companion model was discontinued for the home market and then in July and August the four-cylinder Vignale Vanguard saloon, and the Ensign Estate were deleted completely. Temporarily the Vanguard Six was also produced for export only, between August 1961 and June 1962, when the manual model was reintroduced in the UK. Front disc brakes became available as an option in July.

The STI combine was concentrating more and more on its extremely successful Triumph range of advanced and well-appointed saloon and sports machinery and the very name 'Standard' was a handicap in some markets. Nevertheless, in February 1962 a new Ensign De Luxe saloon and Estate car were released, to meet a demand from disgruntled and enthusiastic original model owners. The four-cylinder engine had been enlarged to 2138 cc, developing 75 bhp net at 4,100 rpm, and the car also used larger and more powerful front drum brakes and was further refined within. In this Ensign De Luxe form, saloon and estate models were both available, priced at £848 and £1,013 respectively. The Vanguard Six saloon and estate models cost £991 and £1,101 at this time.

But as the Triumph badge appeared on an ever-growing range of sports and, more important, saloon cars, the Standards became rather surplus to requirements, and with the design of the new Triumph 2000 saloon, using a development of the 2-litre six-cylinder Standard engine, there was little point in continuing with the division. In May 1963 production of Ensign and Vanguard models ceased, and Standard-Triumph continued with rapid expansion of their other marque, eventually to become part of the most powerful motor manufacturing combine in British industry.

33 Sunbeam

The Sunbeam concern established a solid reputation for producing good-looking sporting saloon cars early on in their career, and in 1960 this Rootes Group company were offering two models, one of them the Rapier saloon of distinctly sporty character, and the other the Alpine two-seater sports car which did not quite, perhaps, aspire to the title so well as its saloon-car sister.

The Rapier had been introduced originally in 1955, and in 1960 was available in Series III form using a 1494-cc ohv engine. This breathed through twin Zenith 36WIA carburettors and, with a high cr of 9·2:1, produced 78 bhp gross at 5,400 rpm. This was transmitted via a Borg & Beck single dry-plate clutch to a pleasant four-speed gearbox with synchromesh on the upper three ratios, and a spiral bevel final drive was fitted. Laycock de Normanville overdrive was a very attractive option on the car, accentuating its true 'Grand Touring' characteristics, and suspension followed usual Rootes practice of coil-and-wishbone ifs with a semi-elliptically sprung live rear axle. Telescopic shock absorbers were used all round, steering was by Burman recirculating ball system, and the stylish and speedy saloon was priced at £985. A convertible model was also available at £1,042, and for 1960 Lockheed 10-$\frac{3}{16}$-inch diameter front disc brakes had been fitted, with powerful 9-inch rear drums.

Introduced in 1959, the two-seat, two-door Sunbeam Alpine sports tourer featured occasional rear seats for two children in comfort or one 'transverse-mounted' adult in acute discomfort, and used an 83·5 bhp gross version of the 1½-litre Rapier engine. Zenith 36WIP2 carburettors were used on this unit, using the same compression ratio, and this was mated to a higher-geared close-ratio gearbox, again with a Laycock overdrive option. A hypoid final drive was used, the live axle still being semi-elliptic suspended, and the classic coil-and-wishbone ifs system was also retained. Steering was again by Burman recirculating ball, and this very handsome and attractive machine, with its stylish downswept nose and unbroken waist line rising to prominent but 'right-looking' tail fins, was reasonably priced at £971.

In September 1960 the Rapier was modified to accept a hypoid final drive, and then in October the Alpine Series II was released, using a high-torque bored-out 1592-cc version of the original engine. Compression ratio had been slightly reduced to a still-high 9·1:1 (an export 8·5:1 version still being available), and a stiffer crankshaft was fitted to deal with the increased output, bhp now being 85·5 gross at 5,000 rpm, while torque was up by some 5 per cent to 94 lb ft at 3,800 rpm. Carburettor choke size was increased from 28 to 30 mm, and a new Borg & Beck clutch was fitted using a hydrolastic self-adjusting slave cylinder. Minor transmission modifications concerned the overdrive switch positioning and gearbox casing, while maintenance was cut by the elimination of eight chassis greasing points. Wider rear springs improved the ride and several minor trim changes and additions were made. The body shell was very rigid and the ride good, but the steering was rather imprecise although helped by neutral handling. Maximum speed was 100 mph, 0–50 time 9·9 sec and consumption about 31 mpg.

In January a handsome Le Mans hard-top conversion by Harrington was introduced, and then in April the Series III Rapier saloons and convertibles were discontinued, to be replaced by the new IIIA cars using a version of the bored-out 1592-cc Alpine unit. The saloon and convertible '1600' unit produced 80·25 bhp gross (75 bhp net) at 4,500 rpm, with 60·8 lb ft torque at 2,250 rpm. Minor interior alterations were also made, and the new models, still with their overdrive option, were up in price to £1,029 (saloon) and £1,087 (convertible). But the gearbox had to be used all the time to keep usable power on tap, the engine becoming rather healthier further up the range, and, while handling was good, the ride was a little bumpy.

In February 1963 the Alpine Series II reached the end of its life, being replaced by the Series III in March. Available in both sports tourer and GT hard-top trim, the new Alpine had the twin Zenith replaced by a compound Solex 32 PA1A carburettor in July, and in this form produced 80·5 bhp at 5,000 rpm combined with torque figures of 93·4 lb ft at 3,500 rpm. The GT model was slightly lower-powered, with 77 bhp and 91 lb ft, but both now had a servo-assisted braking system, diaphragm spring clutch, adjustable steering wheel and foot pedals, fixed front quarter-lights, and a larger boot (fuel tanks being accommodated within the wings and the spare wheel stowed upright behind the rear compartment). The GT hard-top version also had an attractive walnut fascia, hinged rear quarter-lights, a heater and De Luxe trim as standard. The result was a weight increase from 18¾ cwt to 19¼ cwt for the sports tourer and the GT hard-top model weighed 1¼ cwt more, but the open car could still manage 97 mph maximum, took 10 sec to accelerate from 0–50 mph and averaged a surprising 30 mpg.

In October that year the Rapier Series IIIA reached the end of its run, being replaced by the Series IV saloon. This embodied some of the modifications made to the comparable Hillman Minx and Singer Gazelle models from the Rootes stable in having grease nipples eliminated, 15-inch in place of 13-inch road wheels and different gearing. Plated headlight rims replaced the prominent cowls used previously, the front grille was revised with oblong sidelights/flashers in five-bar side grilles, and rubber insert overriders were fitted. A new walnut-veneer fascia was added, fully instrumented as usual, and in addition an adjustable steering wheel, improved front seating and a fully trimmed boot were offered. The twin-choke Solex carburettor from the Alpine was adopted, with larger inlet valves, modified cylinder head and the lightened flywheel which had appeared in later Series III engines. Power was up to 78·5 bhp net at 5,000 rpm, and more torque was developed lower in the rev range with a peak of 91 lb ft at 3,500 rpm. An 8-inch Borg & Beck diaphragm spring clutch was adopted, and softer springs were used all round. The 10·3-inch front discs used on other Rootes models appeared on the Rapier but with servo-assistance, and the price of the new Mark IV, available only as a two-door hardtop saloon, was £876, Laycock overdrive being an optional extra for £51.

In January 1964 the Series III Alpine was discontinued and replaced by the new Series IV model. This used a slightly modified version of the original body shell with cut-down tail fins and an open radiator air intake with just one grille bar carrying a round badge on its centre. Oblong side-light/indicator units resided beneath the headlights and rubber insert over-riders were fitted. Power output was 82 bhp and a Borg-Warner Model 35 automatic transmission option demonstrated the Alpine's evolution from a sports car in 1959 to a fast, comfortable two-seat tourer in 1964.

September saw a new all-synchromesh gearbox being fitted in the Alpine tourer and GT models, a two-speed blower also being standardized on the GT. In October the Rapier faithfully followed its stable-mate in having the all-synchromesh box installed with the same ratios giving 17·6 mph per 1,000 rpm in top gear, and prices at that time stood at £853 (Alpine sports tourer), and £890 Rapier Mark IV, and £914 Alpine GT.

At Le Mans the previous year there had appeared a team of Ford V8-

engined machines, based loosely upon the Alpine, which ran quite well for part of the annual 24 Hours Race. These Sunbeam Tigers were the basis of a road-car produced for export initially and introduced for the home market in March 1965. Apart from the Series IV-type body shell many changes were made to provide a fast, safe and controllable machine, with the 4261-cc Ford V8 engine installed well back in the chassis. With a huge twin-choke carburettor sitting in the Vee, this unit produced 141 bhp at 4,400 rpm, coupled with 258 lb ft torque at a lazy 2,200 rpm, and this drove via a 10-inch single dry plate clutch to a four-speed all-synchromesh Ford gearbox. To take the heavier loadings, suspension and transmission were strengthened and rack-and-pinion steering provided surprisingly light and accurate control, although it suffered from kick-back on poor surfaces, conditions which also made the otherwise comfortable ride deteriorate markedly. But the Tiger was a car which could go along docilely at very low speeds in top and then rush up to 100 mph in under 30 sec, get from 0–50 mph in only 6·8 sec and still return some 20 mpg. The Tiger was, and is, an extremely attractive motor-car both new and second-hand, and sold on introduction at £1,445 in open form, or £1,505 with the GT hard-top.

In September 1965 the Rootes 1725-cc five-bearing engine appeared, and this produced 85 bhp at 5,500 rpm in the Rapier Series V (using a cr of 9·2:1 and a Solex 32 PA1S twin-choke carburettor) and 92·5 bhp on the Alpine Series V, with a twin Zenith-Stromberg 150CD carburettor set-up. 'Rootes 1725' insignia appeared on the cars' front wings and on the Alpine's boot; an alternator replaced the dynamo in both models and the Rapier used an angled gear lever common to the other Rootes 1725-cc saloons. The Rapier also had a twinned exhaust manifold and self-adjusting rear brakes, while the Alpine had additional ventilators, the rear seat carpeted as a luggage space rather than padded for comfort. The automatic option was removed after few customers had taken the bait! Price for the Rapier was up to £908, while the Alpine stood at £878. Performance figures were, as usual, impressive for the class the Rapier represented, maximum speed being 95 mph, 0–50 mph time under 10 sec and fuel consumption figure about 26 mpg. The Alpine was quicker, but just as comfortable in GT form, with a flat-out speed of 98 mph, 0–50 acceleration time of 9 sec and, with its twin carburettor arrangement and sleeker shape, an economy of about 30 mpg.

In September 1966 reversing lamps were introduced as standard on the further refined Alpine and, despite Chrysler's ever-growing interest in the Group, the Tiger retained its smooth Ford V8 engine. But in October a new Sunbeam model appeared, the first all-new one since the Alpine in July 1959 (and even this was a version of the Hillman Imp, fully described in the Hillman chapter and in this guise being dubbed the Sunbeam Imp Sport). Twin Zenith-Stromberg 125CD side-draught carburettors were used on a 10:1 cr version of the 875-cc light alloy engine, and it produced a healthy 51 bhp net at 6,100 rpm. The Girling drum brakes were servo-assisted, and externally the car was distinguishable by a single horizontal bar and motif on the nose, 'Imp Sport' badges on doors and engine compartment, and louvres in the engine cover. In May 1967 front wheel camber was reduced to zero and the brake servo was shifted to the engine compartment to leave more room in the front boot.

Then, in October, the Sunbeam version of the low-roof-line fastback Hillman Californian was announced, dubbed the Sunbeam Stiletto. This was an exceedingly attractive and luxuriously trimmed little car, using the 51-bhp Imp Sport engine, combined with its rally-proved strengthened suspension, zero camber front wheels and servo brakes, and it featured a black Vinyl-covered roof, dual small-diameter headlamps, a padded fascia with circular instruments, three-spoke, leather-rimmed steering wheel and Amblair ventilated upholstery. Radial ply tyres were standard on this model. Reclining front seats were almost Continental in their high standard of support and comfort, but, in common with the other fast-back Imp variants, rear seat head- and leg-room were a little limited. With its superbly quick and direct gear-change and good handling qualities – despite a marked inclination to wander in cross-winds – this Stiletto was the most expensive car in the Imp range at £726. Top speed was over 88 mph, and the little car could scuttle from 0–50 mph in only 10 sec. All this combined with a still astonishing 35 mpg to complete a very pleasant pair of Sunbeam small cars.

At the same time as the Stiletto's debut, an all-new Rapier appeared, clad in a decidedly bizarre-looking pillarless two-door four-seat body. Although the new shell was considerably larger than the original Rapier, the roof-line was $2\frac{1}{4}$ inches lower, glass area was enormous and weight was cut by about 1 cwt. In many respects the Rapier closely followed the Humber Sceptre model, using a similar two-piece prop-shaft, strut-type ifs, steering and brakes. But apart from the underframe and the lower tail panel, the shell was built up from pressings peculiar to this model alone, and with pillarless construction, all windows winding down complete to leave an open-sided roof panel carrying enormous front and rear screens, most of the car's strength being derived from below the waistline. Dual headlamps were set in a horizontal grille of aluminium bars, while the rear quarter pillars were in black Vinyl with emblems and 'Rapier' capital lettering. The rear lights were grouped in vertical clusters and a matt fascia was fitted with ventilation vents at either end, extractors being placed beneath the rear screen.

The $9.2:1$ cr, twin Zenith 150CDS-carburetted 1725-cc engine was used, producing 88 bhp net (94 gross) at 5,200 rpm. Borg-Warner automatic transmission was optional with Laycock overdrive on third and top manual gears as standard. The result was a lavishly equipped and extremely comfortable motor-car, with a top speed of about 27 mpg. As with other Rootes models, overdrive was docile and responsive, its Burman recirculating ball steering system being heavy at parking speeds but lightening considerably on the open road. The ride was good, noise level was commendably low and apart from its odd appearance – which just didn't grow on the public as they said it would – the new machine was well up to the standards set by the earlier car.

In November the Alpine had the self-adjusting rear brake mechanism removed – a system which seldom seems to have worked out well on British production cars – and then in November 1968 both Alpine variants – the sports tourer and GT hard-top – were discontinued. Tiger production had sadly ceased in June 1967, and Sunbeam had now bowed out of the sports car market entirely, concentrating purely on well-finished, quick but not really sporting saloon cars instead.

In 1968, the release of the 1969 models showed the year-old Rapier, the Imp Sport and the Stiletto to be essentially unchanged, although the Imps did have new seats and instrument panels as adopted by the other Rootes marques and the Sport lost its reclining seats and became the cheaper Singer Chamois Sport model. But a high-performance 'prestige' version of the Rapier was introduced, titled the Rapier H120. This used a Holbay-developed version of the twin-carb 1725-cc engine, the tuning company having made a good reputation for itself with down-draught Ford-based Formula 3 racing engines. The result was an engine using Holbay-developed cylinder head and manifolding with Rootes' own camshaft, two Weber 40DCOE twin-choke carburettors replacing the twin Strombergs of the standard car. Flat-top pistons were used in place of the slightly dished standard ones, cr rising to 9·6:1, and with reshaped ports, balanced combustion chambers and modified exhaust valves, double springs and lightweight tubular push-rods, power output was 105 bhp net at 5,200 rpm. Final drive ratio was up from 4·22 to 3·89:1 and with no automatic option the H120 had the Alpine close-ratio all-synchromesh gearbox with overdrive on top and third. Externally a vestigial spoiler appeared, formed into the boot-lid, while the grille mesh was matt black and side stripes appeared with suitable badges and insignia. Top speed was close on 107 mph, 0–50 time down to under 8 sec and fuel consumption not bad for such performance at about 27 mpg. The wider section tyres improved road-holding slightly but made the steering even heavier, though it was still a comfortable and even quicker form of transport. It was, however, rather expensive at £1,634, but had a certain distinction all of its own.

34 Tornado

Tornado Cars Ltd of Rickmansworth were one of the many small but enthusiastic small-quantity GT car manufacturers in business at the start of the 'sixties; their story is in several ways typical of some of their contemporaries.

Tornado entered the decade with two Typhoon models; two- and four-seater open and closed sporting cars which were sold in kit form only. In August 1960 two new models were announced, the 997-cc 105E Ford-powered Tempest and the 2-litre Triumph TR3-engined Thunderbolt. Both were available as complete fully assembled cars or in component form, and again both open and closed, two- and four-seater variants were available.

The basis of the Tempest was a 3-inch tubular ladder-frame with the glass-fibre body shell supported on channel outriggers and side frames. Coil-and-wishbone ifs with rack-and-pinion steering was standard, while at the rear a live axle was coil-sprung and located by lower radius arms, an inclined upper torque reaction link and a Panhard rod. The two-seat models had a wheelbase of 7 feet 2 inches, while that of the four-seaters was 14 inches longer. Four full seats were provided in the open-style body, but the closed shell restricted the rear seats to occasional use only. The shell itself was a study in curves – too many of these – with high humped wings front and rear giving a rather broken-backed look. Standard or tuned 105E Ford engines were available, with BMC A-Series and Standard-Triumph units as optional equipment. Turning the scales at only 9¾ and 10½ cwt respectively, the two- and four-seat Tempests were in the same power/weight ratio class as contemporaries such as the Marcos. Kit prices were £595 and £655 (two-/four-seaters), and rose expensively to £1,167 and £1,250 complete.

The Thunderbolt was similarly styled and based on a similar chassis frame, but the tracks, front and rear, were 2 inches wider. (Wheelbase lengths were the same as those for the two Tempest models.) Other differences included larger and wider drum brakes, and a 15- instead of 7-gallon fuel tank. The standard-tune TR3 engine was supplemented by a Ford Consul unit in union with a Moss gearbox, but the Triumph engine/gearbox/overdrive package would seem to have been preferable. Thunderbolt prices were £795 and £855 (two-/four-seaters) in kit form, and £1,500 and £1,665 complete. A GT hard-top of a rather ungainly domed shape was available for the two-seater model.

Tornados appeared widely in club competition, but the company was obviously catering to the widest possible enthusiast market with its myriad variants, and it produced a near-estate model in September 1960. This unlikely looking machine was dubbed the Sportsbrake, and the shell was available in Tempest, Typhoon and Thunderbolt form. It retained the basic curvilinear shape below the waistline, while a gently arched roof extended from the wrap-round windscreen to the tail, which incorporated a top-hinged tail door and rear screen. Long curved side windows were let into the superstructure sides. This was £49 more than the basic models, and effectively was an inexpensive, yet quite quick, utility car with that important touch of individuality. The whole range was rather over-priced, however.

The basically unhappy looks of these early models can hardly have been in their favour, and were not perpetuated in an all-new model announced by the Rickmansworth concern – the Tornado Talisman. Much more attractive – not unlike a Lancia GT of the 'fifties – the new model was small, with a straight waistline from the hooded headlamps to the rear edge of the wide-opening doors, curving down gently into unobtrusive tail fins. A divided nostril air intake appeared in the attractively pointed nose, and with a wrap-round screen and large side windows, the roof-line sloped gracefully to the tail, carrying a high-mounted and quite steeply raked windscreen.

The result was exceptionally well-balanced and attractive, and was fitted to the backbone chassis of 3-inch diameter 16 swg tubing, the two main backbone longerons being only 1 foot apart. Six tubular cross-members formed the ladder frame, four outriggers with channel-section side pieces carrying the one-piece body on rubber mountings. Unequal length wishbone suspension was used all-round with co-axial coil spring/damper units front and rear. Two trailing links and the fixed-length drive shafts completed rear wheel location and Girling 9-inch diameter disc brakes were used at the front with 7-inch rear drums. With rack-and-pinion steering the Talisman was interesting in incorporating a collapsible steering column (from the Triumph

Herald) to minimize accident injury risk. A Cosworth-Ford 1340-cc Classic engine and transmission was standard, producing around 75 bhp from its twin-Weber carburettors. Optional final drive ratios of 4·1 and 4·5:1 were offered, and with a useful and illuminated boot capacity, a well-instrumented dash panel, two-speed screen wipers and washers as standard, the new model was priced at £1,299 on release.

The 11·3-cwt vehicle was very much a driver's motor-car, accelerating well from 0–50 mph in just over 7 sec, and touching 102 mph flat-out. Handling was firm and responsive, the Talisman being stable and pretty neutral until the tail let go and slid out in a gentle and easily controlled oversteer. Turning circle for this sporting four-seater was tiny, and its Cosworth-tuned engine not uneconomical at about 25 mpg.

In May 1962, two Talisman versions were announced; from then on it was available in GT or Touring form. The GT was virtually as originally released, but now featured a Smiths heater system as standard. Basic price was raised slightly to £915, but dropped overall to £1,259 with tax, while the Touring variant was fitted with the standard 1340-cc Ford engine, using a single Zenith carburettor but the company's own four-branch exhaust manifold. This, it was claimed, increased output from standard Ford saloon figures to 55 bhp, and without heater, tachometer, and dual-speed wipers, price was fixed at £1,142 for what was still a very pleasant and attractive little four-seater. At the same time Talisman kits were offered at £875 (GT) and £795 (Touring), and with a production rate of two to three cars a week delivery was quoted as being six to eight weeks.

During this time Colin Hextall and Bill Woodhouse in the company's club-racing Talismans were cleaning up in their classes and providing excellent publicity, and when Ford released their 1498-cc engine the Talisman was fitted with a tuned version producing some 85 bhp in GT trim, or 60 bhp in Touring tune.

But the Talisman in this form was to be the Rickmansworth company's last fling, and, quietly and unreported, they faded from the scene, production ceasing before the middle of the decade that they had entered so enthusiastically.

35 Triumph

In the 1950s the Triumph concern emerged as a major sports car manufacturer, with cars well in the forefront of technical innovation. The TR2, for example, was the first British production car to have disc brakes fitted as standard. Widespread competition success confirmed the image of the sporting Triumph.

In 1960 the company were offering only two basic models, the TR3A sports and the small 1-litre Herald saloon which was interesting in that it featured all-independent suspension at a time when ifs with a live rear axle was virtually universal in vehicles of this class.

The TR3A was a high-performance development of the earlier TR3, having a 100-bhp 1991-cc four-cylinder engine breathing through twin SU semi-downdraught carburettors. Transmission was via a 9-inch single dry plate Borg & Beck clutch to a four-speed gearbox, with optional overdrive and synchromesh on all but first gear. Girling 11-inch front discs were standard, with broad 9-inch diameter drums at the rear, and coil spring ifs was used with a half-elliptic suspended live rear axle. The car was quick, and firmly suspended; a true sports car with somewhat 'he-man' characteristics. The body was classically Triumph, a squared-off shell with front wing styling sloping down along the bonnet sides across high doors to a raised and chunky tail. Both convertible and hard-top versions were available, and in 1960 they cost £991 and £1,040 respectively. They both offered considerable performance potential, and as genuine 'sports' cars were great fun to drive.

The little Herald saloon was available in two versions; a two-door four-seat saloon, and a two-door two-seat coupé. It was styled by Michelotti in Italy and had a pert compact appearance, with small tail fins and an angular roof line. A double-backbone chassis was used with body panels bolted to it, while a front-hinged all-enveloping bonnet gave first-rate access to the 948-cc four-cylinder engine which had appeared in original form in the old Standard 8. The unit gave 34·5 bhp at 4,500 rpm, cr was 8:1 and a single Solex downdraught carburettor was fitted. The coupé had a high-output unit, with a cr of 8·5:1 and twin SU carburettors, but this only produced 45 bhp at 5,800 rmp.

A 6¾-inch Borg & Beck sdp clutch was used, feeding a four-speed gearbox, with synchromesh on the upper three ratios. Alford & Alder rack-and-pinion steering was fitted, and the Herald models had a uniquely tight turning circle of 25 feet, making them incredibly manoeuvrable and easy to park. Suspension was the usual coil-spring-and-wishbone ifs, but an independent rear end used swing axles and a transverse leaf spring. The effect of this was to give the little Herald quite good general handling properties, but when it was pushed too far loss of adhesion was sudden. As the nose dropped, the rear-wheels assumed exaggerated positive camber and the up-edged tyres lost their grip. Prices of the all-independent Heralds were reasonable at £702 for the saloon and £730 for the coupé.

A twin-carburettor saloon was introduced in September 1959, and the convertible – initially for export only – was announced in March 1960. In June 1960 styling ridges were applied to the quarter panel behind the fixed-head coupé's side windows, and in August the convertible became available on the home market at £766.

The Triumph design team responsible for this range consisted of Messrs H. G. Webster, C. Wigginton, A. E. Ballard and N. Rose. (On the styling side, Michelotti were to continue to collaborate very successfully with Standard-Triumph in coming years.)

In February 1961, the larger-engined Herald 1200 was first produced, to be announced in April. It used a large-bore 1147-cc version of the 1-litre power unit, and had 'Herald' lettering above the grille with '1200' insignia on the boot. An attractive walnut veneer fascia was introduced, while a lockable glove box, white rubber bumpers, improved seats with a fixed rear seat squab and a heater were all standardized. Saloon, fixed-head coupé and convertible models were available.

Meanwhile, the 1-litre saloon had demonstrated a maximum speed of about 71 mph and an overall consumption of 37 mpg, while the twin-carburettor coupé was good for 76 mph and 39 mpg, in the latter respect doubtless aided by its better shape. Meanwhile the TR3A with overdrive was capable of achieving 110 mph, and still managed as much as 34 mpg – these Triumphs really were economical.

With the announcement of the 1200, the 1-litre Herald became the economy Herald S model, and in May a handsome estate car version of the 1200 was announced. In March, however, the short-lived 948-cc saloon had been discontinued, and in June it was to be followed by the twin-carburettor model, the fixed-head coupé and the convertible. In October only the 1-litre Herald S survived, running alongside the 1200s, and front disc brakes became available as an optional extra common to both 1-litre and 1200 models.

In September, when over 80,000 TR3s had been built, came the long-awaited debut of a new Triumph sports car, the TR4, initially released for export only. The new model, with its typically square-cut and chunky Michelotti body, used a four-cylinder 2138-cc engine producing 105 bhp gross at 4,600 rpm. A four-speed all-synchromesh gearbox was fitted, while coil spring ifs and a half-elliptic rear end were retained. Apart from its styling, and these mechanical aspects, the new car was very similar to the TR3, although the latter had a narrower chassis. The TR4 was reasonably priced at £1,095 in open and £1,146 in closed forms, and an interesting innovation was the introduction of a Surrey top, the roof panel detaching to leave a fixed rear screen still in place. Wind-up side windows completed cockpit protection.

The new model had a 0–50 mph time of just over 7 sec, covered the standing quarter mile in 17·5 sec, and had a top speed of 110 mph. Again a front-hinged bonnet was used, giving easy access to the engine and front suspension.

There were now the five versions of the Herald (1200 saloon, coupé, convertible and estate, and the 1-litre Herald S) being built in company with the newly released and much in demand TR4; the TR3 was still being built to fulfil export orders, until it was discontinued in April 1962.

Then, in May, the new Triumph Vitesse was announced, similar to the Herald but having a six-cylinder 1596-cc underbored Standard Vanguard engine. Front disc brakes were fitted as standard, while the Herald-type front-hinged bonnet had angular flared wings carrying diagonally mounted dual headlamps. Aluminium bumpers further distinguished the car, together with 'Vitesse' script insignia. The six-cylinder engine gave 70 bhp at 5,000 rpm, and the gearbox, with synchromesh on the top three ratios only, was available with overdrive. The Herald's 25-foot turning circle was also retained. But the basic Herald shell was very cramped for rear-seat passengers' legs, and the whole family were very close to being 2+2 cars rather than true four-seaters.

The company was meanwhile extending its range still further, with the announcement in October of a small brother to the TR4 sports. Named the Spitfire 4, this was an 1147-cc machine developed from the Herald. It used the same backbone of twin box-section members running the length of the car, splaying out fore and aft to accept engine and suspension. The Herald chassis also had an outrigger system to which the body was bolted, but the new sports car's Michelotti-styled shell, with its more slender version of the Herald-type nose, recessed headlights and barrel sides, was an all-welded structure with its own sills and transverse stiffeners (thus it did not need strengthening outriggers). Apart from softer springing for the lighter car, suspension was identical to the Herald, with unequal length wishbones and inclined coil springs at the front and a transverse leaf spring with swing axles and radius arms at the rear.

Power came from a twin SU HS2-carburetted high-compression version of the Herald 1200 engine, turning out 63 bhp at 5,750 rpm, an increase of more than 50 per cent over standard tune. The rack-and-pinion steering gave a turning circle of only 24 feet, while the standard Herald four-speed remote change transmission was fitted, still with sychromesh on all but first.

The new car was instantly in demand. It was small, sleek and attractive, handled well up to the point of no return, and was quick for its size with a maximum speed of 93 mph and 0–50 mph acceleration in 12 sec. Consumption was around 35 mpg, and price was attractive at £729.

A further addition was made to the Herald range in March 1963, production of the new 12/50 model having commenced the previous December. Externally the standard skylight sun-roof identified the new type, while a heater and front disc brakes were also standard. The 1147-cc engine had a high-compression head (cr of 8·5 instead of 8·0:1) and produced 51 bhp at 5,200 rpm as opposed to 39 at 4,500 in standard tune. The 12/50 was also just over $\frac{1}{2}$ cwt heavier than the 1200, but had a lot to offer as a small 'luxury' family saloon, being very well finished, if still lacking in rear-seat leg-room. The price of the 12/50 was £635. The sun-roof, incidentally, also became optional on the Vitesse from March.

In September 1963 overdrive and a hard-top became available as options for the best-selling Spitfire, and the Vitesse saloon and convertible were modified with a restyled fascia carrying additional tachometer and temperature gauges. By then bigger news was already a month old, the company having extended its operations into the medium saloon-car market with the introduction of the Triumph 2000, announced in August.

This model was almost completely new, only the 1998-cc six-cylinder engine having been inherited, via the Vitesse, from the Standard Vanguard. Mr Harry G. Webster, Standard-Triumph's Director of Engineering, had produced a unitary construction body shell which gained its strength from longitudinal and transverse box-section sills, giving a very rigid centre section despite the use of four doors, mated with robust engine-bay and boot structures. All-independent suspension was arranged to concentrate its loads into this centre section rather than at the shell's extremities. The ifs system was unusual in having single forged lower links braced by a rearward mounting channel section radius rod, both carried in large rubber bushes. Ford-like Macpherson struts, with co-axial springs and rack-and-pinion steering completed the system. At the rear two semi-trailing triangular arms of cast aluminium alloy located the wheels, while coil-springs picked-up in depressions formed in the arms and cups built into the body shell. Telescopic dampers were mounted aft of the axle line independent of the coil springs to operate at maximum arm movement. The whole assembly, complete with cross-members and the differential, was rubber-mounted to the shell and could be removed in unit.

The six-cylinder engine was tuned to produce 90 bhp as opposed to its original 80, breathing through twin Stromberg 1·50CD carburettors fed from a 14-gallon long-range tank. The engine was installed at an inclination of 8 degrees to the right to provide room for the ancillaries, while transmission was via a Laycock diaphragm-spring clutch to the all-synchromesh TR4 gearbox (although now using different gear ratios). A Lockheed disc/drum braking system incorporated a vacuum servo, and extras included Laycock de Normanville overdrive on third and top gears, and Borg-Warner Model 35 fully-automatic transmission.

The styling, again by Michelotti, was clean and graceful, a lip to the rear edge of the roof being reminiscent of the Herald, while dual headlights in cut-outs above the full-width horizontal slatted grille gave an aggressive look. The interior was luxuriously equipped, even with fully reclining front bucket seats, while boot space was modest but considered sufficient. Engineer Webster's conception had been to produce a car striking a good balance between performance and economy, with comfortable accommodation for four or five, and an overall size conducive to manœuvrability and ease of parking. The new car had a top speed of 93 mph, accelerated from 0–50 mph in 10·9 sec and managed about 29 mpg touring. The original price was £1,087, and by 1969 over 100,000 had been produced.

The Herald S was discontinued in January 1964, having been the cheapest Triumph on the market for nearly three years (1-litre Herald production in that time totalling 69,578). Slight modifications to the 2000 resulted in the redistribution of some controls, the fitting of electric screen washers, a parcels shelf in front of the driver, anti-vibration bush around the gearlever and altered front disc pad areas to eliminate squeal.

In October the Herald 1200 coupé was deleted. It had never been an attractive machine and a mere 1,633 were produced. Then the Spitfire Mark I was deleted in December, being replaced by the improved Mark II model which was announced in March 1965. Engine output was up from 63 to 67 bhp with the addition of a four-branch exhaust manifold, and a diaphragm clutch was fitted. Internally upholstery was deeper, carpet kick pads, black leathercloth fascia and door cappings (replacing the ugly bare paintwork of the Mark I) were adopted, while outwardly five horizontal grille bars were used and 'Mark II' emblems appeared on the boot.

At the same time the TR4A sports car was announced, being the first all-independent model in the TR range. Externally the grille bars were wider spaced, sidelights joined repeater indicators in chromed housings on the wings, stainless steel beading extended from them to the rear edges of the doors, and 'TR4A' emblems sprouted. A wood-veneer fascia was fitted and the handbrake dropped down between the seats. A four-branch exhaust with twin down-pipes was added, and with the better breathing induction system power output was up to 104 bhp at 4,700 rpm. But top speed was down slightly in this heavier model, standing at 108 mph with a 0–50 mph time of 8·4 sec. Overall fuel consumption was still excellent at 30 mpg, however.

The rear end of the TR4 chassis had to be entirely redesigned to accept the Triumph 2000 irs system used, and this provided both a more comfortable ride and less 'hoppy' road holding. A special TR4A version retaining the rigid live axle hung on semi-elliptics continued to be produced for export, featuring the new trim changes and more powerful engine. But at that time, in its four production years, 40,300 live axle TR4s had been built. The new TR4A was priced at £968 on release.

In July 1965 the Vitesse 'six' was modified with Stromberg 1·50CD carburettors replacing the SUs previously used, and then in September came an exciting development when Triumph introduced a front-wheel drive saloon.

This new model, the 1300, was based quite closely upon the 2000, Michelotti having skilfully shrunk the body to suit a wheelbase 9½ inches shorter. Structurally, the new shell was similar to the 2000, and its irs system was almost identical to the 2000/TR4A arrangement. In true 2000 fashion the interior was plush and comfortable, equipment included very deep front seats tilting to give instant height and rake adjustment, while the steering wheel position was also adjustable. Wheelbase was kept as long as possible to provide maximum space inside and the passenger compartment was only about 1½ inches shorter than that of the 2000.

The design team, including Mr A. E. Bollard and Mr D. E. Eley in addition to Messrs Webster and Michelotti, had developed a Standard-Triumph wartime patent for the fwd system used. This had been for a sump transmission to be used in the Bug parachute vehicle. The four-speed all-synchromesh gearbox was mounted below the normal clutch/flywheel assembly of the longitudinally-mounted engine, driving forward beneath the block with an integral pinion and gearbox output shaft in the final drive. The result was a heavy but very directly-controlled unit with low centre of gravity, driving large 13-inch wheels through double-jointed shafts. The Herald 1147-cc engine was bored out to 1296-cc, given a four-port de-siamesed head and brought up to 61 bhp specification before having the new transmission added.

The front-wheel drive 1300 was impressively well finished, and fairly quiet, although gearlever movement was considerable. There was a fair amount of roll but the ride was good and the car was very stable. The new engine pushed it along at 83 mph, from 0–50 mph in just over 13 sec and with an overall fuel consumption of about 26 mpg – well down on its more modestly engineered brethren.

In the following month the estate car version of the 2000 appeared, with the roof-line curved down in a pleasing sweep to meet a neatly chopped-off tail. The large tail-gate opened upwards and the car was only 1 cwt heavier than its saloon predecessor. Prices of the new models were £797 for the 1300 and £1,373 for the 2000 Estate.

In November 1965 a horn ring replaced the bar on the 2000s, and in January 1966 the Herald 1200s appeared with aluminium non-rust silencers fitted, soon followed by diaphragm clutches as standard. In June the exhaust system of the TR4A was modified. The first 1967 2000s were produced in August, to be announced in October; these had black rubber overrider inserts, full-flow ventilation with extractor ducts over the saloon's rear window and beneath it in the Estate's tail-gate, and with heater controls on top of a walnut veneer centre console. Perforated leather seats were fitted and an ashtray and air vents occupied the fascia centre. In September a spate of changes saw the Herald 12/50 lose its '12/50' wing badges, and in the Vitesse the 1596-cc engine was replaced by the 1998-cc 2000 unit, the model thus becoming the 'Vitesse 2-litre'. New emblems appeared in the grille and on the tail, while a three-spoke leather-rimmed steering wheel, reversing light, larger diaphragm clutch and bigger brakes were also standardized.

The company had run Spitfire fast-back models in the Le Mans 24-Hours race with some success, and in October 1966 a similarly-styled shell appeared in the new GT6, using the 1998-cc six-cylinder engine once again mounted in the Spitfire backbone chassis. A large power-bulge in the bonnet gave clearance over the 95 bhp twin Stromberg 1·50 CD-carburetted engine, while a non-divided grille also aided frontal recognition. The fast-back styling included small quarter windows behind the doors, but broad quarter pillars produced large blind spots. The rear screen was let into an opening tail-gate above a broad parcels shelf and luggage area, and the price was £883. This new GT6 combined a claimed top speed of 107 mph with a 0–50 mph time of 7·8 sec. Unfortunately the GT6 retained the Herald-based swing axle suspension of the Spitfire and this gave rise to a car whose limit was very marked, and which, with its rear track changing over road excrescences, tended to run in a 'straight line' as though it had a hinge in the middle. The original GT6 was not a very good motor-car from such an otherwise impressive stable.

The Spitfire evolved further in January 1967, when the 1296-cc engine used in the 1300 model was fitted, albeit with a conventional transmission and rear-wheel drive. The folding hood became an integral non-removable fitting, and the front bumper was raised to fit right in front of the undivided radiator air intake, rubber inserts fitting into the overriders. The rear bumper, without overriders, was similarly raised, reversing lights were standardized, a veneer fascia was added and the company badge on the bonnet deleted. With twin SU HS2 carburettors, and a cr of 9:1, this new engine gave 70 bhp net at 6,000 rpm and the Spitfire Mark III thus produced had a top speed of 95 mph, accelerated from 0–50 mph in 10·1 sec, and could still average around 36 mpg – still good value for £717.

In August 1967 the Herald 1200 convertible and estate and 12/50 were discontinued, and replaced by the 1296-cc-engined 13/60 model. The compact Herald saloons had long been the mainstay of Standard-Triumph production, and on their deletion 55,400 12/50s had been produced, together with 50,982 1200 convertibles and estates.

Their replacement retained the pert Michelotti styling from 1959, but with the flared frontal line to the wings used on the Vitesse, and carrying single headlamps flanking a horizontally barred grille. Instruments were grouped in two dials on the fascia, with control switches on a recessed panel in the centre, a combined washer/wiper switch on right and an ashtray on top. Front disc brakes, heater and washers were all standard, while a sun-roof on the saloon was optional. Convertible and estate versions were also offered, prices ranging from £700 for the saloon, £755 for the convertible, to £774 for the estate.

With a cr of 8·5:1 and just one side-draught Stromberg carburettor, the engine in these models produced 61 bhp at 5,000 rpm. This was as in the standard 1300, but whereas the front-wheel drive saloon weighed 18 cwt, the conventional 13/60 model was just under 17 cwt. The result was a 0–50 mph time of 11·3 sec as opposed to the 13·2 sec achieved by the 1300, although the maximum speed of 82 mph was a fraction slower. Fuel consumption was about the same, but probably for aerodynamic reasons was worse than that of the twin-carburettor Spitfire Mark 3 using a tuned version of the same engine.

A logical move now was to produce a high-performance version of the more modern 1300 design, and so at the same time the 1300TC was released, using a 75 bhp version of the Spitfire engine, and introducing a brake servo. 'TC' badges in Rover style appeared on the wings, and the new version touched 90 mph flat out, 0–50 time was down to 10·5 sec and fuel consumption was again – strangely – improved at about 30 mpg. At £874, an increase of only £39 at the time, this was very worth while. The Herald 1200 saloon was retained at £627.

The final model was a revision of the TR4A, the main feature being the standardization of a petrol injection engine for the first time in a British production car. This TR5 PI used a 2498-cc six-cylinder engine in place of the trusty old 'four'. This had a cr of 9·5:1, and with Lucas electronic fuel injection produced 150 bhp at 5,500 rpm, with 164·1 lb ft torque at 3,500 rpm. Roadster and hard-top coupé versions were available, with stiffer rear suspension, larger power brakes with a fail-safe device, and an improved interior. This featured a non-reflective wooden fascia with round face-level air vents at each end, rocker control switches, Ambla upholstery and a very taut and flap-free weather-proof fitted hood. An offset 'TR5' badge on the bonnet and '2500' insignia on the rear wings above repeater flashers betrayed the new car's identity and with overdrive an optional extra, the new TR had a top speed of about 118 mph and accelerated from 0–50 mph in only 7 sec. Fuel consumption was fairly low at 20 mpg. The open version was priced at £1,212, the hard-top costing an extra £43.

The TR4A was discontinued in August 1968 when 28,500 had been built, and the company's final models of the decade began to appear in the following month. The GT6 Mark II was the first, its handling deficiencies being largely overcome by the adoption of a reversed lower wishbone at the rear, using the transverse leaf spring as an upper link to both spring the wheels and give them almost parallel vertical movement (rubber-doughnut universal joints in the drive shafts helped to eradicate the huge camber changes resulting from the original swing axle layout). Flexibly mounted adjustable radius arms provided fore-and-aft location. Externally the Mark II GT6 could be distinguished by its raised bumper, blanketing the radiator air intake in Spitfire Mark III style. Handling was vastly improved, and the GT6 became pleasantly fast and safe, although that large rear-quarter blind spot remained. Price was £1,125, and by March 1969 4,399 had already been produced.

A similarly modified irs system, only the dampers being different, was also adopted for the Vitesse Mark II. The power output of the 2-litre 'six' was raised to 104 bhp at 5,300 rpm, with the adoption of a TR-type cylinder head giving longer ram-action ports, and a new camshaft profile. At £951 for the saloon and £998 for the convertible this was still the cheapest six-cylinder car on the home market. Top speed was up to 101 mph, and 0–50 mph time was only 8·2 sec. The six was not too economical at 26 mpg, but still very competitive for its size. New 'sculptured' wheels were an external sign of the times, being used on both the Vitesse and the GT6.

Another new model to use them was the 2·5 PI saloon, which had a detuned 132 bhp version of the Lucas-injected TR5 PI engine. With a four-speed manual gearbox as standard, and overdrive or full Borg-Warner automatic transmission as options, the new car proved extremely good – very smooth and quiet, with a lively response to the throttle and good handling capabilities. It had a maximum of 108 mph, a 0–50 mph time of 7·5 sec and managed about 20 mpg. The price of this true 'grand touring' car was £1,450. For less sporting motorists the standard 2000 model continued in production.

In January 1969 the rebodied TR6 appeared, using the same inner body structure as the TR5 but with new external panels styled by Ghia. The new body featured a shallow full-width oval air intake and a sharply cut-off tail, and was a great improvement over the original TR4-type styling. The tail allowed an increase in the size of the boot while a zipping rear window in the hood was a useful hot-weather feature. A new three-spoke padded steering wheel was fitted, and everything inside was matt finished to decrease reflective glare. All details complied in full with US safety regulations, while the 150 bhp Lucas-injected engine was as before. The pressure pump in this system had earlier been moved from under the bonnet to a cooler mounting in the tail which prevented fuel vaporization at embarrasing moments. Minor alterations to the suspension killed a tendency to transfer from understeering stability to oversteering brinkmanship when lifting off in a corner – a front anti-roll bar causing a 1-inch track increase. Weight was up slightly from 20¼ cwt to 21½ cwt but the better shape maintained the top speed of 117 mph plus, while 100 mph cruising represented a mere 3,860 rpm in overdrive top.

Some 3,100 TR5 PIs had been built when the TR6 was released, in addition to 8,594 normally carburetted export models. At the time of writing 3,720 TR6s had been built, together with 112,274 of the evergreen Herald 1200s, 96,140 1300s (including TCs), 2,609 2·5 PI saloons, 106,793 2000s and 2,398 Vitesse Mark IIs. The Spitfire Mark III had proved a most successful sports car export with 37,321 built to date, and with more models in the range than ever before, the 'sixties ended with Triumph having reached a new height of production in terms of advanced and sophisticated machinery. Few other companies in the British industry can match their record of growth and development.

36 Turner

Jack Turner's small company was based at Pendeford Airfield, Wolverhampton and produced a range of small sports cars based on proprietary components. These achieved considerable popularity in the late 'fifties and early 'sixties, being particularly successful among the club-racing fraternity.

137

In 1960 the works offered a model with a choice of tuned 948-cc Austin or 1097-cc Coventry Climax engines. These were fitted in an orthodox chassis frame using twin tubes as a main structural member. Coil-and-wishbone independent front suspension came from the A35, while the rear axle, borrowed from the same source, was sprung by twin laminated torsion bars and located by twin radius arms, a torque reaction link and Panhard rod. Rack-and-pinion steering was used, and the machine was clad in a reasonably well made Sprite-like glass fibre body shell, with a small two-seat cockpit and thrust-forward almost full-width radiator 'mouth'. Girling 8-inch drum brakes were standard on the basic 948-cc model with $8\frac{9}{16}$-inch front discs as an optional extra.

Weather protection took the form of rigidly-framed side-screens and a well-designed and simple to erect removable hood. Other good features were the sizeable boot (accessible through a locking boot lid), a comfortable driving position (once the bolt-down adjustment had been set), and comprehensive instrumentation. Poor points were the general lack of trim within the cockpit, a difficult-to-reach handbrake on the far side of the transmission tunnel from the driver, and the installation of the fuel filler within the boot.

In all, this was a light and agile little car, its well-located rear axle and well-balanced cornering characteristics making it more than a match for the comparable Mark I Sprite. With the Climax engine installed the Turner was considerably faster too. A representative yardstick of its performance was given by the model with a tuned 948-cc engine modified by Alexander Autos and Marine Ltd, distributors for South-Eastern England. (They added a light-alloy cylinder head with twin $1\frac{1}{2}$-inch SU carburettors in place of the standard $1\frac{1}{4}$-inch units, an optional 'Super Sports' camshaft, and a very close ratio gearbox.) The result was a slightly intractable and harsh round-town sports car which impressed with its speed and cornering power in the country. Its close gear ratios, particularly the high bottom gear, could prove a burden at times, but with a maximum speed of just under 100 mph, a 0–50 mph time of around 10 sec and economy of some 35 mpg this was a pleasant specialized sports car. Generally, the Turner shared some of the rough finish and high noise-level of its contemporary small-quantity production sports cars, but at £815 in basic assembled form (with 948-cc engine), or £645 in 'kit' form, it gathered a band of enthusiastic owners. Much of the production was exported, and at this high point in the small sports car industry's proliferation, Turner Cars were doing quite well.

A glass-fibre moulded hard-top became available in March, improving cockpit protection and top speed performance by its better air-flow. The Climax-engined version continued to attract enthusiasm from its owners and respect from its opponents. It could touch 65 mph in second gear and an exhilarating 90 mph in third, still cornering safely and surely with its direct but stiff-feeling rack-and-pinion steering and easily-provoked oversteering characteristics. Top speed was around 102 mph, 50 mph came up in 9·5 sec from rest and when driven hard consumption was about 28 mpg – by no means excessive. With the Climax engine 9-inch front disc brakes and 8-inch rear drums were standard, and the 1960 price (complete) was £1,099 (the basic price being around £775). A useful optional extra was a self-locking differential, costing £57.

Development and production continued in modest numbers through 1961, the 105E Ford engine in modified form being introduced to augment the BMC and Climax FWE units. Assembly was claimed to take under twenty-four hours and only basic tools were required, while prices for the kit stood at £550 for the 1-litre models or £800 for the more sophisticated Climax version.

Then in 1962 an all-new Turner GT saloon model appeared. This used a radically different chassis design, with a sleekly-styled partially stressed glass-fibre skin mounted on a steel unitary chassis structure. It was introduced at the Racing Car Show in January, being offered in kit form with either modified 105E Ford or standard FWE Climax engines for £850 and £1,000 respectively. Centre-lock wire wheels, disc brakes, close-ratio gearbox and wood-rimmed steering wheel were all included in the standard specification.

A low nose with a shallow elliptical radiator air intake sloped up towards a raked windscreen, rounded roof line and gently wrapped-round rear window, while the headlights were set well back in the wings in cut-outs. Two wide-opening doors were fitted and with occasional four-seat accommodation this very different, and very much more expensive to produce, Turner was offered alongside the sports two-seaters.

In 1963 five-main-bearing Ford 1500 engines were standardized in the range, and the GT was priced at £870 kit or £895 assembled (not including purchase tax), while the two-seater versions were available for £699 as a kit. But this was a difficult period for small manufacturers and the Wolverhampton company failed to keep its head above water. Its sporting and individualistic products went the way of so many others about this time.

37 TVR

Even by the motor industry's standards this Lancashire-based company has had a chequered career, and its fortunes fluctuated throughout the decade. The original TVR had been produced by designer Trevor Wilkinson (from whose christian name the initials are derived) in 1957. Available in kit form, this Mark I was a two-seat fixed head coupé with tubular backbone chassis and a choice of either a supercharged 1172-cc side-valve Ford or single ohc Coventry Climax 1100 engine. In 1959 Layton Sports Cars Ltd was formed, with Henry Moulds, David Scott-Moncrieff, and Trevor Wilkinson among the directors, to produce this car, and in 1960 the stumpy little TV₁R coupé was generally available with MGA 1500 (Mark II) and later 1600 (Mark IIA) engines.

These vehicles used a tubular chassis with all-round independent suspension by a system of trailing links and torsion bars borrowed from the VW front end. The bodywork was in glass-fibre, featuring a fashionably long down-swept nose, the whole of the section forward of the front wheels and above the waistline hinging to give first-rate access to the engine (MG or Climax units were still available to customer specification). Two small doors gave access to the cockpit, with the back axle and extreme tail immediately behind a small luggage compartment, back of the seats. The car was available complete or in component form, and with a little time and skill a very pleasant personalized GT car could be produced from the 'kit'. With an all-up weight of only 15 cwt and the 79·5 bhp MGA 1600 engine installed, the TVR could accelerate from 0–50 mph in about 9 sec, had a top speed of 98 mph and returned approximately 33 mpg. Although the all-independent suspension was hard and uncoprommising, handling was very predictable, but some bump-steering at speed was a problem. Worm-and-peg steering was direct and quick, while 11-inch drum brakes all-round were powerful and effective (although these were replaced by disc units at the front in 1961).

Three basic models were offered, using a 997-cc 105E Ford engine for £1,003, the MGA 1600 unit for £1,183, or the 1216-cc Coventry Climax FWE (as used in the Lotus Elite) for £1,431.

In 1961 small quantity production continued, two new companies, TVR Cars Ltd and Grantura Engineering Ltd being formed to handle marketing and production. The former was liquidated in 1962, but Grantura Engineering continued with Chester car dealers Keith Aitcheson and Bryan Hopton in command, in association with one time BRM engineer Ken Richardson, and Arnold Burton of the Montague Burton concern. Under this diverse management a new Mark III model was shown in New York in April 1962, and fortunes were revived by orders to the tune of some 1½ million dollars.

In the Mark III, designer John Thurner, who had joined TVR from Rolls-Royce in 1958, dispensed with Wilkinson's original trailing arm ifs/irs system. The rear king posts, being rubber-mounted on the trailing arms, had allowed rear-wheel steering, which, to say the least, could be disconcerting. So a coil-and-wishbone system was adopted fore-and-aft, and the four-main-tube backbone chassis redesigned accordingly with extra triangulation to increase torsional rigidity, and at the expense of an even more massive 'transmission' tunnel in the car's confined interior. Triumph-Herald front suspension parts were used in conjunction with some of TVR's own, and rack-and-pinion steering was adopted, with Girling 10¾-inch front disc brakes and TR-type 9-inch rear drums. A competition department had been formed under Ken Richardson, and in addition to the standard MGA 1622-cc engined model, a Le Mans-type tuned unit was optional. This featured an HRG cross-flow light alloy head, with 9·5:1 cr, twin Weber DCOE dual-choke carburettors and produced 108 bhp at 6,000 rpm as opposed to the standard 90 bhp at 'five-five'. The MGA gearbox was retained with close ratios available, and with further attention to sound insulation and to interior appointment (already to a surprisingly high standard of comfort and appearance) price was fixed at £1,182.

During this period the works competitions cars put up some reasonable performances in minor events (although their international forays were pretty disastrous). In most respects these cars were identical to the production variants – engine and gearbox changes were made, of course, but apart from this and the absence of extraneous interior trim, the only additions were 23-gallon long-range fuel tanks, wide-rim wire wheels and racing tyres.

In 1963 the Mark III model was replaced by the new MGB-powered TVR 1800, using the same coil-and-wishbone all-independent suspension system, but with slight revision to the spring rates and damper settings. The new engine in standard trim produced 94 bhp net at 5,500 rpm from its 1798 cc and this gave a maximum speed of nigh-on 120 mph, with acceleration to match. A major characteristic of the car was its sure-footed handling, the precise steering and throttle control combining to give the driver complete command over the car's attitude. The disc/drum brakes were again very powerful, and on occasion they could be locked. Although entry to the cockpit was still pretty difficult for the tall or portly, the low seating position, wedged in firmly between the door and large chassis-hugging tunnel, was very snug and gave a great sense of security. The price of the new model, hardly differing at all externally from the Mark III, was £872 basic or £1,054 including tax.

With this TVR 1800 as the sole model, the company continued in production, but at all times its finances were rather stretched. Jack Griffith Incorporated in America had, during this period, fitted a V8 Ford engine into the TVR chassis – and were rather surprised to find that it did fit – and this version entered production with the 200 bhp engine in a slightly beefed-up chassis. Other modifications included a stronger prop-shaft and an extra coil-spring/damper on each rear suspension unit, replacing the single damper used previously and giving added acceleration wind-up resistance.

But the arrangement with Griffith lasted only a short time, and early in 1965 the home market Mark III 1800 was replaced by the Mark IV, which had improved weight distribution (the engine having been moved forward), slightly revised door trim, a wooden fascia on the still very high scuttle and TR4 front suspension uprights and brake calipers. The tail was also cut off short in a Kamm design, and a huge rear screen which made for excellent visibility was wrapped over the sloping roof.

The company was still ambitious beyond its resources, however, particularly in its attempt to enter the luxury car market in 1965 with a handsome body design by Fiore, based on a lengthened V8-powered chassis. In appearance Fiore's body was similar to that of the later Aston Martin DBS. It was to be built by Fissore in Italy, an arrangement doomed by a prolonged dock-strike, if by no other factors. TVR Cars Ltd went into liquidation, and their new luxury car, the Trident, did not see the light of day in quantity. In September 1965 their assets were acquired by Mr Arthur Lilley and his son Martin, who became Managing Director of the new company – TVR Engineering.

The 1800 was continued with its MGB engine, eventually appearing in 1800S form with 95 bhp at 5,500 rpm to push it from 0–50 mph in about 9 sec, and give a respectable maximum speed of 107 mph, with fair comfort and very good control. The V8 version was continued as the TVR Tuscan at a price of £2,365 in 1967, using the 4727-cc Ford V8 engine. The Tuscan had really good performance, streaking from 0–50 mph in only 4·9 sec, and having a maximum speed of no less than 140 mph.

Late in 1966 a Sunbeam Imp-based model, using a pretty Fiore-designed Fissore-built four-seat body on the Rootes chassis platform, appeared at the Turin Motor Show. Named the TVR Tina this interesting little car in 2+2 coupé and four-seat open forms was also shown at Earls Court in the following year, but it was not seriously put into production. The 1800, however, continued. It was renamed the TVR Vixen, still using the MGB engine in its standard form, although the new 1599-cc Ford GT engine, producing 95·5 bhp gross at 'five-five' could be specified. Mated via a diaphragm spring clutch to an all-synchromesh Ford gearbox this smooth and willing power unit soon replaced the MGB engine in standard cars.

The BMC engine was rather more torquey, giving a higher top speed and better acceleration in the higher gears, but the standard MG gear ratios were not so useful as those in the Ford bore. Fuel consumption was better at low speeds with the 1600 unit, but with both Weber chokes open the MGB engine was rather more efficient in converting fuel into power. Acceleration from 0–50 mph occupied 7·5 sec, better than the 1800, but 0–90 time was some 2 sec slower. Overall fuel consumption was about the same, 26 mpg. The car retained the cornering capabilities of the earlier models, although the drawbacks of rather dead steering and minimal luggage space persisted. The interior was still very well-appointed for a car which was certainly not mass-produced and priced at only £1,387.

For 1969 the Tuscan was continued, to order only, and the Heron-head Crossflow 1600 Ford engines were adopted for the pretty little Vixen S2 models, which still had the 'traditional' TVR body shape. The S2's engine produced 93 bhp gross at 5,400 rpm, with 102 lb ft peak gross torque at 3,600 rpm. The Ford all-synchromesh gearbox was retained, and with the well-proven tubular backbone chassis, Girling disc/drum brakes and Alford & Alder rack-and-pinion steering. The price was up to £1,583.

The Ford V6 3-litre engine attracted TVR engineers just as it had others before them, and a Tuscan V6 model appeared in an externally standard shell. Its 2994-cc engine produced 136 bhp net at 4,750 rpm and, with maximum torque figures of 193 lb ft at only 3,000 rpm the result was a very fast motorcar. Top speed was close on 125 mph, 0–50 mph acceleration occupied only 6 sec and fuel economy was excellent at around 26 mpg. This model was priced at £1,930 total in 1969, with the S2 series including the standard version at £1,487, the S2 Sport at £1,666 and the Super Sport variant at £1,787.

In 1966 TVR produced around eighty-five cars in the mill at Blackpool, in 1967 the total rose to 200, and in 1968 to 250 cars. In 1968 the company purchased some land at Marton, Blackpool, initially to use for a new body and paint shop, which it planned to concentrate production in by the end of 1969. Thus TVR was in a strong position at the end of a decade of fluctuating fortunes, producing pleasantly individual, well-built and good-mannered cars.

38 Vanden Plas

This member of the erstwhile British Motor Corporation produced luxury versions of cars in the basic BMC range throughout the 'sixties. The Vanden Plas Princess models represented a particular kind of staid, yet surprisingly quick, opulence, ranging from the trim little 1100 to chauffeur-driven VIP saloons and limousines.

For 1960 their luxury saloon was the A99-based 2912-cc six-cylinder 3-litre Princess. Mechanically this was similar to the A99 and Wolseley 6/99, and on its introduction in October 1959 was found to offer luxury of quite a high order. Manual overdrive and automatic transmission versions were available, priced at £1,396 and £1,467 respectively. They featured additional sound-proofing, deep and plush upholstery and great use of wooden veneers and extra equipment.

The big Princess limousine and saloon used a 3995-cc six-cylinder engine, producing a maximum of 150 bhp at 4,100 rpm from a single Stromberg carburettor and a 6·8:1 cr. A Borg & Beck 10-inch sdp clutch transmitted drive to a four-speed gearbox with synchromesh on the upper three ratios only, and a Hardy Spicer divided prop shaft was mated to a hypoid bevel back axle. Borg-Warner automatic transmission was optional, and this very stately and ponderous machine used coil-spring ifs with a semi-elliptic back axle. Servo-assisted Lockheed 12-inch drum brakes were fitted all round, and with Cam Gears cam-and-peg steering (power-assistance optional) this 41¾-cwt car was available in saloon or limousine form at £3,046.

In May 1960 these 'Princess' models became the 'Vanden Plas Princess' range, and from December the coronet insignia was blocked-in with red enamel on the 3-litre, and black enamel on the 4-litre versions. From January 1961 the 4-litre models were continued to special order only, and in July the Mark II 3-litre appeared with a twin exhaust system, increased power, floor change and a redesigned fascia panel. The Mark Is finally ceased production in October, and July 1962 saw the introduction of optional power-assisted steering. The Mark II's development continued into 1963, stronger seat runners and a new reduced-bore exhaust system being introduced in March, and an automatic boot light was added in October. In that month, for the coming year, a new Princess model was announced, this being the Vanden Plas luxury variant of the transverse front-engined, front-wheel drive 1100. This model used twin SU carburettors, and its luxury appointments included auxiliary lights, wooden fascia, full carpeting and trim, and a sunshine roof among the optional extras. Production did not start for some time, however, the first models leaving the production lines in January 1964.

Then, in June, the Mark II 3-litre was discontinued, for BMC had con-cluded an arrangement with Rolls-Royce to use their FB60 3909-cc six-cylinder engine. Using the quiet overhead inlet, side-exhaust cylinder head design, this engine used a 7·8:1 cr and twin SU HS8 carburettors, producing a smooth 175 bhp gross at 4,800 rpm. Peak torque was 218 lb ft at 3,000 rpm, and a Borg-Warner Model 8 automatic transmission was standard. This used three speeds and a torque converter and drove to a 3·15:1 hypoid bevel back axle. Coil-and-wishbone ifs with lever arm dampers and an anti-roll bar were used, with half-elliptic leaf springs and telescopic shock absorbers at the rear. 'Hydrosteer' power-assisted steering was also standard, and servo-assisted 10-inch Lockheed front disc brakes were fitted with 10-inch drums, 3 inches wide, at the rear. Farina's body styling had been modified to remove the rather undignified-looking sharp-pointed tail fins, and the tail line was now low and smooth, with rounded-off wing tips. Vertical tail light clusters had

143

also been replaced by horizontal ones, and with '4 litre Princess R' insignia, this not-very-rich man's Rolls-Royce was priced at £1,994.

Windscreen and rear-window rake had been reduced to give extra room inside, and the back seat was moved 1½ inches further aft to increase leg-room. Fold-away picnic tables with plated inserts to hold glasses or cups were included, and the wooden-trimmed, plushly carpeted and well-appointed interior was really quite attractive.

Extra torsional rigidity was gained in the shell's redesign, and smaller 13-inch wheels and lower-rate springs, improved handling noticeably, the Princess R being notably stable, running in a straight line hands-off with no trouble at all. The power-steering was rather dead, however, and one short-coming on early numbers was that the front suspension carrier, mounted on rubber to kill noise-transmission, was free to skew slightly, and this caused cornering problems until modified. The characteristic understeer of the earlier cars was much reduced, however, by the lighter weight of Rolls' aluminium engine. This was quite spritely too, pushing the car from 0–50 mph in 9·3 sec, and to a maximum speed of about 107 mph. Consumption was not a star attraction at about 14 mpg, however.

No major change occurred in the Vanden Plas luxury range until June 1967, when the 1275-cc engine became an optional unit for the 1100. Then in October a true 1300 model was introduced, and the Mark II Princess 1100 also made its debut with cut-back tail fins, larger rear light clusters, ventilated wheels, front wing repeater indicators, restyled front seats and trim, and '1100 Mark II' insignia. In March 1968 the 1100 was discontinued completely in favour of the 1300, however, and this was followed in May by the discontinuation of the rather dated-looking 4-litre saloon and limousine.

Vanden Plas went on to produce the new Daimler limousine for 1969, and apart from minor changes to the interior décor of the 1300, that completed their nineteen-sixties' programme.

39 Vauxhall

This British arm of America's vast General Motors Corporation produced a huge variety of saloon cars during the past decade, typified by well-designed, smooth engines and precise gearboxes, but marred by softly suspended and often rather garishly decorated body shells. However, towards the end of the period, the company also produced some very attractively styled motor-cars, and with their sophisticated canted ohc engines ended the decade on a high note.

In 1960 Vauxhall were producing the Victor, Velox and Cresta models, all large-sized four-door saloons with comfortable accommodation for four people, and room for two more at a pinch. They were not startling mechanically, were fast in a straight line, understeered rather sloppily through corners, and were softly comfortable.

The Victor F Series II, current at the start of the period, had been introduced in February 1959, with an angular and rather bizarre body shell based
very closely on American styling thought of the 'fifties. Wrap-round front and
rear screens were much in evidence, and other features of the Series II were
a full-width radiator grille, single central bonnet rib, protruding oval sidelights and smooth side panels. The Victor F was powered by an oversquare
four-cylinder engine of 1508-cc producing 55 bhp gross at 4,200 rpm. Carburation was by a single Zenith 34 VN, and cr was only 7·8:1. Transmission was
via a 7¼-inch single dry plate clutch to a three-speed all-synchromesh gearbox
with column change, thence through an open tubular propeller shaft to a
hypoid bevel final drive. Coil-springs with unequal-length wishbones and an
anti-roll bar provided independent front suspension, while a rather poorly-
located rear axle was sprung on semi-elliptics. Vauxhall used their own
telescopic shock absorbers, Burman recirculating ball steering and Lockheed
drum brakes – 8 inches in diameter all round, with two leading shoe units at
the front. Standard, Super, De Luxe and Estate versions were offered, their
prices of between £716 and £858 comparing very well indeed with similar-
sized saloons from the opposition.

The larger PA series Velox and Cresta models used a common six-cylinder
variant of the Victor's engine, two extra cylinders of exactly the same dimensions being added to give a capacity of 2262-cc. A single Zenith 34 VNT carburettor was used, with the 7·8:1 cr, to produce a healthy 82·5 bhp gross at
4,400 rpm. Again a simple all-synchromesh three-speed manual gearbox was
fitted, with an 8-inch Borg & Beck sdp clutch, open tubular propeller shaft and
hypoid bevel final drive. Suspension was similar to the Victor, although 9-inch
Lockheed drums were standard for the PAs, which were some 3 cwt heavier
than the Fs. The Velox was the standard six-cylinder model, with the Cresta
as the better trimmed and equipped leading car in the range, and alternative
Friary Estate variants of both were available. Here again prices were fairly
low for the high cruising speeds and straight-line performance provided,
ranging from £929 for the Velox saloon, through £1,014 for the Cresta model
to £1,222 (Velox Friary) and £1,309 (Cresta Friary). But the poorly located
rear axle readily allowed wheel-spin on bumps or through corners and
spoiled the otherwise comfortable ride. Top speed was 98 mph, and acceleration from 0–50 mph took only 10·4 sec. Fuel consumption stood at around
27 mpg – not bad for such a spritely large car.

In July 1960 servo-assisted braking became optional on the Velox and
Cresta PAs, and in August the ugly Victor was modified with chrome cappings to the headlamp cowls (apart from on the standard saloon model),
full-length side flutes carrying 'Victor' lettering, a deeper rear screen and
vertical fluting on the lower boot lid, with a turn-button lock built into the
number plate. The Velox and Cresta were also modified, with the PASX and
PADX Series variants appearing.

These used 'square' six-cylinder engines of 2651 cc; the compression ratio
was up to 8·1:1, and with an automatic-choke Zenith carburettor, output
was up to 94 bhp net (113 gross) at 4,600 rpm. Peak torque was 147 lb ft
gross at 2,400 rpm, and while retaining the three-speed all-synchromesh
gearbox, Laycock overdrive now became optional on middle and top.
A full GM Hydra-Matic three-speed epicyclic transmission was also available,

145

with a fluid coupling giving effort multiplication in first and reverse. The wheels were up a size from 13 inches to 14 inches, and combined sidelight/indicator units appeared in oblong mounts. Tail fins were more pronounced, hefty housings below combining indicators and tail lights. In manual form the big new Velox and Cresta models were capable of about 95 mph.

In July 1961 production of the Victor F Series II ceased, and in September a number of changes in the range were announced. These included the introduction of the Victor FB models, and of the high-performance VX 4/90, while further modifications were made to the PA Cresta and Velox.

The new Victor body shell was similar to the existing PAs, but with a less pronounced curve in the side panels and a prominent fold-styling along the waistline. Flat bonnet and boot panels were used, the tail curving down sharply and, with its flat side panels, the whole shell looked rather like a tank without a turret – only rather more attractive. A full-width grille incorporated headlights, while individual front seats were provided with a bench at the rear for comfortable four-/five-passenger accommodation. The 1508-cc four-cylinder engine had an 8:1 cr, and produced 49·5 bhp at 4,600 rpm, with peak torque of 80·4 lb ft net at 'two-two'. The new shells were roomier, lower and lighter than their predecessors, allowing higher gearing to be used with softer springs and a better ride. The three-speed all-synchromesh gearbox was standard, but an optional four-on-the-floor transmission was offered – Vauxhall being well to the fore in offering a sychromesh bottom gear in a multi-ratio gearbox. Again, Standard, Super and De Luxe variants were offered, at prices ranging from £744 for the spartan standard model to £847 for the De Luxe and £861 for the company's own Luton-built Estate. But the rear axle of these latest Victors still made its presence felt, they rolled rather excessively and with a high degree of understeer were not the most pleasant of cars to drive along a twisting road. Motorway driving was a different matter, however, and then only the rather restricted driving position could be genuinely criticized.

The VX 4/90, meanwhile, shared the new shell but had a much-modified engine. This featured a cast aluminium-alloy cylinder head with smoothed porting, 9·3:1 cr and inclined aluminized valves. Solid-skirt pistons were fitted, and the unit breathed through a twin-downdraught Solex system, mounted on a water-heated manifold. With a high-lift camshaft an extra 600 rpm was achieved, and power rose no less than 44 per cent to 71·3 bhp net (81 gross) at 5,200 rpm, torque also increasing by some 8 per cent to 87·2 lb ft net at 2,800 rpm. An 8-inch clutch replaced the standard 7¾-inch system, and large 10½-inch Lockheed disc front brakes were fitted, with 14-inch wheels all round. With no real need to look to economy in this performance model, a lower-than-standard rear axle ratio was used (4·125 instead of 3·9:1), and alterations to spring rates, damper settings and roll bar sizes stiffened the suspension. Unpleasantly low-geared steering was retained, but the four-speed all-synchromesh gearbox was standard along with complete instrumentation. Price was announced as £971, and this fast touring car (though still slower than the Velox/Cresta range) was capable of about 90 mph, a 0–50 mph time of under 12 sec and economy of some 27 mpg. The slightly stiffened suspension gave a gentle and controllable transition from understeer to oversteer in corners and although roll was still considerable, its characteristics were an advance on those of the basic Victors.

July 1962 saw the discontinuation of the PASX Velox and PADX Cresta saloons and Estates, these models being replaced in October when the new PB range was released. The new releases, using the same names, featured body shells generally similar to the Victor FB, but with pronounced styling ridges on the waistline and generally sleeker and more angular appearance. As with the FB, these shells were lighter than their predecessors, with servo-assisted front disc brakes as standard, and optional overdrive and Hydra-Matic transmission available in addition to the faithful old three-speed column-change basic unit. The theme of these alterations was to retain well-proven existing mechanical parts, mounted in new and lighter shells. The 2651-cc 'six' drove through higher gear ratios to produce a top speed of about 93 mph, a 10-sec 0–50 mph time and consumption around 24 mpg. Some improvement in acceleration had been gained, but the nicely styled and well-equipped new models were still generally rather imprecise, with low-geared steering and a lack of sure-footedness.

That same month the Victor FB Estate de Luxe appeared, with full-length chrome beading along the sides, decorative wheel trim, leather-covered individual front seats, standard heater, screen washers and full carpeting.

Major modifications to the FBs followed in July 1963, when the 1508-cc engine was discontinued, and in September a new 1595-cc engine was announced, being used in the Victors and the tuned VX 4/90. The new engine was well oversquare, and with an 8·5:1 cr and single Zenith 34VN carburettor, produced 58·5 bhp net at 4,600 rpm. An optional 7:1 cr low-compression head was available, with which power was down to 51·3 bhp at 'four-two', respective torque figures being 84·3 and 81 lb ft. A Borg & Beck 8-inch clutch was fitted, driving to all-synchromesh three- or four-speed manual transmissions, and while large 9-inch Lockheed drums were standard at the front (8-inch drums rear), the 10·5-inch diameter discs used on the VX 4/90 were an attractive option. Again the coil-and-wishbone ifs system with semi-elliptic rear was used. Other changes included a regrouped instrument panel, new rear number plate housing, round sidelight/indicator units wrapping round the wings with 'Victor' lettering, and an anodized aluminium grille with six horizontal bars and six black vertical ones. De Luxe models were further refined, using walnut veneer fascia, rear-seat arm-rests, integral ash-trays, and black hub-cap centres.

The new 1595-cc VX 4/90 had a 9·3:1 cr, retained the twin Zenith set-up (two 36 WIP-3s with 28-mm chokes) and produced 73·8 bhp net at 5,200 rpm, with peak torque of 91·8 lb ft net at only 2,800 rpm. That September the PBSX Velox and PBDX Cresta models had their final drive ratios raised from 3·70 to 3·90:1, and in November parallel Estate models were released, these being conversions by Martin Walker Ltd, of Folkestone. Full six-seat accommodation was offered, arm rests folding down to separate the bench seats for four-passenger use, while the rear seat squab also folded completely flat to offer a large freight space. Glass-fibre roof and upwards-hinging rear door were used, and the price was fixed at £1,305.

The big news that September was the release of Vauxhall's first small-capacity saloon car for many years, the 1057-cc Viva HA. At a time when other manufacturers had been producing cars of this class within minimal overall dimensions, the Vauxhall engineers decided that passenger and luggage accommodation was more important than overall size, and so produced a car having much in common with the Opel Kadett (Opel being the German counterpart of Vauxhall within General Motors). Two doors were used, to facilitate production of a stiff and economical shell.

Great attention was paid in Vauxhall's publicity to rust-proofing the new HA Viva body-shell. The whole of the underside was sprayed with bituminous sealer, and the inside of the body sills was also treated with bituminous aluminium paint to prevent rot from within. Finally, the new Viva was the first British car to use acrylic lacquer paint finish, which is resistant to atmospheric attack and does not need polish, while aluminium was used for the grille's bright metal mouldings. However, these precautions seem to have been to limited avail, for shell deterioration remained quite a problem.

The 1057-cc four-cylinder engine was unusual in having ball-jointed rocker pivots instead of a shaft, wedge-shaped combustion chambers with inclined valves and a smooth port design feeding from a single downdraught Solex B30 PSE carburettor. A massive crankshaft was used, and with an 8·5:1 cr (7·3:1 optional), peak bhp was 44 net at 5,000 rpm (40 bhp low-compression) with peak torque of 59·1 lb ft at 2,800 rpm. This unit was mated to a delightful four-speed all-synchromesh gearbox with very short and precise operation via a 6½-inch Borg & Beck diaphragm spring clutch, unusual in that it was cable-operated. With modern flexibly-mounted engines, it was felt that this method was more effective, as well as being cheaper than the hydraulic system. A short, double universal joint propeller shaft drove aft to the live axle with a short Kadett-like torque tube and hypoid bevel final drive.

A front suspension cross-member was bolted to the chassis through rubber blocks, carrying upper and lower wishbones on either side to locate the wheels, with a transverse leaf spring (again like the Kadett) on the level of the lower ones. This consisted of three thin leaves, with interposed rubber blocks, and Vauxhall-made telescopic shock absorbers picked-up on the lower wishbone. At the rear the semi-elliptic leaf springs were relieved of tramp-inducing twist by the torque tube, stabilizing the car against dive and squat. Low-geared rubber-mounted rack-and-pinion steering was used, and 8-inch diameter Girling drum brakes appeared all round, again with two leading shoes at the front. Servo-assisted discs were optional at only £12 extra, and the new Viva was priced at £527 (standard) and £566 (De Luxe).

The most attractive feature of the new model was undoubtedly its quick gearbox, for although adhesion and cornering power were good it rolled a lot, giving an odd lurch as it settled into corners. Again this Vauxhall suffered from very low-geared steering. The ride was rather bouncy on very springy seats, and body resonance intruded at speed, a shortcoming which was to persist in HA and HB models until the end of the decade.

Production of the Viva was extended from Luton to a new plant at Ellesmere Port in July 1964. In September the much-maligned steering ratio was raised slightly, new-style door trim adopted, and the choke control repositioned, while the De Luxe had thicker front-seat squabs, better arm rests,

1. The AC Ace was influenced by the 166MM Ferrari of the 1950s, looking every inch a thoroughbred. The body was modified in March 1961, with sleeker profile and smaller grille. This example is a 1962 2.6-litre Ford-engined option. Its chic lines have led to its appearance in TV advertising.

3. In 1962, the production thrust of AC sporting models switched to the Cobra, inspired by recently-retired American racing driver, Carroll Shelby. The Cobras were built, virtually in their entirety, at AC's English factory and shipped to Shelby American in Santa Fe (and later Venice, California) for installation of the Ford V8 power unit which endowed the car with its spectacular performance. Good examples now fetch spectacular prices.

2. The AC Aceca two-seat coupe was based on the same tubular steel chassis as the Ace, and its aluminium body was similarly coach-built. Craftsmanship was impressive, and its performance brisk with a 0-60mph time of 9.4 seconds, and a top speed for the Bristol-engined version of over 128mph.

4. The Series II is widely considered the finest of the suave Alvis TD21 3-litre models. Developments in this 1963 version include Dunlop disc brakes all round, and fog lamps faired into the fresh-air ducts each side of the grille. The seven-bearing engine produced 152.3 lb of torque.

1. The ponderous and unwieldy Armstrong-Siddeley Star Sapphire was the swansong model in a range of solid, soundly-engineered, but unexciting and outmoded cars. The marque had been launched in 1919, but by 1960, it had run out of energy…

2. In 1960, the Series II Aston Martin DB4 Coupe was a potent machine by anybody's standards. The six-cylinder engine's 240 bhp enabled the car to exceed 140mph and sprint from rest to 50mph in just over 7 seconds. No slouch even today.

3. Aston Martin finished the decade with a flourish. The DBS was the first of a new series of cars designed by the company's own designer, Bill Towns rather than by Touring of Milan. The knife-edge nose profile was hailed as an immediate success but would not survive changing fashions.

4. The basic Austin Mini's engine grew to 998-cc in Mark II form. The car provided a glimmer of new thinking amidst the staid and outdated designs of the early 1960s Austin model range. Today, the Mini is a collectors' icon with its own clubs and events. Thousands survived in daily use into the 2000s.

1

2

3

1. The angular Farina-styled Austin A40 of 1960 had a 948-cc version of the A-series engine (as also fitted to the Austin-Healey Sprite Mark I). It was fitted with a Zenith downdraft carburettor, and produced a modest 34bhp at 4,750 rpm. Amazingly, this outdated model remained in production until 1967.

2. The A55 Cambridge Farina Saloon, seen here in its customary two-tone paintwork, symbolised late '50s affluence, and was only slightly less prestigious than the Rover P4. The car used BMC's 1489-cc B-series power unit, and as a result, its performance was unexciting. The A55s were solidly built and many examples have stood the test of time.

3. The A60 Cambridge replaced the A55 in late 1961. The car was restyled with less-pointed rear wings offering cut back tips, a contrasting raised waistline flash, and new rear light clusters. The 1622-cc MGA engine was used to raise the car's performance by providing an improved 61bhp at 4,550 rpm.

4. The 1961 Austin Mini-Cooper was a radical departure for the staid BMC company. BMC had formed an association with the Cooper Car Company to build performance versions of the new Mini. Externally, the new model featured a redesigned eleven bar grille and Austin Cooper badges on the bonnet and boot lid.

4

5

5. The Cooper's transverse engine was a derivative of the A-series unit, starting out at 997-cc before being enlarged to 998-cc in 1964. Twin 1¼-inch SU carburettors fed the modified head, with its larger valves and double valve springs. The gear linkage was an improved straight-shift lever via a remote rod unit, instead of the early Mini's "pudding stirrer" lever, bolted directly onto the gearbox.

1. The Mini-Cooper S appeared in March 1963 with the 1071-cc model, followed by the 1275-cc S in April 1964. The tuned engine produced 75 bhp, accelerating the car from 0-50mph in under 8 seconds, and giving it a top speed of 98mph. Wide-rim ventilated steel wheels finished in Old English White remained a popular option.

2. The car's badging was subtle by 21st Century standards, but understated is always best. The magic "S" denoted a significant extra 20bhp in a car weighing under 1500lbs. This is a genuine example, but the availability of reproduction badges means that the little chrome S falsely dignifies some dubious cars.

3. The last big executive Austin saloon, known simply as the "3-Litre" was announced in 1967. It used the MGC 7-bearing, 6-cylinder engine delivering drive to the front wheels. Exactly 9,992 examples were built between 1967 and 1971, when the model was phased out. Despite its "ugly duckling" looks, the car had very stable handling and retained its following into the 2000s.

4. The end of the '60s saw the arrival of the Austin Maxi, the replacement for the A60 medium-sized saloon range. The company's hopes for the future rested on this new model which was equipped with overhead-cam engine technology, a 5-speed gearbox, front-wheel drive, and a 5-door hatchback layout that was ahead of its time. The model was solid and practical, but certainly not pretty.

1. The beginning of the '60s saw an old favourite, the Austin-Healey 100/6, evolve into the 3000 Mark 1. The changes were very subtle on the outside but quite significant on the inside. The redesigned engine block achieved 2,912-cc and 124 bhp, and the car was also equipped with front disc brakes. By the end of the decade, the model had been phased out but is now one of the most prized British collectors' cars from this period. This example is pictured at an historic Brooklands rally.

2. The Bristol 407 was the first model to use a specially-manufactured Chrysler V8 power unit. The 250bhp engine gave a maximum speed of 126mph and a 0-60 time of under 10 seconds. By keeping to its traditional styling, Bristol, survived into the 2000s and continues to produce quirkily exclusive cars, though in very small numbers. Examples from the '60s are still seen in daily use.

3. The Bond Equipe GT used Standard-Triumph parts including a Herald Chassis, suspension, brakes, and engine. Standard Vitesse doors were incorporated into its glass-fibre shell. Few have survived.

1. Daimler's Majestic Major saloon used a 4 1/2-litre version of the company's light-alloy V8. Despite the car's excessive weight, it still outperformed many sports cars of the day with a top speed of over 120mph!

2. The Daimler 2 1/2-litre saloon combined the Jaguar Mark II body shell with a version of the company's SP250 V8 engine. This was lighter than the six-cylinder XK unit.
The result was a car that outperformed the smaller-engined Jaguar Mark IIs, but has never been perceived by collectors as being quite so prestigious.

3. The Daimler SP 250 Dart was both light (having a glass-fibre body) and powerful (with its 140 bhp V8 engine). The combination results in a genuine top speed of 120mph. The styling has not stood the test of time – being seen as controversial when new!

4. The Elva Courier Mark IV was a sleek and well-finished-sports car. It provided a choice of the 1798-cc MGB, or 1498-cc Ford Cortina GT engine. Examples became fairly rare into the 2000s.

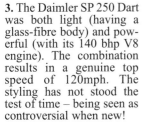

5. The Fairthorpe Electron Minor was available as either a self-assemble kit, or as a finished runner. Original engine choices were based on the smaller Standard-Triumph types. The body styling is reminiscent of the Mark I Sprite.

1. More than 1,250,000 examples of Ford's 105E and 123E Anglia range were sold between 1959 and 1967. The model provided a much-needed boost to Ford's small car image in the British market. It featured an overhead valve engine, four-speed gearbox, and a jaunty reverse slope to its rear window. Many, like this example, have been tuned, to which the Anglia was wonderfully responsive. Lowered suspension and wider wheels improved handling.

3

2. The Mark I Cortina proved an instant success, and over 60,000 cars were sold in the first three months of production, making it Ford's most successful British car of the early '60s.

3. The Mark II Cortina appeared in 1966 with a more chunky, squared-off body. A year into production, the model received a 1600-cc cross-flow engine which replaced the earlier 1500. Rostyle wheels were a favourite option.

5

4. The Ford Corsair was designed as a slightly larger alternative to the Cortina, and gave genuine five-seat accommodation. Starting life with the 1498-cc Kent engine, the car was fitted with a German-designed V4 from 1965. The razor-edge nose styling never really made it…

5. The Capri Classic is a model, which has improved with age. In period, its rather way-out styling, largely derived from the Anglia, looked out of place in a larger car. Today it is sufficiently kitsch to be considered retro beautiful.

1. The Mark III Zodiac was at the top of the mid-'60s Ford range, with its American styling cues. In 1966, the model was replaced by the more technically advanced Mark IV. Good surviving examples are hard to find.

2. Frontal aspect of the 1968 Gilbern Genie, two years into this successful design's production run. The headlights are slightly recessed into each wing and the broad flat- vented bonnet and wide, tapering grille give the car a time-less appeal.

3. The Genie's side elevation confirm that the design's lines have stood the test of time very well. The attractive glass-fibre body, designed by Frieze and Smith, provides a pleasing glass-to-body-work proportion. This car was for sale when photographed, being marketed as a practical means of transport rather than as a valued classic.

4. Nor does the Genie disappoint from the rear. Mechanically, the model was strong, using the long-lasting 2994-cc Ford V6. The steering, brakes, and rear axle were MGB parts. The Genie was available both fully-assembled and in kit form.

1. The G4 was Ginetta's most successful '60s model, both in terms of road and competition use. Powered by a choice of Ford engines, over 500 were produced between 1961 and 1969. Into 2008, based in Leeds, the company still thrived. Their G20 model had become the present day equivalent of the G4, with both road and race versions available.

2. Bertone influence is immediately apparent in the Gordon- Keeble GK1's styling. It was originally powered by a 4.6-litre Chevrolet engine, which made it a very exciting machine. Examples are now extremely rare as only eighty were produced in the period.

3. The Hillman Minx had been the company's middle-sized saloon since pre-war years. The Rootes Group struggled on into the '60s with models that belonged in the '50s. This 1961 series IIIC was the final version of the Minx. The new-shape Super Minx finally superseded it. However, these cars are still sought after into the 2000s, embodying real charm from a bygone age.

4. The Hillman Imp was something completely different: a small, light, rear-engined car, with a sophisticated all-alloy power unit. The Imp was a serious rival to the Austin/Morris Minis. Always good in competition, this example was still racing forty years later, equipped with such modern components as these Compomotive wheels.

1. The big Humbers were the most iconic of the marque's '60s models. This 1966 Hawk is one of the last of its kind. Shown here picking up a businessman outside his office, this image reflects the Hawk's target market. The surviving Humber name was applied to other Rootes products such as the Super Minx, which was somewhat unconvincingly rebranded as the Humber Sceptre.

2. In September 1968, the all-new Jaguar XJ6 was introduced, equipped with the in-line XK engine unit in both 2.8 and 4.2-litre capacities. Its instantly recognizable, classic Jaguar styling makes it seem much more modern than it really is.

3. The Mark II Jaguar has to be one of the greatest car designs ever. Popular to this day, with companies such as Beacham producing upgraded new cars from old shells. The example featured here is in (latterly favoured) red, with chrome wire wheels. In recent years, this livery has become something of a cliché. Carmine Red was just one of 23 original colour options, while chrome wires were a rarely-seen and expensive option. Most contemporary owners opted for standard steel wheels.

4. The Jaguar E-Type was the '60s' most iconic sports car. It was introduced in 1961 with the 3.8-litre XK engine from the top of the Mark II saloon car range. The body shape breathed pure 'sports car' in every line. Ownership in the 21st century remained exclusive, as prices for good examples remained high, and running and maintenance costs are greater than for the decade's mass-market sports cars, such as the MGB.

1

2

1. The allure of a large-capacity American V8 attracted Jensen, just as it had attracted Bristol, especially when fitted into its glass-fibre bodied chassis. By 1964, their engine had grown from 5916-cc to 6276-cc as fitted to the Jensen CV8 shown here. These cars proved extremely tough and long-lived. They are familiar from TV advertising, and are seen on the roads daily.

2. Lotus founder Colin Chapman, took the opposite approach to Jensen. He believed in small lightweight sports cars with compact but powerful engines. The Elan was the perfect example. It combined these attributes with stunning styling to create one of the decade's most iconic cars. The Elan went on to become the star of *The Avengers* TV series, driven by the legendary, and equally gorgeous, Emma Peel.

3. Lotus also undertook tuning work for other car manufacturers. The most famous example of this line was their association with Ford during the '60s. This relationship produced a Lotus-improved version of the best-selling Cortina. The Mark II variant was launched in 1967. This larger car had somehow lost the spirit of the original version, and is not so sought after.

4. The Lotus Elite was the predecessor to the Elan. It was a fast sports coupe that, for a road car, had hitherto unimagined handling capabilities. Accordingly, it was a competition success from the outset.

5. Marcos produced this very sleek GT car during the '60s. It started life with the Ford 997-cc Anglia engine, and progressed (via the 1340-cc Ford 109E, Volvo 1800, and Ford Cortina 1500-cc units) to the 1600-cc Ford cross-flow power unit in 1967. Finally, the Ford 3-litre V6 was installed. The bodyshell was glass-fibre with wooden frame and floors. This example is a 1600 GT.

3

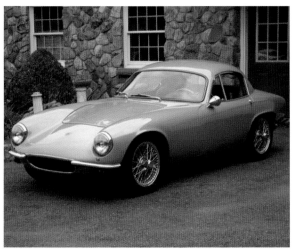

4

5

1

1. The MGB roadster was announced in July 1962, replacing the MGA. It continued to sell for the rest of the decade. A coupe version, the MGB GT, arrived in 1965. It was an immediate success in Britain and in MG 's traditional export markets (America, Australia, New Zealand, and South Africa). The model found a market wherever open-top motoring was popular. It is one of the world's most used and useable '60s classics. Many factors contributed, including the availability of replacement parts (in-cluding new body shells), and the many clubs that support the model. Most importantly, MGBs are still fun to drive on modern roads.

2. An MG 1100 engine bay. The model was launched in October 1962, a twin carburettor version of the basic 1100. Producing 52 bhp, the improved engine gave a top speed of 87mph. Coupled with excellent front-wheel drive traction and great cornering power, this made for a lively little car.

2

3

3. By the early '60s, the MG Magnette had a Mark III Farina-designed body, in common with other medium-capacity BMC saloons.

4

4. The MG 1300 was deliberately aimed at a more sporty market, as was the Cooper S. The new variant featured a walnut dashboard, circular instruments, and a three-spoked, leather-rimmed steering wheel. The engine was a 1275-cc unit similar to the Cooper S's, providing the respectable top speed of 95mph.

1

1. The Morgan 4/4 kept its very traditional looks during the '60s, as it has done ever since. This 1968 4/4 is entirely at home amongst cars many years its junior, at Brands Hatch Morgans in Kent. Note the original painted wire wheels. This Ford 1600 cross flow-powered car would still fetch a good price on their forecourt.

2. The rear view shows the Morgan's stepped mudguards, faired-in spare wheel, and obligatory luggage rack.

3

2

4

3. The Morgan has a functional '60s interior, four-spoke steering wheel (with chrome boss), a walnut fascia, round instrument dials, and a stubby gearlever.

4. The winged 4/4 badge has the patina of 40 years' exposure to the elements.

1. By 1968, the Morris Minor saloon had reached the heady heights of 1098-cc. With its surprisingly aerodynamic shape, the Minor's performance and handling belied its reputation for being the district nurse's car of choice.

2. A splendid Morris Minor Traveller in Trafalgar Blue. The ash framing of this shooting brake has to be kept varnished or it will become stained and deteriorate.

This model is well loved and many remain in daily use, the writer recently saw one driving along New York's Park Avenue. The car is equally at home in town or country.

3. and 4. Front and rear views of the Morris Cooper. The badging was subtly different to that of the Austin version. This is a 1968 998-cc Cooper Mark II. Its grille has larger horizontal chrome bars, and small plastic cameo Morris badges. Almond Green with an Old English White roof is one of the '60s' classic Cooper colour schemes.

14

1. The Morris Oxford was the Morris version of the ubiquitous BMC medium-range saloon. By the 1960s, this solid and respectable car was already old fashioned, but it still had its place in the market.

2. The Morris 1800 was a transverse-engined, front-wheel drive car designed as a successor to the Oxford. It was a generic BMC medium-range saloon, and like its predecessor was available in all of the company's marques. It used a transverse version of the 1798-cc MGB unit.

3

3. The Reliant Scimitar used the 2994-cc Ford Zodiac V6 engine, installed in a cross-braced box section steel chassis carrying glass-fibre bodywork. The model lasted extremely well as glass-fibre does not rust. The styling was pretty futuristic when it first came out, and the car looks "modern" to this day.

4. Riley's version of the Mini was the Elf. The car had an extended boot with tiny tail fins, and the traditional Riley grille grafted onto its restyled nose. Although they are interesting, none of the Mini variants ever challenged the popularity of the Austin Morris originals.

4

1. The Kestrel was the Riley-badged version of the 1100 range. Like so many other famous makes in BMC's '60s line-up, Rileys had been reduced to mere badge-engineered versions of the basic Austins. This meant that BMC models competed against one another for sales. The manufacturer also had to bear the cost of altering its assembly lines for up to five different variants of the same basic car: hardly cost-effective.

2. Very few traditional Riley enthusiasts, loyal to the company's innovative pre-war cars would be fooled into buying this Riley 4/Seventy-two. The car was just a badge-engineered Austin Cambridge. Despite this, the cars were very well made and many have survived in good shape. This 1969 model is photographed at a club meeting.

3. Deliveries of the new four-door Rolls-Royce Silver Shadow began in 1966. This was one of the very first examples, photographed against a suitably classic English backdrop.

1. The traditional P5 Rover received a revamp in 1962, with the introduction of the lowered-roofline Coupe version. This gave the car a more sleek and attractive appearance, without losing its Rover *gravitas*.

2. A magnificent Rover P5B stands for sale in a classic car showroom. The model represents the zenith of big Rover development, being endowed with the GM-based V8 engine of 3500-cc, as fitted from August 1967.

3. The Rover P6 was considered very avant-garde when it first appeared in October 1963. The design was a complete departure from the stuffy, upright, dignified cars usually associated with the company. Indeed, it was almost a young man's car. The model started out with a 2000-cc engine, and was designated the Rover 2000. It then became the 2000 TC (twin carburettor). In 1968, the car was equipped with the light-alloy 3500-cc V8 (already fitted to the P5B) and re-designated the Three-Thousand-Five.

1. In October 1967, the Sunbeam version of the low-roofline Hillman Californian was announced. It was dubbed the Sunbeam Stiletto. Using the Imp Sport engine of 51 bhp and featuring upgraded handling and interior, the car was the most expensive in the Imp range, retailing at £726.

1

2. The Sunbeam Alpine was a very attractive little sports car. It started life in 1959 and various improved versions were launched throughout the '60s. These included the Tiger model, which had a 4261-cc Ford V8 engine. This Mark IV had a slightly modified version of the original body shell, with cut down tail fins, and a revised grille.

3. The glass-fibre body of the Tornado Tempest was soundly constructed on a tubular ladder-frame, and had channel outriggers and side frames. The high humped body had both critics and admirers.

4. The Tornado Talisman appeared in 1961 and was compared in appearance to the Lancia GT of the previous decade. It was powered by a Cosworth-Ford 1340-cc Classic engine, which produced 75 bhp. Only 186 examples were produced between 1961 and 1964, making this a fairly rare car. In period, they achieved considerable club-racing success.

2

3

4

1. The Triumph TR4 was introduced in 1961 as a replacement for the TR3, and was steeped in '50s styling. Michelotti, who was responsible for the look of most Triumphs during the decade, was responsible for the design. The new model had a four-cylinder 2138-cc engine, producing 105 bhp, mated to a four-speed all-synchro-mesh gearbox.

2. In 1960, the Triumph Herald two-door, two-seat coupe was available with twin SU carburettors. This boosted the original 948-cc engine's output to 45 bhp. This model was priced at £730.

3. Dating from 1967, this is one of the last of the Triumph Herald 1200 convertibles. Some 50,982 1200 convertibles and estates were produced. The convertible version has out-survived the saloon.

1

2

1. The Triumph Spitfire 4 was introduced in October 1962, complete with an 1147-cc engine developed from the Herald. It also used the Herald's chassis and running gear. It became an instant success in the small sports car market, looking more streamlined and futuristic than its rival, the Spridget, but history has conferred it with a slightly less rugged image.

2. The GT6 fastback joined the Triumph sports car range in October 1966. Early cars had handling problems, which were due to the use of the swing-axle Herald suspension: notorious for rear-wheel tuck under. This was corrected on the Mark II version pictured here.

3

4

3. The six-cylinder Triumph Vitesse made its debut in May 1962. It was based on the Herald design layout. In September 1965, a 1998-cc unit replaced the original 1596-cc, and the Vitesse 2-litre was born. This is a 1967 example. A 2-litre badge is visible in the centre of the grille.

4. The Turner Mark I was offered either assembled or in kit form, with a choice of engines: the 948-cc Austin, or the 1097-cc Coventry Climax. This example, owned in 2008 by Nigel Taylor, is a BMC-powered car.

5

6

4. The Turner Mark I was offered either assembled or in kit form, with a choice of engines: the 948-cc Austin, or the 1097-cc

Coventry Climax. This example, owned in 2008 by Nigel Taylor, is a BMC-powered car.

5. The TVR Griffith 200 was inspired by America's Jack Griffith Inc. Griffith had tried to fit a 200 bhp

Ford V8 into the standard TVR 1800 chassis, and was somewhat surprised to find that this was possible.

1. The original TVR Tuscan was a V8 version of the 1800 body shape. It was equipped with the 4727-cc Ford engine, providing a 0-50mph time of just 4.9 seconds, and a top speed of 140mph. Many of these cars have been renovated and remain in use.

2. The Vixen S2 used a Ford 1600 Heron-head Crossflow engine, which produced 93 bhp at 5,400 rpm. These cars remain highly collectible and prices for good examples are steadily rising.

1

2

3. Over 300,000 Vauxhall Victor FBs were built at the Luton factory between 1961 and 1964. The styling is typical of Vauxhalls of this period; with General Motors design clues shining through.

3

1. The HA Viva was Vauxhall's first small-capacity saloon car for many years. Powered by a 1057-cc engine that featured novel ball-jointed rockers, the car was very boxy in appearance.

2. Vauxhall entered the '60s with the PA Cresta as its flagship model. Heavily influenced by American styling, with their wrap-around windscreens, two-tone colour schemes, tail fins, and acres of chrome, these cars appealed to a brasher clientele. A fine example is shown here. This is a PADX model, photographed at a show.

3. The Viva range was restyled in September 1966. The HB series had more flowing lines, with an upswept rear wing line following American styling trends of the period. This is the estate version, introduced in June 1967.

4. The Victor FD replaced the old VX 4/90 model in June 1967. The new styling, with its up-swept waistline, reflected the trend seen in the new Viva. But although the car still showed the influence of American styling, this was more restrained that at the beginning of the '60s.

1

1. The Wolseley 18/Eighty-Five upheld the time honoured coding of all Wolseley models. The 18 stood for the cubic capacity, in this case 1800-cc, and the 85 signified the brake horsepower. This was a badged version of the Austin 1800.

2. In common with other badge-engineered marques in the BMC stable, Wolseley had badged variants of the best-selling Austin 1100 and 1300 series. These cars had various luxury extras to justify their higher price, such as reclining seats, walnut dashboards, and twin carburettors.

3

2

3. This Wolseley 16/Sixty is a handsome old beast. Despite being outdated, the model survived until 1969. It was the re-badged equivalent of the Austin Cambridge, but (like the Austin) it had only a single carburettor. The MG and Riley models used the twin-carburettor version of the MGA 1622-cc engine.

4. Up to 1965, the Wolseley 1500 sold steadily. It reflected a tradition of quality, and had an upmarket feel for a small saloon. The car looked classic and cute, rather than outdated. This was certainly a case of the Wolseley brand stimulating sales. This model range enjoyed a sales renaissance into the 2000s...

4

23

1

1. The Wolseley Hornet was a re-badged version of the Austin Mini. Like the Riley Elf, it had an extended boot with small fins, in addition to the traditional Wolseley grille grafted onto the Mini front panel. This particular example was put up for sale in 2007-08, having had only one owner since its first registration in 1964. It was in extremely fine original condition, being completely unrestored. The car was a testament to the fact that many British cars of the '60s were extremely well made.

2. The handsome Rochdale Olympic was offered originally with variety of sporty Ford and BMC engines, making it pretty potent. Examples of this model remained in daily use into the 2000s.

3. The cool-looking Unipower GT used stock Mini-Cooper parts to good effect and sold strongly through the late '60s.

2

3

4

4. The Falcon shell, together with its associated chassis frame and tubular body formers, was designed to accept Ford mechanical parts. This example appeared to require a little renovation.

improved insulation and a fitted boot carpet added. An Estate model, the Bedford Beagle, was converted from the parallel Bedford 8-cwt van, by Martin Walker. That September the Victor FB Series was discontinued, along with the 2651-cc Velox/Cresta engine, which was to be replaced by a new 3294-cc unit.

In October the new FC101 Victor and VX 4/90 models were announced, and the big-engined PBS51 and PBD51 Velox and Cresta were unveiled. The Victor 101 models offered more room, more refinement and more comfort than hitherto, with interior space increased by using curved side panels and windows, giving an extra 4 inches of width at shoulder level. The basic chassis platform was very much as before, but the new welded shell produced a considerably stiffer unit. Once again elaborate anti-rust measures were publicized, and interior comfort was of a high order, separate front seats being standardized in the De Luxe and VX 4/90 models. The heater system was much improved and new-design quarter-lights adopted to reduce wind noise when open. The 1594-cc engine was unchanged, apart from a cr increase to 9:1, while development had produced a quieter fan and reduced induction roar. Mechanical clutch operation was introduced with a bell-crank system, and even lower-geared steering and rear-suspension noise insulation were introduced. Girling self-adjusting rear drum brakes of 9-inch diameter were standardized, with duo-servo rear operation (although the VX version retained its front discs, redesigned to fit in 13-inch wheels).

The new 3·3-litre Velox and Cresta had 115 bhp net at 4,200 rpm, and produced peak torque figures of 175 lb ft at 2,200 rpm. The three-speed all-synchromesh gearbox was retained with its four-speed option available, and both overdrive and Hydra-Matic transmissions could be specified. The Cresta offered bench, individual or reclining front seats in leather. All models had acrylic paintwork, although Vauxhall were never quite to attain the image of longevity they seem to have searched for for so long. The new Velox/Cresta series also, incidentally, gained variable-speed wipers, a twin exhaust system and, on the Cresta only, integral reversing lamps.

But the 101 Victor's duo-servo braking system was removed in April 1965, as the disadvantages of rapid wear and fade – discovered in America shortly after the war – apparently still persisted. That same month GM Powerglide automatic transmission replaced the Hydra-Matic version as optional equipment, and power-assisted steering was added.

In May, the new Super Luxury Viva was introduced, featuring restyled Ambla upholstery, a padded fascia rim, lockable glove box, twin horns, water-temperature gauge and extensive exterior embellishment with 'SL' insignia. A 'Super-Traction' limited-slip differential became optional equipment on the 101 and VX 4/90s, and in June Powerglide was offered for them as well. July saw the Viva's pedals off-set to the right, with amber indicators and sidelights incorporated in new clusters. Then in September walnut veneer fascias became standard on the Victor De Luxe models, and the Super-Traction differential standard on the VX 4/90.

In October new Viva De Luxe 90 and SL 90 models were introduced, with two-branch exhaust manifold, large-bore tail-pipe, bigger valves in a high-compression 9:1 cylinder head and a Zenith 150CD carburettor. Output was 53·8 bhp at 5,400 rpm, with 60·4 lb ft torque at 3,200 rpm. Servo front disc brakes were standardized, and the new SL90 was good for a maximum of about 82 mph, with acceleration from 0–50 mph in 13 sec and economy of around 33 mpg. The standard model could manage 75 mph flat out, 0–50 mph in 14 sec and around 33 mpg again, so noticeable increase was only made in maximum speed. The Beagle Estate also appeared in Mark II form with a padded fascia and coloured side flash, but further up the range big changes were being made.

The PB Velox and Cresta models were discontinued, to be replaced by the PC models with completely new bodies, again giving considerably more interior space. The name Velox was dropped, the two new models being the standard Cresta and improved Cresta De Luxe. Vauxhall styling pedigree was evident in the new shells, although the upswept waistline over the rear-wheel arches was a new departure, reflecting then-current American practice. Extensive sound-damping was applied to the body and a larger boot, larger fuel tank and deep and plush bench seats were standard in the basic model. Heater output and distribution were improved, and circular instruments replaced rectangular ones.

The new shell was even closer to what was claimed to be the optimum tubular shape for a unitary automotive structure, and was rather heavier than its predecessors. Accordingly, a rather more powerful engine was fitted, with higher-lift camshafts, different valve springs and a new Zenith WIA42 carburettor. Power was up to 123 bhp at 4,600 rpm, while peak torque was 176·1 lb ft at 2,400 rpm. A new diaphragm spring clutch was fitted, with the three-speed gearbox as standard and close-ratio four-speed, overdrive and fully-automatic systems as optional equipment. An auxiliary leaf spring was added to the rear suspension, taking load on suspension depression and preventing bad sag under heavy loading without affecting the ride quality of the otherwise still very soft suspension. Transverse axle location was improved by a chassis tie-rod which had originally been fitted to locate the differential pinion flange. A larger front anti-roll bar was fitted, and with optional power-assistance, the already light steering and dead-feeling servo-assisted brakes made the new Cresta a bit of a 'lady's car'. The standard model had single headlights, the De Luxe had dual units, and prices were £956 and £1,058 respectively.

A new luxury model joined the range in 1966; the Vauxhall Viscount. Using the new Cresta shell, the Viscount featured a black-grained fabric-covered roof and most of the optional Cresta equipment as standard. Power-assisted steering, electrically wound windows, heated rear screen, Powerglide transmission and a high degree of all-round luxury were Viscount features. The Powerglide automatic system (using two ratios and a torque converter) and the optional four-speed manual transmission were similar to those offered for the Cresta, and the new model was priced at £1,483.

This family of big saloons were all in the high-90 mph speed bracket, the basic Cresta reaching 50 mph from rest in only just over 7 sec, and returning about 20 mpg, while the Viscount, with its automatic transmission, could top 98 mph, took 3 sec longer to reach 50 mph from rest and for a car of its class was reasonably economical at around 18 mpg.

The Viva range was restyled in September 1966, when the spartan-looking HA Viva range was discontinued. The HB series replacement model featured a new and very attractive body shell, with a bigger engine and redesigned suspension. The new style looked a little strange, largely on account of 12-inch wheels, but basically was shapely, with a flattened nose, sharply up-swept waistline and curved side panels (by-products of the curves were increased panel stiffness and improved sound insulation). Interior rear-seat hip room was greatly increased by lengthening the wheelbase and widening the track. The old transverse leaf ifs system was scrapped, coil-and-wishbones replacing it, while the rigid rear axle was also on coil springs, located by four links, the upper pair forming an A-bracket locating on the differential casing, a lower pair acting as trailing radius arms. The front suspension, steering and engine mounts were carried on a rubber-insulated sub-frame (this means of damping noise deriving from the inertial mass of the engine bearing on the sub-frame was later used to great effect in the Jaguar XJ6).

The engine was bored-out to 1159-cc, and bigger valves were fitted. With a redesigned exhaust system, this engine produced 47 bhp at 5,200 rpm in standard form, the 90 specification raising this figure to 69 bhp at 5,800 rpm. Carburation differed, the standard model using a Zenith IZ and the 90 retaining its Stromberg 150 CD, while without the torque tube of the HA models the propeller shaft was longer; the 90, with its higher rpm, used a thicker than standard shaft. The 90 also retained the HA final drive ratio of 4·125:1, while the new HB standard ratio was higher at 3·89:1.

This new Viva was smoother and quieter than the HA, though still resonating at speed, but its handling was more comfortable and predictable, roll was fairly limited and basic cornering characteristics were pleasantly neutral. Five new Vivas were released, prices ranging from £579 to £708.

Other alterations appearing at this time included walnut fascia and trans-mission tunnel panelling on the VX 4/90, minor trim changes to the Victor 101 (with heaters now standard on the Super and Estate, and also on the basic Cresta).

Automatic transmission became optional equipment for the De Luxe and SL Vivas in January 1967, and at the same time a Brabham performance conversion was approved by the works. Jack Brabham's Surrey-based conversion business had been developing Viva tuning equipment for some time, and the engine of the 'Brabham-Viva' used twin Stromberg carburettors and a free-flow exhaust system, producing 79 bhp. This conversion was optional on De Luxe 90 and SL90 models, being externally identifiable by a contrasting colour paint bar across the nose, wrapping round into a flash along either side.

In June 1967 the very pretty HB Viva Estate range was introduced, in four trim variants, and in August the Victor 101 FC range, including the VX 4/90, was discontinued, being replaced by the all-new Victor FD and 2000 FD models.

While the Vivas had looked like smaller versions of the larger Vauxhall saloons, the new Victors resembled expanded Viva variants. The new shell was slender and delicate-looking, inheriting the up-swept waistline, sloping tail, and more accentuated barrel sides; overall, their proportions were very sleek and attractive. The all-new engine featured a single overhead camshaft driven by an internal-toothed rubber belt, operating inclined overhead valves.

A five-main-bearing crankshaft was used, with H-section con-rods and die-cast aluminium pistons, and the cylinders were inclined at 45 degrees to the vertical to maintain a low overall height and provide a smooth induction tract shape. Hemispherical combustion chambers were used with an 8·5:1 cr in both basic 1599-cc and 2000 1975-cc units, single Zenith 36IV down-draught carburettors also being common to both units. The 1600 produced 83 bhp gross at 5,800 rpm, with 90 lb ft torque at 3,200, while figures for the 2-litre were 104 bhp at 5,800 rpm and 116 at 3,200 respectively.

Transmission included a diaphragm spring clutch (for the first time in a Victor) but the four-speed gearbox was fundamentally as before (the 'standard' three-speed only being seriously intended for export models). Following HB Viva practice, coil-and-wishbone ifs was fitted, with rack-and-pinion steering, while at the rear a coil-sprung rigid axle was located by four parallel trailing links and a Panhard rod. Dampers were mounted remotely from the coil springs at the rear, so all suspension functions were independent of one another. Track was wider than on the 101 at the front by 3 inches and at the rear about half that, while the 1600 used 9-inch drum brakes all round, with front servo-assisted discs optional. The 2000 used the discs as standard, but 10·3 inches in diameter as opposed to 9·06 inches on the 1600 options.

With the floor-change gearbox, separate front seats were standard, and upholstery throughout was sumptuous and thick, although this limited rear seat leg-room somewhat – particularly with the front seats adjusted to their full extent. Great attention was also paid to producing a safe motor-car.

But experience with the 2000 showed that the ridiculously low-geared steering persisted, and that the high degree of understeer could be embarrassing on tight roundabouts. The new Victors were quick and comfortable, however, and were good transport for the average motorist. The price of the basic model was only £819: four-speed gearbox, separate front seats and disc brakes being extras. The 2000 was priced at only £910, so they still offered great value for money.

Although it had distinct limitations, delighting only in fast open-road work or medium-pace country jaunts, the 2000 was quite impressive statistically, having a maximum speed of about 95 mph, a 0–50 mph time of under 10 sec and overall fuel consumption of some 26 mpg.

May 1968 saw a further model released, this being the luxurious Ventora saloon, combining the 3·3-litre push-rod six-cylinder engine with the new FD Victor shell. In revised form the 'six' produced 140·2 bhp gross at 4,800 rpm, with 185·7 lb ft torque (gross) at 2,400 rpm. The four-speed all-synchromesh manual transmission was standard (GM Powerglide automatic could be specified). The Ventora was luxuriously equipped, although internally it did not challenge the limousine-like appointments of the continuing Viscount model. Compared with the rather noisy new Victors, the Ventora was quiet and comfortable, riding well on its soft suspension, although on undulating surfaces this led to a rather sickening motion. Maximum speed was an impressive 102 mph, the 0–50 mph time was 2 sec better than the Victor 2000 and fuel consumption was reasonable at 22 mpg. Price was £1,158.

Introduced that same month, the Victor 3300 Estate used the same basic amalgam of engine and body shell and, with similar options to those of the Ventora available, was an attractive buy at £1,184. For the room and comfort these big Vauxhalls offered, they were very competitively priced. Also introduced were Victor FD Estates in 1600 and 2000 forms.

In March production of the Viva GT had started. This hot-rod type creation used the single ohc engine of the 2000 with twin Zenith 150CDS variable-choke carburettors boosting gross output to 112 bhp at 5,400 rpm, with a peak of 125 lb ft gross torque at 3,400 rpm. Its matt-black bonnet sported twin air scoops, and it had chromed wheel trims and quadruple exhaust tail-pipes. It appeared to be little more than an exaggerated example of 'cowboy engineering'. Indeed, it was not all that powerful, and certainly lacked the competition breeding of its more expensive – but honest – Ford counterpart, the Escort Twin Cam. As with all these later Vauxhall saloons, adhesion and general road-holding was reasonable though in comparison with other sporting saloons the new GT was soft, wallowy and again endowed with a high degree of understeer, the front-end ploughing into sharp corners (although in fairness its stability in fast curves was a good point). Top speed was just on 100 mph, acceleration from 0–50 mph took 7·9 sec, and average consumption was about 23 mpg. This 'GT' was priced at £1,063 but by the end of the period the company had realized their mistake and a more muted GT was released for 1970.

Then, in June, the 1599-cc ohc engine was installed in a Viva shell, the result being the Viva 1600 model, available in saloon De Luxe and SL forms, or as an Estate. Again the four-speed transmission was adopted, with the Borg-Warner 35 automatic transmission optional. The normal well-balanced Vauxhall brakes were used, with 8·4-inch front discs and 8-inch rear drums. Improvements in acceleration and performance were unfortunately offset by very poor fuel consumption, and the appeal of this model was limited accordingly (the price was £797). Early in October 1968 new four-door Viva models appeared and, with £8 being added to all Viva prices on the addition of a GM collapsible steering column, this latest modification was accompanied by a further rise of some £48 overall. Access, already very good with only two wide-opening doors, was improved in terms of convenience. Modified door locks were added, plus ash-tray-carrying arm-rests, and relocated, simpler to operate, panel switches. But the heater system perpetuated another short-coming, apparently being either fully on or fully off, with no comfortable mid-point. In De Luxe, 90 De Luxe, SL and 90 SL forms, four-door prices ranged from £797 to £845, while the 1600 model was priced at £890 on introduction.

With this final modification adding to an enormous range of Viva, Victor and Cresta models, plus the Ventora and Viscount, Vauxhall came to the end of a decade of considerable development. Producing saloon cars aimed at a very large portion of the average motoring public they have always offered quite good value for money, even if some aspects of their design philosophy have seemed at odds with the company's firmly British background.

40 Wolseley

From its earliest beginnings as the Wolseley Sheep Shearing Company in the nineteenth century, this old firm became one of the great racing-car manufacturers of the heroic age, and later gained a tremendous reputation for building solid, reliable, well-equipped, middle-class saloons – production of which continued under BMC until into the 'sixties.

For 1960 a new standard-trim fleet 1500 model joined the normally quite luxurious 1500, both being B-Series engined stable-mates of the Riley One-Point-Five, but using a single SU HS2 carburettor and a cr of 7·2:1, producing 50 bhp gross at 4,200 rpm. A four-speed gearbox was used, and, unlike the sporty torsion bar Riley, coil-and-wishbone ifs was used. Otherwise the models were similar, and the pleasant but rather slow and sluggish Wolseley 1500s sold for £705 (fleet model) and £751 (family saloon).

The very first of BMC's Farina-styled medium saloons had been the Wolseley 15/60, and in this form the spacious four-door car produced 55 bhp gross at 4,400 rpm. It was nicely trimmed inside, with the classic Wolseley radiator grille and illuminated badge, and, as staid and reliable transport with just that important touch of individuality, was priced at £936.

Heading the range was the 6/Ninety-Nine, C-Series engined six-cylinder 3-litre model, also Farina-styled, but with longer wheelbase, wider track and generally more room; a parallel model to the Austin A99 Westminster, in fact. The long-stroke 2912-cc engine had an 8·23:1 cr, and twin SU HS4 carburettors, producing 112 bhp gross at 4,750 rpm. A three-speed all-synchromesh gearbox was used with overdrive on top and second as standard, but a Borg-Warner automatic transmission could be specified. With coil-and-wishbone ifs, and a semi-elliptic rear, the big Wolseley used Lockheed 10·8-inch front disc brakes and 10-inch rear drums, steering being by a cam-and-lever system. This model was priced at £1,254 with overdrive, or £1,325 automatic for 1960.

Modifications occurred in May, interior boot and bonnet hinges appearing on the 1500s, with chrome side-trims extended to the headlights without the original circled 'W' motifs. The 15/Sixty adopted new ash-trays with stubbing plates, as common in the rest of the medium Farina range, and a new rear number plate lit by two bulbs in a bumper casing appeared on the 6/Ninety-Nine. In August this model's roof lamps were repositioned, changing from vertical to horizontal fittings, and in September sealed beam headlamps were also standardized.

A new 16/Sixty Farina appeared in September 1961, using the 1622-cc engine in single-carburettor form, lower-rated than the comparable MG and Riley models. Detail suspension changes and slight increases in wheelbase and track gave a better ride and slightly more room inside, and Borg-Warner 35 transmission became an optional extra. The new body shell had lower and less obtrusive tail fins, plain side moulding tips, overriders moved outwards and side grilles with a central horizontal bar over mesh. A new 3-litre model, the 6/110, was introduced, with power raised by a change of camshaft and improved breathing to 120 bhp net at 4,850 rpm. Suspension modifications included fitting a telescopic shock absorber as a Panhard rod to provide lateral axle location, and increases were again made in interior space.

October saw the old 6/Ninety-Nine and 15/Sixty models discontinued, and also the introduction of a Wolseley Mini variant, the Hornet. This used the same extended-tail shell as the Riley Elf, again with the 34-bhp engine and differed only in name and external adornment at this time. The new Hornet was priced at £672, the 16/Sixty at £992 and the 6/110 at £1,342. The 1500, meanwhile, was given a new grille incorporating the sidelight/indicator units, and was called the Mark III, still being available in both fleet and family model trim.

In June 1962 new rear springs appeared on the 16/Sixty, and in July power-assisted steering and air-conditioning became optional extras for the 6/110. Motor Show time in October saw further changes, leathercloth being replaced by leather on the wearing parts of the Hornet seats, with improved rear seat design and baulk-ring synchromesh on the upper gear ratios, while a wax thermostat was fitted on the 1500 to improve the heater output. Duotone paintwork with standard slotted wheel discs and screen washers appeared on the medium Farina saloon, and minor light and ash-tray changes were made to the 3-litre car.

January 1963 found more powerful heaters appearing in the Hornet, and in February the Mark I was replaced by the new Mark II model with a 998-cc engine, and two-leading-shoe front brakes similar to the Riley. In May a new narrow bore exhaust was fitted to the 6/110, new telescopic dampers improved the Hornet in September, and in October a boot courtesy light was added to the 3-litre model.

The following year, 1964, was a year of change for Wolseley, with a Mark II 6/110 replacing the Mark I in March. Overdrive was optional rather than standard now, with a new four-speed gearbox and 13-inch wheels replacing 14s. Self-adjusting brakes were used, and reclining front seats and picnic tables were also standard equipment, and this very much more refined machine maintained the solid, dependable and comfortable reputation set by the earlier models. But it suffered from marked roll, dead steering and a rather high noise-level, although the 98 mph top speed and 0–50 time of 11 sec were commendable.

Hydrolastic suspension was standardized on the Hornet in September, with the diaphragm clutch, visor, mirror and combination starter/ignition switch modifications of the other BMC Mini models, and in October the visors and a greaseless prop-shaft were added to the 6/110. In November the visors and mirror were added to the 1500 model, and in these forms the four Wolseleys entered 1965.

A new Wolseley 1100 model became available in September that year, with walnut veneer and a twin carburettor engine as used in the comparable Riley Kestrel, and in May the reclining front seat option was made available for both types.

Few major alterations followed, although in June 1967 a 1275-cc engine was offered as optional for the 1100, appearing in October as standard in the Wolseley 1300 which replaced the 1100 entirely in February 1968. In the meantime a Mark II 1100 had been produced in October 1967, with the cut-back tail fins and AP automatic transmission available as an option, and in

March a Wolseley 18/Eighty-Five had appeared, being a variant of the big BMC 1800 saloon, with the traditional grille, reversing light built into the rear bumper, rubber insert overriders, walnut fascia and power-assisted steering as standard. Automatic transmission was an optional extra and the new model was priced at £1,105.

In March 1968 the 6/110 3-litre saloon was discontinued, the Hornet, 1300, 16/Sixty and 18/Eighty-Five continuing into 1969 to complete a decade of BMC/Wolseley badge engineering.

41 The Specialists

Britain has always been a particularly prolific producer of small motor manufacturing businesses, but during the 'sixties the accent has changed considerably. Early on, the Ford 8- and 10-based special craze was coming to an end, and in its place a hefty market for Mini-based variants grew up.

In 1960 Ashley Laminates and Falcon Shells were both producing glass-fibre shells accepting Ford mechanical parts, while the latter also built their own chassis frames with separate tubular body-formers to carry the thin glass-reinforced plastic body. LMB Components of Guildford produced a ladder-frame chassis for sale as the basis of a Ford-powered special, this using semi-swing axle ifs and double cantilever transverse rear leaf springs. Speedex at Luton were also producing road/race Austin 7-based 750 Formula shells, their foremost competition exponent, Jem Marsh, developing the wooden Marcos at this time.

For 1961 Watford Sports Cars produced a rakish but not very attractive-looking Cheetah based on the almost universal ladder-frame chassis and Ford components, and running concurrently was the EB Debonair, a two/four seater GT model very much resembling a Bristol in its austerely handsome lines and capable of accepting a variety of power units. Mini components appeared in the streamlined and well-finished but rather uncomfortably short wheelbase Musketeer of 1962, produced in small numbers by Butterfield Engineering in Nazeing, Essex. This was available in kit form, with an 850 engine for £848 and with a 1000 unit for £892 – which was rather expensive. It was quite well equipped, however, and there were a large variety of optional extras offered, but its Mini basis and odd appearance were not in its favour.

Falcon continued in 1962 with their Terrier-produced tubular chassis and own glass-fibre shells, their kits being available with Ford 105E and 109E units, or Climax 1100-cc, 1220-cc and MGA 1600 engines. The cars were light and attractive, priced at around £750 for a mid-range model complete with engine. LMB had taken over marketing of the Debonair GT, produced by EB (Staffs) Ltd, the model featuring Leslie Ballamy-designed ifs and a live rear axle well located by radius arms, a Panhard rod and coil-spring/

damper units. The 109E Ford Classic engine was standard with the Debonair, the model selling for £820 in kit form.

Throughout this period Rochdale Motor Panels from Lancashire produced consistently attractive, well-designed and well-made kits for a small GT model, the Rochdale Olympic. It was cheap at under £600 with a BMC A-Series or a Ford 105E engine, and offered distinctive yet attractive looks combined with occasional four-seat accommodation. A Riley 1·5-litre engine could also be specified, and in the light yet adequately stiff glass-fibre body-chassis unit this produced vivid performance well into the 100-mph bracket.

Elva, Fairthorpe, Gilbern, Lotus, Marcos, Tornado, Turner and TVR were also producing kit cars at this time but have already been described in detail.

By 1963 the Ford 8-10 economy special fad had died, the high-revving Ford push-rod ohv engine or Mini-component cars taking their place. Falcon produced a particularly attractive, sleek and low 515 model, available in kit form and using the 1498-cc Ford engine and all-synchromesh gearbox. David Ogle, the stylist, had produced a pretty globular SX1000 GT model using Mini-Cooper 997-cc mechanicals and an exceptionally high degree of interior refinement and exterior finish. Deep-Sanderson also produced a Mini engine/transmission/suspension package, clothed in sleek glass-fibre GT bodywork, with the engine at the rear to give a low nose and good forward visibility. It was priced at £750 and offered individuality in an unusual way. Heron Plastics had been producing a GT kit of their own for some time, with coil-and-wishbone ifs and a swing-axle rear end and offering attractive two-seat accommodation with either Anglia or Classic engines for from around £730. Rochdale were now offering their extremely attractive and successful Olympic with the 1498-cc Ford engine tuned to produce around 72 bhp, but kit price had now risen to £735, and the completely assembled car sold for £950 – still inexpensive for a very pleasant little motor-car.

Further Mini-based projects were revealed right at the beginning of 1964, test pilot-cum-racing driver Dizzy Addicott having devised a very streamlined glass fibre DART shell designed to accept sub-frames, suspension and engine from the BMC fwd range. Later, the Mini Marcos was to appear, resembling this early model quite closely, as did the Mini-Jem model. Paul Emery Cars somewhat half-heartedly introduced a tiny Imp-based rear-engined Emery GT, the prototype being panelled in aluminium and later production models having glass-fibre shells.

Diva Cars were building handsome long-nosed GTs mainly for club racing use at this time, but some of them appeared in road trim with a variety of Ford engines installed in varying states of tune.

At the beginning of 1966 a new Mini-based variant, destined to become the most refined and attractive of them all, was announced: the Unipower GT. This sleek rear-engined model used a 998-cc transverse-mounted Cooper engine in a robust tubular space-frame chassis, the whole being clothed in a two-door two-seat glass fibre body of particularly attractive appearance. It was probably the most attractive Mini-based model to date and was produced in some quantity by Universal Power Drives Ltd, of Perivale, Middlesex. It was unusual, and improved, by using its own coil-spring/damper suspension system and not relying on Mini components in this design area.

THE SPECIALISTS   The Unipower was progressively developed and refined and reached the end of the decade still in production and selling well.

The latter part of the decade saw few new specialist manufacturers coming forward, other than those already dealt with in the main body of the text. In 1967 the Ogle SX1000 reappeared under Fletcher Marine auspices as the Fletcher GT, using 850-, 1000- and 1300-cc engines, and another Mini variant was the basically similar Cox GTM, using the BMC engine/transmission/suspension subframe at the rear of a sheet steel chassis clad in glass-fibre bodywork. The Camber GT, and later Maya GT were similar ventures destined for limited success, but come the end of the decade very few more serious attempts had been made to break into the small-quantity motor manufacturing business. With the death of the Ford-engined special movement, and the development by the leading small manufacturers of more and more refined machinery, only Unipower were significantly successful in producing a variant based on a popular mass-produced car.

A.C.

Model and Type	Bore mm	Stroke mm	Cap. cc	C.R.	Vlves.	b.h.p. at r.p.m.	Grs.	Brks.	W/base ft. in.	O.L. ft. in.	O.W. ft. in.	O.H. ft. in.	Track ft. in.	Dry wt. cwt.	Intro./Discon.
Ace 2 dr. spts.	65·0	100·0	1,991	9·0	sohc	102·5(g) 4,500	4	drum	7 6	12 7½	4 11½	4 1	4 2	16	Oct '53/Jul '63
Ace-Bristol 2 dr. spts.	66·0	96·0	1,971	8·5	ohv/p	105 5,000	4	drum	7 6	12 7½	4 11½	4 1	4 2	16	'56/Jul '63
Aceca 2 dr. cpé.	65·0	100·0	1,991	9·0	sohc	102·5 (g) 4,500	4	drum	7 6	12 9½	5 1	4 4	4 2	18	'54/Feb '63
Aceca-Bristol 2 dr. cpé.	66·0	96·0	1,971	8·5	ohv/p	105 5,000	4	drum	7 6	12 9½	5 1	4 4	4 2	18	'56/Jan '63
2·6 Ace 2 dr. spts.	82·55	79·5	2,553	9·2	ohv/p	170 5,500	4	disc/drum	7 6	12 8½	4 11½	4 11	4 2	15½	Oct '61/Jul '63
2·6 Aceca 2dr. spts.	82·55	79·5	2,553	9·2	ohv/p	170 5,500	4	disc/drum	7 6	12 9½	5 1	4 4	4 2	–	Oct '61/Nov '62
Greyhound 2 dr. cpé	66·0	96·0	1,971	9·0	ohv/p	125 6,000	4	disc/drum	8 4	15 0	5 5½	4 4½	4 6	20	Oct '59/July '63
Cobra 289 2 dr. spts.	101·6	72·9	4,727	11·0	ohv/p	280 5,750	4	disc	7 6	12 7½	5 1	4 1	4 4½	18	Oct '62/Feb '69
427 2 dr. conv.	107·7	90·62	6,997	–	ohv/p	– –	4/3A	disc	8 0	14 6	5 7	4 3	4 8	27½	Oct '65/Oct '66
428 2 dr. conv.	104·9	101·1	7,016	10·5	ohv/p	345(g) 4,600	4/3A	disc	8 0	14 6	5 7	4 3	4 8	27½	Jan '67/–
428 Fastback cpé.	104·9	101·1	7,016	10·5	ohv/p	345(g) 4,600	4/3A	disc	8 0	14 6	5 7	4 3	4 8	28½	Mar '67/–

Alvis

Model and Type	Bore mm	Stroke mm	Cap. cc	C.R.	Vlves.	b.h.p. at r.p.m.	Grs.	Brks.	W/base ft. in.	O.L. ft. in.	O.W. ft. in.	O.H. ft. in.	Track ft. in.	Dry wt. cwt.	Intro./Discon.
3-litre 2 dr. sal. (Ser. TD21)	84	90	2,993	8·5	ohv/p	115 4,000	4/3A	disc/drum	9 3½	15 8½	5 6	5 0	4 7⅝	29½	Sep '58/Oct '63
3-litre 2 dr. sal. (Ser. TE21 SIII)	84	90	2,993	8·5	ohv/p	130 5,000	5/3A	disc	9 3½	15 8½	5 6	5 0	4 7⅝	29	Oct '63/Mar '66
3-litre (Ser. TF21)	84	90	2,993	9·0	ohv/p	150 4,750	5/3A	disc	9 3½	15 8¾	5 6	5 0	4 7⅝	29½	Mar '66/Sep '67

Armstrong-Siddeley

Model and Type	Bore mm	Stroke mm	Cap. cc	C.R.	Vlves.	b.h.p. at r.p.m.	Grs.	Brks.	W/base ft. in.	O.L. ft. in.	O.W. ft. in.	O.H. ft. in.	Track ft. in.	Dry wt. cwt.	Intro./Discon.
Star Sapphire 4 dr. sal.	97	90	3,990	7·5	ohv/p	165(g) 4,250	3A	disc/drum	9 6	16 2	6 2	5 2	4 9⅞	34½	Oct '58/Jul '60

Aston Martin

Model and Type	Bore mm	Stroke mm	Cap. cc	C.R.	Vlves.	b.h.p. at r.p.m.	Grs.	Brks.	W/base ft. in.	O.L. ft. in.	O.W. ft. in.	O.H. ft. in.	Track ft. in.	Dry wt. cwt.	Intro./Discon.
DB4	92	92	3,670	8·25	dohc	240 5,500	4	disc	8 2	14 8¼	5 6	4 4	4 6	26¼	Oct '58/Aug '63
DB4GT	92	92	3,670	9·0	dohc	302 6,000	4	disc	7 9	14 3⅜	5 6	4 4	4 6	24½	Sep '59/Mar '63
DB5	96	92	3,995	8·75	dohc	282 5,500	4/5	disc	8 2	15 0	5 6	4 4	4 6	28·9	Sep '63/Aug '65
DB6	96	92	3,995	8·9	dohc	282 5,500	5/3A	disc	8 5¾	15 2	5 7¾	4 5½	4 6¼	30	Oct '65/–
DBS	96	92	3,995	8·9	dohc	282 5,500	5/3A	disc	8 6¼	15 0½	6 0	4 4¼	4 11	36	Oct '67/–
Volante	96	92	3,995	8·9	dohc	325 5,750	5/3A	disc	8 5¾	15 2	5 6	4 5½	4 6¼	32·5	Oct '67/–

Austin

Model and Type	Bore mm	Stroke mm	Cap. cc	C.R.	Vlves.	b.h.p. at r.p.m.	Grs.	Brks.	W/base ft. in.	O.L. ft. in.	O.W. ft. in.	O.H. ft. in.	Track ft. in.	Dry wt. cwt.	Intro./Discon.
Mini	62·94	68·26	848	8·3	ohv/p	34 5,500	4	drum	6 8 5/32	10 0¼	4 7½	4 5	3 11 7/16	12½	Aug '59/Oct '67
Mini Countryman	62·94	68·26	848	8·3	ohv/p	34 5,500	4	drum	7 0 5/32	10 9⅞	4 7½	4 5½	3 11 7/16	13	Mar '60/Oct '67
Mini-Cooper	62·43	81·28	997	9·0	ohv/p	55 6,000	4	disc/drum	6 8 5/32	10 0¼	4 7½	4 5	3 11 33/32	12¾	Aug '61/Jan '64
Mini-Cooper 'S'	70·64	68·26	1,071	9·0	ohv/p	67·5 6,500	4	disc/drum	6 8 5/32	10 0¼	4 7½	4 5	4 0 33/32	13¾	Mar '63/Mar '64
Mini-Cooper	64·58	76·2	998	9·0	ohv/p	55 5,800	4	disc/drum	6 8 5/32	10 0¼	4 7½	4 5	3 11 33/32	13	Jan '64/–
Mini-Cooper 'S'	70·64	61·91	970	10·0	ohv/p	64 6,500	4	disc/drum	6 8 5/32	10 0¼	4 7½	4 5	4 0 33/32	12½	Jun '64/Jan '65
Mini-Cooper 'S'	70·64	81·33	1,275	9·75	ohv/p	76 6,000	4	disc/drum	6 8 5/32	10 0¼	4 7½	4 5	4 0 33/32	12½	Apr '64/–
Mini Mk II 1000	64·58	76·2	998	8·3	ohv/p	38 5,250	4	drum	6 8 5/32	10 0¼	4 7½	4 5	3 11 7/16	12½	Oct '67/–
Mini Mk II 1000 Countryman	64·58	76·2	998	8·3	ohv/p	38 5,250	4	drum	7 0 5/32	10 9⅞	4 7½	4 5½	3 11 7/16	13	Oct '67/–
A35 Countryman	62·94	76·2	948	8·3	ohv/p	34 4,750	4	drum	6 7½	11 5⅞	4 8	5 4	3 9¼	–	1956/Sep '62

Austin

Model and Type	Bore mm	Stroke mm	Cap. cc	C.R.	Vlves.	b.h.p. at r.p.m.	Grs.	Brks.	W/base ft. in.	O.L. ft. in.	O.W. ft. in.	O.H. ft. in.	Track ft. in.	Dry wt cwt.	Intro./Discon.
A40	62·94	76:2	948	8·3	ohv/p	34 4,800	4	drum	6 11 13/32	12 2	4 11 3/8	4 8 3/4	3 11	15 5/8	Jun '58/Sep '62
A40 Countryman	62·94	76:2	948	8·3	ohv/p	34 4,800	4	drum	6 11 9/32	12 2	4 11 3/8	4 8 1/4	3 11	15 1/2	Sep '59/Sep '61
A40 Mk II	64·58	83-72	1,098	8·5	ohv/p	48 5,100	4	drum	7 3 3/64	12 1 1/8	4 11 3/8	4 8 3/4	3 11	15 5/8	Sep '61/Nov '67
A40 Mk II Countryman	64·58	83-72	1,098	8·5	ohv/p	48 5,100	4	drum	7 3 3/64	12 1 1/8	4 11 3/8	4 8 1/4	3 11	15 1/2	Sep '61/Nov '67
A55 Cambridge Mk II	73·025	89	1,489	8·3	ohv/p	53 4,350	4	drum	8 3 7/16	14 10 1/8	5 3 1/2	4 11 3/4	4 1 7/8	20 5/8	Sep '58/Oct '61
Cambridge Mk II Countryman	73·025	89	1,489	8·3	ohv/p	53 4,350	4	drum	8 3 7/16	14 10 1/8	5 3 1/2	5 0	4 1 7/8	22 3/4	Sep '60/Oct '61
A60 Cambridge	76:2	89	1,622	8·3	ohv/p	61 5,100	4/3A	drum	8 4 1/4	14 6 1/2	5 3 1/2	4 10 1/8	4 3 3/8	21 1/2	Oct '61/Feb '69
A60 Countryman	76:2	89	1,622	8·3	ohv/p	61 5,100	4/3A	drum	8 4 1/4	14 9 1/8	5 3 1/2	4 10 1/8	4 3 3/8	22 3/4	Oct '61/Feb '69
A99 Westminster	83·34	89	2,912	8·3	ohv/p	108 4,750	3	disc/drum	9 0	15 7 1/2	5 8 1/2	5 0 1/2	4 6	29 3/4	Jul '59/Sep '61
A110 Westminster	83·34	89	2,912	8·3	ohv/p	120 4,750	3	disc/drum	9 2	15 8	5 8 1/2	5 0	4 5 1/8	31 1/2	Sep '61/Jan '68
1100	64·58	83-73	1,098	8·5	ohv/p	48 5,100	4	disc/drum	7 9 1/2	12 2 3/4	5 0 3/8	4 5	4 3 1/2	16	Sep '63/Mar '68
1100 Countryman	64·58	83-73	1,098	8·5	ohv/p	48 5,100	4	disc/drum	7 9 1/2	12 2 3/8	5 0 3/8	4 5	4 3 1/2	16 1/4	Mar '66/–
1300	70-61	81-28	1,275	8·8	ohv/p	60 5,250	4	disc/drum	7 9 1/2	12 2 3/4	5 0 3/8	4 5	4 3 1/2	16 1/2	Oct '67/–
1300 Countryman	70-61	81-28	1,275	8·8	ohv/p.	60 5,250	4	disc/drum	7 9 1/2	12 2 3/4	3 0 3/8	4 5	4 3 1/2	16 5/8	Oct '67/–
1800	80-26	89	1,798	8·4	ohv/p	84 5,300	4	disc/drum	8 10 1/8	13 8 1/4	5 6 3/4	4 8	4 8	22 3/4	Oct '64/–
1800S	80-26	89	1798	9·5	ohv/p	95·5 5,700	4	disc/drum	8 10 3/8	13 8 27/32	5 6 7/8	4 8 5/16	4 8	22 3/4	Sep '69/–
3 Litre	83·34	89	2,912	8·2	ohv/p	118 4,500	4/3A	disc/drum	9 7 1/2	15 5 1/8	5 6 1/4	4 8 3/32	4 8 3/32	29 5/8	Oct '67/–
Maxi	76:2	81-28	1,485	9·0	sohc	74 5,500	4	disc/drum	8 8·8	13 3	5 4	4 6·5	4 5-8	19 1/8	Apr '69/–

Austin-Healey

Model and Type	Bore mm	Stroke mm	Cap. cc	C.R.	Vlves.	b.h.p. at r.p.m.		Grs.	Brks.	W/base ft. in.	O.L. ft. in.	O.W. ft. in.	O.H. ft. in.	Track ft. in.	Dry wt. cwt.	Intro./Discon.
Sprite Mk. I 2 dr. spts. (AN5)	62·9	76·2	948	8·3	ohv/p	42·5	5,000	4	drum	6 8	11 5¼	4 5½	4 1¾	3 9¾	58/	Mar '58/May '61
Sprite Mk. II 2 dr. spts. (AN6)	62·9	76·2	948	9·0	ohv/p	46·5	5,500	4	drum	6 8	11 0¾	4 5	4 1¾	3 9¾	13½	May '61/Oct '62
Sprite Mk. II 2 dr. spts. (AN7)	64·58	83·72	1,098	8·9	ohv/p	55	5,500	4	disc/drum	6 8	11 0¾	4 5	3 11¾	3 9¾	14	Oct '62/Mar '64
Sprite Mk. III 2 dr. spts. (H/AN8)	64·58	83·72	1,098	9·0	ohv/p	59	5,750	4	disc/drum	6 8	11 0¾	4 7	4 0½	3 9¾	13¾	Mar '64/Oct '66
Sprite Mk. IV 2 dr. spts. (H/AN9)	70·64	81·33	1,275	9·0	ohv/p	65	6,000	4	disc/drum	6 8	11 0¾	4 6⅞	4 0½	3 10 19/32	13½	Oct '66/–
3000 Mk. I 2 dr. spts. (BN7/BT7)	83·34	89	2,912	9·03	ohv/p	124	4,600	4	disc/drum	7 7¾	13 1½	5 0	4 1	4 2	21¼	Mar '59/Jun '61
3000 Mk. II 2 dr. spts. (BN7/BT7)	83·36	89	2,912	9·03	ohv/p	130	4,750	4	disc/drum	7 8	13 1½	5 0½	4 2	4 2	21¼	Jun '61/Feb '64
3000 Mk. III 2 dr. spts. (BJ8)	83·36	89	2,912	9·03	ohv/p	150	5,250	4	disc/drum	7 8	13 1½	5 0	4 2¾	4 2	22¾	Feb '64/Jan '68

Bentley

Model and Type	Bore mm	Stroke mm	Cap. cc	C.R.	Vlves.	b.h.p. at r.p.m.		Grs.	Brks.	W/base ft. in.	O.L. ft. in.	O.W. ft. in.	O.H. ft. in.	Track ft. in.	Dry wt. cwt.	Intro./Discon.
S2/S3 Series	104·14	91·44	6,230	8·0	ohv/p	–	–	4A	drums	10 3 10 7	–	–	–	5 0	39/ 40¾	Aug '59/Oct '65
T-Series	104·14	91·44	6,230	9·0	ohv/p	–	–	4A	discs	9 11½	16 11½	5 11	4 11¾	4 9½	40¾	Oct. '65/–

Bristol

Model and Type	Bore mm	Stroke mm	Cap. cc	C.R.	Vlves.	b.h.p. at r.p.m.	Grs.	Brks.	W/base ft. in.	O.L. ft. in.	O.W. ft. in.	O.H. ft. in.	Track ft. in.	Dry wt. cwt.	Intro./Discon.
406	68·69	99·64	2,216	8·5	ohv/p	105 4,700	4	disc	9 6	16 6	5 8	5 0	4 8	27	Aug '58/Oct '61
407	98·55	84·07	5,130	9·0	ohv/p	250(g) 4,400	3A	disc	9 6	16 7	5 8	5 0	4 6½	31½	Oct '61/Feb '64
408	98·55	84·07	5,130	9·0	ohv/p	250(g) 4,400	3A	disc	9 6	16 1½	5 8	4 11	4 6½	31	Oct '63/–
409	99·31	84·07	5,211	9·0	ohv/p	250(g) 4,400	3A	disc	9 6	16 1½	5 8	4 11	4 6½	30	Oct '65/–
410	99·31	84·07	5,211	9·0	ohv/p	250(g) 4,400	3A	disc	9 6	16 1½	5 8	4 11	4 7	30	Oct '67/–

Daimler

Model and Type	Bore mm	Stroke mm	Cap. cc	C.R.	Vlves.	b.h.p. at r.p.m.	Grs.	Brks.	W/base ft. in.	O.L. ft. in.	O.W. ft. in.	O.H. ft. in.	Track ft. in.	Dry wt. cwt.	Intro./Discon.
SP 250	76·2	69·85	2548	8·2	ohv/p	140 5,800	4/3A	Disc	8 8	13 4¼	5 0½	4 2¼	4 2	20	Sep '59/Sep '64
Majestic	86·36	107·95	3794	7·5	ohv/p	147(g) 4,400	3A	Disc	9 6	16 4	6 1¼	5 2¾	4 9	34½	Oct '54/Mar '60
DK 400/A/B Limousine	95·2	107·95	4617	7·0	ohv/p	167(g) 3,800	4	Drum	10 10	18 1	6 5	5 10⅜	5 3	42	Oct '54/Mar '60
Majestic Major	95·25	80·01	4561	8·0	ohv/p	220 5,200	3A	Disc	9 6	16 4	6 1¼	5 2¾	4 9	36½	Oct '59/Jun '68
2½-Litre V8 250	76·2	69·85	2548	8·2	ohv/p	140 5,800	4/3A	Disc	8 11⅜	15 0¾	5 6¾	4 8⅜	4 7	28¼	Oct '62/Oct '69
Sovereign	92·07	106	4235	8·0	dohc	245 5,500	4/3A	Disc	8 11⅜	15 7¾	5 6¾	4 6½	4 7¼	30	Oct '66/Oct '69
New Sovereign (2·8)	83	86	2791	9·0	dohc	180 6,000	4/3A	Disc	9 0·9	19 9½	5 9¼	4 4·9	4 10¼	33	Oct '69/–
New Sovereign (4·2)	92·07	106	4235	8·0	dohc	245 5,500	4/3A	Disc	9 0·9	15 9½	5 9¾	4 4·9	4 10¼	33	Oct '69/–
4·2 Limousine	92·07	106	4235	8·0	dohc	245 5,500	3A	Disc	11 9	18 10	6 6½	5 3¾	4 10	42	Jun '68/–

Ford

Model and Type	Bore mm	Stroke mm	Cap. cc	C.R.	Vlves.	b.h.p. at r.p.m.	Grs.	Brks.	W/base ft. in.	O.L. ft. in.	O.W. ft. in.	O.H. ft. in.	Track ft. in.	Dry wt. cwt.	Intro./Discon.
Consul Mk. II 4 dr. sal. (204E)	82·55	79·5	1,703	7·8	ohv/p	59 4,200	3	disc/drum	8 8½	14 6¼	5 8¾	5 1½	4 5	21½	Feb '56/Apr '62
2 dr. dhc.												5 0¾		22	
4 dr. Est.												5 3½		22	
Zodiac Mk. II 4 dr. sal. (206E)	82·55	79·5	2,553	7·8	ohv/p	86 4,200	3	disc/drum	8 11	14 10½	5 8¾	4 11¾	4 5	22¾	Feb '56/Apr '62
2 dr. hc.												5 1		23½	
4 dr. Est.												5 4		23½	
Zephyr Mk. II 4 dr. sal. (206E)	82·55	79·5	2,553	7·8	ohv/p	86 4,200	3	disc/drum	8 11	14 10½	5 8¾	4 9	4 6	24½	Feb '56/Apr '62
2 dr. dhc.												5 1		23½	
4 dr. Est.												5 4		23½	
Anglia 2 dr. sal. (105E)	80·96	48·41	997	8·9	ohv/p	39 5,000	4	drum	7 6½	12 9½	4 8½	4 8	3 10½	14¾	Sep '59/Dec '67
2 dr. Est.										12 10		4 9½		15¾	
Classic 2/4 dr. sal. (109E)	80·96	65·07	1,340	8·3	ohv/p	54 4,900	4	disc/drum	8 3	14 2¾	5 5¼	4 8	4 2	18¾	Jun '61/July '62
Classic 2/4 dr. sal. (116E)	80·96	72·7	1,498	8·3	ohv/p	59·5 4,600	4	disc/drum	8 3	14 2¾	5 5¼	4 8	4 2	18¾	July '62/Jul '63
Anglia Super 2 dr. sal. (123E)	80·96	58·17	1,197·8	8·7	ohv/p	48·5 4,800	4	drum	7 6½	12 9½	4 8½	4 8	3 10½	14¾	Nov '62/Nov '67
Capri 2 dr. cpé. (Ser. 109E)	80·96	65·07	1,340	8·3	ohv/p	54 4,900	4	disc/drum	8 3	14 2¾	5 5¼	4 5¾	4 1½	17⅜	Sep '61/Jul '62
Capri 2 dr. cpé (Ser. 116E)	80·96	72·7	1,498	8·3	ohv/p	59·5 4,600	4	disc/drum	8 3	14 2¾	5 5¼	4 5¾	4 1½	17⅜	July '62/July '64
Zephyr 6 Mk. III 4 dr. sal. (213E)	82·55	79·5	2,553	8·3	ohv/p	98 4,750	4	disc/drum	8 11	15 0½	5 9	4 9	4 6	24½	Apr '62/Jan '66
4 dr. Est.												4 9½		25⅞	
Zephyr 4 Mk. III 4 dr. sal. (211E)	82·55	79·5	1,703	8·3	ohv/p	68 4,800	4	disc/drum	8 11	15 0½	5 9	4 9	4 6	24½	Apr '62/Jan '66
4 dr. Est.												4 9½		26	
Cortina de luxe 2/4 dr. sal. (113E)	80·96	62·99	1,198	8·7	ohv/p	48·5 4,800	4	disc/drum	8 2	14 0½	5 2½	4 8¼	4 1½	15½	May '62/Sep '66
4 dr. Est.												4 9¼		17½	
Cortina Super 2/4 dr. sal. (118E)	80·96	72·7	1,498	8·3	ohv/p	59·5 4,600	4	disc/drum	8 2	14 0½	5 2½	4 8½	4 1½	16¼	Jan '63/Sep '66
4 dr. Est.												4 9½		18¼	
Cortina GT 2/4 dr. sal. (118EGT)	80·96	72·7	1,498	9·0	ohv/p	78 5,200 rpm	4	disc/drum	8 2	14 0½	5 2½	4 9	4 1½	18¾	Apr '63/Sep '66
Cortina-Lotus 2 dr. sal. (125E)	82·55	72·75	1,558	9·5	dohc	105 5,500	1	disc/drum	8 2	14 0½	5 2½	4 7	4 3¼	16½	Jan '63/Sep '66

Ford

Model and Type	Bore mm	Stroke mm	Cap. cc	C.R.	Vlves.	b.h.p. at r.p.m.	Grs.	Brks.	W/base ft. in.	O.L. ft. in.	O.W. ft. in.	O.H. ft. in.	Track ft. in.	Dry wt cwt.	Intro./Discon.
Corsair 2/4 dr. sal. (120E) 4 dr. Est.	80·96	72·7	1,498	8·3	ohv/p	59·5 4,600	4/3A	disc/drum	8 5	14 9	5 3½	4 7½	4 2½	17½ 20½	Oct '63/Sep '65
Corsair GT 2/4 dr. sal. (120GT)	80·96	72·7	1,498	9·1	ohv/p	78 5,200	4	disc/drum	8 5	14 9	5 3½	4 7½	4 2½	17½	Oct '63/Sep '65
Corsair V4 2/4 dr. sal. (3004E) 4 dr. Est.	93·66	60·35	1,663	8·9	ohv/p	81·5 4,750	4	disc/drum	8 5	14 9	5 3½	4 7½	4 2½	19¼ 21¾	Sep '65/–
Corsair V4 GT 2/4 dr. sal. (3006E) 4 dr. Est.	93·66	72·42	1,996	8·9	ohv/p	93 4,750	4/3A	disc/drum	8 5	14 9	5 3½	4 7½	4 2½	19½ 22½	Sep '65/Nov '66
Corsair 2000 4 dr. sal. (3006E)	93·66	72·42	1,996	8·9	ohv/p	93 4,750	4/3A	disc/drum	8 5	14 9	5 3½	4 7½	4 2½	19½	Nov '66/–
Zephyr V6 Mk. IV 4 dr. sal. (3008E) 4 dr. Est.	93·66	60·35	2,495	8·9	ohv/p	118·5 4,750	4/3A	disc	9 7	15 5	5 10⅗	4 8⅕	4 10⅗	25½ 27¼	Mar '66/–
Zephyr Mk. IV 4 dr. sal. (3010E) 4 dr. Est.	93·66	72·42	1,996	8·9	ohv/p	93 4,750	4/3A	disc	9 7	15 5	5 10⅗	4 8⅕	4 10⅗	24½ 26¼	Mar '66/–
Zodiac Mk. IV 4 dr. sal. (3012E) 4 dr. Est.	93·66	72·42	2,994	8·9	ohv/p	144 4,750	4/3A	disc	9 7	15 5	5 10⅗	4 8⅕	4 10⅗	26¼ 28	Mar '66/–
Cortina Mk. II 1300 (Ser. 3034E)	80·97	62·99	1297	9·0	ohv/p	52 5,000	4	disc/drum	8 2	14 0	5 4·9	4 6¾	4 5½	16⅞	Sep '67/–
Cortina Mk. II Estate 1300	80·97	62·99	1297	9·0	ohv/p	52 5,000	4	disc/drum	8 2	14 1½	5 4·9	4 6¾	4 5½	18⅞	Sep '67/–
Cortina Mk. II Estate 1600	80·97	77·62	1599	9·0	ohv/p	64 4,800	4	disc/drum	8 2	14 1½	5 4·9	4 6¾	4 5½	19¼	Sep '67/–
Cortina Mk. II 1600 (3036E)	80·97	77·62	1599	9·0	ohv/p	64 4,800	4	disc/drum	8 2	14 0	5 4·9	4 6¾	4 5½	18	Sep '67/–
Cortina Mk. II GT (3036E)	80·97	77·62	1599	9·0	ohv/p	82 5,400	4	disc/drum	8 2	14 0	5 4·9	4 6¾	4 5½	18	Sep '67/–
Cortina-Lotus Mk. II (3020E)	82·55	72·8	1558	9·5	dohc	106 6,000	4	disc/drum	8 2	14 0	5 4·9	4 6	4 5½	18	Mar '67/–
1600E (3036E)	80·97	77·62	1559	9·0	ohv/p	82 5,400	4	disc/drum	8 2	14 0	5 4·9	4 6	4 5½	18	Oct '67/–
Executive 4 dr. sal. (3022E)	93·66	72·42	2,994	8·9	ohv/p	144 4,750	4/3A	disc	9 7	15 5	5 10⅗	4 8⅕	4 10⅗	26¼	Oct '66/–
Escort 1100 (3024/3026E)	80·98	53·29	1,097·8	9·0	ohv/p	53(g) 5,500	4	drum	7 10½	13 3¾	5 1¾	4 5	4 1¾	14⅞	Jan '68/–
Escort 1300 (3026/3032E)	80·98	62·99	1,297·7	9·0	ohv/p	63(g) 5,000	4	drum	7 10½	13 3¾	5 1¾	4 5	4 1¾	15	Jan '68/–
Escort 1300GT (2026E)	80·98	62·99	1,297·7	9·2	ohv/p	75(g) 5,400	4	disc/drum	7 10½	13 3¾	5 1¾	4 5	4 1¾	15	Jan '68/–

Ford

Model and Type	Bore mm	Stroke mm	Cap. cc	C.R.	Vlves.	b.h.p. at r.p.m.	Grs.	Brks.	W/base ft. in.	O.L. ft. in.	O.W. ft. in.	O.H. ft. in.	Track ft. in.	Dry wt. cwt	Intro./Discon.
Escort Twin Cam (3026E)	82·55	72·75	1,558	9·5	dohc	115(g) 6,000	4	disc/drum	7 10½	13 3¾	5 1¾	4 5	4 1¾	15¼	Jan '68/–
Escort Estate (1100 & 1300)*	–	–	–	–	–	– –	–	–	7 10½	13 5	5 1¾	4 6	4 1¾	17¼	Mar '68/–
Capri 1300	80·97	62·99	1,297·7	9·0	ohv/p	52 5,000	4	disc/drum	8 4¾	13 11¾	5 4¾	4 2¾	4 5	17¼	Jan '69/–
Capri 1300GT	80·97	62·99	1,297·7	9·2	ohv/p	64 6,000	4	disc/drum	8 4¾	13 11¾	5 4¾	4 2¼	4 5	17½	Jan '69/–
Capri 1600	80·97	77·62	1,599	9·0	ohv/p	64 4,800	4	disc/drum	8 4¾	13 11¾	5 4¾	4 2¾	4 5	17½	Jan '69/–
Capri 1600GT	80·97	77·62	1,599	9·0	ohv/p	82 5,400	4	disc/drum	8 4¾	13 11¾	5 4¾	4 2¾	4 5	18¼	Jan '69/–
Capri 2000GT	93·66	72·44	1,996	8·9	ohv/p	93 5,500	4	disc/drum	8 4¾	13 11¾	5 4¾	4 2¾	4 5	18⅞	Jan '69/–
Capri 3000GT	93·66	72·42	2,994	8·9	ohv/p	128 4,750	4	disc/drum	8 4¾	13 11¾	5 4¾	4 2¼	4 5	21¼	

*details omitted may be taken from corresponding saloon version table

Hillman

Model and Type	Bore mm	Stroke mm	Cap. cc	C.R.	Vlves.	b.h.p. at r.p.m.	Grs.	Brks.	W/base ft. in.	O.L. ft. in.	O.W. ft. in.	O.H. ft. in.	Track ft. in.	Dry wt. cwt.	Intro./Discon.
Minx (Ser. IIIA)	79·0	76·2	1,494	8·5	ohv/p	50·2 –	4/3A	drum	8 0	13 6·7	5 0¾	4 10½	4 1	19·4	Sept '59/Sep '60
Minx (Ser. IIIB)	79·0	76·2	1,494	8·5	ohv/p	50·2 –	4/3A	drum	8 0	13 6·7	5 0¾	4 10½	4 1	19·4	Sep '60/Jul '61
Minx (Ser. IIIC)	81·5	76·22	1,592	8·3	ohv/p	52·8 –	4/3A	drum	8 0	13 5½	5 0¾	4 10	4 3¾	19	Aug '61/Aug '63
Minx (Ser. V)	81·5	76·22	1,592	8·3	ohv/p	52·8 –	4/3A	disc/drum	8 0	13 6·7	5 0¾	4 11½	4 1	19·2	Sep '63/Sep '65
Minx (Ser. VI)	81·5	82·55	1,725	8·4	ohv/p	65 –	4/3A	disc/drum	8 0	13 6·7	5 0¾	4 11½	4 1	19·2	Sep '65/Mar '67
Husky (Ser. II)	76·2	76·2	1,390	8·0	ohv/p	51(g) 4,400	4	drum	7 2	12 5½	5 0½	4 11½	4 1	18	Mar '60/Aug '63

Hillman

Model and Type	Bore mm	Stroke mm	Cap. cc	C.R.	Vlves.	b.h.p. at r.p.m.	Grs.	Brks.	W/base ft. in.	O.L. ft. in.	O.W. ft. in.	O H. ft. in.	Track ft. in.	Dry wt. cwt.	Intro./Discon.
Husky (Ser. III)	76·2	76·2	1,390	8·0	ohv/p	40·5 4,200	4	disc/drum	7 2	12 5½	5 0½	4 11½	4 1	18½	Aug '63/Dec '65
Super Minx (Mk. I)	81·5	76·22	1,592	8·3	ohv/p	53·5 —	4/3A	disc/drum	8 7	13 10¼	5 3¾	4 10¼	4 3¾	20½	Oct '61/Apr '67
Imp	68·0	60·375	875	10·0	sohc	39 —	4	drum	6 10	11 7	5 0¼	4 6½	4 1·3	13¾	May '63/–
Imp Californian	68·0	60·375	875	10·0	sohc	39 —	4	drum	6 10	11 7	5 0¼	4 4½	4 2·6	14·1	Oct '67/–
New Minx	81·5	71·6	1,496	8·4	ohv/p	60 —	4	disc/drum	8 2½	14 0	5 3½	4 8	4 4	17½	Nov '66/–
Hunter	81·5	82·55	1,725	9·2	ohv/p	74 —	4/3A	disc/drum	8 2½	14 1½	5 3½	4 8	4 4	18¾	Aug '66/–

Humber

Model and Type	Bore mm	Stroke mm	Cap. cc	C.R.	Vlves.	b.h.p. at r.p.m.	Grs.	Brks.	W/base ft. in.	O.L. ft. in.	O.W. ft. in.	O.H. ft. in.	Track ft. in.	Dry wt. cwt.	Intro./Discon.
Hawk (IA, II, III)	81	110	2,267	7·5	ohv/p	73 4,400	4	disc/drum	9 2	15 4¾	5 9½	5 1	4 8⅞	28½	Oct '59/Sep '64
Hawk (IV)	81	110	2,267	7·5	ohv/p	78(g) 4,400	4/3A	disc/drum	9 2	15 4	5 10	4 11¼	4 8¾	28·9	Oct '64/Jan '68
Super Snipe (II)	87·3	82·55	2,965	8·0	ohv/p	121 4,800	3/3A	disc/drum	9 2	15 4½	5 10	5 1	4 8⅞	29	Oct '59/Sep '60
Super Snipe (III & IV)	87·3	82·55	2,965	8·0	ohv/p	121 4,800	3/3A	disc/drum	9 2	15 8	5 10	5 1	4 8⅞	28⅞	Oct '60/Sep '64
Super Snipe (V)	87·3	82·55	2,965	7·5	ohv/p	132·7 5,000	3/3A	disc/drum	9 2	15 7½	5 10	4 11¾	4 8⅞	31½	Oct '64/Jun '67
Sceptre (Mk. I)	81·5	76·2	1,592	9·1	ohv/p	— —	4	disc/drum	8 5	13 9½	5 3¼	4 9	4 3¾	22	Jan '63/Sep '65
Sceptre (Mk. III)	81·5	82·55	1,725	9·2	ohv/p	85 —	4/3A	disc/drum	8 5	13 11	5 3¼	4 9	4 3¾	21½	Sep '65/Sep '67
New Sceptre	81·5	82·55	1,725	9·2	ohv/p	94 —	4/3A	disc/drum	8 2½	14 1½	5 4⅔	4 8	4 4	19½	Sep '67/–
Imperial	87·3	82·55	2,965	7·5	ohv/p	124 —	4/3A	disc/drum	9 2	15 7½	5 10	4 11¾	4 8·9	32½	Oct '64/Jun '67

Jaguar

Model and Type	Bore mm	Stroke mm	Cap cc	C.R.	Vlves.	b.h.p. at r.p.m.	Grs.	Brks.	W/base ft. in.	O.L. ft. in.	O.W. ft. in.	O.H. ft. in.	Track ft. in.	Dry wt. cwt.	Intro./Discon.
3·8 Mk. II	87	106	3,781	8·0	dohc	220(g) 5,500	4/3A	disc	8 11$\frac{3}{8}$	15 0$\frac{3}{4}$	5 6$\frac{3}{4}$	4 9$\frac{1}{2}$	4 7	28$\frac{1}{4}$	Oct '59/Sep '67
3·4 Mk. II	83	106	3,442	8·0	dohc	210(g) 5,500	4/3A	disc	8 11$\frac{3}{8}$	15 0$\frac{3}{4}$	5 6$\frac{3}{4}$	4 9$\frac{1}{2}$	4 7	28$\frac{1}{4}$	Oct '59/Sep '67
2·4 Mk. II	83	76·5	2,483	8·1	dohc	120(g) 5,750	4/3A	disc	8 11$\frac{3}{8}$	15 0$\frac{3}{4}$	5 6$\frac{3}{4}$	4 8$\frac{5}{8}$	4 7	27$\frac{1}{2}$	Oct '59/Sep '67
Mk. IX	87	106	3,781	8·0	dohc	220(g) 5,500	4/3A	disc	10 0	16 4$\frac{1}{2}$	6 1	5 3	4 10$\frac{3}{16}$	34$\frac{1}{2}$	Oct '58/Sep '61
Mk. X	87	106	3,781	8·0	dohc	255 5,500	4/3A	disc	10 0	16 10	6 4$\frac{5}{16}$	4 6$\frac{1}{2}$	4 10	35	Oct '61/Oct '65
E Type 3·8	87	106	3,781	9·0	dohc	265(g) 5,500	4	disc	8 0	14 7$\frac{5}{16}$	5 5$\frac{1}{4}$	4 0	4 2	22	Mar '61/Oct '65
3·8S	87	106	3,781	8·0	dohc	220(g) 5,500	4/3A	disc	8 11$\frac{3}{8}$	15 7$\frac{3}{4}$	5 6$\frac{3}{4}$	4 6$\frac{1}{2}$	4 7$\frac{1}{4}$	30	Sep '63/Sep '67
3·4S	83	106	3,442	8·0	dohc	210(g) 5,500	4/3A	disc	8 11$\frac{3}{8}$	15 7$\frac{3}{4}$	5 6$\frac{3}{4}$	4 6$\frac{1}{2}$	4 7$\frac{1}{4}$	30	Sep '63/–
Mk. 10 4·2 & 420G	92·07	106	4,235	8·0	dohc	255 5,400	4/3A	disc	10 0	16 10	6 4$\frac{5}{16}$	4 6$\frac{1}{2}$	4 10	35	Oct '64/Oct '66/+
E-Type 2 + 2	92·07	106	4,235	9·0	dohc	265(g) 5,400	4/3A	disc	8 9	15 4$\frac{1}{2}$	5 5$\frac{1}{4}$	4 2	4 2	27	Mar '66/Sep '68
420	92·07	106	4,235	8·0	dohc	245 5,400	4/3A	disc	8 11$\frac{3}{8}$	15 7$\frac{3}{4}$	5 6$\frac{3}{4}$	4 6$\frac{1}{2}$	4 7$\frac{1}{4}$	35	Oct '66/–
240	83	76·5	2,483	8·0	dohc	133(g) 5,500	4/3A	disc	8 11$\frac{1}{4}$	15 0$\frac{3}{4}$	5 6$\frac{1}{4}$	4 9$\frac{1}{2}$	4 7	27$\frac{1}{2}$	Sep '67/–
340	83	106	3,442	8·0	dohc	210(g) 5,500	4/3A	disc	8 11$\frac{1}{4}$	15 0$\frac{3}{4}$	5 6$\frac{1}{4}$	4 9$\frac{1}{2}$	4 7	27$\frac{1}{2}$	Sep '67/–
E-Type 4·2	92·07	106	4,235	9·0	dohc	265(g) 5,400	4	disc	8 0	14 7$\frac{5}{16}$	5 5$\frac{1}{4}$	4 0	4 2	23	Oct '64/Sep '68
XJ6 2·8	83	86	2,792	9·0	dohc	180(g) 6,000	4/3A	disc	9 0$\frac{4}{5}$	15 9$\frac{1}{2}$	5 9$\frac{1}{2}$	4 4$\frac{4}{5}$	4 10$\frac{3}{5}$	30$\frac{1}{4}$	Oct '68/–
XJ6 4·2	92·07	106	4,235	8·0	dohc	245(g) 5,500	4/3A	disc	9 0$\frac{4}{5}$	15 9$\frac{1}{2}$	5 9$\frac{1}{2}$	4 4$\frac{4}{5}$	4 10$\frac{3}{5}$	30$\frac{3}{4}$	Oct '68/–
Series 2 E-Type	92·07	106	4,235	9·0	dohc	265(g) 5,400	4	disc	8 0	14 7$\frac{5}{16}$	5 5$\frac{1}{4}$	4 0	4 2	23$\frac{3}{4}$	Oct '68/–
Series 2 E-Type 2 + 2	92·07	106	4,235	9·0	dohc	265(g) 5,400	4/3A	disc	8 9	15 4$\frac{1}{2}$	5 5$\frac{1}{4}$	4 2	4 2	26$\frac{1}{2}$	Oct '68/–

Jensen

Model and Type	Bore mm	Stroke mm	Cap. cc	C.R.	Vlves.	b.h.p. at r.p.m.	Grs.	Brks.	W/base ft. in.	O.L. ft. in.	O.W. ft. in.	O.H. ft. in.	Track ft. in.	Dry wt. cwt.	Intro./Discon.
541R	87	111	3,993	7·4	ohv/p	– –	4	disc	8 9	14 8	5 3	4 5	4 4	29	Oct '56/Sep '60
541S	87	111	3,993	7·4	ohv/p	135 –	3A	disc	8 9	14 10	5 7	4 6	4 7¼	28	Oct '60/Sep '63
CV8 Mk I	105	86	5,916	9·0	ohv/p	330 4,600	3A	disc	8 9	15 4	5 7	4 7	4 9	31	Oct '62/Oct '63
CV8 Mk II	108	86	6,276	9·0	ohv/p	330 4,600	3A	disc	8 9	15 4	5 7	4 7	4 9	31	Oct '63/Jul '65
CV8 Mk III	108	86	6,276	9·0	ohv/p	330 4,600	3A	disc	8 9	15 4	5 7	4 7	4 9	31	Jul '65/Oct '66
Interceptor	108	86	6,276	10·0	ohv/p	330 4,600	4/3A	disc	8 9	15 8	5 9	4 5	4 9	32	Oct '66/–
FF	108	86	6,276	10·0	ohv/p	330 4,600	4/3A	disc	9 1	15 11	5 9	4 5	4 9	34	Oct '66/–

MG

Model and Type	Bore mm	Stroke mm	Cap. cc	C.R.	Vlves.	b.h.p. at r.p.m.	Grs.	Brks.	W/base ft. in.	O.L. ft. in.	O.W. ft. in.	O.H. ft. in.	Track ft. in.	Dry wt. cwt	Intro./Discon.
Magnette III	73·025	89	1,489	8·3	ohv/p	63·5 5,000	4	drum	8 3 3/16	14 10⅛	5 3½	4 11¾	4 1⅞	21½	Feb '59/Oct '61
Magnette IV	76·2	89	1,622	8·3	ohv/p	68 5,000	4/3A	drum	8 4¼	14 10⅛	5 3½	4 10⅛	4 3⅜	21½	Aug '61/Apr '68
MGA 1600	73·395	88·9	1,588	8·3	ohv/p	79·5 5,600	4	disc/drum	7 10	13 0	4 10	4 2	4 0¾	17½	Jul '59/Mar '61
MGA 1600 Mk II	76·2	89	1,622	9·0	ohv/p	90 5,500	4	disc/drum	7 10	13 0	4 10	4 2	4 0¾	17¾	Jun '61/Jun '62
MGA Twin Cam	73·395	88·9	1,588	9·9	dohc	108(g) 6,700	4	disc	7 10	13 0	4 10	4 2	4 0⅞	18¾	May '58/Jun '60
Midget Mk. I	62·94	76·2	948	9·0	ohv/p	46·4 5,500	4	drum	6 8	11 5⅝	4 5	4 1¾	3 9¾	12½	Jun '61/Mar '64
Midget Mk. II	64·58	83·72	1,098	8·9	ohv/p	56 5,750	4	disc/drum	6 8	11 5⅝	4 5	4 1¾	3 9¾	13	Mar '64/Oct '66
Midget Mk. III	70·61	81·28	1,275	8·8	ohv/p	64 5,800	4	disc/drum	6 8	11 5⅜	4 6⅞	4 0⅝	3 10 15/16	13½	Oct '66/–
MGB	80·26	89	1,798	8·8	ohv/p	95 5,400	4	disc/drum	7 7	12 9 3/16	4 11 15/16	4 1⅜	4 1¼	18⅛	Jul '62/–
MGC	83·362	89	2,912	9·0	ohv/p	145 5,250	4	disc/drum	7 7	12 9¾	4 11 15/16	4 2¼	4 2	22	Oct '67/Jul '69

MG

Model and Type	Bore mm	Stroke mm	Cap. cc	C.R.	Vlves.	b.h.p. at r.p.m.	Grs.	Brks.	W/base ft. in.	O.L. ft. in.	O.W. ft. in.	O.H. ft. in.	Track ft. in.	Dry wt. cwt	Intro./Discon.
1100	64·58	83·72	1,098	8·9	ohv/p	55 5,500	4	disc/drum	7 9½	12 2¾	5 0⅜	4 5	4 3½	15½	Oct '62/Mar '68
1300	70·61	81·28	1,275	8·8	ohv/p	60 5,250	4	disc/drum	7 9½	12 2¾	5 0⅜	4 5⅞	4 3½	15½	Oct '67/–

Morgan

Model and Type	Bore mm	Stroke mm	Cap. cc	C.R.	Vlves	b.h.p. at r.p.m.	Grs.	Brks.	W/base ft. in.	O.L. ft. in.	O.W. ft. in.	O.H. ft. in.	Track ft. in.	Dry wt. cwt	Intro./Discon.
Plus 4	83	92	1,991	8·5	ohv/p	100 5,000	4	disc/drum	8 0	12 0	4 8	4 4½	3 11	15¾	Oct '58/Jun '62
4/4 (Ser. III)	81	48·4	997	8·9	ohv/p	41 5,000	4	disc/drum	8 0	12 0	4 8	4 3	3 11	12¾	Sep '60/Oct '61
4/4 (Ser. IV)	81	65	1,340	8·5	ohv/p	56 4,900	4	disc/drum	8 0	12 0	4 8	4 3	3 11	13	Oct '61/Feb '65
4/4 (Ser. V)	81	72·75	1,498	9·0	ohv/p	83 4,600	4	disc/drum	8 0	12 0	4 8	4 3	3 11	13	Jan '66/Jan '68
4/4 '1600'	81	77·6	1,598	9·0	ohv/p	93 4,750	4	disc/drum	8 0	12 0	4 8	4 3	3 11	13	Jan '68/–
Plus 4	86	92	2,138	9·0	ohv/p	105 4,750	4	disc/drum	8 0	12 0	4 8	4 4½	3 11	15¾	Jun '62/Jan '69
Plus 4 Plus	86	92	2,138	9·0	ohv/p	105 4,750	4	disc/drum	8 0	12 8	5 1	4 3	4 1	15½	Oct '63/Dec '66
Plus 8	88·9	71·12	3,528	10·5	ohv/hyd	184(g) 5,200	4	disc/drum	8 2	12 6	4 9	4 2	4 2	16¾	Oct '68/–

Morris

Model and Type	Bore mm	Stroke mm	Cap. cc	C.R.	Vlves.	b.h.p. at r.p.m.	Grs.	Brks.	W/base ft. in.	O.L. ft. in.	O.W. ft. in.	O.H. ft. in.	Track ft. in.	Dry wt. cwt.	Intro./Discon.
Mini	62·94	68·26	848	8·3	ohv/p	34 5,500	4	drum	6 $8\frac{5}{32}$	10 $0\frac{1}{4}$	4 $7\frac{1}{2}$	4 5	3 $11\frac{7}{16}$	$12\frac{1}{2}$	Aug '59/–
Mini Traveller	62·94	68·26	848	8·3	ohv/p	34 5,500	4	drum	7 $0\frac{5}{32}$	10 $9\frac{7}{8}$	4 $7\frac{1}{2}$	4 $5\frac{1}{2}$	3 $11\frac{7}{16}$	13	Sep '60/–
Mini-Cooper	62·43	81·28	997	9·0	ohv/p	55 6,000	4	disc/drum	6 $8\frac{5}{32}$	10 $0\frac{1}{4}$	4 $7\frac{1}{2}$	4 5	3 $11\frac{13}{32}$	$12\frac{3}{4}$	Aug '61/Jan '64
Mini-Cooper 'S'	70·64	68·26	1,071	9·0	ohv/p	67·5 6,500	4	disc/drum	6 $8\frac{5}{32}$	10 $0\frac{1}{4}$	4 $7\frac{1}{2}$	4 5	4 $0\frac{1}{32}$	$13\frac{3}{4}$	Mar '63/Mar '64
Mini-Cooper	64·58	76·2	998	9·0	ohv/p	55 5,800	4	disc/drum	6 $8\frac{5}{32}$	10 $0\frac{1}{4}$	4 $7\frac{1}{2}$	4 5	3 $11\frac{13}{32}$	13	Jan '64/–
Mini-Cooper 'S'	70·64	61·91	970	10·0	ohv/p	64 6,500	4	disc/drum	6 $8\frac{5}{32}$	10 $0\frac{1}{4}$	4 $7\frac{1}{2}$	4 5	4 $0\frac{1}{32}$	$12\frac{1}{2}$	Jun '64/Jan '65
Mini-Cooper 'S'	70·64	81·33	1,275	9·75	ohv/p	76 6,000	4	disc/drum	6 $8\frac{5}{32}$	10 $0\frac{1}{4}$	4 $7\frac{1}{2}$	4 5	4 $0\frac{1}{32}$	$12\frac{1}{2}$	Apr '64/–
Mini Mk II 1000	64·58	76·2	998	8·3	ohv/p	38 5,250	4	drum	6 $8\frac{5}{32}$	10 $0\frac{1}{4}$	4 $7\frac{1}{2}$	4 5	3 $11\frac{7}{16}$	$12\frac{1}{2}$	Oct '67/–
Mini Mk. II 1000 Traveller	64·58	76·2	998	8·3	ohv/p	38 5,250	4	drum	7 $0\frac{5}{32}$	10 $9\frac{7}{8}$	4 $7\frac{1}{2}$	4 $5\frac{1}{2}$	3 $11\frac{7}{16}$	13	Oct '67/–
Minor 1000	62·94	76·2	948	8·3	ohv/p	37 4,800	4	drum	7 2	12 4	5 1	5 0	4 $2\frac{5}{8}$	14	Oct '56/Sep '62
Minor 1000	64·58	83·72	1,098	8·5	ohv/p	48 5,100	4	drum	7 2	12 4	5 1	5 0	4 $2\frac{5}{8}$	14	Sep '62/–
Minor 1000 Traveller	62·94	76·2	948	8·3	ohv/p	37 4,800	4	drum	7 2	12 4	5 1	5 0	4 $2\frac{5}{8}$	15	Oct '56/Sep '62
Minor 1000 Traveller	64·58	83·72	1,098	8·5	ohv/p	48 5,100	4	drum	7 2	12 4	5 1	5 0	4 $2\frac{5}{8}$	15	Sep '62/–
Oxford V	73·025	89	1,489	8·3	ohv/p	53 4,350	4	drum	8 $3\frac{3}{16}$	14 $7\frac{7}{8}$	5 $3\frac{1}{2}$	4 $11\frac{3}{4}$	4 $1\frac{7}{8}$	$20\frac{3}{4}$	Mar '59/Oct '61

Morris

Model and Type	Bore mm	Stroke mm	Cap. cc	C.R.	Vlves.	b.h.p. at r.p.m.	Grs.	Brks.	W/base ft. in.	O.L. ft. in.	O.W. ft. in.	O.H. ft. in.	Track ft. in.	Dry wt. cwt.	Intro /Discon.
Oxford VI	76·2	89	1,622	8·3	ohv/p	61 5,100	4	drum	8 4¼	14 6½	5 3½	4 10½	4 3½	21½	Aug '61/–
Oxford V Traveller	73·025	89	1,489	8·3	ohv/p	53 4,350	4	drum	8 3$\frac{3}{16}$	14 7⅜	5 3½	4 11¾	4 1⅞	22¾	Sep '60/Oct '61
Oxford VI Traveller	76·2	89	1,622	8·3	ohv/p	61 5,100	4	drum	8 4¼	14 6½	5 3½	4 10½	4 3½	23	Aug '61/–
1100	64·58	83·73	1,098	8·5	ohv/p	48 5,100	4	disc/drum	7 9½	12 2¾	5 0⅜	4 5	4 3½	16	Aug '62/Mar '68
1100 Traveller	64·58	83·73	1,098	8·5	ohv/p	48 5,100	4	disc/drum	7 9½	12 2⅜	5 0⅜	4 5	4 3½	16¼	Mar '66/–
1300	70·61	81·28	1,275	8·8	ohv/p	60 5,250	4	disc/drum	7 9½	12 2¾	5 0⅜	4 5	4 3½	16½	Oct '67/Feb '68
1300 Traveller	70·61	81·28	1,275	8·8	ohv/p	60 5,250	4	disc/drum	7 9½	12 2¾	5 0⅜	4 5	4 3½	16⅝	Oct '67/–
1800	80·26	89	1,798	8·4	ohv/p	84 5,300	4	disc/drum	8 10⅛	13 8¾	5 6¾	4 8	4 8	22¾	Mar '66/–
1800S	80·26	89	1,798	9·5	ohv/p	95·5 5,700	4	disc/drum	8 10⅜	13 10$\frac{27}{32}$	5 6⅞	4 8$\frac{5}{16}$	4 8	22¾	Oct '68/–

Reliant

Model and Type	Bore mm	Stroke mm	Cap. cc	C.R.	Vlves.	b.h.p. at r.p.m.	Grs.	Brks.	W/base ft. in.	O.L. ft. in.	O.W. ft. in.	O.H. ft. in.	Track ft. in.	Dry wt. cwt.	Intro./Discon.
Sabre 4 2 dr. spts.	82·6	79·5	1,703	8·8	ohv/p	73 4,400	4	disc/drum	7 6	13 9	5 1	4 2	4 0	16½	Mar '61/Dec '63
Sabre 6 2 dr. spts.	82·55	79·5	2,553	8·3	ohv/p	98 4,750	4	disc/drum	7 6	13 9	5 1	4 2	4 0	17¾	Oct '62/Sep '64
Scimitar GT 2 dr. cpe (SE4)	82·55	79·5	2,553	8·3	ohv/p	120 5,000	4	disc/drum	7 8	13 11	5 3	4 3½	4 3½	19¾	Sep '64/Oct '66
Scimitar GT 2 dr. cpe (SE4A)	93·66	72·42	2,994	8·9	ohv/p	144 4,750	4	disc/drum	7 8	13 11	5 3	4 3½	4 3½	19½	Oct '66/–
Rebel 2 dr. sal. (FW4)	55·88	60·96	598	8·4	ohv/p	28 5,250	4	drum	7 5	11 6	4 10	4 7½	3 11	11	Sep '64/Jan '68
Rebel 2 dr. sal. (FW4B)	60·5	60·96	701	8·4	ohv/p	31 5,000	4	drum	7 5	11 6	4 10	4 7½	3 10⅖	11	Oct '67/–
Rebel 2 dr. Est. (FW4BEZ)	60·5	60·96	701	8·4	ohv/p	31 5,000	4	drum	7 5	12 1¼	4 10	4 7½	3 10⅖	11	Dec '67/–

Riley

Model and Type	Bore mm	Stroke mm	Cap. cc	C.R.	Vlves.	b.h.p. at r.p.m.	Grs.	Brks.	W/base ft. in.	O.L. ft. in.	O.W. ft. in.	O.H. ft. in.	Track ft. in.	Dry wt. cwt.	Intro./Discon.
One-Point-Five	73·025	89	1,489	8·3	ohv/p	63·5 5,000	4	drum	7 2	12 $9\frac{1}{4}$	5 1	4 $11\frac{3}{4}$	4 $2\frac{7}{8}$	$17\frac{1}{2}$	Jan '60/Apr '65
Elf	62·94	68·26	848	8·3	ohv/p	34 5,500	4	drum	6 $8\frac{5}{32}$	10 $10\frac{5}{16}$	4 $7\frac{1}{2}$	4 5	3 $11\frac{7}{8}$	$12\frac{1}{2}$	Oct '61/Nov '62
Elf	64·58	76·2	998	8·3	ohv/p	38 5,250	4	drum	6 $8\frac{5}{32}$	10 $10\frac{5}{16}$	4 $7\frac{1}{2}$	4 5	3 $11\frac{7}{8}$	$12\frac{1}{2}$	Jan '63/Oct '69
Four/Sixty-Eight	73·025	89	1,489	8·3	ohv/p	63·5 5,000	4	drum	8 $3\frac{3}{16}$	14 $10\frac{1}{8}$	5 $3\frac{1}{2}$	4 $11\frac{3}{4}$	4 $1\frac{7}{8}$	$21\frac{1}{2}$	Apr '59/Oct '61
Four/Seventy-Two	76·2	89	1,622	8·3	ohv/p	68 5,000	4	drum	8 $4\frac{1}{4}$	14 $10\frac{1}{8}$	5 $3\frac{1}{2}$	4 $10\frac{1}{8}$	4 $3\frac{3}{8}$	$21\frac{3}{4}$	Sep '61/Oct '69
Kestrel 1100	64·58	83·72	1,098	8·9	ohv/p	55 5,500	4	disc/drum	7 $9\frac{1}{2}$	12 $2\frac{3}{4}$	5 $0\frac{3}{8}$	4 5	4 $3\frac{1}{2}$	16	Sep '65/Jan '68
Kestrel 1300	70·61	81·28	1,275	8·8	ohv/p	60 5,250	4	disc/drum	7 $9\frac{1}{2}$	12 $2\frac{3}{4}$	5 $0\frac{3}{8}$	4 $5\frac{7}{8}$	4 $3\frac{1}{2}$	16	Oct '67/Oct '69

Rolls-Royce

Model and Type	Bore mm	Stroke mm	Cap. cc	C.R.	Vlves.	b.h.p. at r.p.m.	Grs.	Brks.	W/base ft. in.	O.L. ft. in.	O.W. ft. in.	O.H. ft. in.	Track ft. in.	Dry wt. cwt.	Intro./Discon.
Silver Cloud II	104·14	91·44	6,230	8·0	ohv/p	— —	4A	drum	10 3	17 $7\frac{3}{4}$	6 $2\frac{3}{4}$	6 $5\frac{1}{2}$	5 0	39	Aug '59/Sep '62
Phantom V	104·14	91·44	6,230	8·0	ohv/p	— —	4A	drum	12 0	19 10	6 7	6 $5\frac{1}{2}$	5 4	41	Sep '59/Oct '68
Phantom VI	104	91·4	6,230	9·0	ohv/p	— —	3A	drum	12 0	19 10	6 7	5 9	5 4	$51\frac{1}{2}$	Oct '68/–
Silver Cloud III	104·14	91·44	6,230	9·0	ohv/p	— —	4A	drum	10 4	17 $7\frac{1}{4}$	6 2	5 $4\frac{3}{4}$	5 0	39	Oct '62/Sep '66
Silver Shadow	104·14	91·44	6,230	9·0	ohv/p	— —	4A/3A	disc	9 $11\frac{1}{2}$	16 $11\frac{1}{2}$	5 11	4 $11\frac{3}{4}$	4 $9\frac{1}{2}$	40	Oct '65/–

Rover

Model and Type	Bore mm	Stroke mm	Cap. cc	C.R.	Vlves.	b.h.p. at r.p.m	Grs.	Brks.	W/base ft. in.	O.L. ft. in.	O.W. ft. in.	O.H. ft. in.	Track ft. in.	Dry wt. cwt.	Intro./Discon.
Eighty 4 dr. sal. (P4)	90·49	88·9	2,286	7·0	oh/in sv/ex	77 4,250	4	disc/drum	9 3	14 10¼	5 5⅝	5 3¾	4 4½	28¾	Jul '59/May '62
Ninety-Five 4 dr. sal. (P4)	77·8	92·075	2,625	7·8 8·8	oh/in sv/ex	102 4,750	4	disc/drum	9 3	14 10¼	5 5⅝	5 3¾	4 4½	29¼	Sep '62/Jul '64
One Hundred 4 dr. sal. (P4)	77·8	92·075	2,625	7·8	oh/in sv/ex	104 4,750	4	disc/drum	9 3	14 10¼	5 5⅝	5 3¾	4 4½	29	Jul '59/Jul '62
110 4 dr. sal. (P4)	77·8	92·075	2,625	7·8 8·8	oh/in sv/ex	123 5,000	4	disc/drum	9 3	14 10¼	5 5⅝	5 3¾	4 4½	29½	Sep '62/Jul '64
3-Litre 4 dr. sal. (P5)	77·8	105	2,995	8·75	oh/in sv/ex	115 4,500	4/3A	disc/drum	9 2½	15 6½	5 10	5 0¼	4 8	32¼	Sep '58/Aug '67
2000SC 4 dr. sal. (P6)	85·7	85·7	1,978	9·1	sohc	99 5,000	4/3A	disc	8 7⅜	14 10¼	5 6	4 7¼	4 5⅜	24½	Oct '63/–
2000 TC 4 dr. sal. (P6)	85·7	85·7	1,978	10·0	sohc	124 5,500	4	disc	8 7⅜	14 10½	5 6	4 7¼	4 5⅜	25	Oct '66/–
3·5 Litre 4 dr. sal. (P5B)	88·9	71·1	3,528	10·5	ohv/p	184 5,200	3A	disc	9 2½	15 6½	5 10	5 0¼	4 8	31¼	Sep '67/–
Three Thousand Five 4 dr. sal. (P6B)	88·9	71·1	3,528	10·5	ohv/p	184 5,200	3A	disc	8 7⅜	14 11¾	5 6	4 7¾	4 5⅜	25½	Apr '68/–

Singer

Model and Type	Bore mm	Stroke mm	Cap cc	C.R.	Vlves.	b.h.p. at r.p.m.	Grs.	Brks.	W/base ft. in.	O.L. ft. in.	O.W. ft. in.	O.H. ft. in.	Track ft. in.	Dry wt. cwt.	Intro./Discon.
Gazelle (IIIA/IIIB)	79	76·2	1,494	8·5	ohv/p	64(g) 4,600	4	drum	8 0	13 7½	5 0¾	4 11½	4 1	20	Sep '59/Jul '61
Gazelle (IIIC)	81·5	76·2	1,592	8·3	ohv/p	52·8 4,100	4/3A	drum	8 0	13 7½	5 0¾	4 11½	4 1	20	Jul '61/Aug '63
Gazelle (V)	81·5	76·2	1,592	8·3	ohv/p	52·8 4,100	4/3A	disc/drum	8 0	13 8½	5 0¾	4 10	4 3¾	20	Sep '63/Sep '65
Gazelle (VI)	81·5	82·55	1,725	8·4	ohv/p	62·5(g) 4,200	4/3A	disc/drum	8 0	13 10½	5 0¾	4 10	4 3¾	19½	Sep '65/Mar '67
New Gazelle	81·5	82·55	1,725	9·2	ohv/p	74 5,000	3A	disc/drum	8 2½	14 0	5 3½	4 8	4 4	18¼	Nov '66/Feb '70
Vogue (I/II)	81·5	76·2	1,592	8·3	ohv/p	58 4,400	4/3A	disc/drum	8 5	13 9¼	5 2¼	4 10¼	4 3¾	21	Jul '61/Sep '64
Vogue (III)	81·5	76·2	1,592	9·1	ohv/p	78·5 5,000	4/3A	disc/drum	8 5	13 11	5 3	4 10	4 3¾	21	Oct '64/Sep '65
Vogue (IV)	81·5	82·55	1,725	9·2	ohv/p	80(g) 5,000	4/3A	disc/drum	8 5	13 11	5 3	4 10	4 3¾	21	Sep '65/Aug '66
New Vogue	81·5	82·55	1,725	9·2	ohv/p	80(g) 5,000	4/3A	disc/drum	8 2½	14 1½	5 3½	4 8	4 4	18	Aug '66/Feb '70

Singer

Model and Type	Bore mm	Stroke mm	Cap. cc	C.R.	Vlves.	b.h.p. at r.p.m.	Grs.	Brks.	W/base ft. in.	O.L. ft. in.	O.W. ft. in.	O.H. ft. in.	Track ft. in.	Dry wt. cwt.	Intro./Discon.
Chamois (Saloon)	68	60·375	875	10·0	sohc	39 5,000	4	drum	6 10	11 9¼	5 0¼	4 6½	4 1½	13¾	Oct '64/Feb '70
Chamois (Sport)	68	60·375	875	10·0	sohc	42(g) 5,000	4	drum	6 10	11 9¼	5 0¼	4 6½	4 1½	14¼	Oct '66/Feb '70
Chamois (Coupé)	68	60·375	875	10·0	sohc	42(g) 5,000	4	drum	6 10	11 9¼	5 0¼	4 4½	4 1½	14	Apr '67/Feb '70

Standard

Model and Type	Bore mm	Stroke mm	Cap. cc	C.R.	Vlves.	b.h.p. at r.p.m.	Grs.	Brks.	W/base ft. in.	O.L. ft. in.	O.W. ft. in.	O.H. ft. in.	Track ft. in.	Dry wt. cwt.	Intro./Discon.
Ten Companion	58	76	803	8·0	ohv/p	37(g) 5,000	4	drum	7 0	12 0	4 10	4 11	4 0½	15¼	Jun '55/Jan '61
Ensign de Luxe	86	92	2,138	8·15	ohv/p	75 4,100	4	drum	8 6	14 3½	5 7½	5 0	4 3½	22¾	Feb '62/May '63
Ensign	76	92	1,670	8·0	ohv/p	60 4,000	4	drum	8 6	14 3½	5 7½	5 0	4 3½	22¼	Oct '57/Aug '61
Vanguard	85	92	2,088	7·5	ohv/p	68(g) 4,200	4/3A	drum	8 6	14 3½	5 7½	5 0	4 3½	23	Oct '58/Jul '61
Vanguard Six	74·7	76	1,998	8·0	ohv/p	80 4,400	4	drum	8 6	14 3½	5 7½	5 0	4 3½	22¾	Oct '60/May '63

Sunbeam

Model and Type	Bore mm	Stroke mm	Cap. cc	C.R.	Vlves.	b.h.p. at r.p.m.	Grs.	Brks.	W/base ft. in.	O.L. ft. in.	O.W. ft. in.	O.H. ft. in.	Track ft. in.	Dry wt. cwt.	Intro./Discon.
Rapier (III)	79	76·2	1,494	9·2	ohv/p	73 5,400	4	disc/drum	8 0	13 6½	5 0¾	4 10	4 1¾	20⅛	Sep '59/Apr '61
Rapier (IIIA)	81·5	76·2	1,592	9·1	ohv/p	75 5,100	4	disc/drum	8 0	13 6½	5 0¾	4 10½	4 1¾	20⅛	Apr '61/Oct '63
Rapier (IV)	81·5	76·2	1,592	9·1	ohv/p	78·5 5,000	4	disc/drum	8 0	13 7¼	5 0¾	4 9¼	4 3¾	20⅛	Oct '63/Sep '65
Rapier (V)	81·5	82·55	1,725	9·2	ohv/p	91(g) 5,500	4	disc/drum	8 0	13 7¼	5 0¾	4 9¼	4 3¾	20⅛	Sep '65/Jun '67
New Rapier	81·5	82·55	1,725	9·2	ohv/p	94(g) 5,200	4/3A	disc/drum	8 2½	14 6½	5 4¾	4 7	4 4	20	Oct '67/–
Rapier H120	81·5	82·55	1,725	9·6	ohv/p	106 5,200	4	disc/drum	8 2½	14 6½	5 4¾	4 7	4 4	20	Oct '68/–
Alpine (I)	79	76·2	1,494	9·2	ohv/p	83·5(g) 5,300	4	disc/drum	7 2	12 11¼	5 0½	4 3½	4 3	18½	Jul '59/Oct '60
Alpine (II/III)	81·5	76·2	1,592	9·1	ohv/p	80 5,000	4	disc/drum	7 2	12 11¼	5 0½	4 3½	4 3	18¾	Oct '60/Jan '64
Alpine (IV)	81·5	76·2	1,592	9·1	ohv/p	82 5,000	4/3A	disc/drum	7 2	13 0	5 0½	4 3½	4 3¾	19	Jan '64/Sep '65
Alpine (V)	81·5	82·55	1,725	9·2	ohv/p	99(g) 5,500	4	disc/drum	7 2	13 0	5 0½	4 3½	4 3¾	19	Sep '65/Jan '68
Tiger (Mk. I)	96·5	73	4,261	8·8	ohv/p	164(g) 4,400	4	disc/drum	7 2	13 0	5 0½	4 3½	4 1¾	22	Mar '65/Jan '67
Tiger (Mk. II)	101·6	73	4,737	9·3	ohv/p	200 4,400	4	disc/drum	7 2	13 0	5 0½	4 3½	4 1¾	22	Jan '67/Jun '67
Imp Sport	68	60·375	875	10·0	sohc	51 6,100	4	drum	6 10	11 7	5 0¼	4 6½	4 2½	14⅛	Oct '66/–
Stiletto	68	60·375	875	10·0	sohc	51 6,100	4	drum	6 10	11 7	5 0¼	4 4½	4 2½	14	Oct '67/–

Triumph

Model and Type	Bore mm	Stroke mm	Cap. cc	C.R.	Vlves.	b.h.p. at r.p.m.	Grs.	Brks.	W/base ft. in.	O.L. ft. in.	O.W. ft. in.	O.H. ft. in.	Track ft. in.	Dry wt. cwt.	Intro./Discon.
Herald Coupé	63	76	948	8·5	ohv/p	45 5,800	4	drum	7 7½	12 9	5 0	4 3¼	4 0	14¾	May '59/Jun '61
Herald Saloon	63	76	948	8·0	ohv/p	34·5 4,500	4	drum	7 7½	12 9	5 0	4 4	4 0	15	May '59/Jan '64
Herald Convertible	63	76	948	8·5	ohv/p	45 5,800	4	drum	7 7½	12 9	5 0	4 4	4 0½	15	Mar '60/Jun '61
Herald 1200 Coupé	69·3	76	1,147	8·0	ohv/p	39 4,500	4	drum	7 7½	12 9	5 0	4 3¼	4 0	15¼	Feb '61/Oct '64
Herald 1200 Convertible	69·3	76	1,147	8·0	ohv/p	39 4,500	4	drum	7 7½	12 9	5 0	4 4	4 0½	15½	Feb '61/Sep '67
Herald 1200 Saloon	69·3	76	1,147	8·0	ohv/p	39 4,500	4	drum	7 7½	12 9	5 0	4 4	4 0	15¼	Feb '61/–
Herald 12/50 Saloon	69·3	76	1,147	8·5	ohv/p	51 5,200	4	disc/drum	7 7½	12 9	5 0	4 4	4 1	16	Mar '63/Aug '67
Herald 13/60	73·7	76	1,296	8·5	ohv/p	61 5,000	4	disc/drum	7 7½	12 9	5 0	4 4	4 1	16	Sep '67/–
1300	73·7	76	1,296	8·5	ohv/p	61 5,000	4	disc/drum	8 0⅝	12 11	5 1¾	4 6	4 5	17	Sep '65/–
1300TC	73·7	76	1,296	9·0	ohn/p	75 6,000	4	disc/drum	8 0⅝	12 11	5 1¾	4 6	4 5	17	Sep '67/–
Vitesse	66·75	76	1,596	8·75	ohv/p	70 5,000	4	disc/drum	7 7½	12 9	5 0	4 4½	4 1	17¼	May '62/Sep '66
Vitesse 2 Litre	74·7	76	1,998	9·5	ohv/p	95 5,000	4	disc/drum	7 7½	12 9	5 0	4 5¾	4 1	17¼	Sep '66/–
TR3A	83	92	1,991	8·5	ohv/p	100(g) 5,000	4	disc/drum	7 4	12 7	4 7½	4 2	3 9	18¾	Jan '58/Apr '62
TR4	86	92	2,138	9·0	ohv/p.	100 4,600	4	disc/drum	7 4	13 0	4 10	4 2	4 2	18½	Jul '61/Jan '65
TR4A	86	92	2,138	9·0	ohv/p	104 4,700	4	disc/drum	7 4	12 9⅝	4 10	4 2	4 1¾	19	Jan '65/Jul '67
TR5	74·7	95	2,488	9·5	ohv/p	150 5,500	4	disc/drum	7 4	12 9⅝	4 10	4 2	4 1¾	19¼	Aug '67/Dec '68

Triumph

Model and Type	Bore mm	Stroke mm	Cap. cc	C.R.	Vlves.	b.h.p. at r.p.m.	Grs.	Brks.	W/base ft. in.	O.L. ft. in.	O.W. ft. in.	O.H. ft. in.	Track ft. in.	Dry wt. cwt.	Intro./Discon.
TR6	74·7	95	2,498	9·5	ohv/p	150 5,500	4	disc/drum	7 4	12 11	4 10	4 2	4 2¼	20¾	Jan '69/–
Spitfire Mk. I	69·3	76	1,147	9·0	ohv/p	63 5,750	4	disc/drum	6 11	12 1	4 9	3 11½	4 1	13½	Oct '62/Dec '64
Spitfire Mk. II	69·3	76	1,147	9·0	ohv/p	63 5,750	4	disc/drum	6 11	12 1	4 9	3 11½	4 1	13¾	Dec '64/Jan '67
Spitfire Mk. III	73·7	76	1,296	9·0	ohv/p	75 6,000	4	disc/drum	6 11	12 3	4 9	3 11½	4 1	14	Jan '67/–
GT6	74·7	76	1,998	9·5	ohv/p	95 5,000	4	disc/drum	6 11	12 1	4 9	3 11	4 1	16	Oct '66/Sep '68
GT6 Mk. II	74·7	76	1,998	9·25	ohv/p	104 5,300	4	disc/drum	6 11	12 3	4 8	3 11	4 1	17	Oct '68/–
Vitesse 2 Litre Mk. II	74·7	76	1,998	9·25	ohv/p	104 5,300	4	disc/drum	7 7½	12 9	5 0	4 5¾	4 1½	18¼	Oct '68/–
2000	74·7	76	1,998	9·0	ohv/p	90 5,000	4	disc/drum	8 10	14 5¾	5 5	4 8	4 4	21¾	Aug '63/–
2·5 PI	74·7	95	2,498	9·5	ohv/p	132 5,450	4/3A	disc/drum	8 10	14 5¾	5 5	4 8	4 4	22¼	Sep '68/–

Vanden Plas

Model and Type	Bore mm	Stroke mm	Cap. cc	C.R.	Vlves.	b.h.p. at r.p.m.	Grs.	Brks.	W/base ft. in.	O.L. ft. in.	O.W. ft. in.	O.H. ft. in.	Track ft. in.	Dry wt cwt.	Intro./Discon.
Princess 3 Litre	83·34	89	2,912	8·23	ohv/p	108 4,750	3/3A	disc/drum	9 0	15 8	5 8½	5 0	4 5 13/16	29⅞	Oct '59/Jun '64
Princess 4 Litre	87·3	111·1	3,993	6·8	ohv/p	120 4,000	4/3A	drum	11 0⅜	17 11	6 2½	5 10	5 2½	41	Aug '57/May '68
Princess 1100	64·58	83·72	1,098	8·9	ohv/p	55 5,500	4	disc/drum	7 9½	12 2¾	5 0⅜	4 5	4 3½	16¾	Oct '63/Mar '68
4 Litre Princess R	91·44	95·25	3,909	7·8	oh in/ sv ex	175 4,800	3A	disc/drum	9 2	15 8	5 8½	4 11	4 6 15/16	31	Aug '64/May '68
Princess 1300	70·61	81·28	1,275	8·8	ohv/p	60 5,250	4	disc/drum	7 9½	12 2¾	5 0⅜	4 5⅞	4 3½	17¼	Oct '67/–

Vauxhall

Model and Type	Bore mm	Stroke mm	Cap. cc	C.R.	Vlves.	b.h.p. at r.p.m.	Grs.	Brks.	W/base ft. in.	O.L. ft. in.	O.W. ft. in.	O.H. ft. in.	Track ft. in.	Dry wt. cwt.	Intro./Discon.
Victor F	79·37	76·2	1,508	7·8	ohv/p	48·5 4,200	3	drum	8 2	14 0	5 4	4 10	4 2	19	Feb '59/Jul '61
Victor FB	79·37	76·2	1,508	7·8	ohv/p	48·5 4,800	3	drum	8 4	14 5¼	5 4	4 8	4 3¼	18·9	Sept '61/Jul '63
Victor FB	81·64	76·2	1,595	8·5	ohv/p	58·5 4,800	3	drum	8 4	14 5¼	5 4	4 8	4 3¼	18·9	Sept '63/Sept '64
Victor FC 101	81·64	76·2	1,595	9·0	ohv/p	76 4,600	3	drum	8 4	14 6¾	5 4¾	4 7¼	4 4½	20¾	Oct '64/Aug '67
Victor FD	85·73	69·24	1,599	8·5	sohc	83(g) 5,600	4	drum	8 6	14 8¾	5 7	4 4½	4 6	20·7	Aug '67/–
Victor FD 2000	92·25	69·24	1,975	8·5	sohc	104(g) 5,500	3	disc/drum	8 6	14 8¾	5 7	4 4½	4 6	20·9	Aug '67/–
VX 4/90 FB	79·37	76·2	1,508	9·3	ohv/p	71·3 5,200	4	disc/drum	8 4	14 5¼	5 4	4 8	4 3¼	20	Sept '61/Sept '64
VX 4/90 FC	81·64	76·2	1,595	9·3	ohv/p	73·8 5,600	4	disc/drum	8 4	14 6¾	5 4¾	4 7¼	4 4½	20¼	Oct '64/Aug '67
Velox PA	79·37	76·6	2,262	7·8	ohv/p	82(g) 4,400	3	drum	8 9	14 10	5 7	4 9	4 6	22¼	Sept '57/Jul '60
Velox PA	82·55	82·55	2,651	8·1	ohv/p	94 4,400	3	drum	8 9	14 10	5 7	4 9	4 6	22¾	Jul '60/Jul '62
Cresta PA	79·37	76·6	2,262	7·8	ohv/p	82(g) 4,400	3	drum	8 9	14 10	5 7	4 9	4 6	22½	Sept '57/Jul '60
Cresta PA	82·55	82·55	2,651	8·1	ohv/p	94 4,400	3	drum	8 9	14 10	5 7	4 9	4 6	22¾	Jul '60/Jul '62
Velox PB	82·55	82·55	2,651	8·5	ohv/p	94·6 4,800	3	disc/drum	8 11½	15 2	5 10½	4 8½	4 8¼	23·7	Oct '62/Sept '64
Velox PB	92·07	82·55	3,294	8·5	ohv/p	115 4,800	3	disc/drum	8 11½	15 2	5 10½	4 8½	4 8	24	Sept '64/Oct '65
Cresta PB	82·55	82·55	2,651	8·5	ohv/p	94·6 4,800	3	disc/drum	8 11½	15 2	5 10½	4 8½	4 8¼	23·7	Oct '62/Sept '64
Cresta PB	92·07	82·55	3,294	8·5	ohv/p	115 4,800	3	disc/drum	8 11½	15 2	5 10½	4 8½	4 8	24	Sept '64/Oct '65
Cresta PC	92·08	82·55	3,294	8·5	ohv/p	140(g) 4,800	3	disc/drum	8 11½	15 7	5 9¾	4 8½	4 8¼	25	Oct '65/–
Viva HA	74·3	60·96	1,057	8·5	ohv/p	44·2 5,200	4	drum	7 7½	12 11	4 11¾	4 5¼	4 0	14	Sept '63/Sept '66

Vauxhall

Model and Type	Bore mm	Stroke mm	Cap. cc	C.R.	Vlves.	b.h.p. at r.p.m.	Grs.	Brks.	W/base ft. in.	O.L. ft. in.	O.W. ft. in.	O.H. ft. in.	Track ft. in.	Dry wt. cwt.	Intro./Discon.
Viva HB	77·7	60·96	1,159	8·5	ohv/p	56·2 5,200	4	drum	7 11 4/5	13 5 3/5	5 3	4 5	4 3	15 1/4	Sept '66/–
Viva 1600 HB	85·73	69·24	1,599	8·5	sohc	83(g) 5,600	4	disc/drum	7 11 4/5	13 5 3/5	5 3	4 5 1/4	4 3	17·8	Jun '68/–
Viva GT HB	92·25	69·24	1,975	8·5	sohc	112(g) 5,600	4	disc/drum	7 11^4	13 5 3/5	5 3	4 5 1/4	4 3	18·5	Mar '68/–
Viscount	92·08	82·55	3,294	8·5	ohv/p	140(g) 4,600	2A	disc/drum	8 11 1/2	15 8 3/5	5 9 4/5	4 8 1/2	4 8 1/2	27	Jun '66/–
Ventora	92·08	82·55	3,294	8·5	ohv/p	140(g) 4,600	4	disc/drum	8 6	14 8 3/4	5 7	4 4 1/2	4 6	22·7	Feb '68/–
Victor 3300	92·08	82·55	3,294	8·5	ohv/p	140(g) 4,600	4	disc/drum	8 6	14 8 3/4	5 7	4 4 1/2	4 6	24	May '68/–

Wolseley

Model and Type	Bore mm	Stroke mm	Cap. cc	C.R.	Vlves.	b.h.p. at r.p.m.	Grs.	Brks.	W/base ft. in.	O.L. ft. in.	O.W. ft. in.	O.H. ft. in.	Track ft. in.	Dry wt. cwt.	Intro./Discon.
1500	73·025	89	1,489	7·2	ohv/p	48 4,200	4	drum	7 2	12 7 3/4	5 1	4 11 3/4	4 2 7/8	17 1/2	Jan '59/Apr '65
6/Ninety-Nine	83·34	89	2,912	8·23	ohv/p	108 4,750	3	disc/drum	9 0	15 7 1/2	5 8 1/2	5 0 1/2	4 6	29 1/2	Jul '59/Oct '61
6/One Hundred & Ten	83·34	89	2,912	8·3	ohv/p	120 4,750	3	disc/drum	9 2	15 8	5 8 1/2	5 0	4 5 13/16	31	Sep '61/Mar '68
15/Sixty	73·025	89	1,489	8·3	ohv/p	53 4,350	4	drum	8 3 3/16	14 7 3/8	5 3 1/2	4 11 3/4	4 1 7/8	21 1/4	Dec '58/Oct '61
16/Sixty	76·2	89	1,622	8·3	ohv/p	61 5,100	4/3A	drum	8 4 1/4	14 6 1/2	5 3 1/2	4 10 1/2	4 3 3/8	21 1/2	Jan '62/–
Hornet	62·94	68·26	848	8·3	ohv/p	34 5,500	4	drum	6 8 5/32	10 10 5/16	4 7 1/2	4 5	3 11 7/8	12 1/2	Oct '61/Nov '62
Hornet Mk. II/III	64·58	76·2	998	8·3	ohv/p	38 5,250	4	drum	6 8 5/32	10 10 5/16	4 7 1/2	4 5	3 11 7/8	12 1/2	Feb '63/–
1100	64·58	83·72	1,098	8·9	ohv/p	55 5,500	4	disc/drum	7 9 1/2	12 2 3/4	5 0 3/8	4 5	4 3 1/2	16 3/8	Sep '65/Feb '68
1300	70·61	81·28	1,275	8·8	ohv/p	60 5,250	4	disc/drum	7 9 1/2	12 2 3/4	5 0 3/8	4 5 7/8	4 3 1/2	16 1/2	Oct '67/–
18/Eighty-Five	80·26	89	1,798	8·4	ohv/p	84 5,300	4	disc/drum	8 10 3/8	13 10 27/32	5 6 7/8	4 8 5/16	4 8	23	Mar '67/–

Index

Note: the numbers in brackets refer to illustrations, page and number.
Headings in bold denote main entries in text.

List of Plates

1 AC 428 Convertible; AC Cobra chassis; AC Cobra 4-7-litre; Aston Martin DB6 GT and Volante Convertible; Aston Martin DBS bodyshell base unit; Aston Martin DBS in body shop

2 Austin Mini Mk II; 1959 Morris Mini Minor; Austin 1100 Mk II; 1963 Morris 1100; Morris 1300 Traveller; Morris 1800 Mk II

3 Austin 1800 Mk I; BMC factory interior; Austin Maxi; Austin Maxi cornering hard; Austin 3-litre

4 Austin-Healey 3000; Austin-Healey Sprite Mk II; Bentley S-Series at speed; Bentley T-Series; Bond Equipe GT4S; Bond 1300

5 Bristol 409; Daimler Majestic Major; Daimler Limousine; Fairthorpe Rockette

6 Ford Popular; Ford Anglia 100E; Ford Anglia 105E; Ford Escort; 1961 Ford Capri; Ford Capri 3000GT XLR; Ford Classic; Ford Cortina

7 Ford Lotus-Cortina Mk II; Ford Cortina Mk II Estate; Ford Corsair 2000 De Luxe; Ford Corsair 2000 Estate; Ford Zephyr Mk III; Ford Zephyr Mk IF De Luxe Estate; Ford Prefect interior; Ford Mk IV Executive Zodiac interior

8 Gilbern Invader; Gilbern Invader chassis; Ginetta G15; Gordon GT chassis; Gordon-Keeble

9 Hillman Minx 1600; Hillman Imp; Sunbeam Imp Sport; Humber Hawk Estate

10 Jaguar polishing shop; Jaguar 3-8 Mk II racing; Jaguar E-Type racing; Jaguar 240; Jaguar E-Type 242; Jaguar XJ6

11 Jensen 5415; Jensen C-V8; Jensen FF; Lagonda Rapide

12 Lotus Elites in body shop; Lotus Elan SE; Lotus Elan chassis; Lotus Elan Plus-2; Lotus 7; Lotus Europa

13 Original Marcos; Marcos GT; Mini Marcos; MGA 1600 coupe"; MG 1100; Morgan Plus 8

14 Morris Minor; Reliant Sabre; Reliant Rebel; Reliant Scimitar; Reliant Scimitar GTE

15 Rolls-Royce Silver Shadow; Rolls-Royce interior; Rover 2000; Rover 2000 front suspension, rear suspension and body frame

16 Rover 95; Rover 3-Litre; Rover 3500; Rover 3i-litre V8 engine; Rover 2000 TC engine

17 Standard Ensign; Standard Vanguard Six Estate; Standard Vanguard saloon; Standard Vanguard six-cylinder engine; Sunbeam Rapier; Sunbeam Alpine cockpit; Sunbeam Tiger

18 Triumph TR3A; Triumph TR4; Triumph TR4 front suspension; Triumph TR4A chassis; Triumph Spitfire; Triumph GT6; Triumph Spitfire, late model; Triumph TR6

19 Triumph Herald line-up; Triumph 1300 TC; Triumph Vitesse Mk II; Triumph 1300 interior; Triumph 2000 saloon; Triumph 2500 PI engine; TVR bodyshell production; TVR Tina convertible

20 TVR Vixen S2; Vauxhall Victor F-Series; Vauxhall Cresta PA; Vauxhall VX 4/90; Vauxhall Victor FB; Vauxhall Viscount PCE; Vauxhall Victor 101 Super; Vauxhall Victor FD 2000

21 Vauxhall Viva HA; Vauxhall Viva HB; Wolseley 1500; Wolseley 6/110; Unipower GT; Vauxhall Viva GT

23 Action photos; Jaguar XJ6; Jensen Interceptor; Vauxhall Victor; TVR; Jaguar E-Type and Daimler SP250

24 Action photos: MG Midget; Triumph Spitfire; Triumph GT6 Mk II; Ford Cortina and Hillman Hunter; Triumph GT6 Mk II rear suspension Action photos: MGB racing; Lotus-Elan racing; Sunbeam Alpine at Le Mans

List of Plates for the colour section

1 AC Ace; AC Aceca; AC Cobra; Alvis TD 21

2 Armstrong-Siddeley Star Sapphire; Aston Martin DB4; Aston Martin DBS; Austin Mini

3 Austin A40 [Farina]; Austin A55 Farina Saloon; Austin A60 Cambridge; Austin Mini Cooper; Mini Cooper engine bay

4 Austin Mini Cooper S; Badge detail of Cooper S; Austin 3-litre; Austin Maxi

5 Austin Healey 3000 Mk1; Bristol 407; Bond Equipe

6 Daimler Majestic Major; Daimler 2 ½ litre saloon; Daimler SP 250 Dart; Elva Courier Mark IV; Fairthorpe Electron Minor

7 Ford 105E Anglia; Ford Cortina MkI; Ford Cortina MkII; Ford Corsair; Ford Capri Classic

8 Ford Zodiac MkIII; Gilbern Genie front, back and side shots

9 Ginetta G4; Gordon-Keeble GK1; Hillman Minx series IIIC; Hillman Imp

10 Humber Hawk; Jaguar XJ6; Jaguar Mark II; Jaguar E-Type

11 Jensen CV8; Lotus Élan; Lotus Cortina; Lotus Elite; Marcos 1600 GT

12 MGB Roadster; MG 1100;MG Magnette; MG 1300

13 Morgan 4/4;Morgan 4/4-rear view; Morgan 4/4 interior;
Morgan 4/4-badge detail

14 Morris Minor saloon; Morris Minor traveller; Morris Cooper front and
rear views

15 Morris Oxford; Morris 1800; Reliant Scimitar, Riley Elf

16 Riley Kestrel; Riley 4/Seventy-two; Rolls-Royce Silver Shadow;

17 Rover P5 Coupe; Rover P5B; Rover P6

18 Sunbeam Stiletto; Sunbeam Alpine; Tornado Tempest; Tornado Talisman

19 Triumph TR4; Triumph Herald; Triumph Herald Convertible

20 Triumph Spitfire 4;Triumph GT6; Triumph Vitesse; Turner Mk1; TVR
Griffith 200; TVR Grantura

21 TVR Tuscan; TVR Vixen; Vauxhall Victor FB

22 Vauxhall HA Viva; Vauxhall Cresta PA; Vauxhall Viva HB; Vauxhall Victor
FD

23 Wolseley 18/Eighty-five; Wolseley 1100;Wolseley 16/Sixty; Wolseley 1500

24 Wolseley Hornet; Rochdale Olympic; Unipower GT; Falcon Shell